...panion Volume to . . .

Preaching Through the Bible, Volume One

A Com

Preaching Through the Bi

PREACHING THROUGH THE BIBLE

Volume Two

by
ERIC W. HAYDEN

Preface by
DR. WILBUR M. SMITH

ZONDERVAN PUBLISHING HOUSE
GRAND RAPIDS, MICHIGAN

Printed in the United States of America

FOREWORD

It has now been nearly ten years since one Sunday morning in London, I walked into a small church not far from where Spurgeon's tabernacle stood for such a long time, and heard a man preach to a small congregation of middle class people. His sermon was an expository survey of one of the Minor Prophets and it was superbly done. I said to myself then that if this young man continues this kind of preaching he will be heard from. The young man was the author of this book, Eric W. Hayden, who from the beginning of his ministry was determined to be a Biblical expositor.

Now there are, we might say, five different ways in which a minister may give himself to Biblical preaching. Some, and this requires great ability and certainly the direct leading of the Holy Spirit, can devote a whole year to a single chapter of the Word of God, such as Dr. Martyn Lloyd-Jones has done with the first chapter of Ephesians, and other rich portions of the Scriptures. Others may devote a long period to preaching through a single book of the Bible, as Dr. Donald Barnhouse took four years to preach through the Epistle to the Romans. Others will preach through the New Testament, six or eight, or ten sermons on each of the Gospels, and on the other books proportionately, as Dr. Harry Ironside did. Nearly all of his expository works are the fruit of this kind of a ministry. Then, of course, as all ministers know who desire to base their preaching upon the Word of God, there is the plan of preaching a series of sermons on some Biblical theme, as the Parables, the Person and Work of the Holy Spirit, etc. Finally there is the method adopted by the author of this book, in which there is one sermon devoted to each book of the Bible, made up of some introductory material and then the exposition of some prominent chapter in the book, as here the first sermon is on the second chapter of Genesis. This is the method followed so successfully by, among others, Dr. J. Vernon McGee, pastor of the Church of the Open Door in Los Angeles, California.

In 1964 Mr. Hayden published his well-received volume, *Preaching Through the Bible*, in which he devotes one chapter to each book of the Bible and surveys its principal teachings. This, of course, is, comparatively, adequate for the smaller books of the Bible, but it takes a great deal of skill to cover in one sermon the principal themes of such books as Isaiah, Acts, Hebrews, etc.

To carry on a ministry like this, three things are absolutely basic. First of all, if one is going to preach every Lord's day from the Word of God in extended series such as this, he must believe that the Scriptures are the inspired Word of God, a conviction that will give him what the Apostle called "much assurance." The reason why hundreds of ministers are not expositors of the Scriptures is that they have lost confidence in the Word of God. In the second place, such an expositor will have to be a dedicated student of the Bible, not simply one who believes and reads it for his own soul, but who will necessarily spend hours every week in a careful study of a given passage or book. This will require diligence of the first order, the shut door, and the alert mind. Finally, to carry on this kind of a ministry, one must be living according to the statutes and commandments and ideals of the Word of God. He must be allowing life in Christ, as set forth in the Scriptures, to be the determinate factor of his personal life.

I am very happy to commend this new volume by my friend, Mr. Hayden. I am sure it will prove a blessing to a great number of clergymen, and, I trust, laymen on both sides of the Atlantic, and will encourage many young men to similarly devote themselves to a lifelong study and exposition of the oracles of God.

WILBUR M. SMITH

San Marino, California

AUTHOR'S PREFACE

Sir Arthur Conan Doyle's Sherlock Holmes once said to Dr. Watson: "You know my methods. Apply them." In 1964 in my book *Preaching Through the Bible, Volume One,* I tried to explain the method of Bible teaching that I have followed in every church in which it has been my privilege to be pastor. I did this believing that others might like to apply the same method to their own church situation. From reading many reviews of the book, and from personal letters of appreciation received, it seems that a real need has been met. It has been encouraging to hear from ministers and pastors who have begun to preach through the Bible. Some of them have confessed that their Bibles, like their hymnbooks, have been divided into favorite and less well-known sections.

Preaching Through the Bible, Volume One is only part of my method. Besides taking my people through a book of the Bible each Sunday (explaining briefly the authorship and background before pinpointing the original theme and abiding message of the book by expounding what I call a "key text") I also deal with one "famous" chapter from each book at the mid-week meeting for Bible study. Usually I begin this series of "famous" Bible chapters when the "preaching through the Bible series" is well underway, when I am approaching the end of the Old Testament. My people have then acquired quite a good understanding of the whole Bible and its message, and are eager to delve deeper into the Word.

In *Preaching Through the Bible, Volume One,* it was not possible to give in each chapter a skeleton outline of the books of the Bible. Now in this second volume it is possible to do this and thus I can set the "famous" chapter being studied in its context. The chapter is also studied with the help of a simple outline. These two outlines (of the complete book and of the single chapter) I print with colored chalk on two large blackboards before the Bible study meeting begins. Some may think it is better to write on the board while one is speaking (the late Dr. G. Campbell Morgan's method), but for this one needs to be able to print quickly and legibly. I find it is better to be like an army commander who shows his officers the map and battle diagrams *before* the engagement with the enemy—they then know where they are going! By writing the notes on the blackboards before the meeting, it enables early-comers to copy them in their notebooks. They can then leave room to add further notes during the course of the lecture.

This is my method, and so that others may apply it and find it a blessing to themselves and their congregations I issue them in this book form. The outlines (of book and chapter) are but "bare bones," and admittedly I have not exhausted the flesh that could be put upon the skeleton. That is for others to do as they adopt this method of teaching their people or as they study the Bible personally.

One or two reviewers of the first volume suggested that some of the messages in *Preaching Through the Bible* could be given at the midweek meetings. This second volume shows why this need not be so. It could be *books* of the Bible on Sunday, *chapters* on a weeknight.

A few reviewers said that equal space was given to small books of the Bible (the Minor Prophets, Obadiah or Philemon) in Volume One, as to larger books, like the Book of Psalms. This second volume explains the reason. Through the Bible book by book, Sunday by Sunday, is only a beginning; the study of "famous" chapters is only a continuation; there is more to follow. The Bible is an inexhaustible mine and there are many varied ways of "preaching through" it.

Volume One was reviewed by a few liberal theologians. Knowing my conservative evangelical beliefs they regretted that "the scholarship of half-a-century had been overlooked." We have not overlooked this modern scholarship. We have studied it and found much of it unsatisfying. We prefer to accept the more God-honoring scholarship of the conservative evangelical school.

The "divine library" of sixty-six books has more than sixty-six famous chapters. The selection in this book is my own. They are the chapters to which the Holy Spirit has led me during my ministry.

In *Preaching Through the Bible, Volume One*, Dr. Sidlow Baxter in his generous Foreword described the work as "a bird's eye view" not "a surveyor's ground-plan." In this second volume the bird has flown nearer the ground, and the surveyor has begun to draw his plan. Here is more detail than in the first volume. In Volume One, to change the metaphors, a telescopic view of the Bible was taken; now a more microscopic view is our aim. A brief reminder is given of the character and contents of the whole book at the beginning of each chapter, but then the message of the well-known chapter is dealt with. The subjects are diverse, but as with any study of the Word of God, diversity in unity is clearly seen. Here are messages of challenge and comfort given centuries ago, and yet are extremely pertinent for our own day and generation.

I have tried to be comprehensive in content, spiritual in emphasis, and practical in application, that ministers, missionaries, students and laymen might all be helped and encouraged in their study of the Bible and in their personal lives.

ERIC W. HAYDEN

Leominster, Herefordshire, England

CONTENTS

OLD TESTAMENT

NEW TESTAMENT

WHAT WE ARE AND WHY

Genesis 2

The Book of Genesis is the book of beginnings or origins: the beginning of the material universe, the human race, sin and salvation, family life, a godless civilization, the nations of the world, the confusion of languages—in fact, the beginning of everything we know. The fact that so-called "intellectuals" tend to dismiss this book, must not prevent the Christian from studying it and avowing his belief in it as part of God's revelation. It is not, of course, a scientific treatise couched in twentieth-century scientific terms, but there are no scientific inaccuracies to be found in its pages.

The theme of Genesis is, "The Failure of Man Met by the Salvation of God," and a convenient outline of the book is as follows:

    I. CREATION (1-5)
    II. DILUVIAN (6-9)
    III. NATIONS (10, 11)
    IV. GENERATIONS (12-50)
        A. *Abraham* (12-25)
        B. *Isaac* (26)
        C. *Jacob* (27-36)
        D. *Joseph* (37-50)

The purpose of the Book of Genesis then is primarily to acquaint us with the purpose of creation and man's part in it. The final creative act of God was that of man. Later the psalmist cries out in wonder, "What is man?" He is awed (in Psalm 8) by man's position, authority and enduement as the apex of creation. The purpose of the rest of creation was to focus light upon man. The earth and all living creatures were prepared for man's enjoyment and pleasure.

This "famous" second chapter of Genesis answers the psalmist's rhetorical question; it tells us what we are and why. It teaches us that man is the crown and culmination of God's creative acts; it shows us that there is in man the promise and potency of Godlikeness.

Why chapter two and not chapter one? The fact is, we have two accounts of the creation of the world and mankind in these early chapters. What is called "the catastrophic theory" explains this dual account. After verse one of the first chapter we must assume that the earth was made waste and empty by divine judgment as described in Jeremiah 4:23-26. There is sufficient geological evidence to support this theory of a great world-wide catastrophe. In chapter one we have only a brief outline, giving the general pattern of creation; in chapter two we have more detail. In the first chapter we have God in relation to the universe He created; here in chapter two we have God in relation to man.

An outline of chapter two may be given in this form:

    I. THE COMPLETION OF THE UNIVERSE (verses 1-6)
       A. *The Earth and Sky*
       B. *Plants and Beasts*
   II. THE FORMATION OF MAN (verse 7)
 III. THE DESCRIPTION OF THE GARDEN (verses 8-17)
 IV. THE CREATION OF WOMAN (verses 18-23)
  V. THE INSTITUTION OF MARRIAGE (verses 24, 25)

I. THE COMPLETION OF THE UNIVERSE (verses 1–6)

What majestic wording here, as in chapter one, for the creative work of God! We have simple statements of fact, no involved scientific terms, but how much more dignified than talking about puddles and protoplasm!

The author's statement here is that God has finished His work of creation, and there is never a purpose of God that is not brought to a successful conclusion. What is it that He completed or "finished"?

A. *The Earth and Sky.* By this we mean the material, terrestrial globe, and also the spiritual, atmospheric and astronomical spaces. All "the host" of them probably refers to the stars, for "hosts" is used in that sense in the Bible as well as in the sense of the hosts of angels or redeemed inhabitants of heaven. Obviously at this point in creation it is the stars, planets, satellites and other heavenly bodies that are meant.

B. *Plants and Beasts.* These were created next, the trees and vegetable matter first that the animals might find fodder. It is possible to translate verse 5 as: "As yet no plant of the field was upon the earth, and no herb of the field had as yet sprung up." This does two things: it makes us realize that God's great intention was the creation of man, that the creation of the world was for man; but it must also then be accepted that if nothing living in the plant world was created, then the first man needed no such food to sustain him. And this creates a difficult problem! From Genesis 1 we know that animals were created before man, and they would need vegetation.

How did God mark the completion of His work? By "resting on the seventh day" (verse 2). This was not the rest of exhaustion as was the Saviour's when asleep in the boat. This was the rest of satisfaction. Exhaustion would give the idea of work interrupted; satisfaction affirms that the work was completed. It was final; nothing could be added to it. Then in verse three we are told that God blessed this seventh day and sanctified it. In chapter one we see that "blessing" implies fruitfulness and dominion. The Sabbath day should therefore be a day of fruitfulness and a day that dominates the other days of the week in the lives of God's people. "Sanctified" means set apart in a special sense for God and for the worship of God. What a noble concept of the Lord's Day this is! Today we keep the first day of the week and rejoice not so much in creation, but in redemption. On the first day of the week the Lord Jesus Christ arose from the dead, and on the same day of the week the Holy Spirit was later sent forth.

II. THE FORMATION OF MAN (verse 7)

In this small section we have a dignified description of the origin of man. There is no hint here of any evolutionary process from some lower species of animal. The famous statistician George Gallup once said: "I could prove God statistically. Take the human body alone— the chance that all the functions of the individual would just happen is a statistical monstrosity." No, it did not "just happen." The word "formed" means literally "molded." We need not imagine God molding with His fingers a man out of wet clay. The earth was created by the divine Word. Man may have been molded in the same way.

Our chapter is entitled *What We Are and Why*. In a rather striking and bizarre play the central character lies dead and a policeman bends over his body. "What's his name?" asks the policeman. A voice in the crowd replies "Man." With pencil hovering over notebook the policeman says: "How do you spell it?" How do we spell man? How do we analyze him, define him? Formed from dust but at the same time a "living soul." We have personalities and power to think and reason. We have consciences that tell us right from wrong. We have natural life (physical), and the potential for supernatural (spiritual) life. We have moral natures also. What a contrast with the animals from which some say we have evolved! How fitted we are for life in a world of spiritual and moral values. How we should emphasize the spiritual and minimize the physical and material. We were made on the same day as the animals, but what a gulf between us—and the secret is that man alone was made in the divine image.

God is a Spirit and so this likeness is in the realm of the spiritual. We were not created *looking like* God (that is, in physical appearance), but so that exercising reason, freewill and faith we might *look to* God and have spiritual fellowship with God—a privilege not accorded to the rest of creation. All this was marred by the Fall, but it has been renewed to us in Christ (Ephesians 4:24; Colossians 3:10).

III. THE DESCRIPTION OF THE GARDEN (verses 8-17)

For those who like to pour scorn upon this early narrative and talk of it in terms of myth, legend and so on, let us note that particular care is taken to give the Garden of Eden a specific geographical location. We cannot, of course, place the site with any accuracy today. It seems to have been east of Palestine, possibly in Mesopotamia.

But we do know why it was created: first (verse 8), that man might be put there as a proof of God's love and consideration for him. Here was his most favorable condition for daily living in communion with God and later for his great battle against Satan and evil. Thus it was made both aesthetically beautiful and appetizingly satisfying (verse 9); the trees "pleasant to the sight" and "good for food." In the center was "the tree of life," which some commentators take to mean a tree whose fruit was designed to be eaten by man, that physical decline and decay might be arrested and the body prepared for "translation" like Enoch or Elijah as the world became overpopulated. Another tree was the tree of "the knowledge of good and evil." Why was this necessary if man was created with a conscience? The tree was not meant to be eaten like the Tree of Life; it was planted in Eden as a moral test for mankind. The inhabitants of Eden were given the "run" of the Garden except for this one tree. Its importance is not that it might have made Adam and Eve as knowledgeable as God, but that Adam was commanded not to touch it, and he deliberately disobeyed God (verse 17). The punishment for disobedience was death. Many commentators state at this point that physical death was the punishment. How severe a punishment that alone, for Adam must have seen animals and insects die. But physical death did not come immediately. He did not see Eve drop dead at his feet like Ananias and Sapphira before Peter. Adam and Eve did die eventually, after the due process of decay and waning powers had set in. But as soon as they ate of the tree they died spiritually. They discovered what Isaiah later pronounced—sin separates between a holy God and a sinner. God particularly stressed "the day" that Adam ate he should die—so on that day it must have been spiritual death, for he continued to live physically.

IV. THE CREATION OF WOMAN (verses 18-23)

Through these early chapters there is a distinction between "created" and "made." Created means bringing into existence out of nothing; made is the process of making something from already existing material. Adam was made out of existing soil; now Eve is made from Adam's body.

Just as many people believe Adam and Eve picked an apple (although apple is not mentioned), so many think that Eve was made from Adam's ribs and that man now has one less rib than a woman! The word translated "rib" means "side" (Revised Version). The Hebrew means "flank."

The "operation" was performed under an anesthetic—it was while Adam slept. This was not merely to save Adam inconvenience, but also to prevent him from seeing God at work, for all other creations were made out of sight of Adam.

Why was woman made? Verse 18 tells us because God saw that

it was not good for a man to be alone—he had physical and emotional and spiritual needs that could only be met and expressed in marital and family relationships. Eve was also to be a "helpmeet" for Adam, that is, a helper in his daily activities and primarily in his worship of God. The Hebrew for "helpmeet" means literally "a match for him"! Its real meaning is that woman is man's counterpart; there is a "fitting in" and a response to one another. In verse 23 there is a play upon words which bears this out. The Hebrew for man is "ish," and God said the woman should be called "isha," as we have man and wo*man*.

In the middle of this wonderful account of God's making of Eve we have another naming: God allows Adam to give names to the animals. Obviously Adam had very clear perception of the true nature of these animals for he named them appropriately (verses 19, 20). Names, for the Easterner, are very important. They not only have meanings but they fit in with the character of the person. It has been suggested that as Adam was naming these animals, he saw them going about in pairs and so realized his own need of a companion.

V. THE INSTITUTION OF MARRIAGE (verses 24, 25)

These two verses are supremely important. No understanding of Matthew's and Mark's references to divorce can be had until we understand this divine concept of human marriage. Our Lord's enemies only went back to Moses' regulations when discussing divorce with the Saviour. Christ always went back to these two verses, to God's original intention for mankind.

Here we have the inviolability of marriage. When God has joined a man and woman together He has made a union which no man has any right to undo. In God's mind there is a non-existence of divorce.

The marriage is consummated here not by any religious, civil or legal ceremony, but simply through the sexual act. Thus the Apostle Paul later writes that a man who visits a prostitute is married to that woman. According to the laws of our land a marriage is null and void only if it has not been consummated physically.

Why is all this included here? Certainly not for Adam and Eve's sake, but so that later under inspiration of the Holy Spirit the Apostle Paul could write of the Church and its fellowship with the Lord. He is able to talk of the intimacy of the Church's union as between a man and his wife.

WHY THE CALENDAR WAS CHANGED

Exodus 12

The Book of Exodus is the sequel to Genesis. The first book of the Bible describes man's failure and fall; the second is the account of how God hastened to the help of mankind by offering to redeem him. In Genesis we have God's promise; in Exodus His procedure. "Redemption" is the key word of the book and the theme is, "Redemption through Blood." "Exodus" means "way out" or "departure," and the Book of Exodus contains the record of the departure of the children of Israel from Egyptian bondage. An outline of the whole book is as follows:

I. REPRESSION (1–13)
   The Saviour (Moses): His Birth, Call and Contests
II. REDEMPTION (14–19)
   The Journey: Red Sea, Wilderness, Mount Sinai
III. REVELATION (20–34)
   The Laws: Moral, Social and Spiritual
IV. REALIZATION (35–40)
   The Tabernacle: Begun, Built and Blessed

In order that Pharoah, king of the Egyptians, should allow God's people, the children of Israel, to leave the land of oppression and captivity, God sent down a series of plagues or judgments upon the oppressors. The last plague of the series forms the subject of a "famous" Bible chapter, Exodus 12. This is the outline of the chapter:

I. THE INSTITUTION OF THE PASSOVER (verses 1–13)
   A. *The Slaying of the Lamb*
   B. *The Sprinkling of the Blood*
II. THE REGULATIONS FOR POSTERITY (verses 14–28)
   A. *The Seven Days Without Leaven*
   B. *The Story of the Ordinance*
III. THE DESCRIPTION OF THE PLAGUE (verses 29–36)
   A. *The Smiting of the First-born*
   B. *The Spoiling of the Egyptians*
IV. THE EVACUATION OF THE PEOPLE (verses 37–42)
   A. *The Swelling of the Numbers*
   B. *The Solemnity of the Occasion*
V. THE ADDITIONS TO THE PRECEPTS (verses 43–51)

    A. *The Seclusion of the Home*
    B. *The Sincerity of the Gentiles*

In this chapter then we witness the final conflict between God's chosen saviour (Moses) and the self-appointed oppressor of God's people (Pharoah).

The theme of the chapter is familiar to most Christians for it concerns the Passover Feast. When a film was made of the sinking of the *Titanic* it was entitled *A Night to Remember*. In this chapter we have *the* night to remember, a night so memorable that the Jewish calendar was changed. Until this great event the Jewish year began with the month of harvest; now by divine command it is to begin with the remembrance of the Passover. From autumn and harvest to springtime and a feast that reminded them of God's redemptive plan. It is sometimes thought that Adam and Eve were created in the autumn, for the autumn fruits were ripe on the trees in the garden. If that is true then the remarkable change in the calendar is seen. Nor was this the only change God made in the calendar. As we saw in Genesis 2, God sanctified the seventh day; in the New Testament it is the *first day* that is observed as the Lord's Day, because of another memorable event, the Resurrection of Jesus Christ. The Passover outshone the autumn celebration of harvest; the Christian Lord's Day outshines the old Jewish Sabbath; and the believer's "second birthday" is brighter than his ordinary day of birth.

After Exodus 12, whenever a Jew looked at his calendar, it would remind him of the terrible experience of repression, the awful bondage which man's own failure and sin had brought upon him. It would remind him of his redemption, the day when God led him forth out of captivity into liberty; of revelation, the time when God saw fit to reveal His will, giving mankind certain laws and commandments that would make life together possible; and realization, that is, that man was now able to commune and have fellowship with God through worship in His ordained sanctuary.

I. THE INSTITUTION OF THE PASSOVER (verses 1–13)

    A. *The Slaying of the Lamb.* Looking back from the New Testament vantage point it is easy to see how this section is so typical of the Lord Jesus Christ.

First, the lamb was in its *prime*—"a male of the first year" (verse 5). When Jesus died on the cross He was no longer the Babe of Bethlehem. He had grown "in wisdom and stature," but He was still only thirty years old.

Note also the *purity* of the lamb—"without blemish" (verse 5). So Peter refers to the Lord (I, 1:19). So Pilate found Him to be without fault. He was the sinless Son of God, the Lamb of God without blemish.

The Passover lamb was killed for a *purpose*. For four days it had been set apart (verses 3, 6). In the same way Jesus entered Jerusalem four days before He was crucified. God's purpose, however, was predetermined long before that—from before the foundation of the world.

So we could go on in minute detail: roasting with fire (typical of the Lord's agonizing sufferings), and not a bone broken.

B. *The Sprinkling of the Blood.* Again this is typical. The slaying of the lamb had resulted in the shedding of blood. Now the blood must be sprinkled with the [paint brush] hyssop, being applied to the doorway of the home. Christ's death is in vain unless the shed blood is applied by faith for the cleansing of sin.

The blood was put in a basin and stood on the threshold. Then the side posts and the lintel were sprinkled, thus a cross was formed, "putting the X in Exodus"! This surely denotes that an open confession of Christ is necessary by believers today. All passers-by, as well as the angel of death, could see clearly the saving mark of the blood that Passover evening. God could have arranged for the red cross to have been painted on the rooftops so that the angel of death would see it clearly (like hospitals in wartime made the cross visible to aircraft), but He wanted it to be a witness to man as well.

Some Jews believe that the "lintel" was a small lattice window immediately above the front door. If that is correct then perhaps that is where the woman who harbored Joshua's two spies "bound a scarlet cord" so that she was preserved when the city was captured. The blood then stood for preservation and substitution—"a lamb has died here in my place," the eldest son of the family could say.

No wonder our Lord took over this feast of the Passover on that "dark betrayal night" and transformed it into the memorial meal we now know as the Lord's Supper or Communion Service. The Passover was said to "represent the perfect unity of Israel as a nation: one meal, at one table, eaten whole and eaten entirely." So the Lord's Supper represents the unity of the Church. At the Lord's Table we are "all one in Christ Jesus."

II. THE REGULATIONS FOR POSTERITY (verses 14-28)

We must be careful to distinguish between two sets of regulations in this chapter. One set is for the first observance of the Passover. It had to be eaten quickly and the people were to be dressed, ready to depart in a hurry. The more detailed regulations are now given for posterity, for those who will keep this feast as a future memorial to that first occasion.

A. *The Seven days Without Leaven.* The leaven, like the Lamb, is typical. It is often a symbol of corruption, passion and sin. For seven days—seven being the number of completion, perfection—for seven days bread without leaven was to be eaten. The house was to be searched, the leaven removed the day before the Passover.

This leaven consisted, as far as we can tell, of a piece of fermented dough left over from the previous baking. This lump of dough was "hidden" or dissolved in the kneading trough before the flour was added, or else hidden in the flour itself before kneading began. Fermentation is a process that implies corruption and so it came to stand for sin in various forms.

Ought we not approach the Lord's Supper as these people approached the Passover, having searched out the leaven, having examined ourselves and burned up the leaven of hypocrisy, resentment, greed, jealousy, and all the rest?

B. *The Story of the Ordinance.* There was once a man who, when asked what he believed, said that he believed what the Church believed. When asked what the Church believed he said, "The same as I believe!" Asked next what he and the Church believed he replied: "The same thing!" The reference in this subsection to a satisfactory explanation always being given to the children about the meaning of the Passover feast is a lesson for us today. It has been well-said that we should never do anything we do not understand in religion, especially regarding the two ordinances of baptism and communion. It is also important to train the children of the church in doctrine.

III. The Description of the Plague (verses 29-36)

It has been said that if only Pharaoh had taken heed of the previous plagues a great many innocent lives would have been saved. But it is human nature, depraved nature, to disregard the judgments of God until too late.

A. *The Smiting of the First-born.* The angel of death smote all the eldest in the land, from Pharoah's prince to Pharoah's prisoners, cattle as well as human beings. We are not told if God used natural or supernatural means. Some think it was natural, that is, that some great and terrible disease fell suddenly like an epidemic. Why was this catastrophe confined to the first-born? Because the eldest child is usually the joy and hope of the parents.

The blow fell at night, when all terrors seem more terrible. It is at night that the Bridegroom will come!

A great cry went up, and it is hard for western minds to comprehend the easterner's wail of lamentation for the dead.

The result was, however, that Pharoah let the people of God go, and we expect he was glad to see them go!

B. *The Spoiling of the Egyptians.* The word "borrowed" here is misleading. It really means "asked of." By direct command of God the Israelites asked the Egyptians for their riches and they were exceedingly glad to give them, perhaps to atone for the suffering they had inflicted and to act as an incentive to hasten their future journey. Some have thought of this "spoiling" as immoral, as deceitful, but it was only just payment for the property left behind by the Israelites.

There is an alternative explanation: "spoil" may be translated as "snatch away to safety." In that case the Egyptians were saved from feeling revengeful against the Israelites after the last plague and parted on good terms—a hardly likely explanation in view of the subsequent chase.

IV. THE EVACUATION OF THE PEOPLE (verses 37–42)

A. *The Swelling of Their Numbers.* Six hundred thousand men now leave Egypt. Besides that there were the women and children, in all about 1,200,000 people. After two hundred years the seventy had grown to this fantastic size. But we must remember they were now a "mixed multitude." Besides Israelites there would be Egyptian slaves, prisoners of war who took advantage of the turmoil and confusion to make their escape with God's people. There would also be converted Egyptians. A motley crew indeed! Criminals, hangers-on, camp followers, and at the same time "cunning" (in the sense of clever) craftsmen who one day would be used in the erection of God's Temple.

This is typical of the Christian Church. The spiritual nucleus is the true Israel, the truly born-again church members. Besides them we have the nominal church members, the "dead wood" upon the church roll.

B. *The Solemnity of the Occasion.* A night to be "much observed" is twice repeated in this section. The Hebrew means "of watching" or "of keeping in mind." It is a word that was used in connection with celebrations and vigilance. This solemn occasion was to be perpetually remembered in a fitting and reverent manner. The great workings of God, the display of His power, the exercise of His grace, this is not to be a nine-day wonder but a constant remembrance.

V. THE ADDITIONS TO THE PRECEPTS (verses 43-51)

These extra regulations about the future observance are probably put in because of the mixed multitude that came out of Egypt.

A. *The Seclusion of the Home.* One house for one family was to be the rule. The "communal living" of atheistic communism is entirely unscriptural. Then the feast was not to be divided up and parts taken from one home to another. The symbolism of the meal would be destroyed like that. The eating of the *whole* of the lamb in *one* united home was to be the rule.

B. *The Sincerity of the Gentiles.* No stranger, no foreigner, that is, no non-Jew, no Gentile could eat of the Passover unless he was sincere in wanting to do so. How could his sincerity be tested? By seeing if he had kept the law by being circumcised. The man who became an Israelite through circumcision was so sincere that he became a privileged person and could enjoy all the privileges of the Hebrew religion. In the same way the Lord's Table is only for those who have "put on Christ," by belief and by baptism.

THE GREATEST DAY OF THE YEAR

Leviticus 16

"Access to God" is the theme of the book of Leviticus, the keyword being "communion." "The holiness of God," it has been said, "shines like a white fearful light upon the whole book." How then can sinful man approach such a God? The answer is in the intricate system of the priesthood and the involved system of sacrifices and offerings. The priesthood reveals how it is possible to appropriate the divine provision indicated by the offerings. No man could bring his own sacrifice with which to appease God; it had to be given to the priest, the go-between or mediator between man and God. Thus sin was dealt with in three ways: by substitution (some other life taking the place of the sinner); by imputation (that is, the transference of the sinner's guilt to another); and death (the death of the one upon whom the guilt is laid).

An outline of the Book of Leviticus is as follows:

    I. OBLATIONS (1–7)
        A. *Things Offered to God—the Burnt, Meal, Peace, Sin and Trespass Offerings*
        B. *Instructions to the Priests*
    II. CONSECRATIONS (8–10)
        The Consecration of the Priests
    III. REGULATIONS (11–22)
        Laws to do With Uncleanness and Purification—Beasts, Childbirth, Leprosy
    IV. CONVOCATIONS (23–25)
        A. *Special Assemblies*
        B. *Calendar Dates*
    V. BENEDICTIONS (26)
        The Blessings of Obedience
    VI. AFFIRMATIONS (27)
        Laws Concerning Vows

The "famous" chapter comes within Section III, Regulations, and it deals with the Day of Atonement. This is the greatest day in the religious year for the Jewish people, for on this day provision was made for dealing with the whole question of sin, known and unknown. It has been called "The Good Friday of the Old Testament."

Elsewhere in this book we find that this is the only day of the year for which fasting is prescribed (as well as in verses 29 and 31). This was to be the outward expression of their sorrow and repentance for sin. All other feasts were times of rejoicing. These other feasts are given all together in chapter 18, but this greatest day of the year is so important, so unique, that it stands alone.

Chapter 16 has a backward and a forward look, backward to the death of Nadab and Abihu for sacrilege, forward to the all-sufficient Atonement which God has provided for His people. Naturally for us this forward look is to the cross of Calvary where God's final and ultimate Atonement for sin was worked out.

The outline of Chapter 16 is this:

    I. PREPARATION (verses 1–19)
        A. *Aaron* (verses 1–10)
        B. *The Priests* (verses 11–14)
        C. *The People* (verses 15–19)
   II. PURIFICATION (verses 20–22)
        A. *The Animal* (verse 20)
        B. *The Ritual* (verse 21)
        C. *The Terminal* (verse 22)
  III. INSTRUCTION (verses 23–28)
        A. *The Dress* (verses 23, 24)
        B. *The Flesh* (verse 25)
        C. *The Happiness* (verse 28)
  IV. INSTITUTION (verses 29–34)
        A. *The Date* (verse 29)
        B. *The Duties* (verses 31-33)
        C. *The Duration* (verse 34)

I. PREPARATION (verses 1–19)

In this first section we have a description of the divine preparations necessary by three classes of people for the ceremony and ritual of the Day of Atonement to be effective: Aaron the high priest; the priests, Aaron's son and family assistants; and the people themselves. Before final purification can come adequate preparations must be taken.

A. *Aaron.* Jewish tradition maintains that for seven days Aaron lived apart, in solitude from his fellow men, in a special place reserved for him, and there read and re-read God's ordinances regarding the Atonement. The night before the great occasion he spent sleepless. So we notice too that his attire is in keeping with his attitude—his dress is not the distinctive, ornate robes of the high priesthood but the linen garments, the emblem of purity, simplicity and humility. The more ornate dress was heavy, restricting movement. Thus it was that the Lord Jesus Christ made His Atonement in the form of a man, a servant, not in the robes of His eternal glory. He "humbled Himself" for His death upon the cross.

Aaron's attitude was one of penitent repentance; he came before God offering a bullock and a ram. He used incense as a "smoke screen," preventing his seeing the divine Presence in the Holy Place. Seven times he sprinkled blood on the mercy seat to expiate his own sins. He went in sideways and came out backwards, speaking of his reverence, almost reluctance, to enter God's presence, and then his further reluctance to leave.

B. *The Priests.* Aaron's offering was not only for himself but for "his house" (verse 6), his sons who were in the priesthood with him. The word "house" in verse 11 refers to the order of the priests, and Aaron repeats his confession to include them—not only his immediate family or household, but all the priests ("the house of Aaron," Psalm 135: 19).

C. *The People.* A goat was the animal chosen for the offering of the people. A bullock had been the animal sacrifice for Aaron and the priests. Two goats were selected and a "lot" was drawn from an urn to decide the fate of the two beasts. As the blood was sprinkled for himself so Aaron must now sprinkle it for the people.

II. PURIFICATION (verses 20-22)

There is a dual emphasis here—the purification of the sanctuary and of the people. The people needed purifying because of their sins of commission and omission, of presumption, willfulness and of ignorance. The emphasis that day was upon the cleansing of all sin in all its forms.

A. *The Animal.* A goat, according to Deuteronomy 14:4 was a "clean" animal. It was kept alive for it was to become a scapegoat. The root meaning of the word is "removal," reminding us of Psalm 103:12—"As far as the east is from the west, so far hath he removed our transgressions from us." The goat was sent away *the sins of the people heaped upon its head,* into the wilderness.

B. *The Ritual.* All this took place in the tabernacle court. First there was the symbolic transference of human sin to the animal sacrifice. The word "iniquities" implies a willful departure from the laws of God and can be translated "crookedness." The ordinary sacrifices performed upon the altar were for unwillful sinning, sins of ignorance; the scapegoat was for willful and unwillful sinful acts. "Transgressions" means "acts of rebellion." "Sins" means "deviating from the right path." The ritual of the Day of Atonement then covered all forms of sinning for all the people for all the days of the ensuing year.

C. *The Terminal.* A terminal is where trains are turned around that they might begin their return journey, but it can also mean the extremity or end. The scapegoat was driven into the wilderness to the very end, the end of the road, the end of its strength. It went into an uninhabited place, a solitary place, "a land which is cut off," that is, cut off from the encampment of Israel. Some suggest that it was driven over a precipice. A Jewish legend tells of a scarlet thread hung up where the track finished at the edge of the precipice. If it turned white then the sins of the people were forgiven—"though your sins be scarlet they shall be as white as snow"!

III. INSTRUCTIONS (verses 23-28)

After Aaron had performed his duties in the Holy of Holies he had to lay aside his linen garments and don once more his high priestly dress to complete the ritual in the outer court. The divine instructions cover the priest's dress, the animal's flesh and the resultant happiness.

A. *The Dress.* Aaron had been in close contact with the goat. The sins heaped upon this animal had defiled it and so Aaron himself was contaminated. Thus his clothes must be washed. If only Christians today understood something of the defiling nature of sin, its great contamination! Even the sacrifice for sin was defiling and Aaron must wash himself and his clothes. He could not return to the camp and the people until he had rid himself of ceremonial uncleanness.

B. *The Flesh.* The flesh of the bullock and of the other goat (the one not chosen as the scapegoat) was now burned. This was done outside the camp as a sign that their forgiven sins could never rise up again against them in judgment—it was final; they had obtained full remission.

C. *The Happiness.* Aaron is now able to return to the camp full of joy, happy because he has entered God's presence without dying, rejoicing because he has been the people's mediator and has obtained for them forgiveness of sin. In the same way the Lord Jesus Christ "*for the joy* that was set before him endured the cross, despising the shame" (Hebrews 12:2). The people too are happy, knowing that an atonement has been made and God's wrath appeased. We know from a later chapter that the jubilee trumpet was sounded at the end of the Day of Atonement, announcing with joy the people's release from the bondage of sin.

IV. THE INSTITUTION (verses 29-34)

As with the first Passover meal, the first Day of Atonement was to become regularly celebrated, and in this section we have the divine instructions which are to be observed on all future occasions. The Day of Atonement was to become an institution, the greatest day in the year for God's people.

A. *The Date.* It was to be observed once a year, on the tenth day of the seventh month. The Jews have always referred to it as "the Day." The strange thing is, however, that this day, with its interesting and impressive ritual, this foreshadowing of the cross of Calvary, this institution that has caught the imagination of poet, hymn writer and painter (Holman Hunt's famous canvas *The Scapegoat*) is not mentioned again in the Old Testament. Yet when the writer of the letter to the Hebrews wishes to explain the Atonement of Jesus Christ he cannot write without bringing in this great Old Testament day (Hebrews 9 and 10).

B. *The Duties.* Fasting and rest were to characterize the observance of this institution. Fasting is described as "afflicting your souls." In other words fasting is not going on a slimming diet; nor is it to be used as a weapon for getting one's own way or opinions noticed (i.e. a "hunger strike"). Fasting is always connected with the soul and a person's spiritual condition in God's Word. The aim of fasting is personal holiness or power in service. Sin is self-gratification; fasting is abstinence so that self may be lost in a fresh sight of God and a fresh spiritual experience entered into. Rest from daily toil was also enjoined by God upon His people for this day. They must be wholly taken up with what was being done for them.

C. *The Duration.* Although Scripture is silent about the future observance of this day, it was nevertheless instituted as "an everlasting statute." Continual sinning needed continual atonement. Even the abolition of animal sacrifice has not caused this day to be unobserved by God's ancient people. The orthodox Jew today believes that this day is no longer dependent upon animals and ancient rites, tabernacles or temples, but on repentant hearts. The fasting continued, and we believe "the fast" referred to in Acts 27:9 refers to the Day of Atonement, a day of rest and fasting that resulted in a late sailing for the Apostle Paul.

Thus the day continued to be observed, retaining a spiritual significance even when the sacrificial elements had to be abandoned. For the Christian today, however, it is interesting as a shadow, a type of Jesus Christ, the Great High Priest, who on Calvary entered into the holy place, a place not made with hands, and appeared before a holy God, His Father, as the once and for all sacrifice for sin, surpassing all that had gone before. The greatest day of the year for the believer in Christ is the day of *the* Atonement, surpassing and superseding all others, the day on which Christ died "according to the scriptures" (I Corinthians 15:3).

THE JUSTICE AND MERCY OF GOD

Numbers 35

As its name implies, the Book of Numbers has to do with numbering, or the census taken of the children of Israel as they were being marshalled for their march into the Promised Land.

The book is complementary to Leviticus. After communion must come service, and the theme of Numbers is "Qualifications for Service." The word "service" is used over forty times in the Authorized (King James) Version and is frequently translated "warfare" in other versions. The Christian's daily witness to the truth is a life-and-death struggle against the forces of evil and the powers of darkness.

An outline of Numbers may be given as follows:

I. PREPARATION FOR THE PILGRIMAGE (1-10)
   Census—Service—Separation
II. INTERRUPTIONS ON THE PILGRIMAGE (11-19)
   Complaints—Mutiny—Apostasy
III. CONTINUATION OF THE PILGRIMAGE (20-36)
   Prospects—Promises—Preparations

Our "famous" chapter then comes in the third section: "The Continuation of the Pilgrimage." It also comes in the third subsection which deals with the preparations being made for the very careful division and regulation of the Promised Land. It is, in fact, the "famous" chapter passage that describes the cities of refuge. We entitle it *The Justice and Mercy of God* because here, after all the failure, rebellion, complaints and so on of God's people, we see the unwearying patience and perpetual faithfulness of God giving His children a further proof of His justice and mercy. This famous chapter can be divided like this:

I. CITIES AND SUBURBS (verses 1-8)
II. REFUGE AND REVENGE (verses 9-15)
III. MURDER AND MANSLAUGHTER (verses 16-23)
IV. JUDGE AND JURY (verses 24-32)
V. DEATH AND DEFILEMENT (verses 33, 34)

Before the Second World War experiments were being made in England with "garden cities." Since that war and the advent of the Town and Country Planning acts, and as a result of enemy bombing, more daring schemes for city centers and suburbs have been tried.

The aim of the planners is for better designed living accommodation, more compact shopping, out of town factories, and healthier living in general. Thus we come to the first section of this famous chapter:

I. CITIES AND SUBURBS (verses 1-8)

Here we see something of God's care for His people. Special consideration is given to those whose whole life is given up to His service, the Levites.

Forty-eight cities were to be set aside for the support of the Levites. The Levites were to live among those to whom they ministered. This would make their priestly services available to all and at the same time be more convenient for the collection of the tithe system.

Around each city was to be "an open space" or "suburb" as it is translated in the Authorized Version. On this land it was not permitted to build houses or plant vineyards. It was more like London's Green Belt than the ordinary suburb of a big city which is usually "ribbon building" of domestic houses and local shops.

Before entering Caanan the Levites had lived around the tabernacle. In the Promised Land they were to be dispersed among the tribes. As full time workers they were to be taken care of and supported in a financial and material way. They were not to sow, till and reap themselves. In order that they could give necessary instruction in the things of God to the people, they were not to be entangled in the affairs of this life, they were not to serve tables, but have plenty of time for prayer and preparation for divine work.

This is a foreshadowing of the New Testament emphasis upon the honor in which the full time worker for Christ and the Church is to be held and his material needs supplied. The Apostle Paul states that we are to "communicate" or "share with" the teacher of the Word, if we are taught in that Word. This is where the Anglicans with their parish system and their vicarages and rectories built near the church are more Scriptural than most churches who frequently put their minister in a manse miles from the church and in a neighborhood far removed from those who frequent the church.

II. REFUGE AND REVENGE (verses 9-15)

Among these forty-eight Levitical cities were to be appointed six cities of refuge, three on either side of the river Jordan. These special cities were to be places of asylum for accidental killings. The cities of refuge were obviously selected from among the Levitical cities as they would thus be near a place where was to be found a man of high religious principle able to judge difficult and borderline cases of killing.

Verse 12 describes how the killer could find sanctuary in these cities from the "avenger," that is, the representative of the family of the slain man whose duty it was in this primitive society to avenge or vindicate the death of the victim. An intolerable shame rested upon a family's name until such a death had been avenged. This divine provision of a city of refuge was designed to take the responsibility away from the avenger and place it into the hands of an impartial tribunal or court of law, the "congregation."

The emphasis in Scripture is always upon the sacredness of human life. Occasionally, however, a man might kill another unintentionally, accidentally. For premeditated murder there was no excuse; but for killing under impulse, strong provocation, or some other excuse, God's mercy provided this way out so that divine justice might still be satisfied. These cities of refuge were not like the later sanctuary knockers of medieval times, that murderers might escape justice. The entry into a city of refuge by an escaping killer meant not escape from justice, but examination, inquiry, explanation and the execution of justice. Killing is sin, whether premeditated or unintentional, and God's justice must be satisfied. But in place of the death penalty the slayer would be shut up in the city of refuge until the death of the high priest.

III. MURDER AND MANSLAUGHTER (verses 16-23)

In order that there might be no miscarrying of justice, a clear distinction is now drawn between murder and manslaughter.

The fundamental distinction between willful murder and unintentional manslaughter is one of intention, and so everything hinges on what kind of weapon is used. Today, in this mid-century of violence, the murder weapon is often a clue to motive. So in verse 16 we are told that if the weapon is one of iron then he is a willful murderer; he has killed deliberately, after careful planning. If the killer has looked around for the right size and weight of stone, or wooden instrument such as a club, then there has been premeditation and it is plain murder. From verse 20 it is clear that if no weapon were used, but a push over a cliff top or from the roof of a house was the method of killing, and it was intentional, then murder was committed. On the other hand, if there was no intention of killing, and the "weapon" was a mere piece of farming equipment, then it was manslaughter. One of the most graphic pieces of writing is in C. H. Spurgeon's sermons (Vol. 1899, p. 221) in which he describes a farm laborer who accidentally killed a man in this way.

IV. JUDGE AND JURY (verses 24-32)

The accidental killing has occured; manslaughter has taken place; the killer has run for his life and is safe within the nearest city of refuge. Now what happens? In this section directions are given for legal procedure. A tribunal, a judge and jury, has to be chosen from the elders, appointed by the congregation. If the findings are that the killing was after all murder, then the city no longer remained a refuge to the killer. If manslaughter was proved, then the unfortunate killer could not buy his freedom; he must await the death of the high priest. The death of one high priest and the ordination of a new one marked in these ancient times the beginning of a new era, as with the coronation of a king or the election of a president in England or America today. There is also a Jewish tradition that the man's liberty was connected with the high priest because the high priest should have carried out such a ministry of intercession for the people during his life time that murder or manslaughter should have been impossible in Israel. A killing proved that he had not prayed sufficiently, he had failed in his duty, and so it was only fair to release the killer upon the priest's death.

V. DEATH AND DEFILEMENT (verses 33, 34)

Two major world wars and the mounting toll of road deaths have tended to make modern man hold human life cheap. It is never so in Scripture. Life comes from God—He is the Fount of all life, and so human life is sacred. In this section God's people are told plainly that if it were possible for a man to purchase his freedom after killing another then this results in the cheapening of human life, and ultimately that would corrupt the nation. Because God dwelt in the midst of Israel they must do nothing in the way of violence or unholiness that would defile the nation.

In the light of these sections in this "famous chapter" is it lawful to interpret the cities of refuge as a type of Jesus Christ? Many think so on the basis of Hebrews 6:18—"We . . . who have fled for refuge to lay hold upon the hope set before us." There are difficulties of interpreting the cities in this way as a type of Christ. First, the city of refuge was provided only for the accidental killer, not for the intentional, willful murderer. The Lord Jesus Christ died for those who "know not what they do," that is, those who sin unintentionally, *and* for those who deliberately break His commands, who through willfulness are living in rebellion against God.

Then, there were six cities but there are not six Christs. Again, the slayer could leave the city of refuge, if he wished to jeopardize his life, but there is eternal security for the believer. No man can pluck him out of Christ's hand. Then, too, the fugitive had only to set foot in the city's suburbs for safety. But it does the seeking sinner no good to stay at a distance from Christ or the cross; he must come near and stand upon "redemption ground." The precincts of the church or Sunday school do not save—only Christ and Calvary.

Perhaps the greatest argument against the city being a type of Christ is that within the city walls the killer was restricted. But the Christian life is not a restricted life—it is liberty not bondage! The city of refuge is in many ways an inadequate picture of the saving and keeping work of Christ. What it is a type of is the Christian Church. The true church welcomes sinners of all kinds, intentional and unintentional. As there were six cities so there are many churches of different denominations. A man who has come into church membership can leave it again, though not thereby losing his salvation.

There is no Scriptural account of any person taking advantage of a city of refuge. Neither in any well-known book of Scriptural typology (such as Patrick Fairbairn's) is there any reference to these cities being a type of Christ (Fairbairn does not allude to Hebrews 6:18). The words in Hebrews, with the phrase "lay hold" refer to the sanctuary of the altar (holding on to the horns of the altar) not to a city of refuge. There was no holding on to be done in the city. The refugee had but to put his foot within the city boundary to be safe. In Scripture a city never stands for one person, it always stands for a group or collection of people. Thus the city of refuge is not the Person of Christ, but the people of God, His Church.

THE YEAR OF RELEASE

Deuteronomy 15

"Deuteronomy" means "the second law." The Book of Deuteronomy does not contain new laws but is a repetition, a copy of those originally given. The children of Israel who had come out of Egyptian bondage had now died. The old teaching had to be given to the new generation. In this twentieth century there is seen to be a need for treading the old paths and the Puritan commentaries. Devotional works are being revived and reread. So it was that God saw the necessity for reminding His children of the laws and commandments formerly given. Thus in Deuteronomy six sermons by Moses, delivered in the plains of Moab, are recorded. These are the final words of the great leader of God's people and his emphasis is on "obedience" (the book's key word), and "Man's Motive of Obedience to God" (the book's theme).

The book can be outlined as follows:

I. RETROSPECT (1–4:43)
Historical Review (cf. Numbers 10–32)
II. DECALOGUE (4:44–11)
God's Covenant Repeated
III. PRECEPTS (12–26)
Civil, Domestic and Religious Regulations
IV. BENEDICTIONS (27–30)
Blessings and Curses—Responsive
V. PROSPECT (31–34)
Exhortation Regarding the Future

This "famous" chapter then comes in the third section and is about the Sabbatical year or the year of the Lord's release. In America this year is kept and honored among Christians more than in Great Britain. Colleges release their tutors and lecturers for twelve months that they might do research or write a book; churches release their minister or pastor that he might visit the Holy Land. Originally, however, the year of release was instituted because God's people were an agricultural community and the land needed a periodic rest in order to insure fertility. From that economic character of the year it later developed into a social convenience and its scope was enlarged to cover various situations. It is likely that the year began on the Day of Atonement.

It is quite remarkable, but in 1958 the state of Israel reported that for the first time since the days of the second temple in the first century Jewish farmers in Israel obeyed this command to observe the sabbatical year. Fifteen villages, affiliated with the movement known as Poalei Agudat, ceased to cultivate their land for twelve months. It has been estimated that over 5,000 people in 1958 decided to observe once again the "year of release." In spite of privation and even famine the law has once again been observed.

As the title suggests, the Sabbatical year occured every seventh year. Seven, in Scripture, is the number of completion or perfection. There are seven days to a week. For the Hebrew of old there was one feast day in each seventh month, and every seven years there was the year of release. The culmination of the sabbatical years occurred each fifty years when the jubilee was celebrated with the blowing of the jubilee trumpet.

This famous chapter falls into the following divisions:

> I.   THE REMISSION OF DEBTS (verses 1–6)
> II. THE ALLEVIATION OF NEED (verses 7–11)
> III. THE LIBERATION OF SLAVES (verses 12–18)
> IV. THE CONSECRATION OF CATTLE (verses 19–23)

I.   THE REMISSION OF DEBTS (verses 1–6)

It must be understood that these debts were not loans for the purpose of purchasing luxuries or entering into business transactions. These were not debts that had occurred through buying a house or expanding one's business. Ordinary trading debts belonged to a different category and did not come under the year of release. These were debts that had been contracted because a man had fallen upon hard times—misfortune or calamity had befallen him. Neither must it be assumed that the debts were automatically wiped out forever. It may have been of a temporary nature, for the seventh year only, a brief respite from paying high rates of interest. That is logical, for if it meant the cancellation of the debt forever, people would have been tempted to get into debt during the sixth year so that it would be cancelled in the seventh! That explains why the non-Jew (the "foreigner" of verse 3 did not share in this year of release. A debt contracted by a Gentile would probably be a business debt incurred while staying temporarily in the land.

One commentator states that in this section "we get near to the heart of God, full of compassion and mercy." Not only was the man in debt blessed by the year of release, but the money lender also, for he would have to trust God to supply his needs for twelve months while he was not receiving his repayments and interest. God is no man's debtor and in verse 6 we see that the man who thus foregoes his just exacting of the debt will be divinely blessed.

Surely there are three abiding lessons from this section for Christians. First, we ought to acknowledge our own spiritual indebtedness to Christ who has forgiven all our sins and blotted them out like a cancelled debt *forever*. Never again can the penalty for sin be exacted; Christ paid it all on the cross. Next, we must learn to be long-suffering and patient to those who are in difficulties, who are passing through stringent times. Finally, God expects the Christian to use his money wisely, putting it to good use, that it might do good to others. It is good to take up an offering at the Lord's Table of Communion, calling it "the Benevolent Fund."

II. THE ALLEVIATION OF NEED (verses 7-11)

For the Jew of old the modern proverb was applicable: "Charity begins at home." The Jewish proverb said: "The poor of thine own city should be helped before those of another city." Today the orthodox Jew is renowned for his charity, and as a race the Jews are known for their helping of each other. Thus in this section the emphasis changes from the compassionate heart of God to the tender-heartedness of man (verse 7). If the hand of a man is shut tight then that is an outward sign of an inward condition—tightness of heart. With the advent of the seventh year the temptation would be to refuse help to a needy neighbor, knowing that no repayments would be made for twelve months. Such a thought was covetousness, not charitableness (verse 9). "What am I going to get in return?" is still a prevalent thought among Christians and hinders direct giving to God's work and suggests bazaars, rummage sales and other money-raising efforts. The Lord loved a cheerful giver in the Old Testament as well as in the New! Generosity is a divine quality (verse 10) and giving should always be accompanied by pleasure and satisfaction knowing that it is a divine spiritual law that it is "more blessed to give than to receive."

But suppose we give to those who are in such circumstances that they can never hope to repay us? Then we must trust to the Lord to recompense us (verse 11). And suppose we cannot really afford to give when a need is made known or an appeal for help comes? We give sacrificially as Christians knowing that "my God shall supply all your need" (Philippians 4:19).

III. THE LIBERATION OF SLAVES (verses 12-18)

This is not such a drastic change of subject matter as might appear at first sight. A man's misfortune in those ancient days might have been so bad that even a loan of money from a friend could not save him. In order to avoid utter destitution he would have to sell himself temporarily and become a member of another's household, earning food and shelter for himself by doing menial service. In other words he sold himself into service for another; he became a slave! The slavery of the Old Testament must never be confused with that of the New. The Hebrew slave was comparatively well looked after for the master was governed by divine law in his treatment of his servants. There were rules and regulations governing his bodily injury and so forth. It was not so in the case of the slaves of the Greeks and Romans.

In the seventh year a voluntary slave or bondman was automatically set free and the master was obliged to equip him for his new freedom so that he could begin life again with confidence. There is a lovely thought in the original language of verse 14. It may be translated: "Thou shalt adorn him with a necklace." The sign of the slave was an iron and leather collar—a dog collar! By contrast the freed slave was adorned with a necklace of goods given him by his former master. As we sometimes speak of "showering gifts" upon people, so the slave was given cattle, food and drink to "set him up" in his new freedom. The spur for this was the memory of Egyptian bondage by the Hebrew master. Remembering how all God's people were once enslaved and then set free by God Himself, liberated with a goodly share of Egyptian spoil, the master liberated his slave in the year of release with a "necklace" of good things (verse 16).

If a slave liked his master and had been treated well during his time of service then he need not take advantage of the regulations for the year of release. He could elect to remain a slave forever. The sign of that decision would be a hole bored in the slave's ear. The servant would place his ear against a post and the awl or brace and bit would drill the hole. Verse 17 infers that similar requirements were in force for women servants during this year of release.

The abiding spiritual lesson is easy to perceive. Once we were in bondage to Satan, servants of sin. The Holy Spirit worked in our hearts as we came under the sound of the Gospel and one day we took advantage of the year of release. Nothing had to be paid for "Jesus paid it all, All to Him I owe." Jesus did it all, and more than that He put a necklace about us, giving us all the peace and joy and privileges of the Christian life. Now, however, we become willing slaves, "bond-slaves" as the Apostle Paul termed it, "branded" with the mark of ownership of Jesus Christ.

IV. THE CONSECRATION OF CATTLE (verses 19-23)

In the Book of Exodus it had been decreed that the firstlings of the cattle of the children of Israel should be sanctified or consecrated to the Lord. This we presume was in gratitude for the sparing of the first sons when those of the Egyptians were overtaken by death on the night of the Passover. Now verse 20 implies a special service and place for this consecration. No male "firstling" of any herd or flock was to be "worked" but instead sacrificed to the Lord. Verse 21 governs the sacrifice itself: the animal had to be unblemished. If found to be lame, or deformed in any other way, then it had to be eaten within the gates (verse 22) with the blood poured out upon the ground (verse 23). In other words, only the best is good enough for

God—a lesson that Christians are a long time learning—the best of our possessions and the best of our service. It is said that in England a Christian says: "Here comes a missionary on furlough. I must give her my coat and buy myself a new one." Our attitude should be: "I must make my old coat last a bit longer and buy the missionary a new one"! That which is shoddy, tumble-down and second-hand must never be "palmed off" on to the Lord or placed in His house—especially if we would not give it "space" in our own home! How easy it is to perform conscientious service for an earthly master (for financial gain) and yet do "slipshod" work for our heavenly Master—merely because His reward is to come!

> Take my life and let it be
> Consecrated, Lord, to Thee.
>
> ❋   ❋   ❋
>
> Take myself, and I will be,
> Ever, only, all for Thee.

OUR SUPERNATURAL RESOURCES

Joshua 6

Joshua is the first of the Old Testament historical writings and is named after the hero of the book. In these pages is recorded the arrival of God's people in the Promised Land. The book is crowded with military incidents and many critics are adverse in their judgment because of the warlike nature of it. It must be remembered, however, that God, because of His righteous nature, is perpetually antagonistic to sin. Joshua then is a description of "surgery" rather than "murder."

The book is also a continuation of Deuteronomy and Joshua himself is privilged to continue and complete what Moses left unfinished. The key word is "possession" and the theme: "Possessing our Possessions." An outline of the whole book is as follows:

    I. INVASION (1-5)
   II. CONQUEST (6-12)
  III. PARTITION (13-22)
  IV. DECEASE (23, 24)

Our "famous" chapter comes within Section II, the conquest of the land. The first stage of the campaign has to be the conquest of Jericho. God gave this victory to inspire confidence for future battles. The spies had reported: "The people is greater and taller than we; the cities are great and walled up to heaven" (Deuteronomy 1:28). But Jericho fell, and this one victory inspired confidence in Joshua and in God for the future. So it is in the spiritual life for young believers. The first successful battle with Satan after conversion helps greatly for the future. The lesson has to be learned that "each victory will help you some other to win."

Modern archaeology confirms the Word of God at every point. Spade work at the site of Jericho provides evidence of the falling of the walls and then the destruction of the city by fire. There may have been a secondary cause, such as an earthquake. If so, then it was a miracle that it occurred at the critical time. We prefer to entitle the chapter *Our Supernatural Resources* and to look beyond natural explanations.

The outline of Chapter 6 is:

    I. DIVINE INSTRUCTION (verses 1-7)
   II. HUMAN EXECUTION (verses 8-14)

38

III. Divine Intervention (verses 15-20)
IV. Human Devastation (verses 21-24)

I. Divine Instruction (verses 1-7)

God always likes His work done in His own way and so He gave specific instructions regarding Jericho and its conquest. They were to be carried out to the very letter. But first let us look at the city itself. As standards went in those days, it was strongly fortified. Keller, in *The Bible as History*, describes it as "a master-piece of military defence." There were two sets of walls, six feet thick. The gap of ten to twelve feet in between was filled with rubble. These walls were twenty-five to thirty feet high with very strong foundations. These details were discovered between 1907 and 1909 by a German-Austrian expedition. Verse one of this famous chapter describes the city as "straitly" shut up, that is securely bolted and barred or barricaded. That there was a curfew in force so that none might enter or leave, is another possible explanation. And this was all "because of Israel"! The inhabitants of Jericho were afraid of God's people! If only Christians who are so afraid of Satan would realize that the devil and his demons are really afraid of God's people!

Old commentators always saw in "shut up" Jericho a picture of the obstinate heart of the unbeliever. Could it not also be a similar thought to Revelation 3:20, the shut up nature of the Church of God until revival comes?

God had already made His plans, however, and He was prepared to wait until the time was right for the execution of His purpose: "See I have given into thine hand Jericho" (verse 2).

The divine instructions are given in verse three following. Summarized they are as follows: Seven priests carrying seven trumpets, followed by the ark of the covenant, were to march around Jericho in solemn procession, preceded by the army of Israel. This was to be done daily, the whole procession returning to the camp at Gilgal each night. On the seventh day they were to march around the city seven times, and then while the trumpets made a great noise, and as the people gave a great shout, the walls would fall down.

The trumpets are important. The Revised Version has "jubilee trumpets," so this was for Israel more of a religious occasion than a military one. If it was the rams' horns that were used then it impresses upon us that God was going to do nothing in a showy, ostentatious manner.

The walking round the walls could have been for several purposes. It would arrest attention; it would impress upon the inhabitants of Jericho the great number of Israelites. Perhaps it was to show the patience of God to Jericho for as Matthew Henry puts it: "God delivers in His way and in His own time."

Dr. Scofield in his Reference Bible illustrates the lesson well in a footnote: "The central truth here is that spiritual victories are won by means and upon principles utterly foolish and inadequate in the view of human wisdom." Writing to the Corinthians the Apostle Paul said: "But God hath chosen the foolish things of the world to confound the wise; and God hath chosen the weak things of the world to confound the things which are mighty; And base things of the world, and things which are despised, hath God chosen, yea, and things which are not, to bring to nought things that are: That no flesh should glory in his presence" (I, 1:27-29). And again: "For though we walk in the flesh, we do not war after the flesh: (For the weapons of our warfare are not carnal, but mighty through God to the pulling down of strong holds;) Casting down imaginations, and every high thing that exalteth itself against the knowledge of God, and bringing into captivity every thought to the obedience of Christ" (II, 10:3-5).

II. HUMAN EXECUTION (verses 8-14)

These verses are a repetition of the divine instructions, but also show how they were carried out or executed by Joshua, the priests, the army and the people in every detail.

What a strange sight it must have been and what a weird effect upon the inhabitants of Jericho it must have had! No war machines were maneuvered into position; no soldiers undermined the walls; no sound was made in the form of popular marching songs; no weapons were in readiness for battle. And what faith all this expressed on behalf of Israel. No wonder the writer of the famous "faith chapter" (see later: *The Westminster Abbey of the Bible*), Hebrews 11, declared: "By faith the walls of Jericho fell down." Wonderful soldiers of faith not to want to trust to their weapons! Imagine the United Nations forsaking orthodox and nuclear weapons and organizing a Christian witness march!

If only we had more faith in God's weapons, in His ways and in the work which He is able to do on our behalf. God wants His work done according to His revealed will. We must keep to His "it is written" and give pride of place to prayer and preaching.

III. DIVINE INTERVENTION (verses 15-20)

On the seventh day it happened! Seven times around they went this day, reminding themselves that seven was the divine number of perfection and completion. They shouted and the walls fell flat. Excavations have revealed that the outer ring fell outward and downhill, while the inner walls fell inward upon the buildings behind and buried them. In the science laboratory we have seen glass tumblers splintered into fragments by the human voice or a musical instrument at a certain pitch. We know of car windshields being shattered by a jet airplane breaking the sound barrier. But is that the explanation here? We must not read into God's Word what is not there. The inspired record does not say that the walls fell, after cracking and crumbling, because of the blowing of trumpets or the shouting of people. If we believe in God and His power as Creator; if we believe in Him as the Author of the natural laws, then we need go no further than to say that this was divine intervention on behalf of God's people.

There are instructions within instructions obeyed in this section. Previously Joshua had been told to spare Rahab and her household because she sheltered and helped the Israelite spies to make their reconnaissance. Now Joshua impresses upon the Israelites the need to honor this promise.

Further a warning is given in verses 17 and 18. All spoil in Jericho was to be looked upon as "accursed." It was not to be taken for personal use. Everything in Jericho belonged to the Lord (verse 19).

We must note that the people were to restrain themselves, and keep themselves from all that defiled in Jericho. The teaching summed up in the phrase, "Let go and let God," can be taken too far. We must never expect God to do something for us that we can quite easily do for ourselves. We have the power to turn off the smutty television show; we can return the book to the public library that is full of immorality; we can stop looking and listening and speaking about sinful practices. As Romans 6:11 puts it, "*Reckon* ye also yourselves to be dead indeed unto sin."

IV. HUMAN DEVASTATION (verses 21-24)

Apart from the salvation of Rahab and her relatives the city was utterly devastated (verse 21). Except for the Lord's gold and silver the city was burned with fire (verse 24). A curse was put upon the city and a ban imposed upon its rebuilding. Five hundred years later the ban was broken, but it cost the builder and his two sons their lives.

Jericho was a frontier fortress, a border town. Now border towns are often a mixed multitude—English, Irish, Scots and Welsh, as the case may be. It is a place of divided loyalties. So in the Christian life there are borderline things. The Bible does not legislate for certain pleasures, amusements and habits. Some of them were unknown in Bible times. But we must apply Bible principles to these doubtful things, at the same time remembering the old adage: "When in doubt —don't"! If these "Jerichos" are not dealt with—the petty pinpricks and doubtful things of the Christian life—then the bigger issues will be overlooked. Deal with them and we shall be able to say: "So the Lord was with Joshua," substituting our name for Joshua's.

THE KIND OF MAN GOD CAN USE

Judges 6

The Book of Judges takes its title from the period of Jewish history known as the "reign of the Judges," that is, civil, religious, and military chieftains in command of God's people between the lives of Joshua and Saul. These "judges" were raised up by God to be the "saviours" of His oppressed people and they were warrior, priest or prophet judges.

No one knows who wrote this book, although tradition holds the view that the author was Samuel. It is a sad book whoever wrote it, for it records a period of ungodliness, decay, degeneration, rebellion and apostasy, although God's people were now in the Promised Land. They had wandered for forty years in the wilderness, but now for a period approximately ten times as long they know spiritual wandering within the land God had promised to give them. The key word of the book is "anarchy" (lawlessness or confusion) and the key text is either 17:6, 18:1, 19:1 or 21:25. The theme and abiding message is, "Proneness to Wander." God's deliverances often occur when conditions seem at their worst. He is able to raise up the right man or the right woman at the right time.

The whole book can be given in outline form as follows:

    I. DECLENSION (1-16)
        A. *Moral and Spiritual*
   II. CONFUSION (7-21)
        A. *Civil and Religious*

The "famous" chapter we entitle *The Kind of Man God Can Use*, and verse divisions are:

    I. THE SITUATION (verses 1-6)
        A. *Idolatry and Impoverishment*
   II. THE PROPHET (verses 7-10)
        A. *Reminder and Rebuke*
  III. THE DELIVERER (verses 11-40)
        A. *Commission, Cowardice, Courage and Confirmation*

I. THE SITUATION (verses 1-6)

This "famous" chapter comes in the first division of the book, Declension. The moral and spiritual declension is summed up in the words of this first verse: "They did evil in the sight of the Lord." In spite of three previous experiences of servitude for idolatrous ways God's people have again become idol worshipers, forgetful of the true and living God who has three times been their patron and defender. The result is that the Midianites, a wandering, warlike people, masters of the art of pilfering and plundering, came upon them, routed them and left them in a state of famine.

The struggle was long and bitter. The Israelites had to take to caves and other hideouts and try to carry on life from such "air raid" shelters. But their enemies were "like grasshoppers (locusts) for multitude" (verse 5). What a description! Not only does it speak of a great number, a swarm of enemies, but it tells of the confused state of the battle rather than a regular, organized, pitched conflict. It was guerilla warfare carried on by an undisciplined mob. Impoverishment and famine resulted.

Frequently the spiritual parallel to the history of Israel in Judges is said to be the professing Christian Church down the ages. Today we are in a state of disruption and disunity. Many Christians hide out of sight in their dens and never witness to the unsaved world. The twentieth-century Christian Church is by and large impoverished spiritually. The idolatry of the world is in our midst: the worship of the god of money, position, possessions, power and learning. This condition went on for seven years for Israel—the number of completion in Scripture. In other words the apostasy of the Church seems almost complete today with its modernist theology and liberal interpretation of Scripture.

II. THE PROPHET (verses 7–10)

In spite of such a tragic situation or condition prevailing, we now see what God is going to do. He does not deliver His people immediately but first prepares the way of deliverance by sending a "preparer" (the prophet) for the deliverer. As Matthew Henry put it: "Before He sent an angel to raise them up a saviour He sent a prophet to reprove them for sin and bring them to repentance."

After seven years' declension the people cry to God (verse 7), not on this occasion primarily to complain of their troubles, but to confess their sins. What marvelous divine patience and graciousness that after seven years' silence He was willing to hear them! In their prosperity they neglected Him; in their poverty He is willing to help them. Their extremity was God's opportunity, as is often the case.

The prophet is unnamed. Nor are we told when and how he delivered God's message. Was it at some solemn fast day held because of their dire straits? It may have been that he was a messenger and went about delivering the same message from den to den, tribe to tribe, family to family. Obviously these things are not told us because God wants us to notice the more important fact: the message itself and the purpose of the prophet.

The message begins with a reminder (verse 8): "I brought you up . . . and out." God had brought them up from Egypt and out of bondage, the very situation in which they find themselves with the Midianites. The reminder is continued in verse 9. The prophet reminds them that not only has God delivered in the past but He has given them the land of those He subdued.

The message closes with a rebuke (verse 10): "I am the Lord your God." They had been ungrateful, they had forgotten that they were under an obligation to Him and that He alone should be worshiped and served. "Ye have not obeyed my voice." Their sin was disobedience. Such a sin includes others: reliance upon self, self-will, pride and so forth.

Once again we must keep in mind the New Testament spiritual parallel, the Church. How we need to remind ourselves continually of what God has done for the Church which He purchased with His own blood. We need to read and reread standard works on the history, progress and expansion of the Church like *The Story of the Church* (A. M. Renwick) or *The Unquenchable Light* (K. S. Latourette). How disobedient we have been to the leadings of the Holy Spirit!

III. THE DELIVERER (verses 11-40)

This situation was caused by the children of Israel themselves; it was their own sinfulness. The prophet was the first part of the divine plan to help them. The deliverer is God's man for the hour, and in this section we see the kind of man God can use in just such an emergency. Of Gideon Dr. Alexander Whyte says: "We are not told to whom we are indebted for the Book of Judges but whoever he was he was a master of the pen, and the story of Gideon is his masterpiece."

First we note his commission. It was given by an angel of the Lord. Some believe it was the pre-incarnate Christ, that is, the Son of God in a temporary human form before He adopted human form for His earthly ministry at the Incarnation. He came to Gideon when he was alone, withdrawn from the world, when about his daily business of threshing. So the Saviour came to fishermen in the New Testament, and so God called Amos and others from the field or farm.

Next we notice Gideon's cowardice. Gideon's character is a mixture of cowardice and courage, humility and haughtiness. He foreshadows Paul who in human weakness discovered divine strength.

Verses 11 to 15 give an account of Gideon's cowardice, but Gideon's view of himself is not how God sees him. The Lord's angel refers to him as "Thou mighty man of valour." God always sees more than what a man is—He sees what He can make of him, what he can become. The words of the commission are, "Go . . . thou shalt save Israel." Fearful and afraid, questioning his fitness for the task (not, however, questioning God's power), Gideon feels unworthy of the honor of such service. As Christians and as churches we must always feel this sense of unworthiness if God is to use us.

Gideon's courage is recorded in verses 25 to 29. He begins by overthrowing his father's altar. Then he uses the same stones to erect an altar to God. The much-needed work of reformation begins with treading under foot the false god Baal that the One true and living God might be exalted. No wonder Dr. Whyte comments: "At every blow of Gideon's swift axe new strength came into his arms." This reformation then began at home. So judgment must begin at the house of God if revival is to come. The Church must put her own house in order if blessing is to overflow to the world. We must relinquish idols and discard every reminder of our idolatry.

Finally, there is confirmation of the commission in verses 36 to 40.

Seeking such confirmation Gideon makes a contract with God. He is ready to become the deliverer of God's people if God will prove that He is with him. He asks for his sign in the same spirit of apology as Abraham in Genesis 18, 30 and 32.

Taking a fleece, a sheepskin rug, he asks God that in the early morning there shall not be dew on both the rug and the ground—only upon the sheep-skin—the ground is to be dry. Not content with this he reverses the procedure and asks for dew on the ground and a dry skin, apologizing, of course, for his seeming distrust. It has become a favorite method of guidance with Christians of all ages! "Let me pass such-and-such an examination and I shall know, O God, that you want me to become a missionary," and so on. But there is more here than a lesson in guidance. The fleece stands for small Israel and the surrounding ground for the Midianites. God could distinguish between them. So the fleece can stand for the New Testament Church. Can God see the distinction between His own people and people of the world? Are we as distinct as sheep and goats? Or, to use the Saviour's metaphor, are we like sheep in the middle of a pack of wolves, fighting for our lives, upholding the truth, proclaiming the Gospel? Have we obeyed the injunction: "Be ye separate and come ye out from among them" (II Corinthians 6:17)?

Dr. Alexander Whyte points out that there is an uninspired, apocryphal addition to the story of Gideon's fleece. A legend has it that Gideon's mother made a mantle out of it and that Gideon wore it beneath his armor, next to his heart. Thus he was always full of hope when others despaired, and cautious when others would have gone to their destruction. Perhaps the legend was formed because of verse 34: "The Spirit of the Lord came upon Gideon." Therein lay his secret. It was not in the fleece of a sheep, but in the Spirit of God. That is the need of every believer and every church, an enduement of God's Holy Spirit, anointing us, filling us, baptizing us, giving us that holy unction without which all service is futile. The Spirit-filled man is the kind of man God can use.

CONTAGIOUS FAITH

Ruth 1

This book of undying loveliness and charms had such an effect on the poet Keats that he referred to it in his *Ode to a Nightingale*—this is the only other book besides Esther that bears a woman's name as title. It is called Ruth because Ruth is the central figure and heroine. What a relief it is to read this small book after the turmoil and warfare of the Book of Judges. It is refreshing, set as it is in the placid scene of Bethlehem during barley harvest. It is a book full of the "milk of human kindness." The theme is, "Rest in Weariness" and it has great typical value, Boaz the "kinsman-redeemer" being a type of Christ. An outline of the book is as follows:

    I.   FROM THE FORBIDDEN LAND (1)
        Ruth's Decision
   II.   IN THE HARVEST FIELD (2)
        Ruth's Subjection
 III.   ON THE THRESHING FLOOR (3)
        Ruth's Cessation
 IV.   AT THE CITY GATE (4)
        Ruth's Remuneration

This "famous" first chapter of the book comes in the first main division, From the Forbidden Land, and sets the keynote of the whole book. The key to understanding the book is to remember the Jewish emphasis upon the significance of names. All persons in this delightful story bear names that describe their characters. A name does more than identify a person for the easterner; it identifies a person's character. Then too the name was expected to exercise or exert an influence upon the person bearing that name. How we need to remember that if we are Christians we bear the name of Christ and that should influence our daily life and conduct, character and bearing.

The keynote of this famous chapter is *Contagious Faith.* How could Ruth have had such love and devotion for Naomi unless the faith of Naomi had created the same sort of faith and quality of faith in Ruth. Ruth learned faith in God from Naomi. Naomi's quiet but strong loyalty to her God produced responsive faith in the heart of Ruth. As believers in Christ we ought to ask ourselves frequently: "Have I heard another say 'Thy God shall be my God' because my faith in Him is so conspicuous and contagious"? If we are witnessing and testifying to our faith, and our life reinforces what our lips declare, then our faith will be contagious.

The chapter will be studied under the following pattern:

    I. The Culmination of Circumstances (verses 1-5)
    II. The Resolve to Return (verses 6-18)
    III. The Attitude Upon Arrival (verses 19-22)

I. The Culmination of Circumstances (verses 1-5)

The book begins with the words: "Now it came to pass." This common phrase in Scripture for the commencement of a book is frequently used to connect a story with preceding events. In this case "famine" refers to the account in Judges 6:3-6. Then too the phrase "now it came to pass" often denotes sorrow or misfortune. So during this severe famine misfortune came to a certain man of Bethlehem, his wife and his two sons.

Famine was one of the periodic scourges in Bible times. Sometimes it was the natural result of lack of rain, disease or blight ruining a crop; at other times it was caused by marauding bands of soldiers or brigands. The Hebrew word for famine means "hunger"; in the New Testament it means "want of food." Almost always in God's Word a famine is related to divine providence and the doctrine of the Fall. In other words a famine is a direct outcome of human sin and God's curse upon the soil. Sometimes God withdrew the fruits of nature from His people because of their disobedience or idolatry. A famine thus represents divine displeasure.

We have seen that in Judges God's people are in the Promised Land. A famine in the land that God promised was "flowing with milk and honey"! Bethlehem means "house of bread," but now it is a place of barrenness, hardship and famine. So is a believer's life when he persists in sinful disobedience to God and His Word.

This "certain man" then left what was considered one of the finest and most fruitful districts and emigrated to a forbidden land, the country of Moab. Perhaps he was wealthy, or maybe "a certain man" infers that he was frightened, having been stripped of all his possessions by a hungry mob. Perhaps he did not intend staying long in Moab, only until the emergency was over. The backsliding Christian does not really want to stay long in the world, he only goes in for a moment with an unsaved friend, to enjoy "the pleasures of sin for a season." "There's no harm," he says, "in one drink, one bet on the dogs or horses, one visit to the theater or some other doubtful place of amusement." Unfortunately the visit often becomes a long stay, as it did with this man from Bethlehem. And as this man took his family with him, so the backslider often takes other believers into the world.

The clue to this man's character is in his name (verse 2): Elimelech. It means "My God is King" or "Unto me shall the kingdom come." Does this tell us that he was an arrogant man, his heart full of pride? By contrast his wife's name was Naomi, meaning "the sweet one," one who did loving and kind deeds. Their two sons were called Mahlon (meaning "sickness") and Chilion (meaning "vanishing" or "consumption"). It would seem then that their names were given to them because of the famine and its effect upon small children.

Elimelech died (verse 3) and we can infer that it was not through old age or infirmity but because he had remained too long in the forbidden land. The wife took no notice of the divine warning and remained in Moab. The sons went a step further and married Moabite girls. How often is this sin of the "unequal yoke" taught and yet some believers persist in marrying unbelieving partners! Divine judgment visited these sons; they too died. Surely the New Testament epitaph to write upon the tombs of Elimelech, Mahlon and Chilion is: "He that will save his life shall lose it."

The names of the wives (verse 4) were Orpah (meaning "ornamented with rich hair") and Ruth (meaning "friendship"). Thus we are left in our story with three widows: one aged and two young women bereft of their husbands. Such are the calamitous circumstances surrounding these three.

II. THE RESOLVE TO RETURN (verses 6-18)

Naomi was in Moab because her husband took her there. But there is no need to remain in a wrong place when the reason for being there ceases to exist. Matthew Henry put it: "When constraint ends; choice begins."

At first the resolve to return was strong with all three widows. They felt ill-fated and that bad-luck was dogging their footsteps every day. It was not uncommon for a famine to last seven years, and in verse 6 we are told how they hear that after ten years there is no longer any famine in Bethlehem. Days of plenty have not yet returned, but better to live in congenial surroundings and have the necessities of life than uncongenial circumstances with luxuries! Better to be in the Lord's land with divine provision than in Satan's country with his luxuries. So these defenseless women begin the fifty mile journey home (at least, home for Naomi) during lawless times. Their resolve was turned into action.

Verse 8 is important. An oriental parting never took place within the home. The parting guest was always accompanied some distance along the road. So the two daughters-in-law go with Naomi to speed her on her way. Naomi stops after some distance and attempts to dissuade them from coming further. If she had done that in the house then they might have tried to keep her; if she had tried to persuade them to leave with her while in the security of their home they might not have been moved by her appeal. Now with house and home far behind she is safe in persuading them to accompany her. First (verse 8) she commends their kindness to her late sons. Because of her indebtedness they need not feel any qualms at going back instead of going on. Our Lord always adopted Naomi's practice and sought to discourage eager followers. If they said: "We will follow Thee whithersoever Thou goest," He replied: "The Son of Man hath not where to lay His head." Sometimes modern evangelistic methods give the impression of making it too easy to enter the Kingdom. Inquirers are not asked to count the cost of discipleship.

The young widows agree to go with Naomi (verse 10), but only with the desire of settlement among the Hebrews, in their land, not with any idea of becoming worshipers of the true God. Naomi next tries sarcasm in order to dissuade them (verses 11, 12). The result is that Orpah turns back but Ruth decides to go on, and her decision is one that includes willingness to become a believer as well as a dweller in the land. Besides wanting to adopt the Jewish way of life she wants to live the life of God (verse 16). Ruth's resolve is a six-fold one: 1. To travel with Naomi anywhere ("Whither thou goest I will go"); 2. To live with Naomi in any place ("Where thou lodgest I will lodge"); 3. To settle with Naomi and anyone else ("Thy people shall be my people"); 4. To adopt Naomi's religion ("Thy God shall be my God"); 5. To die with Naomi at any time ("Where thou diest"); 6. To be buried with Naomi in any place ("There will I be buried"). It does not take much imagination to work out the parallels with Christian discipleship, substituting ourselves for Ruth and the Lord Jesus for Naomi. Are we thus fully and completely committed?

III. THE ATTITUDE UPON ARRIVAL (verses 19-22)

"All the city was astir" (or moved) (verse 19). Imagine it to be some small English village or American "small town"—small town talk, curtain peering, and so forth. It was even more prevalent in Palestine with their close community life and rather crude architecture. What met these prying eyes? "They two." A Jewish rabbi comments: "The purpose of this expression is to indicate that the true Jew and the proselyte (the one who has adopted the Jewish faith) are equal in the eyes of God." One was an old woman, weary and worn, marked and aged by sorrow and suffering (for what a change the ten years evacuation had made!); the other was a young woman, serene of disposition, displaying such unfamiliar loyalty to a mother-in-law of another race. They had to ask: "Is this Naomi"? She was so changed by privation and sorrow that the women of Bethlehem gave her a new name, Marah, or bitter. She who had gone away with all her worldly goods and riches now returned empty and of no reputation, for her husband was dead. But she returned a better and a wiser woman. How often can the backslider testify, looking back upon the barren years away from the Lord, that the experience has been for good, for it has prevented such a lapse recurring and it has been a means of helping others when their faith was faltering.

So Ruth and Naomi returned, and it was barley harvest, that is, April when the Passover festival began. How wonderful in God's time table. Ruth could now avail herself of the old Mosaic law and have the gleaners share of the cut barley, those corners of the field that were left for such as her. Praise God,

> He never is before His time,
> He never is behind!

FIGHTING FOR A RIGHTEOUS CAUSE

I Samuel 17

The First Book of Samuel may be divided into four parts, each section depicting a great character: Eli, Samuel, Saul and David. The predominant theme is, "Prayer Changes Things." The key word of the book is "prayer," the key text being Chapter 12:23, "As for me, God forbid that I should sin against the LORD in ceasing to pray for you."

The outline of the book then is as follows:

    I.   ELI (1—3:18)
        Humility and Ignominy
   II.   SAMUEL (3:19—8)
        Fidelity and Integrity
  III.   SAUL (9—15)
        Jealousy and Instability
  IV.   DAVID (16—31)
        Diplomacy and Intrepidity

It is, of course, impossible to sum up a man's character in two words, but those given in the above outline are carefully chosen to illustrate the salient features and chief tendencies of the person.

Our "famous" chapter is one concerning David, who in the previous chapter has been anointed king of Israel by Samuel.

Although chapter 17 is so well-known, it is not so well-known that this is a difficult chapter textually. Many verses, because of the obscurity of the old Hebrew manuscripts, have been left out in such versions as the Septuagint, the Greek version of the Old Testament. Some of the difficulties are these: in the previous chapter we are told that Saul loved David greatly and made him his armour-bearer (16: 19-23), and yet in chapter 17 he is away from the army during a time of national danger and seems an unheard-of person! Then verses 12 following of this famous chapter are a repetition of what has been said in the previous chapter. Logical explanations can be given of these and other difficulties however. The exploits referred to in chapter 16 may be the slaying of the lion and the bear and not the military deeds of courage; while Saul's mental illness might have prevented him from taking much notice of David on the first occasion. Obviously, as a boy musician, a wandering minstrel, he would not have been taken much notice of in any case. Leaving these difficulties we divide the famous chapter into these sections:

I. The Champion and His Challenge (verses 1-11)
  A. *His Size* (verse 4)
  B. *His Equipment* (verses 5-7)
  C. *His Challenge* (verses 8-10)
II. The Shepherd and His Speech (verses 12-30)
III. The King and His Kindness (verses 31-40)
IV. The Combatants and the Combat (verses 41-54)
V. The Victor and His Virtues (verses 55-58)

One of the great dangers in studying such a famous chapter is that it is so gripping and thrilling that we tend merely to retell it to ourselves, perhaps "dressing it up" in modern speech. C. H. Spurgeon, once preaching upon verse 50 of this chapter began by saying: "A careful perusal of the whole chapter will well repay our pains . . . I want the entire narrative as a text." There is, however, one extremely beneficial way of studying the chapter, that is, by seeing David as a type of Jesus Christ. That must always be kept in mind when studying the chapter under such divisions as we have outlined.

I. The Champion and His Challenge (verses 1-11)

The opposing armies of the Philistines and the children of Israel are encamped upon opposite hills. As was common at that time the chosen representatives of each army were to decide the issue. In one way it is a pity the custom has been dropped! How less devastating would be modern war if an Adolph Hitler could have fought it alone with a Joe Stalin!

Here in this section we are told something of the Philistine's champion: his size, equipment and challenge.

A. *His Size* (verse 4). Goliath was approximately nine or ten feet high. Giants are mentioned several times in Scripture. Sometimes they are called "mighty men" and sometimes "the mighty one." They were men of immense stature and seemed more prevalent before the Flood than afterward. Scripture very wisely tells us that we cannot "by thought add one cubit to our stature" (Matthew 6:27)—not by wishful thinking or by wearing stiletto heels! In the Christian life physical stature is of no importance. A man's real height is whether he can reach heaven when on his knees! Spiritual stature is what really matters. We should strive to "grow up into Him in all things" that we might "grow in grace" and in a knowledge of His Word.

B. *His equipment* (verses 5-7). We know not what Goliath's helmet of brass weighed. We are only told that his coat of mail was 157 pounds weight. The brass greaves or shin guards are also unspecified, but the target or javelin which was carried between his shoulders had a staff like a weaver's beam and an iron head weighing 19 pounds. A servant carried his shield for him. Such were the weapons in which Goliath put his trust. By contrast the Christian must put on "the whole armour of God," putting on each piece "with prayer."

C. *His challenge* (verses 8-10). Goliath refers not to himself as "a Philistine" but (according to the Hebrew) *"the* Philistine." He was the well-known Philistine, the champion whose renown and fame had been spread abroad. His tone is thus proud, defiant, terrifying, boastful. How similar are the pronouncements of the believer's adversary, Satan! How similarly blatant are the giant evils of our time: gambling, drinking, smoking, impure entertainment and the rest.

II. THE SHEPHERD AND HIS SPEECH (verses 12-30)

After the above glimpse of the might of man, Goliath in all his military equipment, we now see something of the quiet workings of the providence of God. David the shepherd boy is brought into the picture in a natural and delightful way. He is his father's messenger, bearer of provisions and supplies to his brothers who are "out at the front." This shepherd boy leaves his sheep for a while without he or his father knowing that God has some greater guardianship in store for him.

Arriving at the Israelite's camp David notices that a bold and boastful enemy champion has struck timidity and fear into the hearts of God's people. At once David is concerned about the honor of God. Like the Lord Jesus Christ, David is filled with righteous indignation. Discouraged by his elder brother from making himself heard, David nevertheless persists and gains a hearing. Eventually his speech upholding the honor of God comes to the ears of the king. David could have been provoked to quarrel with his own brother, but he sees that the real foe is Goliath and he must be dealt with. How the Christian Church needs to learn that lesson! What petty bickering and quarrels there sometimes are among church members, when all the time the real foe is undealt with! Is it not that we are sometimes more concerned about our own honor rather than God's honor? We have a desire to "establish our rights" or "prove our points," whereas our chief concern should be to vindicate God's honor and concern ourself with defeating the evils in the world.

III. THE KING AND HIS KINDNESS (verses 31-40)

The king having now heard of this shepherd boy, David is presented to him and he undertakes to fight Goliath. With great kindness the king tries to dissuade David, excusing him on the grounds of youth (verse 33). This was always a favorite verse of C. H. Spurgeon and other youthful champions of the faith. Paul perhaps had it in mind when he wrote to Timothy: "Let no man despise thy youth" (I Timothy 4:12). It is not physical size that matters in spiritual conflict as we have already seen. Nor is it physical maturity, but spiritual maturity that fits a Christian for spiritual service.

In marked contrast with Goliath David recounts his deeds of prowess, but emphasizes that it was the Lord who delivered him from the lion and the bear (verse 37). Spurgeon has three R's for this section: recollections, reasonings and results. David began by recollecting what God had done for him in the past; from that he reasoned that his coming conflict was a true parallel (as he defended defenseless sheep so now he must defend Israel, God's defenseless sheep); as he was alone in fighting the lion and the bear so he must fight Goliath alone; as he had been up against the sheer brute force of untamed nature so now he was against the brutality of Goliath. From these reasonings he was able to deduce certain results: he could run the same risks again for he was relying on the same God; what God had done once He could do again.

Thus it was that the king kindly suggested to David that he might borrow his armor—not realizing that spiritual equipment available to David and in which David had utmost trust and reliance. Undoubtedly it would have been fine armor, royal equipment, but David had not "proved" (verse 39) it; he was unaccustomed to the "feel" of it; he did not feel "at home" in it, and so he quickly put it off.

IV. THE COMBATANTS AND THE COMBAT (verses 41-54)

We must now beware of assuming that Goliath's weapons were carnal (as Paul puts it) and David's were spiritual. David also had material weapons although not as extensive and complicated as the giant's. David's were the ordinary weapons of a humble shepherd boys, a sling and a stone with four spare "shots." Against these Goliath had a spear, sword and shield. Then too, to "finish off" Goliath, David had to resort to Goliath's own sword. Remembering our title of this famous chapter we can say with Dr. G. Campbell Morgan: "(David) was armed with the profound sense of the righteousness of his cause; the material weapons of David were needed, and on that level they were superior to those of the giant, for they operated ere the sword and spear and the javelin could be brought into use. But it was the sense of the righteousness of his cause which gave inerrancy and strength to the slinging of David." That is what always makes the difference when a Christian or Christian fellowship is engaged in battle—the righteousness of the cause for which we are fighting. We are battling against sin and Satan—Satan who has blinded the eyes and stopped the ears and hardened the hearts of the unbelieving world. He has them in his power. Well, then, we are "good soldiers of Jesus Christ," His champions, dressed in royal armor, engaged in fighting the powers of darkness and wickedness in high places. We would not be half so timid and half-heartened if only we realized we were fighting to promote God's glory, possessed by an overwhelming sense of the righteousness of our cause.

Let us sum up David's preparations then by saying that he relied upon proved weapons. He used that sling every day of his life, in practice if not in earnest. Does that not remind us of II Samuel 1:18,

"Also he (David) bade them teach the children of Judah the use of the bow: behold, it is written in the book of Jasher"? The bow was not a new weapon in those days; it had been used many times previously, in fact it was spoken of in this book of Jasher referred to. But the bow was a neglected weapon and the children of Judah had to learn to become bowmen all over again. They were persuaded to return to a well-tried, trusted weapon, and it was this weapon that felled Goliath—the shepherd's sling. What a spiritual lesson for believers! Today is the age of newfangled gospel weapons. We are supposed to be old-fashioned if we do not hold monthly Sunday evening film services; if we do not put on an entertaining program of brains' trusts, Christian "revues," and the like, all to attract the outsider. But all the while we are forsaking the well-tried weapons of preaching and prayer, weapons ordained of God for the conversion of sinners. Men are saved by "the foolishness of preaching" and preaching in the power and demonstration of the Holy Spirit is the sling that brings giants low.

David's weapons were scorned by the enemy (verse 43), and probably by his brethren and friends. So might ours be, but no matter, when they are ordained, owned and blessed of Almighty God.

V. THE VICTOR AND HIS VIRTUES (verses 55-58)

Dr. Alexander Whyte, in his six volumes of *Bible Characters,* has devoted four chapters to David: David in his virtues, vices, graces and services. Certainly David had many virtues, and in this last section we have a miniature portrait of the victor in battle, with more than a hint at some of his virtues. It was usual in those days to ask who a man's father was in order to find out who the son was (verse 58). David had just laid low the giant and delivered Israel, but he is not the slightest bit proud or puffed up. Instead of bragging about himself or his deed he is modest and refers to himself as "the son of thy servant Jesse the Bethlehemite" (verse 58). Some Christian ministers are known as "evangelist so-and-so's brother," or "Mrs. Bland's husband," that is, they live in the shadow of the other, basking in their reflected glory. David could now have attributed all renown to himself, but he humbly describes himself as "son of Jesse." Many a famous preacher or missionary has come from humble surroundings, has had only a humble upbringing; his forbears have been obscure men and women. William Carey was the son of a village weaver ("miserably poor and seemingly without prospects"); Robert Rowntree Clifford, founder of London's West Ham Central Mission, was the son of a shipyard worker, and so we could continue. But background and breeding are nothing to Almighty God. He chooses whom He wills, calls a man and equips him, then uses him in His righteous cause.

PROMISE-KEEPING

II Samuel 9

The Second Book of Samuel is a story of triumph and tragedy, for it records the rise and fall of King David. After magnificent victories sin creeps in. The theme is, "The Exceeding Sinfulness of Sin." Here is proved to us that in the hour of success then temptation increases. David succumbed and fell. Coveting the wife of another he plotted the death of the husband to gain his selfish ends.

An outline of the book consists of Davids':

    I. REGALITY (1-5)
        His Accession to the Throne
   II. PROSPERITY (6-10)
        His Consolidation of the Kingdom
  III. ADVERSITY (11-19)
        His Sin and Absalom's Revolt
  IV. TESTIMONY (20-24)
        His Thanksgiving and Last Words

Our "famous" chapter comes within the second section of the book, the prosperity that attended the early part of David's reign. No wonder Dr. Alexander Maclaren says of this ninth chapter of Second Samuel "this charming idyl of faithful love to a dead friend and generous kindness comes in amid stories of battle like a green oasis in a wilderness of wild rocks and sand."

Why *Promise-Keeping?* Again we must quote Dr. Maclaren: "Neither his own prosperity, nor the absence of any trace of Saul's legitimate male descendants, made him forget his ancient promise to Jonathan." Not always in time of prosperity do men of position look back to earlier times of struggle and strenuous endeavor. David did, and thought of Jonathan, and how "the soul of David was knit with the soul of Jonathan." Jonathan had once charged him to show "the loving-kindness of Jehovah" and this David now does. David at this point is a man after God's own heart, keeping covenant and showing mercy upon those who might well be considered enemies.

What a message for our modern, everyday world. Promises today seem made to be broken rather than kept, in the international and political realms and in commerce and business. On a plane known to all of us, when we engage in door-to-door visitation, inviting people to Christian churches or evangelistic campaigns, how often they "promise" to come merely to get rid of us so they can get back to their television! Once "the Englishman's word was his bond"; today there is little sacredness regarding the giving of one's word. Such are the lessons to be learned from this great chapter which can be divided as follows:

I. INVESTIGATION (verses 1-4)
II. RECEPTION (verses 5-8)
III. PROVISION (verses 9-13)

I. INVESTIGATION (verses 1-4)

This inquiry after any living descendants of Saul's dynasty must have been some years after David had ascended the throne. Mephibosheth was five years old at Saul's death, but in this chapter we see that he now has a son. While David is keeping his promise now, he had obviously forgotten his obligations for some years. The longer a debt is postponed or a promise unfulfilled, the easier it is to forget all about it. This has happened to some believers. Once, some years ago, they stood up at a "Keswick" missionary meeting and stated their willingness to undergo training for full-time service, but that is now years ago and they are no nearer overseas missionary service than at the time they stood on their feet in answer to the speaker's challenge.

At long last then David asks: "Is there yet any that is left of the house of Saul?" (verse 1). Note how his desire is to show kindness to enemies—Saul was David's sworn enemy. How much easier it is to do kind things for fellow believers who are like-minded. That is not the example and injunction of our Lord however. "But I say unto you, Love your enemies, bless them that curse you, do good to them that hate you, and pray for them which despitefully use you, and persecute you; That ye may be the children of your Father which is in heaven" (Matthew 5:44, 45).

The necessary information about one remaining of Saul's household was given by Ziba, a former servant in that household. He not only told of a living descendant but a lame one, Mephibosheth. In chapter 4 we are told how Mephibosheth had an accident in childhood and so became lame. Lameness, in the Bible, was a dreadful handicap. It unfitted any descendant of Aaron for the priesthood (Leviticus 21:18). It rendered animals unsuitable for sacrifice (Deuteronomy 15:21). It made a man unfit for military service. Usually a man who was lame was derided and taunted (II Samuel 5:6). There are five recorded healing miracles of Jesus of lame people and one by Peter. In Hebrews 12:13 lameness is used figuratively of Christians and their need to walk carefully so that they do not cause others to stumble.

Mephibosheth has been living in obscurity, perhaps out of fear (verse 7), perhaps out of natural humility. He is the son of Jonathan and the grandson of Saul. His life was "a series of disasters, disappointments and anxieties." Among the mountains of Gilead he was brought up by Machir, and there he married and had a son, Mica.

II. Reception (verses 5-8)

David commanded that Mephibosheth be fetched from obscurity and brought to court. Probably he was conducted to court by Ziba, the former servant of Saul's estate and now managing Saul's estate for David.

Lame Mephibosheth presents himself before David, prostrating himself on the ground in spite of his physical disability. He is received by David with much kindness. He is not only a reminder of David's intimate relationship with Jonathan but his very name is an honorable one, for Mephibosheth means "idol-breaker." His deformity is no deterrent to David for it is not for himself but for his father's sake he is receiving him favorably. David saw Jonathan rather than Mephibosheth, and in the same way God the Father sees not us but "Christ in us." When we pray to Him He sees His Son first and His righteousness which we have put on by faith. We may make another spiritual analogy: before our conversion we were deformed by sin. But Christ received us for His Father's sake!

III. Provision (verses 9-13)

Ziba, who has been managing Saul's estate for David, is now ordered by the king to manage it for Mephibosheth, so that Mephibosheth might have an income befitting his position (verses 9, 10). Then he invited Mephibosheth to eat at the king's table daily, "as one of the king's sons" (verse 11). What a parallel with the Gospel. "Come and welcome," "Come and dine" is the invitation of Christ to the sinner. Once we are born again we are sons and daughters of the King of kings and one day will take our reserved place at the "marriage supper" of the Lamb. Until then our Lord manages our estate for us, giving us daily provision, a generous supply of spiritual bounty from "His riches in glory."

We can now summarize Mephibosheth's career like this. He was lame and lost, then loved and lifted. Or we can say he was fallen, fearful and far off, but then he was lifted up, made secure and brought near.

The sequel to the story of Mephibosheth in this famous chapter is this: he lived thus in Jerusalem for seventeen years. Then came Absalom's rebellion. David fled from the capital and is provided with food by Ziba. Asking Ziba where Mephibosheth is, Ziba treacherously replies that Mephibosheth was remaining behind in Jerusalem for his own ends. David thus restores the property to Ziba, taking it away from Mephibosheth. Later, after the rebellion, David found out the truth from Mephibosheth. Mephibosheth had wanted to flee with David but being lame knew he must do so upon an ass. Ziba had refused to procure an ass for him. David believed his story and spared Mephibosheth's life when he put to death other members of Saul's household (chapter 21).

THE SACRED VERSUS THE SECULAR

I Kings 18

The First Book of Kings, which in the Hebrew Bible is one book with the Second, continues the record and completes the story of the Hebrew Kingdom given in the two books of Samuel.

Perhaps the most interesting feature of I Kings is the writer's brief summary of each king, sometimes favorable, sometimes unfavorable, and sometimes approval modified by disapprobation.

An outline of the book may be given in this form:

    I. THE ACCESSION AND REIGN OF SOLOMON (1-11)
       His Wisdom, Wealth, Works and Wickedness
    II. THE DIVISION AND DECAY OF THE KINGDOM (12-16)
       Captivity, Idolatry, Conspiracy and Uncertainty
    III. THE MISSION AND WORKS OF ELIJAH (17-22)
       His Concealment, Contest, Confidence and Courage

The opening scene of the First Book of Kings is a deathbed scene. David, the once rosy-cheeked shepherd boy has become Israel's greatest king and has now come to the end of his life and reign. Next follows a scene of bloodshed: Solomon relentlessly puts to death all rivals after accession to the throne. Then follows a scene of glory. He builds a glorious palace and temple, and his fame, because of his wisdom and wealth, spreads far and wide. Enticed by his wives to idolatrous practices, however, his enemies soon rise against him and he is killed. Then a series of kings succeed him and the story does not really come to life again until we are introduced to the towering and majestic figure of Elijah, the "human lightning flash" as he has been called.

The theme of the book is, "The Lord Reigneth" and the key word "glory." To imagine that this glory is the glory of Solomon or his temple is to miss the purpose of the recorder. Our Lord Jesus Christ compared Solomon's glory with the common lily of Palestine and found that the glory of the latter exceeded the glory of Solomon! It is the greater glory and power of the sovereign God that we are to see in these twenty-two chapters. Our "famous" chapter does just that, coming in the final division of the book, The Mission and Works of Elijah.

Our outline of this "famous" chapter is:

    I. THE PROPHET AND THE SECRET DISCIPLE (verses 1-16)
    II. THE KING AND THE PUBLIC ASSEMBLY (verses 17-20)

III. The People and the Priestly Imposters (verses 21-29)
IV. The Fire and the Supreme God (verses 30-40)
V. The Suppliant and the Answered Prayer (verses 41-46)

Most commentators entitle this well-known chapter "The Contest on Carmel." Our title, *The Sacred Versus the Secular*, reminds us of a comment made by Dr. Alexander Maclaren that this contest has its modern parallel "in the impotence of all other schemes and methods of social and spiritual reformation and the power of the Gospel." The need of Elijah's time was rain; the rain came, in torrents; but God answered by fire. Surely rain and fire are the two outstanding metaphors of spiritual revival. Revival is the need of our time as rain was of Elijah's. Some would have us believe that such an awakening can come about by the schemes and methods of mere man. They would have us believe that the answer to our spiritual drought is "an educated ministry" or "more up-to-date visual/audio methods," "slicker publicity," and so on. The contest was not between Elijah and the prophets of Baal but between Elijah's God and the prophets' god Baal, that is, it was a contest between the sacred and the secular. So today the battle is between those who would secularize the Church of God, bolstering up its organizations and methods, concentrating upon a world-wide union (not spiritual unity), instead of believing in a real Holy Spirit revival in answer to fervent, persistent, believing prayer following upon humiliation and repentance.

I. The Prophet and the Secret Disciple (verses 1-16)

C. H. Spurgeon begins a sermon on verse 12 of this chapter by saying: "I suspect Elijah did not think very much of Obadiah." And I suspect the Apostle Paul would not have thought much of him either, for Paul wrote that it was not enough to believe on the Lord with the heart. There should be confession with the mouth—and Obadiah was a secret disciple! Much has been said in commendation of this man, and a great deal of it is perfectly true. These verses indicate that Obadiah had worshiped God from his youth; that his was a childhood or teen-age conversion (verse 12). Obviously his devotion was not shallow for "he feared the Lord greatly" (verse 3). His piety was practical for when certain prophets of the Lord were persecuted Obadiah sheltered them in safety and secrecy, protecting and providing for them (verse 4). This was no mean feat for there were a hundred persecuted prophets and Obadiah hid them in two caves. Think of the trips by night necessary in order to get their provisions to them without being seen! We have similar "Obadiahs" in the New Testament: Joseph of Arimathea who preserved the body of the Lord at night; Nicodemus who came with his questions to Jesus by night.

Yes, Obadiah was a secret disciple. He loved God and God's

servants, but he kept himself in obscurity in regard to his faith, although observe that he was prominent regarding his official position. His name means "Servant of Jehovah," but that merely expressed the high hopes of his parents when they presented him to the Lord and named him.

His official position was chamberlain to the palace of King Ahab. He was governor to the royal household. Under Ahab's direction he was scouring the countryside for green grass upon which the country's cattle could feed during the terrible time of drought and famine through which they were passing (verse 5). Under the Holy Spirit's influence Obadiah and the prophet Elijah met. Elijah has been in obscurity also, in concealment, but now the time is right for him to come into the open and serve God in the front line of battle. The divine commission is that Elijah must go to King Ahab and tell him that God is going to send the much-needed rain (verse 1). He tells Obadiah to go to Ahab and tell him of the forthcoming meeting there will be between God's prophet Elijah and himself. At once Obadiah seeks arguments for not going. They are now age-old excuses put forward by some Christians: He was afraid for his life and his livelihood! Obadiah did not relish the thought that the king would know of his friendship with the outcast Elijah. Obviously then Ahab did not know of his chamberlain's allegiance and devotion to Jehovah and it was more than his life and job was worth to tell him. To convince Elijah that he was truly a worshiper of the God of Israel he emphasized his hiding of the one hundred prophets, telling Elijah that he can check the story if he wishes (verse 13). Elijah, however, insists that Obadiah must carry the message to King Ahab. How often the secret disciple meets such a crisis. The secret disciple in the office or factory is suddenly challenged by another Christian sent to work in the same place and at long last confession of Christ has to be made. How thankful, after it is all over, is the secret disciple. He receives such joy and assurance that he would not go back to being a secret disciple again.

II. THE KING AND THE PUBLIC ASSEMBLY (verses 17-20)

The meeting between Ahab and Elijah is described by Matthew Henry as "the meeting . . . between as bad a king as ever the world was plagued with and as good a prophet as ever the church was blessed with"!

The king's attitude was rude to say the least. He accused Elijah of "troubling Israel," that is "disturbing Israel." The Hebrew word is connected with "boiling water," and thus came to mean irritate, confuse or cause sorrow. Ahab was thus accusing the prophet of being a disturber of the peace! The insult is thrown back in Ahab's face by the prophet when Elijah points out that by his idolatry, the worship of the false god Baal, his disobedience of God's commands, the king is really the cause of Israel's disastrous situation. Nevertheless the king agrees to do as the prophet directs and promises to convene the people of Israel and all the 450 prophets of Baal to a public assembly on Mount Carmel. It has been suggested that Carmel was chosen by Elijah as being a place where God was formerly worshiped in purity; that it was held in high esteem, and that probably the remains of a former altar to God still stood there. Other commentators suggest that it was ground belonging to the Canaanites and held sacred to their gods in former days.

III.   THE PEOPLE AND THE PRIESTLY IMPOSTERS (verses 21-29)

The sacred and the secular have already met in the persons of Elijah and Ahab. Now there is going to be a contest between them, with the people, who at this time are undecided, as onlookers. By an earnest appeal Elijah tries to make them decide even before they witness the contest: "How long halt ye between two opinions"? (verse 21). "Halt," means "limp" or "hop," not "stop." "How long are you going to hobble at the two forks in the road?" is a possible translation. "Neutral you cannot be" declares the old Sankey hymn. No one can be neutral in matters of religion. He that is not *for* God is against Him according to the Bible. For three and a half years the Israelites have had an opportunity of making their decision, three and a half years of drought and famine, years of divine judgment, yet they have remained unmoved and undecided and still do in the face of Elijah's appeal.

Before setting forth the conditions of the challenge Elijah reminds them of the odds—450 against one! "I, even I only, remain a prophet of the Lord" may be an expression of great loneliness rather than a statement of fact, that he alone remains a true prophet of Jehovah, for we must remember the 100 rescued by Obadiah. Well, in the loneliness and in the minority Elijah is going to "take on" 450 imposters.

The nature of the contest was as follows: upon an altar certain sacrificial animals were laid. No fire was lit. Elijah and his contestants were to call respectively on their g(G)od—the real one would be the one who answered by fire. Does it not seem strange that when the real need of the country was water that Elijah proposed an answer by fire? But if he had said water and rain had come then they could have said it was natural means, but not so with fire.

These terms were agreed to and the priests of Baal set to work. What a graphic description we have here of false religion. Excitement, dancing, slashing with knives, working up into a frenzy—and all for nothing. How Elijah must have enjoyed himself! How he urged them on, encouraging them in their shouting, suggesting that perhaps they had not shouted loud enough for their god to hear! All the while they were only making themselves look more ridiculous!

IV. THE FIRE AND THE SUPREME GOD (verses 30-40)

There was no need to study in great detail the preparations of
the prophets of Baal. There is need to notice Elijah's for in them
is a solemn rebuke to king and people. This famous chapter comes
after the section in the book entitled "The Division and Decay of the
Kingdom." Elijah thus takes twelve stones, a sign that he believes the
division to be wrong, revealing at the same time to the king and his
subjects the true unity of the twelve tribes.

Three times the sacrifice upon the altar is saturated with water.
One wonders where Elijah obtained such a quantity of water in time
of drought! How angry the onlookers must have been to see it wasted!
One explanation that has been given is that it was sea water fetched
especially for the purpose. At any rate here was three-fold affusion,
baptism by pouring. Is it fanciful to suggest that Elijah did it in the
name of the Trinity? Three was the number that spoke of completion,
and that made the altar, the wood and the sacrifice completely un-
combustible.

The next part of Elijah's preparations was most essential—
prayer. The prophet prayed for the fire to fall and the hearts of the
people to be broken. It was not a long prayer. It was direct and to
the point. Fire was wanted so fire was prayed for, and fire then fell.
It was as simple as that. Elijah addressed himself to the One who was
the God of Abraham, Isaac and Jacob in order that the people should
be reminded of their long relationship to this covenant God. Then he
prayed that God's name should be honored, not that his, the prophet's
honor should be vindicated. There then is the secret of revival-pro-
ducing prayer: the forgetting of our own selfish desires for prominence, or eminence for our particular church or denomination; concerned only with God's glory and honor.

God's fire is a consuming fire, so not only did the sacrifice burn
but also the very stones of the altar. The trench of water and the
surrounding ground was dried up. The people were forced to acknowledge the true, supreme God, and the priestly imposters of Baal were
put to death, partly, it has been suggested, because they were apostate
Israelites and thus their lives were forfeit by Deuternomy 13:1-5,
and partly because of their treatment of Elijah, God's true prophet.
They were traitors to God; they had done more than enough evil;
no longer were they to exist to contaminate true religion or perpetuate
a false one.

V. THE SUPPLIANT AND THE ANSWERED PRAYER (verses 41-46)

Again we see the prophet at prayer. How many of us would
have been satisfied with the victory gained on Carmel and left it at
that? But God had only answered by fire. There was still the need
for water. Now Elijah must pray for rain. He was sure the rain was
coming for God had promised it, and Elijah had already assured

Ahab that it was on its way. But God still likes to hear us pray; He still likes to be reminded of His promises. Here also is a lesson to all preachers and prophets: prayer in public is not enough, Elijah must now withdraw to the privacy of Carmel's summit and pray again. So our Lord Himself frequently withdrew from the crowds and His disciples and prayed alone.

Elijah must have been exhilarated after the victory, but he is also humiliated by success and throws himself prostrate on the ground to pray.

His servant is told to tell him when the first indication of rain appears. First it is only as a hand-size cloud. Soon it is sufficient to produce a downpour on the thirsty land. Now completely victorious Elijah acts as the forerunner of Ahab. Perhaps he was invited to ride in the king's chariot as an honor; he preferred to run before, however, not wanting to give the impression to the people of being proud or a position seeker. This famous chapter is full of vivid scenes and swift action. None is more glorious than this last scene. The distance between Carmel and Jezreel was about ten miles. In torrential rain Elijah ran on foot, outrider to the royal chariot!

A MAN AND HIS BLEMISH

II Kings 5

The Second Book of Kings is one with the first in the Hebrew Bible; it continues the same story. But the glory of Israel now changes to downfall. Twenty-one times we read that "so and so did evil . . ." The theme is, "The Casting-off of Restraint." Here is the record of the disobedience of God's people to God, conformity to the surrounding nations, public and private idol worship.

The book opens with the close of Elijah's ministry and continues with the sixty-six years of Elisha's, giving an account of his sixteen miracles. The contents of the book may be given in outline form like this:

     I. ELISHA SUCCEEDS ELIJAH (1, 2)
    II. ELISHA'S SUCCESSFUL MINISTRY (3-18)
   III. THE SUBVERSION OF THE NORTHERN KINGDOM (14-17)
   IV. THE SUCCESSION OF KINGS (18-23)
    V. THE SUCCUMB OF JUDAH (24, 25)

Our "famous" chapter comes within Section II of this outline of the book. It is one of the last of the Elisha stories, probably occurring during the reign of Jehu.

It is an old saying that "there is something bad in the best of us and something good in the worst of us." This chapter gives us a portrait of *A Man and His Blemish*. There are several such characters in Scripture. King Solomon had an "only"; the Rich Young Ruler had a "one thing thou lackest"; and here Naaman has a "but." Oliver Cromwell desired to be painted "wart an' all." All Bible portraits are as true to life as that. Weaknesses, blemishes, faults, foibles, failings—all are put upon the canvas. Did the great Spurgeon smoke cigars?—biographers bring out this blemish. Did the renowned G. Campbell Morgan possess too many suits?—even his daughter-biographer must include that weakness. So Naaman must be presented to us as he really was—a great man, courageous, victorious in battle, *but* . . . a leper!

This chapter may be divided as follows:

     I. A SUFFERER ANXIOUS TO BE CURED (verses 1-8)
    II. A SCORNER ANGRY AT THE MEANS OF CURE (verses 9-13)
   III. A SCEPTIC ACCEPTS THE REMEDY AND IS CURED (verses 14-19)

IV. A Scoundrel Acts Dishonestly and is Cursed (verses
20-27)

I. A Sufferer Anxious to be Cured (verses 1-8)

Naaman was suffering from perhaps the most loathsome disease
in the Old Testament. Leprosy typified sin in all its forms, intellectual,
physical and moral, a foul mind, foul lips and foul acts. Mosaic law
stipulated that the leper must live in isolation "without the camp"
(Leviticus 13:45,46); he must cry out "Unclean!" when approaching
other people. Naaman could be thankful that he did not come under
such restrictions in his deformity and defilement.

Naaman was a man of wealth. No wonder an English proverb
says that "health is better than wealth." The former can never be
bought with the latter. There was no physician who could heal Naaman of his leprosy. Dr. Alexander Maclaren points out that "there is a
'but' in every fortune, as there is a 'but' in every character." Naaman's
fortune was useless for the purpose of buying him health and happiness; it could only make him comfortable in his misery.

Perhaps Naaman's hope of being cured lay dormant until the
"captive maid" gave him hope. Verses 2 to 4 give the process: she
spoke to her mistress who had the ear of the king; the king decided
to write to the king of Israel. How ironical all this is. The regular
channels are being followed. The private must speak to the corporal,
and he to the sergeant,(and the sergeant to the lieutenant, and so on
right up to the general! There was no red tape that could be cut.
Every form had to be filled in! And all this while a man was anxious
to be cured of his dread disease. How much better it is for the sinner.
He has immediate entrance to a pardoning God through Jesus Christ
the Sin-bearer. There is no priest to go through, no ritualism or ceremonies to be observed! And this lengthy procedure did not really help
Naaman at first for the king of Israel thought it was a trick to wage
war (verse 7). Only by prophetic intervention was the situation saved
(verse 8). When will the nations learn that preachers are more important than politicians!

II. A Scorner Angry at the Means of Cure (verses 9-13)

Namaan felt slighted by the physician before he scorned to use
the prescription. He arrived at Elisha's house and the prophet did not
even come out to greet him (verses 9, 10). It would have been customary as well as courteous to meet such a famous person as Naaman
before he arrived at the house, and his dignity was pricked by
Elisha's attitude. Elisha was teaching Naaman a valuable lesson: with
God there is no respect of persons. Naaman was not a great man who
happened to be a leper but a leper who happened to be a great man.
Dr. Alexander Maclaren comments: "A wise doctor will treat the
Prince of Wales just as he will treat the Prince of Wales's stable-boy."

Naaman wanted his position, his power and his possessions taken into account: "I thought, He will surely come out to me" (verse 11). Rich and poor alike are equal in God's sight and should be so to God's servants. Unfortunately it is not always so. Here then, in this subsection we have "a dignified prophet and a dissatisfied peer."

Naaman was dissatisfied with his prescription because it was handed to him on a plate by Elijah's servant (verse 10). The National Health Service in England has meant that doctors cannot spare enough time as they would like with their patients. Often prescriptions are written out as patients enter the surgery or consulting room! Elisha was different, however, for he had prophetic insight and knew all about Naaman's case, his symptoms and background. He knew that the divinely-prescribed remedy was to dip seven times in Jordan. That was too commonplace for Naaman. He wanted Elisha to "strike his hand over the place" (verse 11), implying the motions of a magician with the appropriate incantations! The Revised Version translates it "wave," like a magican waving his wand to perform some magic trick. In any case, Naaman thought that if self-immersion was to be the cure then he had far cleaner and more beautiful rivers in his own country. Naaman's servants hit the nail on the head (verse 13): if only the prescription had been some newly-discovered "wonder drug" instead of an old-fashioned, homespun remedy, then Naaman would have been more ready to follow instructions. What another parallel to the gospel! If only twentieth-century man, clever, scientific, could save himself by his own discoveries and inventions! But God's way of salvation is much simpler; and He will have no other way, for "Neither is there salvation in any other for there is none other name . . ." (Acts 4:12).

III. A SCEPTIC ACCEPTS THE REMEDY AND IS CURED (verses 14-19)

Overcoming his anger Naaman listens to reason. Yes, the Gospel also makes people angry. The message of the cross is an offense. People do not like being called sinners.

Naaman finally submits to Elisha and does as he is told (verse 14). So do we become saved from our sins when we come to Jesus saying "Nothing in my hands I bring . . ."

Not only is Naaman cured but he is converted and makes an open confession. His cure is beautifully described in verse 14—his skin becomes like that of a "little child." In the same way the sinner must become like a little child and be converted and he is then "born again."

Naaman's conversion to the God of Israel is described in verses 15 and 17. In the former verse we also have his confession. It is a public one, before his servants. Then he intends taking some soil back home with him. He may have thought that God was confined to the land of Israel or that He was a God who must be worshiped on holy soil. Before condemning Naaman let us remember our own lack of understanding and discernment of spiritual truths during the early days of conversion. Naaman even thought that God's servant would want money for what he did! The gift is refused (verse 16), teaching us that salvation is free, without money and without price. The hungry and thirsty, as well as the leprous, may come freely.

IV. A Scoundrel Acts Dishonestly and Is Cursed (verses 20-27)

What a character Dr. Alexander Maclaren gives Gehazi: "Gehazi had a sordid soul, like Judas." He adds: "Gehazi's glib ingenuity in lying augurs long practice in the art."

The reality of Naaman's conversion must first be noted. No longer is he arrogant and proud. Why, he dismounts to greet Gehazi, the mere servant of Elisha (verse 21)! Listening to Gehazi's plausible story Naaman freely gives because of his change of heart. Gehazi's sin was not mere dishonesty; it was partly that, but in the main Elisha's judgment upon Gehazi was because Gehazi had done precisely what Elisha had been careful not to do, that is, he gave Naaman the impression that religion was the money-making business so many think it to be. That is why Elisha asks Gehazi: "Is this a time to receive?" Elisha wanted Naaman to have a conspicuous disregard of wealth in order that he might learn of God's free love, untarnished by love of worldly possessions. Because Gehazi's sin was so great his sentence was so severe. He had gotten for himself Naaman's money; now he is given Naaman's leprosy.

We can conclude in no better way than by going back to the maid who began the long process of Naaman's cleansing and conversion. How did she know Elisha could cure leprosy? She did not know, but she had faith in the prophet of the Lord to do anything! What is the "but" in your life? Is it pride? Is it timidity? Is it anxiety? Whatever it is we need that girl's faith to believe that Christ can cure us. And when He has dealt with us we must be like her and become a link in the chain of another's conversion. She could not preach a sermon, but she could tell someone of a God of power who employs ministers to do His will. She may have been in captivity but she was in the place of the Lord's choice, and when we are in the Lord's will then He can use us.

WHAT WE MAY AND MAY NOT DO

I Chronicles 17

"The Constant Activity of God" is the theme of the First Book of Chronicles, summed up by the key word "sovereignty" (key text: "Thou reignest over all"—29:12). The book's title means "Words of Days or Events of the Times." The Greek title is *Omissions*. In other words this is a book of Stop Press News! It is a supplement to the books of Samuel and Kings.

A broad sweep of history from Adam onward (covering something like 3,500 years) is taken, with God choosing, guiding, governing and controlling human affairs.

An outline of the book is as follows:

    I. GENEALOGY (1-9)
        Primeval History (Adam to the Patriarchs)
   II. MONARCHY (10-29)
        National Prosperity (End of Saul to beginning
        of Solomon)

The "famous" chapter of this book is in the second section, the middle reign (David's), leading on to Solomon's. The ark of God had been captured from the Philistines and is now back in the city. David has a renewed desire to build a place for it in the capital, a permanent and worthy resting place. Such a desire was commendable and worthy, but it was not the will of God! In this chapter we see how David is brought into God's presence to learn a lesson that many of us need today. David's desire to do something for the Lord was set in the light of what the Lord was doing, and had been doing, for David. A Christian's relationship with God must always be based upon what God is doing for us and not upon what we think we are doing for Him! So many Christians busy themselves with what they call "Christian service," but it may not be what God requires of us. What we may and may not do must always depend upon His will for us. If God had wanted David at that point in history to build a temple then He would have revealed His will and David would have had to be obedient. But God did not want a temple built by David. If we attempt to do anything for God, however worthy, noble, sacrificial, or God-glorifying it might appear to be, if it is not God's will then we have earned no merit with Him for having done it.

Our outline of this chapter is this:

    I.   Enterprise and Encouragement (verses 1, 2)
   II.   God's Refusal of David's Plan (verses 3-15)
        A. *Ruler not Builder*
        B. *Successor not Predecessor*
  III.   David's Acceptance of God's Plan (verses 16-25)
        A. *Resignation and Revelation*
        B. *Praise and Prayer*
  IV.   Promise and Performance (verses 26, 27)

I. Enterprise and Encouragement (verses 1, 2)

David was rightly dissatisfied that his own house was permanent and beautiful while the ark was still behind curtains and was movable. So God's House of Prayer, the church buildings in which we worship, would be better kept in good repair and tasteful decoration if we thought as much of them as we do our own dwelling places. These we paint and decorate frequently, using the best materials that we can afford. We take care each Spring as to the furnishings and fabric, and yet God's House is frequently to be seen with flaking paint and decaying wood or stone work. Second-hand furnishings and equipment are sometimes placed in God's House which we would never use in our own homes.

Thus there formed in David's heart and mind plans for the erection of a suitable house of worship, an edifice befitting a glorious God. They were enterprising plans, rational and realistic, and the king did well to speak to his minister about the proposition. The result was that his minister encouraged him. Nathan was mistaken, of course (no minister of God is infallible). Nathan did not know the Lord's will any more than David, so he encouraged him in his task.

Sometimes the procedure should be reversed. Ministers need encouragement in their plans and Christian ministry. C. H. Spurgeon has a famous sermon called "Encourage Your Minister!"

David had been saving gold and silver for some time. It is always good to make ample preparation for God's work in the future, then when the work has to be done it is neither done hastily nor in a haphazard manner. A renovation fund in a church enables repairs and redecorations to be undertaken when necessary. An evangelistic fund enables some evangelistic mission or campaign to be undertaken or supported.

II. God's Refusal of David's Plan (verses 3-15)

Nathan was told by God to break the sad news to David—he was not to build the temple. We observe two tragedies here. First, Nathan had tragically misled David, encouraging him to do something which God refused to accept, speaking without seeking to know God's mind and will. Secondly, we see David's tragedy. David had to watch his scheme tumble down before his eyes; his successor was to have the honor of erecting the temple.

It appears that God had been well-satisfied with the humble resting places of the ark. In verse 6 David is reminded that no word came to the Judges to build a temple—their job was to feed the people, not build temples.

God gives His reason to David as to why his services are not required in this direction. If the Judges were teachers and not builders, David was a soldier and not a builder. Verses 7 and 8 describe David's career from shepherd to soldier. God did not choose David because he saw him to be a potential builder; He saw him as a soldier and ruler. As Spurgeon puts it, David had the "aspirations, but not the qualifications." In a later chapter (28:2,3) it is said: "Because thou hast been a man of war, and hast shed blood." There are Christian men who have been prominent on the battlefield, and some of them have been mightily used as gospel preachers, but the temple was to be a "house of peace" for the God of peace and He did not want it built by a man of war.

Let us widen the application for ourselves. How many people after conversion (especially if we have been converted late in life) long to enter the full-time ministry at home or abroad? Doors to training seemed shut, however, and all our wonderful plans and schemes came to nothing and we had to remain at the workbench or behind the shop counter. God knows best and He knows that in a great house there are different vessels.

God now graciously allows David to prepare the way for his successor's work. The erection of the temple is to be Solomon's task, but David can pave the way. The New Testament emphasis is upon one man building upon another's foundation, one sowing and another watering. So God promises that the temple will be built (verses 10, 12). God will always have His work done at the right time, in the right way, and by the right people.

III. DAVID'S ACCEPTANCE OF GOD'S PLAN (verses 16-25)

Not all of us submit to God's will as readily as David did! First we see his resignation, not, as with many of our hymns on the will of God, in minor key; no, David resigns himself jubilantly because of God's revelation to him (verse 10). When God makes clear to us His plan and purpose, His will and way, ought we not to submit gladly? David was so overwhelmed by the fact that God had explained Himself and that He promised to make up to him for his disappointment by blessing him in the future that David is greatly encouraged. God never takes away without bestowing; He never shuts one door without revealing some other avenue of service.

What fellowship with God David is here enjoying! Disappointment is worthwhile if it brings us nearer to God and makes us realize more of His will and of His ways. Thus David can give vent to praise and prayer. The praise is in verses 20-22. The prayer is contained in verse

23. It is one thing to accept God's will when it is so different from our own plans, but it is another thing to go on and praise God for the disappointment and request Him to use it for His own glory! What a heart David had! The plan for the temple was in his heart (verse 2), now this prayer is in his heart (verse 25).

IV. PROMISE AND PERFORMANCE (verses 26, 27)

An early lesson to learn in the art or science of prayer is to remember to plead promises. God must, because He is faithful, answer His own promises. David reminds God of His promise to bless Him. What daring faith David has! What a great concept he has of God's power in blessing! "For ever" are the two words to note. None of God's promises can be revoked or opposed; they will stand for all time and eternity.

BREAD AND CIRCUSES

II Chronicles 9

Our title for this "famous" Bible chapter is taken from Juvenal's *Satires*: "Panem et Circenses." The Roman population of that time wanted but two things, daily food and sport or amusement. That is what the politicians offered them to keep them quiet and that is what most people want today in this affluent twentieth century, this age of "never had it so good." Given sufficient material luxuries, money and enough leisure in which to spend it, and we shall be perfectly happy! So runs the philosophy of millions.

Such was King Solomon's philosophy and it resulted in tragedy. Endowed with much natural ability, possessing a special divine gift of wisdom, yet Solomon failed miserably. He became a slave to the lower side of nature and dragged down his people with him, illustrating the truth of the proverb: "Like king, like people." He sought to solace and drug the people with material splendor but moral and spiritual degradation quickly followed in its wake.

The story of the Second Book of Chronicles, however, is not only the story of Solomon's failure. It also records the failure of formal, centralized worship, a religion of ceremony and ritual, a religion that was lifeless. The theme of the book is, "The Failure of Formal Religion." There was "a paralysis in the life of the king, and a poison in the life of the nation"! Successive kings failed to revive the observance of true religion in the life of the nation.

One commentator has said that it is "impossible to arrange this book in handy divisions," but we give, nevertheless, the following outline:

I. SOLOMON (1-9)
   A. *Building and Blessing the Temple* (1-7)
   B. *Accumulating Wealth and Wisdom* (8, 9)
II. SUCCESSORS (10-36)
   A. *The Divided Kingdom* (10-28)
   B. *Reforms and Revival* (29-36)

Our "famous" chapter comes in the first main division and the second subdivision.

Solomon's wisdom is set out in the Song of Solomon, Proverbs and certain Psalms. In the latter there is no note of repentance as in those composed by David (Psalm 51 for instance). His wealth had

73

come from Caananitish countries round about, some being carried by his navy from distant places like Ophir.

It was Solomon's wisdom that the Queen of Sheba came to find out more about, and this chapter describes her visit.

In outline form the chapter is divided as follows:

    I. THE QUEEN'S VISIT (verses 1-12)
        A. *Question and Answer* (verses 1, 2)
        B. *Seeing is Believing* (verses 3-8)
        C. *Giving and Receiving* (verses 9-12)
   II. THE KING'S PROSPERITY (verses 13-21)
        A. *Silver and Gold* (verses 13-16)
        B. *Furnishings and Fittings* (verses 17-20)
        C. *Animals and Birds* (verse 21)
  III. THE KING'S POPULARITY (verses 22-28)
        A. *Princes and Presents* (verses 22-24)
        B. *Chariots and Horses* (verse 25)
        C. *Reign and Territory* (verses 26-28)
   IV. THE KING'S DECEASE (verses 29-31)
        A. *Summary and Record* (verses 29, 30)
        B. *Death and Burial* (verse 31)
        C. *Son and Successor* (verse 31)

I. THE QUEEN'S VISIT (verses 1-12)

Dr. Alexander Whyte describes the queen thus: "As I see her, (she) came to Jerusalem on the very highest errands. She was moved to undertake her journey by the very strongest and the very loftiest of motives." This queen had heard in Sheba of the name of the Lord and "there was no name of any god given in Sheba that took such hold of the Queen of Sheba's heart as did the name of the God of Israel." Sheba in Matthew and Luke is qualified by the words "queen of the south" (Matthew 12:42; Luke 11:31). There is frequent mention of the place in eastern literature and various are the interpretations. Some say Ethiopia is meant, others say it stands for a group of towns or a district, perhaps synonymous with Beer-sheba.

A. *Question and Answer* (verses 1, 2). Dr. Whyte refutes the suggestion that the queen was frivolous or captious. If she had been either of these then our Lord would not have commended her as He did: "The queen of the south shall rise up in the judgment with this generation, and shall condemn them" (Matthew 12:42). We have perhaps been beguiled by the words used in verse 1—"prove" and "hard questions." In all probability she asked serious, genuine questions about the temple and its worship and ritual, and she received distinct and satisfying answers from Solomon—"He told her all her questions" or "answered all her problems (clever king indeed to be able to satisfy a woman's curiosity!).

Our Lord Jesus Christ was able to say of Himself: "A greater than Solomon is here" (Matthew 12:42). As the Queen of Sheba took her problems to Solomon we may take ours "to the Lord in prayer" and He will hear and answer us.

B. *Seeing Is Believing* (verses 3-8). What did the queen mean by "seeing the wisdom of Solomon"? She was most likely referring to his practical sagacity, the material outcome of his wise intellect. Doubtless he applied his mental prowess to everyday life. She saw his *house* with its beauty and grandeur, its furnishings and fittings. She saw his *food*, its abundance and variety (obviously she was not on a strict slimming diet!) She noted his *servants*, their diligence, dress and deportment. And when she had seen all this then she believed; seeing the truth of the reports that she had heard in her own land she now believed having seen them to be true at first hand.

Our Lord said to Thomas: "Blessed are they that have not seen and yet have believed" (John 20:29). That is the true life of faith for the believer in Christ. The non-Christian always wants visible proof; with the Christian it is a case of "whom having not seen (we) love" (I Peter 1:8). Ought we not to "talk up" Christ and the Church as people talked about Solomon and his temple so that people will want to inquire further into spiritual things?

C. *Giving and Receiving* (verses 9-12). First, the queen gave gifts to Solomon, according to oriental custom. There would have been a camel caravan or train to carry them. Solomon had no need of further wealth, but this was a gesture meant to cultivate further acquaintanceship and confirm future friendship. She gave him gold spices and jewels. In return she received "all her desire," "whatsoever she asked." Perhaps she asked for wisdom rather than wealth, religion rather than riches, spiritual blessings rather than material benefits, questions to do with the eternal and not the temporal. So too we have been promised by our Lord all that we ask for: "ask and it shall be given you." Because we do not ask we have not.

II. The King's Prosperity (verses 13-21)

Solomon undoubtedly also gave tangible gifts at the queen's departure, and in this section we can see that he could well-afford to do so!

A. *Silver and Gold* (verses 13-16). The king's wealth was probably increased that year by something in the region of $1,000,000,000. This came from visiting "chapmen" or traders, and surrounding kings and governors. There is no suggestion that this was unlawfully extracted from them. It was probably willingly given as a tribute rather than a tithe, to gain his favor and support or protection. This wealth was made into shields and placed round the walls of his armory.

B. *Furnishings and Fittings* (verses 17-20). Solomon had a great ivory throne overlaid with gold. It had six steps and a footstool. There were two pedestal lions. On each side were twelve lions. No other kingdom possessed such a work of art of such value. There was probably a canopy overhead, supported by two more lions. Here was unrivaled splendor.

The magnificence of oriental monarchs was indicated by a great display of plate. Golden goblets or drinking vessels would be displayed. Solomon scorned silver for such use—only gold was good enough. We might parody a British prime minister's boast and say that Solomon "had never had it so *gold*"!

C. *Animals and Birds* (verse 21). Apes and peacocks had been imported from Tarshish. These were rare creatures. From I Kings 4: 32, 33, we may assume that Solomon was keenly interested in natural history: "And he spake three thousand proverbs: and his songs were a thousand and five. And he spake of trees, from the cedar tree that is in Lebanon even unto the hyssop that springeth out of the wall: he spake also of beasts, and of fowl, and of creeping things, and of fishes." Some commentators take this to mean that the king went on lecture tours.

III. THE KING'S POPULARITY (verses 22-28)

The king, then, was no stay-at-home. He was popular and much sought after. People came to see him and he went out to see others.

A. *Princes and Presents* (verses 22-24). Surrounding royalty sought out Solomon and like the Queen of Sheba they came with their presents when they visited him to see his wealth and hear his wisdom. Here surely is a parallel to the New Testament story of the Wise Men of the East who came to see the infant King with their gifts of gold, frankincense and myrrh.

B. *Chariots and Horses* (verse 25). Solomon possessed a great many stalls for horses and had a great many chariots and charioteers. Perhaps here is a clue to one of the king's failings. In times of trouble he put more trust in chariots and horses than he did in the living God? Horses have frequently been a man's downfall!

C. *Reign and Territory* (verses 26-28). Here we have the details of Solomon's reign, its extent in territory rather than length or duration. It is as nothing when compared with the kingdom of heaven, the countless hearts over which Jesus holds sway today, and the kingdom over which He will one day reign in person from sea to sea and shore to shore.

IV. THE KING'S DECEASE (verses 29-31)

So far we have been seeing "Solomon in all his glory." We have noted his pomp and power. Now death, "the great leveler," is at work, stripping Solomon of wealth, wisdom, power and popularity. Like every rich man, Solomon could not take his money with him. Living he had been worth millions, dying he was worth nothing! All had to be left behind.

A. *Summary and Record* (verses 29, 30). By contrast with all described so far, the rest of the king's acts are unworthy of individual note. They are all lumped together by two or three minor seers, their works not being considered worthy of being included in the canon of sacred Scripture. We note that he reigned forty years in all.

B. *Death and Burial* (verse 31). At long last Solomon "slept." What a wonderful word the Bible uses for death! Sleep is so peaceful, so restful, so tranquil. He was buried with his ancestors in the capital, with David his father.

C. *Son and Successor* (verse 31). The chapter that begins so gloriously ends on a note of tragedy. Here is the common mistake of a son who thought he could trade on his father's name and popularity and assume the same authority. He tried to carry on and carry all before him as did Solomon. But Solomon had one thing Rehoboam had not—wisdom. Solomon was wise; Rehoboam was a fool, and he paid dearly for his folly.

THE FIRST BIBLE SCHOOL LECTURERS

Ezra 7

The books of Ezra and Nehemiah were originally one book. Ezra is history and Nehemiah deals more with the person of Ezra who figures so prominently in the book bearing his name. Ezra records the return of the exiled Jews to Jerusalem to rebuild the temple. In this book we see the altar erected and the foundations of the temple laid. Opposition interrupts the work. It is overcome, however, and the work is resumed and completed. The building is dedicated, and certain religious reforms are brought in by Ezra. The theme then is, "Overcoming Opposition." The inspiration and strength necessary to overcome such opposition is derived from the Word of God. Several terms are used for God's Word: the Word of the Lord, the Commandments of the God of Israel, the Law of the Lord, and some others.

An outline of the book can be given thus:

I. THE RETURN FROM EXILE (1, 2)
II. THE RESTORATION BEGUN (3)
III. THE RESISTANCE INITIATED (4)
IV. THE RESUMPTION OF THE WORK (5, 6)
V. THE RETURN OF EZRA (7, 8)
VI. THE REFORMATION OF THE PEOPLE (9, 10)

The "famous" chapter comes within Section V, the return of Ezra to Jerusalem. We entitle it *The First Bible School Lecturers* because here Ezra is referred to as "a ready scribe" (verse 6) and "ready" applies to the mind rather than the pen. He means that Ezra's intelligence or mental processes was quick, skillful or diligent. These scribes were first of all royal secretaries; they wrote at dictation or copied word by word the Old Testament documents. By the time of Jesus Christ they had "grown numerically but deteriorated spiritually" (Dr. G. Campbell Morgan). With Ezra we see what God intended they should be—Bible lecturers. Their chief business was not to copy the documents, but to expound and interpret the true meaning of God's law and apply it to everyday life. They were to be God's messengers taking the place of the older prophets. Unlike the prophets they did not receive new revelations, but explained the ones already given, applying their teaching to the constantly changing conditions and circumstances of life for God's people. These men thus became experts in exposition, interpretation and practical application of the Word of God.

Since the great Bible teaching of Dr. Campbell Morgan in West-minster Chapel, London, Bible schools have come into the life of many a church. Sometimes separated from the prayer meeting, at other times a part of it, one night each week is given over to a fellow-ship study of the Word of God, under the supervision of a man called and equipped for the task.

The outline of this "famous" chapter is as follows:

  I. LEAVING FOR JERUSALEM (verses 1-10)
 II. LETTER FROM THE KING (verses 11-26):
     A. *The Largess* (verses 11-20)
     B. *The Levy* (verses 21-24)
     C. *The Law* (verses 25, 26)
III. LOYALTY TO GOD (verses 27, 28)

I. LEAVING FOR JERUSALEM (verses 1-10)

The chapter opens with a long list of names. The list, accord-ing to one commentator, is "clearly abbreviated." What is the point of it, for no such catalog is without point in God's Word? It shows us that Ezra was descended from Seraiah or Jeshua the high priest, and so he is well-fitted for his sacred task. He is a man of learning, a "ready" scribe, intelligent, well-read, able to "take in" and "give out." He is a man of great personal piety and holy zeal in spiritual things (verse 10). Matthew Henry points out what temptations there must have been in Babylon for a man like Ezra. He could have made a study of the stars, astrology could have become his first love, but Ezra kept to the sacred Scriptures. So today, with all the oppor-tunities of higher education, how tempting it is for a man to forsake the ministry and a study of theology (once called the "queen of the sciences") for something that at first sight seems more thrilling or more rewarding (especially from a financial aspect)!

Here in this section of the chapter Ezra teaches us the proper method of Bible study: we first study it as it stands; then we live it out, putting it into practice; finally we teach it to others that they might benefit from it. Notice above all else how Ezra prepared his heart rather than his head. That is the way we should always come to the Scriptures, with a personal sense of unworthiness, with reverence for the Word of God, if need be persevering until the Holy Spirit unlocks the treasure chest. Verse 10 may be summarized: Prepare the heart . . . perform the duties . . . preach the word. . . .

Dr. Alexander Whyte, in his study of Ezra, takes most of his material from this famous chapter. He defines Ezra as a man who has set the pattern of Bible study as we have it today. And he es-pecially notes that "the good hand of his God was upon him" (verse 9). Without that we shall not successfully understand or impart to others the Word of the Lord.

Such was the man who journeyed to Jerusalem on behalf of his countrymen. The journey would have taken four months. Why did he follow on? Why was he not one of the first to arrive in Jerusalem? We are not told directly, we can only assume that God was keeping him back in solitude that he might be prepared for his important task as a Bible lecturer.

II. LETTER FROM THE KING (verses 11-26)

Ezra went to Jerusalem carrying an important document. The contents here are in Aramaic and not in the Hebrew of the Old Testament. The Hebrew language is not resumed until Verse 27. It is thought that Queen Esther, the king's mother, influenced Artaxerxes the king to write on behalf of the Jews.

A. *The Largess* (verses 11-20). The king gave Ezra a large quantity of money to take with him to Jerusalem. The king's largess or bounty was generously given from the royal treasury, further contributions being made by the court and ordinary people of the country. Besides money, vessels for use in the temple were given. Ezra was entrusted with this wealth—obviously he was known as a man of integrity, one who would not use it for his own ends. How similar this is to the New Testament account of the Apostle Paul going to Jerusalem with alms for his fellow countrymen.

How was this money to be used? Here is a lesson for Christians from a heathen king! —"after the will of your God" (verse 18). How frequently we spend our money on clothes, furniture, luxuries, and so forth, without first seeking to know God's will, and without first considering the needs of the mission field or evangelism at home.

B. *The Levy* (verses 21-24). Eastern kings could be either very generous or exceedingly cruel and stringent. This king, besides his own gifts, ordered a levy or compulsory payment, a kind of tax imposition to be raised or collected from the surrounding Persian princes. They were to give approximately $200,000 plus 800 bushels of wheat and 700 gallons of wine and oil. Only those who were temple officials were exempt from this levy.

Again there is a lesson here for Christians, given by heathen. Verse 21 informs us that it was to be done "speedily." How often the giving of money drags on. Appeals and renewed appeals have to be given. The people have to be encouraged to give and then from time to time stirred up again by some embarrassed minister or church treasurer. Giving in Old and New Testaments is not something spasmodic, something that depends upon earnest and eloquent appeal, it is systematic and sacrificial, a definite proportion of one's income set aside for the Lord's work.

C. *The Law* (verses 25, 26) The king's letter empowered Ezra to appoint judges or magistrates, men who themselves already knew God's laws and were willing and able, as Bible lecturers, to teach it to others. While they were, first of all, judicial magistrates, enforcing

God's laws, punishing with penalties any infringement of them, the important part of their work and office was the teaching of God's law and its application to everyday life.

Notice, too, how the civil laws ("the law of the king," verse 26) were to be kept as strictly as the divine laws. This too is New Testament doctrine: "Render unto Caesar the things that are Caesar's" (Matthew 22:21) said our Lord; and Paul enjoined upon believers —"Be subject unto the higher powers" (Romans 13:1). All too many Christians look upon man-made laws as inferior to God's laws and so infringe on them whenever possible.

III. LOYALTY TO GOD (verses 27, 28)

Commentators look upon these verses as being an extract from Ezra's personal memoirs. Once again the true Ezra is revealed, a man who sees God's hand for good in everything; a man who is always ready to acknowledge his indebtedness to divine mercy and grace. Matthew Henry points out that after this letter Ezra could have been excused if he had written the words, "God Save the King"! In view of such royal bounty, such kingly generosity, Ezra could have paid great tribute to the king. Instead he takes the opportunity of ascribing glory to the King of kings. It was God, the King of the universe, who moved the heart of the earthly king to act as he did. How wonderful to remember that God has not changed and today he is capable of moving the hearts of earthly rulers, whether in the Kremlin, White House, or Buckingham Palace!

THE GREATNESS AND DIGNITY OF SERVICE

Nehemiah 6

Nehemiah is the last of the historical books of the Old Testament as Malachi is the last of the prophetical books. No more history is recorded until we reach Matthew's gospel.

In Ezra is recorded the restoration of the altar and the temple. Now in Nehemiah we have the record of the reconstruction of the city walls. Again the lesson is that success depended on obedience to the Word of God and absolute faith in the power of prayer. The Book of Nehemiah opens and closes with prayer. But prayer and human effort go together in this book, the abiding theme being, "The Inseparability of Prayer and Effort."

Ezra was a biography of Ezra, so here in Nehemiah we have biographical details about Nehemiah. We see him as a great man of prayer and the man who overcame bitter opposition from within and without through prayer. The key text of the book is: "We made our prayer unto our God, and set a watch against them day and night" (4:9).

An outline of the book is as follows:

    I.   WORK AND WORKERS (1-7)
        A. *The Building of the Wall*
        B. *The Opponents of the Prophet*
   II.   REPENTANCE AND REVIVAL (8-10)
        A. *Sin Confessed*
        B. *Scripture Expounded*
  III.   CENSUS AND CENSURE (11-13)
        A. *The Population*
        B. *Their Reformation*

Our "famous" chapter comes within the first section or division of the book dealing with the arrival of Nehemiah in Jerusalem, his organization of labor, and his completion of the work much to the discouragement of the enemy.

The significant and operative word in chapter 6 is "so" in verse 15. "*So* the wall was finished." *So*, in spite of opposition; *so*, in spite of grave difficulties; *so*, as a result of keeping to God's direction and methods; *so*, as a result of God's overruling; *so*, as a result of the leadership of one man and his successful efforts to weld his people into a unity; *so*, because of the vision of the greatness and dignity of the task of building for God.

The chapter outline is:

    I. A GREAT WORK (verses 1-9)
        —not forsaken
        A. *The Plotters*
        B. *The Plots*
   II. A GREAT TEMPTATION (verses 10-14)
        —not foreseen
  III. A GREAT VICTORY (verses 15-19)
        —not forgotten

I. A GREAT WORK—*not forsaken* (verses 1-9)

In these few verses we have described the great cunning, subtlety and stratagem of the opponents of God's people. But that did not make Nehemiah forsake his important work. He has too great a sense of the greatness and dignity of service. So ought all Christians to have and then we would not become so easily discouraged when things are difficult.

A. *The Plotters.* Sanballat was a Moabite leader of the opposition, a governor of Samaria. The party spirit governed this man's thinking and acting. This man's descendants continued in the same strain so that the Jews had no dealings with the Samaritans.

Next there was Tobiah, an Ammonite slave, connected by marriage with the Jews. Nehemiah thinks of Tobiah as his chief enemy, so Tobiah comes first in his prayers! How few Christians follow Nehemiah's example. We would if we believed not only that prayer changes things but people as well!

Then there was Geshem, an Arabian, probably the chieftain of some tribe.

B. *The Plots.* An invitation to meet in the plain of Ono was given. Ono was approximately twenty miles north of Jerusalem. Nehemiah could easily have been kidnaped or murdered if he went so far from the city. "Let us meet together"—their reason for issuing the invitation was that they purported to be interested in the common good of God's people, or that they desired Nehemiah's friendship or advice. Beneath the surface, however, is guile. They "thought to do him a mischief," an expression that can mean murder or at least some violence to his person. Perhaps with this invitation there went a hint of reward or personal gain for Nehemiah, for his reply is: "I am doing a great work, so that I cannot come down" (verse 3). This used to be the stock answer of every minister of the Gospel when he was offered (sometimes with the lure of financial gain) alternative employment such as school teaching. The Christian ministry used to be considered the highest vocation of all, and anything else offered and accepted would be taking a step down. The ministry may be long hours, poor pay, fewer professional privileges, but it is still Royal Service. There is a greatness and dignity about it that makes anything else a step down.

The second plot was by letter. Four visits were made with oral invitations to meet. Now a letter that is threatening and libelous in tone is delivered. It suggests that a rumor is going around saying that Nehemiah aims to become king, that is, that he is stirring up a rebellion. This letter would be a small piece of papyrus or leather, perhaps even pottery, and so not being able to be folded or rolled it would be an "open letter" (verse 5) which many could read. The suggestion now is that such a report be discussed between them.

How often are God's servants thus misrepresented by the world and to the world. Even in ministerial circles there is "professional" jealousy, and letters (signed and anonymous) are written and read that would be better unwritten and unread.

Nehemiah is not in the least frightened, however, for his strength is in God (verse 9). Some commentators say this is not only a prayer of supplication by Nehemiah but a resolution: "Now, therefore, O God, I will strengthen my hands." Christian fortitude is greatly needed in the face of criticism and opposition from without and within the Christian Church.

II. A GREAT TEMPTATION—*not forseen* (verses 10-14)

We are now introduced to another schemer, Shemaiah (not mentioned elsewhere in the Bible). He was a prophet (verse 12) who was "shut up." Not, as some suggest, ceremonially unclean or he would not have been able to enter the temple as he mentions. Perhaps the phrase depicts secrecy. Shemaiah wishes to meet Nehemiah in secret, then they would both flee to the temple for sanctuary. Nehemiah, however, is not a priest, so he refuses to break God's law in order to save his own skin.

Verse 14 tells us that quite a succession of prophets and prophetesses were hired to tempt Nehemiah in the same way, all to no avail. Nehemiah's concept of the greatness and dignity of service is so high that he places faithful service above personal safety. Many a servant of God could have an easier life if only he listened to the voice of the tempter: "Don't burn the candle at both ends"; "don't burn yourself out for God, you're still young yet"; "take things easy now you've past middle life," and so on. Like Nehemiah and the Apostle Paul we must be prepared to "spend and be spent," not allowing God's work to suffer because of some lame excuse for slackness.

How plausible is the devil! He suggested to Nehemiah that he might be slain in the night, and being concerned for his personal safety, and concerned for the people who would be left leaderless and defenseless, their work undone again, the devil suggested attractive steps to be taken. The devil knows us well. He knows that self-preservation is a law of nature. He has lost none of his plausibility today when we read of the drift into other occupations by ministers of all denominations.

Like Luther Nehemiah speaks out vocally against the devil, "hurls his ink pot at him" as it were. Sometimes it is wise to resist the devil; at other times it is well to run from him!

Let us note how this section closes with Nehemiah praying for those who have sought to trick and trap him. He is content to acknowledge that "vengeance is mine, saith God," and is not revengeful himself. How often we bear a grudge against some opponent, some critic, and harbor resentment in our hearts for years instead of "letting go and letting God" deal with it and the people concerned.

III.   A GREAT VICTORY—*not forgotten* (verses 15-19)

In the month Elul, that is the time of year corresponding to our August-September, the wall was gloriously completed. This was a noble victory for Nehemiah and a wonderful vindication of his methods, character and attitude. The victory was such that it appeared tragedy to his enemy (verse 16)—"they were much cast down in their own eyes." Within fifty-two days (and doubtless they would have ceased work on the Sabbath) the work was finished. The enemies' chief mortification was that they saw the work had been "wrought . . . of our God."

The devil and those who serve him do not give up easily, however. For a considerable time Tobiah sent a succession of letters to Nehemiah, trying to intimidate him, keeping him in a state of fear and uncertainty. Having seen victory go to Nehemiah, they were trying to make the victory lose some of its sweetness for him. How dreadful that some near (and perhaps dear) to Nehemiah were willing to keep Tobiah informed about Nehemiah so that he could put a false interpretation upon what they said and so write perverted things about him. How often is the servant of God thus misrepresented, and how often are there to be found those who will believe such evil reports!

The great victory of God on behalf of His faithful servant is forever recorded in His Word, however, and will not be forgotten. It will ever abide as a salutary lesson to discouragers, and as a spur to encourage the faithful to continue in well-doing as true servants of the living God.

NOTHING VENTURE, NOTHING WIN

Esther 5

The key word of the Book of Esther is "providence" and the theme, "The Overruling Activity of God." Apart from Ruth this is the only other book bearing a woman's name as title. Although there is no mention of God by name, His finger is here! Although there is no mention of the temple worship, and only one reference to Jerusalem, yet this book is viewed by the Jews with particular sacredness. Dr. A. T. Pierson's alternative title is a good one: "The Romance of Providence." Here in Esther we see the possession and exercise of absolute power by Almighty God.

The three feasts of the book provide an excellent three-fold division for the book:

    I. THE FEAST OF AHASUERUS (1, 2)
        A. *Vashti: Deposition and Divorce*
        B. *Esther: Approval and Appointment*
    II. THE FEAST OF ESTHER (3-7)
        A. *Mordecai: Hounded and Honored*
        B. *Haman: Exposed and Executed*
        C. *Esther: Fasting and Feasting*
    III. THE FEAST OF PURIM (8-10)
        A. *The Jews: Their Avengement*
        B. *Mordecai: His Advancement*

The story of this book is well-known. The king of Persia, while drunk, requires the queen to exhibit herself before his nobles and friends. She refuses and is banished. Another queen is sought and selected, a Jewess, Esther. A conspiracy is formed against the Jews and a great massacre planned. Esther's guardian tells her it is up to her to save the lives of her people. At first fear fills her heart, but she is told that she cannot pick and choose, for as a queen she has responsibility. She is encouraged by the words: "Who knoweth whether thou art come to the kingdom for such a time as this?" (the key verse of the book, 4:14).

Our "famous" chapter comes in the second division of the book, and is a sequel to Mordecai's challenge. Esther takes her life into her hands in order to save her people. *Nothing Venture, Nothing Win* seems an appropriate title. Spurgeon's comment on this familiar proverb in his *Salt Cellars* is: "Some measure of risk must attend all trading.

We must venture all, even to life itself for Christ's cause." Esther ventured and won more than safety for her people—the result of her courageous action was that "the outstretched sceptre of the king was the sign of the Divine rule exercised in that court of earthly pride and pomp" (Dr. G. Campbell Morgan).

Our chapter outline is as follows:

    I. ESTHER'S DARING (verses 1-8)
        A. *Invitation* (verses 1-3)
        B. *Intervention* (verses 4-8)
   II. HAMAN'S DESIGN (verses 9-14)
        A. *Indignation* (verses 9-12)
   II. B. *Incrimination* (verses 13, 14)

I. ESTHER'S DARING (verses 1-8)

In order to gauge Esther's daring, her great courage and adventurous spirit we must go back to the previous chapter (4) and verse 11—"Whosoever, whether man or woman, shall come unto the king into the inner court, who is not called, there is one law of his to put him to death, except such to whom the king shall hold out the golden sceptre, that he may live." That was a reasonable law in such a country. It gave protection to the king against attempts at assassination. But like most sensible laws or restrictions it affected the loyal as well as the disloyal. The queen was bound by the same law as the would-be criminal. Thus Esther takes her life into her hands when she enters the king's presence uninvited. But in order to obtain grace and favor in his eyes she first dresses in royal apparel, (verse 1).

A. *Invitation.* Pleased with her appearance the king offers her an invitation to enter his presence and petition him. This he does by holding out his sceptre. This sceptre would be a thin staff of wood with perhaps a golden ball at its tip. Such action insured Esther of royal protection. It also stood for a favorable reception, which is borne out by the words: "What wilt thou? and what is thy request? it shall be given thee to the half of the kingdom" (verse 3). "Half of the kingdom" some commentators say should not be taken literally; it was a mechanical formula used to imply the promise of ready assistance, the granting of some special favor.

Before making her request known, Esther "touched the top of the sceptre," a sign of her submission, an act of homage. It also revealed that her intentions were peaceable. Finally it meant that she had a desire to be heard.

Surely this well illustrates how believers should come into the presence of God. Before conversion we had to come as we were, in the "filthy rags" of our own righteousness that we might "put on the righteousness of Christ." Now that we are born again we must come in royal apparel, having "put on Christ." Like the king's daughter of the psalmist, we are not only "all glorious within" but our outward clothing is "pure gold." We must come in holy attire into the presence of a holy God.

But we must come clothed with humility and must also come submissively.

B. *Intervention* (verses 4-8). Queen Esther intends to intervene on behalf of her people. At first it seems as if her courage fails her. A feast has been prepared to which she insists Haman should be invited. The king agrees and Haman is sent for. At that feast Esther suggests another feast for the following day, at which the king and Haman shall again be present. If her courage does not fail her then circumstances not mentioned here have come to light making it impossible for her at the first feast to go any further on behalf of her people. Some have suggested that at this point Esther needed more time for prayer and fasting. Others say that she wanted to "work on" the king in private before making a petition to him in public! At any rate here is a great illustration of the overruling providence of God, for the delay meant that Haman's malice and vindictiveness had a greater chance of displaying themselves. Later events proved the delay right and for the best. So it is often with the Christian. Our time is not always God's time; the heavenly timetable does not always coincide with the earthly one, but eventually we find that "all things work together for good to them that love God" (Romans 8:28).

II. HAMAN'S DESIGN (verses 9-14)

A Persian king usually dined in private with his guests in an adjoining hall. During the drinking of wine important guests were admitted to the king's presence. The king would recline and the queen would be seated on a chair; guests sat on the floor.

Haman, elated that such an honor was to be his the following day, went home to talk about it. A similar situation would be: "Tomorrow I'm having tea with the queen at Buckingham Palace," or, "Tomorrow I am to dine with the president at the White House." But on his way home he sees Mordecai in the king's gateway (verse 9) and immediately his elation becomes inflation, followed by indignation and then incrimination.

A. *Indignation* (verses 9-12). It must be remembered that Haman had had a rapid rise to the top of the tree. In no time at all he had become the greatest man in the Persian Empire, next to the king. He is filled with pride, and a proud man is most dangerous and vulnerable. Such a man becomes even more dangerous when his pride has been pricked as it is now. Mordecai, a Jew, would not move out of his way nor bow down to him. Haman would not be content with seeking punishment for the individual—all the Jews must suffer. His anti-Semitism has remained to this day in various parts of the world. No wonder Mordecai has been called "the black spot in (Haman's) sunshine." Haman is now full of malice, and malice always magnifies pinpricks. Malice blinds the eye to reason; malice makes for self-deception. So Haman goes home and pours out his troubles to his wife and children and friends. At the same time he makes the most of his own personal "success story," his wealth and position and his being asked personally to dine with the king and queen.

If we search our own hearts we shall probably find a similar blind spot. It may not be malice or pride (although these are common Christian failings today. It can take many forms, perhaps a feeling of being indispensable and position-loving, holding on to office so that younger people are not given a chance to learn to serve Christ and the Church.

B. *Incrimination* (verses 13, 14). Haman ends his success story with the affirmation that only Mordecai spoils the picture. Immediately Zeresh his wife and their admiring and favor-currying friends are incriminated in the plot. They propose to build a gallows and ask the king's permission to hang Mordecai from it. Note the height of the gallows: approximately nine feet, that is, high enough to let Mordecai swing for all to see, as an example and a spectacle, so adding disgrace to such a death for such a crime.

Great haste is the order of the day. They do not wait until the feast. They go early in the morning to ask the king's permission and obtain the death warrant. The idea is that with Mordecai hanged Haman will be able to enjoy the feast later in the day. The rest of the story is a thrilling illustration of God's providence, His care of His own people, and comes outside the scope of this "famous" chapter.

The final lesson is this: God can use any of us as He once used an Eastern Jewish orphan. Whatever our family background and educational upbringing there is a place in God's purposes for each and every converted person. Also we must notice that in a time of great crisis it is still possible to do God's will.

Esther bears a distinguished place among the women of the Bible. Her name can mean "a star." Before she became queen her name meant "a myrtle." Christians have new natures and "a new name written down in glory." May we be stars, shining brightly in this world of darkness, and one day more brightly when we shine as jewels in His crown.

AN ALL-ROUND MAN

Job 1

The Book of Job has been acclaimed by many, Christians and non-Christians, as a book of outstanding literary merit. Thomas Carlyle wrote of its "simplicity, sincerity and melody."

It is a book in dramatic form with characters and dialogue, being partly in prose and partly poetry. The subject matter commends itself to us all at some time or another for it is "The Problem of Pain." It is not, however, in the words of Dr. G. Campbell Morgan, "a book of solutions, but a revelation of human experience."

"Testing" is the key word by which to remember the book's theme, the key text being: "Though he slay me, yet will I trust in him" (13: 15).

An outline of the Book of Job is as follows:

Prologue (chapters 1, 2): DEPRIVATION OF PROSPERITY
I. PRONOUNCEMENTS BY MEN (3-37)
   The Vilification of Job
II. PRONOUNCEMENT BY GOD (38-42:6)
   The Vindication of Job
Epilogue (chapter 42:7-17): RESTORATION OF PROSPERITY

Our "famous" Bible chapter, the well-known first chapter, forms part of the Prologue—Deprivation of Prosperity, and can be given in the following outline form:

I. JOB (verses 1-5)
   A. *His Personality* (verse 1)
   B. *His Prosperity* (verses 2-4)
   C. *His Piety* (verse 5)
II. SATAN (verses 6-11)
   His Provocation (verses 6-11)
III. GOD (verse 12)
   A. *His Permission* (verse 12a)
   B. *His Prohibition* (verse 12b)
IV. JOB (verses 13-22)
   A. *His Plight* (verses 13-19)
   B. *His Philosophy* (verses 20-22)

I. JOB

Dr. Alexander Whyte describes Job as "the greatest of all the

men of the East." So he became, and so he began, but there was a
time when he was reduced to near nakedness! The Lord gave and
the Lord took away. We are concerned first however with his personality not his prosperity.

A. *His personality.* From verse 1 we conjecture that he was a
farmer, although little or nothing is told us of him, or indeed known
of him. He is, however, accepted in the New Testament as a historical
person.

The book that bears his name describes him as "perfect," that is
complete, an "all-around man," rather than sinless perfection. His
body, mind and spirit were all cultivated, well-developed.

He was an "upright" man. He was "straight as a die" as we say,
a man of integrity and honesty.

His "perfection" and his "uprightness" are two characteristics
that affected others around him. Now there are two Godward attributes listed: Job "feared God." He was more than a religious man,
a man who liked to worship his Creator. His religious life was deep.
He had a great reverence and awe of God. More than that, religion
and morality went hand in hand for this man. So often they are
divorced today. He "eschewed evil." The Revised Standard Version
translates the phrase: "he turned away from evil." Job not only dreaded
the thought of wrongdoing, had a natural repulsion against sin, but
he deliberately turned away from, turned his back on wickedness in
all its forms. So it should be for those who fear God. "The fear of the
Lord is to hate evil" (Proverbs 8:13). "By the fear of the Lord men
depart from evil" (Proverbs 16:6).

B. *His prosperity* (verses 2-4). Job had seven sons and three
daughters and in Jewish eyes this was a sign of great prosperity, the
blessing of God attending a man. Seven is the Scriptural number of
completion and perfection. The fact that he had more boys than
girls was a further sign of God's blessing upon him! Children for
God's ancient people, as they ought to be for Christians today, were
"a heritage of the Lord."

But Job was also a man of "substance": sheep, camels, oxen,
asses. He had a "great household," that is, many servants and workmen
were in his employ. Dr. Alexander Whyte then was right to begin his
character sketch of Job by saying he was the greatest man in all the
East, for that is what God's Word says here. What a revelation of the
truth of the proverb that "honesty is the best policy," that "piety is
the way to prosperity."

How happy was Job in his prosperity. His sons were settled
near him; they had a succession of feasts, perhaps birthdays or holy
days, in one another's homes. Although a separated family they were
not divided, there was inter-communion on special occasions.

C. *His piety* (verse 5) "Job sent and sanctified them." He had
brought his children up in the nurture and admonition of the Lord.

Now that they have left home Job has not relinquished their religious education or his spiritual responsibility toward them. He was still the priestly head of the family and he sacrificed for them, for the sins they had committed, willfully and in ignorance. This he did continuously, not occasionally. Perhaps like Dr. Whyte we have to say of our own families: "We confess with pain and shame and guilt concerning our children, that Job here condemns us ·to our face. We have not wholly neglected them, nor the Great Sacrifice in their behalf. But we have not remembered it and them together at all with that regularity, and point, and perseverance, and watchfulness, that all combined to make Job such a good father to his children, and such a good servant to his God."

II. SATAN

Now comes a swift change of character and scene: from Job to Satan, man to devil, and from earth to heaven. Some commentators assume that this is the oldest book in the Bible for here we see Satan still in heaven, not yet cast out with the fallen angels through sinful pride.

Job, the pious and prosperous man is going to a swift downfall, overwhelmed by calamity. The fault is not his, however. It is not a question of "Who did sin, this man or his father?" Sometimes sin does result in calamity or in chastisement, but with Job it was no fault of his.

His provocation (verses 6-11). One day in heaven the "sons of God," that is, the angelic messengers of God, presented themselves before God and Satan. Satan's work was "going to and fro," a phrase that may mean restlessness and mischief-making, and there will be no end to this "going to and fro" until Satan is eternally bound.

God asks Satan if in his travels he has "considered" Job. Consider here is in the sense of a man buying a secondhand car, rocking it, pushing it, shaking it, looking intently for defects of one kind and another. Satan is able to do that. Not only does Almighty God see into our hearts but Satan too notices our inward state as well as our outward association with certain people, and other objects of our affection. The same Hebrew word is used of an invading army going around the walls of a city looking for weak places, cracks in the defense. Satan thinks he has found the "chink in Job's armor." Satan uses the criticism that non-Christians have ever since used against Christians, that religion is a money-making affair, that missionaries only make "rice Christians." Job is accused by Satan of being pious merely because it suited his ends and contributed toward material prosperity. "Take away Job's goods," says Satan, and "you have taken away his God." "Try it," says Satan to God in a provoking way—"Put forth thine hand. . ." (verse 11).

III. God

Does God appear in a harsh light in this book? We have to remember that when He allows a believer to be tested or tried it is always that he may come forth as gold. He is the divine Refiner. He knows when the process has gone on long enough.

A. *His permission* (verse 12a). God said in effect to Satan: "All right, try it; take away Job's material prosperity." Thus Job is stripped of everything he held dear. God did not do it, He *allowed* it. He has a permissive will. Evil comes from Satan, but only when permitted by God. He overlooks and overrules. God is supreme whatever the devil may do or devise. He cannot touch a hair of our heads unless God permits.

B. *His prohibition* (verse 12b). God allowed Satan to touch Job's possessions, but not his person, not Job himself. Satan is only given limited power, not a free hand. God always says "Thus far and no further" to Satan. The believer is in the hollow of God's hand and none can pluck us out, no man nor demon. Thus heavy blows may come upon us, but we shall not finally go under. The restraining hand of God the Father is upon Satan.

IV. Job

The chapter ends, as it began, with Job, the all-around man.

A. *His plight* (verses 13-19). Satan loses no time but goes from the presence of God to test Job. Notice how crafty Satan is. He often uses with us the same method he used with Job, he touches us through our sons and daughters. Satan tempts them to worldliness. Perhaps after a wonderful conversion we see them backslide. Four messengers come one after another and tell Job what has happened to his children, then his possessions and property. Robbers, fire and a whirlwind (these are the calamities used by Satan) destroy Job's loved ones—all but one solitary witness.

That was only the beginning. If we could go beyond the bounds of this one chapter we should see Job's own property and health, and then his nearest and dearest, his wife, turning against him and his religious faith.

B. *His philosophy* (verses 20-22). In the face of calamity, composure, for "in quietness and confidence shall be your strength" (Isaiah 30:15). Philosophically Job looks at his present situation and sees that he is but back where he started out in life—he brought nothing into the world, and so he can carry nothing out. What a lesson for our materialistic twentieth century—the brevity of life and of earthly possessions; not one of them can be taken into the next life with us.

Then Job acknowledged God's goodness in allowing him to have material blessings for the short while he has enjoyed them—"Blessed be the name of the Lord," he cries. Notice how he views his losses: the Lord took away his possessions not the robbers. How far we have advanced along the Christian pathway when we can acknowledge the hand of God in everything, in adversity as well as in prosperity. How too we ought to worship the Giver of the gifts rather than the gifts themselves. Do we find it more difficult to praise God for what He takes away rather than for what He gives?

Job's attitude is a clear defeat of Satan. Job does not worship God for what God gives him. Job does not forsake his faith when he loses all for he still has the best of all, God Himself. So Job did not "charge God foolishly," that is, he did not rant and rave saying, "Why should this happen to me?" He kept in close communion with God and sought to understand God's ways and will.

The final answer to this chapter is surely in the New Testament:

"There hath no temptation taken you but such as is common to man: but God is faithful, who will not suffer you to be tempted above that ye are able; but will with the temptation also make a way to escape, that ye may be able to bear it" (I Corinthians 10:13) and

"Blessed is the man that endureth temptation: for when he is tried, he shall receive the crown of life, which the Lord hath promised to them that love him" (James 1:12).

THREE PICTURES IN ONE

*Psalm 23**

Psalm twenty-three, perhaps the best-known and well-loved of all the Psalms, is but one of 150 spiritual songs making up the hymn-book of the Jews, the Book of Psalms. Many people, believers and unbelievers alike, have found this the very book for times of trouble or temptation, sorrow or sickness, persecution or poverty. No experience of life that comes to modern man seems unexperienced by the composers of these songs.

The underlying theme of them all is, "The Attitude of Man in the Presence of God," summed up in the key verse (Psalm 29:2): "Worship the Lord in the beauty of holiness." The key word of the book is "worship" and an outline of the whole book of Psalms can be given in this form:

    I. THE FAILURE OF MAN MET BY SALVATION OF GOD (1-41)
    II. REDEMPTION THROUGH BLOOD (42-72)
    III. ACCESS TO GOD (73-89)
    IV. QUALIFICATIONS FOR SERVICE (90-106)
    V. MAN'S MOTIVE OF OBEDIENCE TO GOD (107-150)

It is thus clearly seen that each section of the book corresponds to the theme of each of the books of the Pentateuch, Genesis to Deuteronomy.

Psalm 23 is the most famous of them all, being sung both at weddings and funerals and other special occasions. Here in these six verses the work of Jesus Christ as Saviour is portrayed, and yet the author lived hundreds of years before the Incarnation. A modern Jewish commentary states: "The world could spare many a large book better than this sunny little Psalm. It has dried many tears and supplied the mould into which many hearts have poured their peaceful faith." And such a comment is by one who sees no Messiah, no personal Saviour in the Psalm; he merely accepts it as having national application, having faith to believe that the God who fed his fathers in the wilderness will ever be the same to them.

We entitle the Psalm *Three Pictures in One* because most people only discover two pictures. John Stevenson in 1853 expounds it under two divisions: The Fold and The Banquet. The modern commentary

---

* The material for this chapter first appeared in *The Sunday Companion*, London, England (March, 1961) under the title: *Photos in the Shepherd Psalm.*

(*The New Bible Commentary*) by the Inter-Varsity Fellowship divides it into two parts: Pilgrimage and Hospitality. But there are clearly three pictures here, three portraits of God Himself: Shepherd, Guide and Host. There is a Pastoral Scene, a Pilgrim Study and a Palace Sketch. Using the terms of the photographer we can give an outline of the Psalm in this way:

> I. LANDSCAPE—A Pastoral Scene (verses 1, 2)
> *Security and Serenity*
> II. ACTION SHOT—A Pilgrimage Study (verses 3, 4)
> *Sanctity and Safety*
> III. INTERIOR—A Palace Sketch (verses 5, 6)
> *Satiety and Sovereignty*

I. LANDSCAPE—A Pastoral Scene (verses 1, 2)

The dictionary defines "landscape" as "a picture of a piece of in- land scenery." Seldom is a landscape drawn, painted or photographed without some figure in the foreground to create human interest, to improve the perspective, or create the illusion of distance, size or space. Here in these two opening verses to the Psalm we are intro- duced to the landscape figure—"the Lord," the Good Shepherd. A Jewish rabbi comments: "In a pastoral community the faithful shep- herd stood as the personification of tender care and watchfulness." This term or descriptive name has been used of God previously, by Jacob in Genesis 48:15. It is also found in the prophetic writings: Isaiah 40:11; Micah 7:14; and again frequently in the Book of Psalms.

Differences between the Eastern shepherd and the one to be seen in the highlands of Scotland or the hills of Wales must be noticed. It is possible when traveling in England, Ireland, Scotland or Wales to see sheep unattended in the fields. In fact a warning sign to motorists sometimes draws attention to common land where sheep are likely to be straying along the road. This was unknown in the East. In Palestine the shepherd and the sheep were always in close proximity. The Palestinian shepherd always led his sheep; in Great Britain they are driven. In the east they were known by name, not by marks. Eastern shepherds were always armed. Accepting the author- ship of Psalm 23 as Davidic, we know that David knew how to deal with lions and bears when preserving his father's flock. Sheep largely fend for themselves in Britain. The Eastern shepherd looks after his sheep with great tenderness and kindness; the sheep are entirely de- pendent upon the shepherd in such a hot, dry climate, with plenty of open desert land and dangers by day and night. It is a natural tendency of sheep to go astray and so they need a shepherd to keep them intact, together as a flock. They do not seem to have the natural tendency or insight of the dog or cat; for finding their way home, they are easily lost.

How true all this is of sinful, wayward, lost men and women and the Lord Jesus Christ as the Good Shepherd! When we come to Him in faith for salvation we never want again. That does not mean automatic prosperity or abundance, but it does mean that nothing necessary will be withheld ("The Lord will provide" said Jacob, and Paul's echo is: "My God shall supply all your need"). John Stevenson comments: "This is the mean between two extremes: destitution and superfluity." "I shall not want" applies both to outward circumstances and inward experiences. God's provision results in a contented body and a contented mind. This portrait of the Shepherd then means first of all *security* for the sheep, all their needs supplied, no need for anxious thoughts regarding tomorrow.

Here too is serenity—green pastures and still waters! Rest and refreshment! "Green pastures" means literally pastures of tender grass. The literal meaning of "still waters" is waters of restfulness. These are not only placid waters, a stream with hardly a ripple on the surface; these are waters beside which one can find true rest. How this is needed in our madly rushing world, a jet age, a space age, a noise-abatement age. In a society of nervous tension, mental anxiety and domestic and business worry, this is God's answer. David, of course, is not thinking in terms of temporal blessings alone, but spiritual prosperity, spiritual health, and spiritual freedom from doubts and fears. Here then is the Shepherd's promise of that kind of life we so often sing about and yet so infrequently experience:

> Drop Thy still dews of quietness,
> Till all our strivings cease;
> Take from our souls the strain and stress,
> And let our ordered lives confess
> The beauty of Thy peace.
>
> So shall my walk be close with God,
> Calm and serene my frame.

But notice how it is all a result of the two words "He maketh." This is all of the Shepherd's provision. It does not come from the philosopher's rostrum with his emphasis upon positive thinking; it is not a result of the psychiatrist's couch; it is the gift of the sovereign God, the Good Shepherd. *He* makes us to "lie down," that is, recline. Again the emphasis is upon security and serenity. The pastures are green and budding, tender to the teeth, tasteful to the palate for the sheep; so are God's blessings to the believer. The still waters are soothing to the mind and spirit. God's Word, the Lord's Supper, the preaching of the Gospel—these are the nourishing blades of young grass for the believer's spiritual nourishment and refreshment. Prayer, meditation, Christian fellowship, these are the atmosphere in which the Christian finds peace and tranquillity in the world of today. God Himself is the Fountain for these waters, and He sends them forth for our refreshment. Security and serenity! Now the atmosphere changes to sanctity and safety with an—

II. ACTION SHOT—A Pilgrimage Study (verses 3, 4)

Photographers know all about action shots. Special viewfinders are now incorporated in most cameras, either, "direct-vision" finders or else a white line is incorporated, thus the subject being photographed, a moving object or person, can be followed until the right moment arrives for "clicking" the shutter.

First we have a portrait of the Guide. A Jewish translation of verse 3 is: "He guideth me in straight paths."

What a dramatic change of scene there is here from the green pastures and still waters! We now see a lonely pilgrim on an uphill road, overcome by heat, fatigue, soreness, blistered feet. Several times the walker has taken a wrong turn ("restore" here may mean "to turn back" or "retrieve," or perhaps "rescue" or even "convert"). The path of holiness has been forsaken and now comes a Guide who will lead into the paths of righteousness, the King's highway of holiness and purity. David is emphasizing *sanctity* or holiness of life and character for the believer.

Sometimes we fall into the mistake of making holiness a fetish, a principle irrationally reverenced. We have "holiness conventions" and become enamored of "holiness teaching." Often it is not with us as it was with David—"for his name's sake." The Name of our Saviour, our Master's reputation is at stake if we are not living holy lives. God's glory is ever the aim of the Christian and so all that we do and are is "for his name's sake."

Are we walking in right paths day by day? *He* first led our steps into the way everlasting; He it is who keeps us walking along the highway of holiness. He is our Guide to the sanctified life.

He is also our Guide to *safety*. He will guide us through the most difficult part of the pilgrimage from earth to heaven, the "valley of the shadow of death." There is no need for fear for we are perfectly safe with One who has traveled this way before us. He knows the road and he has dispelled its darkness, turning substance into mere shadow by His Resurrection from the dead!

From the Hebrew it is not sure if the writer meant "the valley of shadows" or "the valley of the shadow of death." Some commentators equate it with the "valley or baca" or the "valley of weeping." There are many such valleys between birth and death! He is with us in them all. On the other hand there may have been an actual valley in Palestine with which David was familiar, called by this name. Because of its its dense foliage, wild beasts, robbers, early darkness, dense shadows, men hated to travel alone through this place and always desired protection.

Whatever danger may be our particular valley of shadows we

can know the safety that comes from the divine Presence with us. With Him as our Companion and Guide we can *walk* instead of having to run through the valley. Bereavement, separation, loneliness, ill health, all are to be found in the valley, but our Guide leads us through to the sunlit meadows on the other side. And He provides us with a rod and staff. The "rod" was the weapon of defense, a club or staff with an iron spike; the staff was the stick upon which to lean as one walked. Our Puritan forefathers used to say that the rod typified the Holy Spirit's power and the staff the Word of God. This is in keeping with Dr. James Stalker's remark that one was for man's own use and the other was for dealing with others. The Holy Spirit is God's gift to the believer; the Bible is our sword for dealing with others.

III. INTERIOR—A Palace Sketch (verses 5, 6)

Interior scenes always present the artist or photographer with difficulties. Exposure and perspective are difficult to get right.

The portrait that makes the interior scene a graphic one is that of One who is described as the Host or Royal Entertainer in His palace.

So many have felt in the past that verses 5 and 6 are a continuation of the pastoral scene. But sheep do not eat in palaces! Sickly lambs may be reared in the shepherd's kitchen, but that is not "for ever," it is only until they can be weaned. Neither is the word here for "house" ever used for a "fold" in Scripture. Here then is an obvious change of scene again, to the palace of the king with its banqueting hall and its tables loaded with food and fine fare. C. S. Lewis is surely too flippant when he likens this scene to a Christian not enjoying his prosperity unless "those horrid Joneses (who used to look down their noses at him) are watching it all and hating it." Dr. Lewis has misunderstood the psalmist. The Jew's comment is better when he says that "in the presence of mine enemies" is a phrase that makes it plain and evident that the believer "is in God's care and their plots to injure him must fail." There is no spirit of vindictiveness here at all.

God is everywhere regarded in Scripture as a generous Host, providing sumptuous fare for sinful men, and here the emphasis is first upon *satiety* or fullness because of the extravagance of the preparations and provision made. The cup "runneth over," it is filled to the brim, to overflowing. The blessings of eternal salvation are truly superabundant, "all things are (ours)" writes the Apostle Paul. Pardon, peace, answered prayer, spiritual fellowship, discernment in spiritual things, promises—these and much more are God's provision for us. "Oil" often stands for the Holy Spirit in Scripture. What a provision is the third Person of the Trinity! He is our Advocate, our Paraclete, our Comforter, our Guide. Having convicted and converted us He anoints, ordains, and fills to overflowing.

Finally there is *sovereignty*. This is the "house of the Lord for ever." Goodness and mercy stand for this side of death; the Lord's house is the other side of the river. Goodness and mercy have been described as twin footmen standing on the coach behind, always with us wherever we go, to servants to see that no evil befalls the guest. Goodness is physical welfare, provision of temporal and material needs; mercy is divine love and guardianship. These two have followed us all our life thus far and will continue to accompany us right up to the moment of death. Goodness for when we are in need, and mercy for when we fall into sin.

After death—the House of the Lord! This is a common phrase in the Bible for the tabernacle or temple of God. We may interpret it in a spiritual sense: enjoyment of God's presence and communion with God forever. "Forever a favoured resident in the courts of royalty" an old commentator puts it. This is the highest of all spiritual privileges awaiting us. There is nothing else, certainly nothing higher. This reminds us of the never-ending Sabbath of eternity in Revelation. In that House, in which are many "mansions" or abiding places, we shall be just souls made perfect, all spots and wrinkles and other blemishes gone—like Him whom we shall see face to face! No wonder C. H. Spurgeon called the Twenty-third Psalm a lark and not a nightingale, for "as it sings it mounts," taking us on wings of song from the fields with the Shepherd, along the dusty road of life with the Guide, to the palace of the King where we dine with the divine Host himself.

WISDOM AND CONDUCT

Proverbs 15

If the Book of Psalms can be termed the believer's manual of devotion, then Proverbs is the Christian's manual of behavior or ethics. Here is a book entirely different from the previous books of the Old Testament. Proverbs is a collection of wisdom sayings, hence the title given to this "famous" Bible chapter—*Wisdom and Conduct*. Truths about life and how to live it are given in this book with brevity and vividness. The ancient method of teaching in times when books were few and bulky was that clear, crisp sayings would be given orally so that they could be remembered and passed on.

The theme of Proverbs is "the Relation of Religion to Life" and so such subjects are dealt with as: our faith and our money, our homes and family life, friendship, love and marriage. Certain types of people are portrayed: the fool, the practical joker, the talebearer, the backbiter, the boaster, the get-rich-quick.

The authorship of the book is composite: Solomon, Hezekiah's wise men, Augur and Lemuel.

Each section of the book begins with the announcement: "The proverbs of Solomon," that is, proverbs given *by* Solomon or *to* Solomon, and passed on by and to others. The outline is as follows:

   I.   THE ATTAINMENT OF TRUE WISDOM (1-9)
  II.   THE PRACTICE OF RIGHT CONDUCT (10-24)
 III.   THE REGARD OF DUE WARNING (25-31)

Our "famous" chapter, which has been called "the original nucleus of the whole collection," the Inter-Varsity *New Bible Commentary* entitles "The Path of Life and the Secrets of a Cheerful Heart." The writer's assumption is that we have attained true wisdom ("the fear of the Lord is the beginning of wisdom") and are now prepared to be "doers of the Word" and not hearers only, thus putting into practice in daily life and conduct, in our relationship with others, all that we have learned from God.

An outline of Chapter 15 is:

   I.   WISDOM REVEALED IN OUR WORDS (verses 1-7)
  II.   WISDOM REFASHIONS OUR THOUGHTS (verses 8-17)
 III.   WISDOM REGULATES OUR DEEDS (verses 18-33)

It must be stressed that these divisions in such a book are somewhat artificial. There is an orderly arrangement in this particular chapter but there is no consecutive, developed argument by the writer (or preacher).

I. WISDOM REVEALED IN OUR WORDS (verses 1-7)

The emphasis in these opening seven verses is that of James 3. Here are words of wisdom about the human tongue, the speech of a God-fearing person.

The Puritan commentator, Charles Bridges, whose commentary Charles Haddon Spurgeon called, "The best work on Proverbs," stressed that in verse 1 we have a valuable rule for personal relationships, family peace and church unity! A soft answer is like water that quenches fire. Grievous words are like oil that quickens fire, adding fuel to flame. How easy it is to yield to irritation of spirit and make a hasty retort, seeking to justify words and actions, insisting upon having the last word. Yes, pride and passion frequently go together. The old adage about counting ten before we speak has some Scriptural basis—the believer's love of divine wisdom is never revealed in hasty words; but it is shown when we govern our tongues.

In verse 2 we are told that a wise man knows how to speak about his knowledge in a right way. Being in control and command of his tongue the believing man does not make hasty pronouncements. He "useth knowledge aright" (Hebrew: adorneth knowledge), that is, the Christian talks about Christ and his Christian faith in well-phrased language, choosing his words carefully. What a condemnation this is of those who would have us use modern jargon, the language of today, when presenting the Gospel. The fool does not bother about nice wording, good phraseology. He has nothing important to talk about, nothing to say about eternity and the things that really matter.

How are the "eyes of the Lord", (verse 3) connected with words? God's inspection of the universe is "minute, exact, unwearied." The ungodly may try and in part suceed in banishing Him from their thoughts, but the believer knows that God sees and hears all, our secret sins included; His glance is so penetrating. He sees, and He hears the words of our mouths when we speak and to whom we speak.

"When grace is in the heart" there is "healing in the tongue" (see margin). The words of a converted man soothe the afflicted and calm troubled waters. By contrast an evil tongue wounds. "Perverseness" here means a twisting, evil intention. Words that are double-edged often recoil upon the person using them.

Verse 5 contains a striking thought: only one child has ever been able and fitted to teach His own parents—the omniscient Christ, and He set an example of humility, obeying His earthly parents, being subject to them.

Christians may be poor and yet rich (verse 6)! Destitute of money they have "treasure"—spiritual riches laid up where none can touch them. The word "treasure" here means "a great store," and this store is God's provision for His believing children. Whereas the possessions of the unbeliever frequently bring sorrow and trouble, embarrassment and dissatisfaction, the spiritual riches of the godly man bring entire satisfaction.

Verse 7 condemns much of our social intercourse as Christians. What time we waste and what opportunities we miss when we talk about any and every subject under the sun except the Lord!

II. WISDOM REFASHIONS OUR THOUGHTS (verses 8-17)

The heart for the Jew was more than a bodily organ, it was the seat of the emotions. The experience of fear, anger, joy, sorrow, was centered in the heart. Sometimes "heart" could stand for a man himself, his personality, his characteristics and attributes. It had also a third meaning, the intellectual and moral faculties, and that is largely how it is used in this section of the chapter.

Sacrifice and prayer are not so much in opposition (verse 8), rather—they are both religious exercises but without efficacy if done without thought and right intent. When done from right motives, however feeble or stumbling the words, however humble the offering, they are accepted by God and He delights in them. Such a conception of prayer by church members today would result in the midweek prayer meeting being transformed.

Verse 9 has been described as "a pendent to what precedes." The final test of a man's religion is not the performance or accomplishment of certain rites or ceremonies, but his pursuit of righteousness. Holiness unto the Lord must be the chief pursuit of the Christian.

The answer to the corporal punishment dispute is not in Gallup polls, parliamentary debate or the findings of psychologists, it is in the Word of God. Scripture commends it. It begins in the home. If only more fathers practiced it then fewer magistrates would have to mete it out! God chastizes His own children; it is educative rather than punative; it recalls us from the path of backsliding. "He that hateth reproof" is the man who has no desire or intention to repent; he only wishes to persist in evil.

Verse 11 is similar to verse 3. God is an omniscient, all-seeing God. If we could see into heaven and see how God not only reads human hearts but also minds, then we would not harbor the resentments we do, nor the impurities of mind.

How difficult it is, and how much grace we need to receive reproof and accept it as from the Lord (verse 12).

The ancients saw what psychologists are only just beginning to realize, that there is a great sympathy between body, soul and mind. Man's face is the index of his spirit as well as the index of the condition of his body. Indigestion of long standing shows on a person's face; the constant, nagging discomfort "draws" the face, contorts it. So there are spiritual ailments that show on the Christian's face. The old commentator expressed it quaintly thus: "The heart sits smiling in the face and looks merrily out of the windows of the eyes." Stephen before his execution had the face of an angel. However sorely tried or tested or tempted we may be, there should be such an inward sense of peace and joy in the Lord through believing that it is revealed in a tranquil, serene countenance.

Verse 14 tells us that the Christian must use his heart and mind to seek after more and more knowledge, spiritual knowledge and understanding. Only a fool believes he has learned enough. "Young people," commented the Puritan, "guard against this folly at every turn." To the maturer Christian he said: "In religion, beware of preferring empty speculations and disputings on matters indifferent, to the rich pasture of the children of God." There's nothing like communal Bible study, the study of God's Word as a Christian fellowship for helping believers to grow in spiritual grace and stature.

The summing-up verse is verse 15. The Christian is not as miserable as he seems to be, was one man's comment! We might add: Nor is he as "green" as he appears to be. The Puritans excelled in living the Christian life as well as talking or writing about it. One of their number could comment on this verse: "(The Christian) can sing in prison as in a palace" and "All his trouble is but the rattling hail upon the tiles of his house, not disturbing his enjoyment."

The saint's little is better than the worldling's all (verse 24) because everything the believer has comes from the Lord and our heavenly Father knows what we need and how much we need. He gives little to those He cannot trust with more!

Verse 17 is a continuation of the previous one. "Dinner" here is a snack given to a passing wayfarer—a humble, frugal meal of herbs or a handful of dates. But it is better to have that when it is a gift of love then a table groaning with food given grudgingly.

III. WISDOM REGULATES OUR DEEDS (verses 18-33)

Words are the dressing up, the audible expression of our thoughts. Deeds are the execution of what we have thought or desired to do. Some people seem to have a gift for stirring up trouble by their words —they open their mouth, as we say, and put their foot in it! In this picture of the wrathful man (verse 18) we must remember verse 1 again and pour water on the flames instead of adding fuel to the fire.

The lazy man is depicted in verse 19. He is one who has planted a hedge about himself so that he is penned in and no matter where he turns he tears himself. Soon he loses heart and lacks initiative to do anything. By contrast the believer should be one who walks on an elevated highway, a modern expressway. "Made plain" means raised up as a causeway. How true this is in our spiritual experience. The more we neglect our devotional life the more sluggish we become.

The family is a God-ordained unit in Scripture—God "set the solitary in families." The same emphasis is in the New Testament—the Church of God is a family. The days seem to have gone in our church life of the family pew, with mother and father and children all sitting together and worshiping together. School trips abroad have put a stop to many people having a family holiday. Verse 20 emphasizes the filial reverence and maternal honor that there should be in a Christian family.

In verse 21 we come to the center and core of our subject, Wisdom and Conduct. Scripture speaks about the pleasures of sin, even if only for a season. The unbeliever has a remarkable appetite for sin. The believer, by contrast, has forsaken sin—he has been cleansed by the precious blood of Christ. He walks by a different path. And it is divine wisdom that helps us to walk along the straight and narrow road.

Political and ecclesiastical truths are found in verse 22. A queen needs her trusty counselors. Experienced counsel guards against indecision and indiscretion, but it is the result of divine wisdom regulating our minds, not based upon human prejudice. So a pastor needs to be surrounded by Christian experience.

A man naturally approves of his own expression of opinion and regards it as sound (verse 23), but too often we want to speak out of turn and give our advice out of season.

The Christian pilgrimage has been mapped out from above (verse 24); it is of heavenly origin and can only truly be seen from the heavenly vantage point. "Above" means "goeth upward," reminding us that the Christian pilgrim must often take the uphill road.

In the first part of verse 25 is a reference to men of position and power who use it to gratify their own ends and oppress others, e.g. the widow, one who has no one to defend her or take her part. Some of God's choicest promises are given to the widow.

"Thoughts of the wicked" in verse 26 means literally "evil schemes." These are an abomination to the Lord. They are an expression of evil thoughts put into action. The Christian's words are a result of the believer's communion and intercourse with the heavenly Father and His Word.

As in the Ten Commandments, so in verse 27 covetousness is condemned. It is a sin that affects more than the individual. Many a family has been plunged into ruin and misery through one man wanting to win at the gambling table or the race track.

The believer is not only careful about money, spending it and making it, but (verse 28) he is careful about words—he thinks before he speaks.

God is near to all if they desire to call on him for salvation. While a man remains rebellious, Christ-rejecting, then God is far removed from him. To the righteous man God is graciously near at all times, closer than a brother.

"The light of the eyes" in verse 30 is not the love-light, but brightness that appears when one is brought good news. "Good report" means good tidings. "Makes the bones fat" means "invigorates the body." Do we feel like that when we hear the Gospel preached?

The man who hears sin reproved (verse 31) and receives the word as divine correction, stays among the wise and associates with Christians in order to have the opportunity of hearing more.

One who refuses to be taught (verse 32) to become wise makes himself small, of no account. He literally throws his life away.

"Of" should be "in" in verse 33. True love, awe, reverence, fear of God is shown by our willingness to be instructed in divine truths. The second part of the verse emphasizes that we must have this humility, this desire to be taught and instructed before we can have the honor of being looked upon as well-informed people. "Humility before Honor" is a good motto for the Christian; it is a motto for the preacher who must indeed become humble before God's Word before He enjoys the honor of proclaiming it.

A SERMON FOR MODERN YOUTH

Ecclesiastes 12

The subtitle of Ecclesiastes is "The Preacher," that is, a speaker at an assembly. This book is, however, more like a diary than a sermon. From verse 1 we are led to believe that Solomon was the preacher; we are not so told that he was the writer. The book is thus in the form of a monologue.

Many have considered the book something of an enigma. It has been a favorite with the atheist or agnostic. This preacher is not himself an atheist however. He is putting himself in the position of a believer trying to live life without God and so the theme is, "The Emptiness of Life Without God." "Vanity is the key word of the book and the key text is 6:12. "Vanity" here does not stand for that foolish personal pride which we label vanity today; the word means emptiness, and the oft-recurring phrase to emphasize this empty life of the backsliding believer is, "Under the sun is no profit." Life is a wearisome, monotonous thing for the worldly man, with little or no progress or lasting satisfaction. Death is only defeat and offers no solution. The only solution is to look at life from the divine point of view. Without God man is "a half-hinge." The book can be given in this outline form:

THE PROBLEM OF LIFE—
    I. STATED (1:1–3)
    II. STUDIED (1:4–10:20)
    III. SOLVED (11:1–12:14)

There are amazing scientific truths in the book. The movements of the winds, the spinal cord system, the circulation of the blood—all are here long before their discovery by scientists.

This book is frequently quoted in the New Testament for there we have set forth the life more abundant that is to be found in Jesus Christ.

Our "famous" chapter comes in the third and final section, the solution to the problem of life. A convenient outline of chapter twelve is:

    I. AN EXHORTATION TO THE YOUNG (verses 1-7)
    II. A DEMONSTRATION FROM EXPERIENCE (verses 8-12)
    III. A RECOMMENDATION FOR HAPPINESS (verses 13, 14)

I. An Exhortation to the Young (verses 1-7)

"Creator" in verse 1 is plural, the plural of majesty and also a reminder of the Trinity. "Let *us* make man," states Genesis. Father, Son and Holy Spirit were all interested in and involved in our creation.

Here surely a strange exhortation is given us. Young people are not reminded of their vim and vigor, or all that life holds in store for them—they are reminded of the speedy decline of life. Because death's decay begins the minute we are born, we should not hold too many high expectations about life, about life's pleasures and amusements. These have a way of turning out most unsatisfactory.

"Youth" here is synonymous with "teen-ager" today—adolescence. Solomon has a word for the "Teddy Boy," the "Mod" and "Rocker" of his time. Those who have little aim or ambition in life, whose career seems purposeless—these are Solomon's congregation. They are to remember that "evil days" are coming, days when the passions or emotions will be lessened, when they will have less sense of urgency in life and active sport will no longer be engaged in. They will be spectators along the sideline. "I have no pleasure in them," that will be their comment. No wonder C. H. Spurgeon appealed to young people: "Do not give God the dregs of your life!" Youth here is connected with choice—youthful days are days of choosing: choosing a career, a life's partner, and so on.

When the brightness of youthful days have gone, Solomon says in the second verse, then old age approaches like a gathering storm. "Sun" and "light" here stand for the forehead; the moon for the soul; the stars for the cheeks; clouds after rain for eyes after crying.

This storm picture is carried on in verse 3, illustrating our waning powers in old age. "Keepers of the house" stands for our arms with which we defend and support others—these will one day tremble with weakness. The "strong men" are our legs, supporting and carrying us; the "grinders" are our "ivory castles," our teeth, eaten away by decay; "windows" stands for failing eyesight. A decrepit picture!

The result of this failing of physical powers is shown in verse 4. The aged person knows but light and erratic sleep, any slight noise awakens. There are fewer desires for being present at public occasions or business. The "daughters of music" stand for a weak and wavering voice.

Weak nervous energy accompanies all this physical weakness (verse 5). This results in loss of courage and daring; we become easily tired, our energy is soon exhausted; we become afraid of high places, stairs and ladders. Our hair whitens and the digestive system becomes weak. "Long home" stands for the grave and eternity. As Matthew Henry aptly comments: "No short preparations must be made for so long a journey."

Four wonderful descriptions of actual death follow in verse 6. One is particularly striking and forms the theme of a gospel song:

"Some day the silver cord will break." This is Solomon's reference to the spinal system of man. When that finally breaks down the separation between soul and body occurs, which is death. The "golden bowl" is the skull. In the Old Testament lampstands were filled with oil for lighting. The flame flickered when the oil was getting low and finally the light went out. "Pitcher broken" really means a dried up fountain. "Wheel" is part of the fountain's machinery for drawing up water. When broken the fountain is rendered useless.

Verse 7 reminds us that we are body and spirit.

Do we find all this rather depressing? Would any well-known evangelist to modern youth take his text or theme from this passage? Well, this is God's exhortation to young people, to remember one's Creator when young, yielding to Him in repentance and faith. The statistics show that the longer Christian commitment is left the more difficult it becomes. "My Spirit shall not always strive with man" (Genesis 6:3).

II. A DEMONSTRATION FROM EXPERIENCE (verses 8-12)

Having addressed himself to youth the preacher now reminisces and then demonstrates from his own experience how he personally tackles the problem of life. He begins by repeating the text of his "sermon": "Vanity of vanities . . ." (verse 8). Without faith in God the world is empty, unprofitable and unsatisfying. The ancient rabbis taught that there were seven vanities, each corresponding with the seven stages of man.

In spite of the godless world in which he lived the preacher made it his business to teach the people (verse 9). He took great pains and care with his teaching. Nothing must be cheated in God's work. Solomon "gave heed," "sought," and "set in order"—that is, he gave heed, pondered, examined and studied. No preparation can be too conscientious when teaching people the things of God. And when the initial "spade work" has been done then the final form must be pleasing and gripping (verse 10). Matthew Henry once commented: "Good matter is not to be spoilt by bad style." "Acceptable" words are to be used by the preacher, not big words that half the congregation will not understand! The preacher's message must be couched in suitable words for an exact representation of the truth of God's Word.

After such preparation the message will be like a "goad," the sharp stick used by the driver of oxen. So many people prefer a "comforting" message from the preacher; Scripture speaks of God's Word being a two-edged sword, cutting and piercing; it is for reproof and correction as well as comfort. On the day of Pentecost the crowd were "pricked in their hearts." Solomon thus uses words as a goad to those who would draw back and as nails to fasten the message for the wavering and to make them less inconstant in their living. Just as a nail is hammered over and "clinched," so the sermon is meant to be retained in the memory for future days.

Much more could be said from the preacher's experience but Solomon hastens to add (verse 12) that if he were to write a book, or book upon book, he could not say any more than he has already said. What a good thing it is when a preacher knows when to stop! If the books were written and read the reading of them would only produce weariness. Solomon has said and written as much as God would have him say and write. Dr. Martyn Lloyd-Jones of Westminster Chapel, London, was once asked in a ministers' fellowship: "Doctor, how long should we preach for?" His reply was: "Until you have nothing more to say. It might take you twenty minutes. It might take me an hour"! Solomon has said enough from his own experience for his hearers to take in and themselves have a new experience of God.

III. A RECOMMENDATION FOR HAPPINESS (verses 13, 14)

In this section we have a final summing up for this famous chapter and of the whole Book of Ecclesiastes. Here is Solomon's recommendations for living a truly happy life, one of lasting happiness. We must "fear" God, and he uses "fear" in the sense of awe, reverence, devotion and love. Such "fear" always results in obedience ("keep his commandments"). The phrase "whole duty" is difficult to explain. "Duty" is in italics so it could mean: "This is every man's duty" or "This concerns every man."

To give strength to his recommendation Solomon adds in verse 14: "For God shall bring every work into judgment." One day, at the Day of Judgment, everything will be judged, things done in secret as well as things done openly. Everything will be brought to light. In that day an account will have to be given; it will be a day of reckoning. To the young (Solomon's congregation) that day may seem far away, but time is like "an ever-rolling stream" and "the Day" will soon arrive. For that reason alone we should "fear God," for—

Fear Him, ye saints, and you will then
Have nothing else to fear.

SUMMER-TIME IN THE SOUL

Song of Solomon 2

The Song of Solomon has always been a greatly misunderstood book. Censure has been passed upon it because of its sensual language and analogies about love. The Jews, however, look upon Proverbs as the outer court of the temple, Ecclesiastes as the holy place, and the Song of Solomon as the holiest of all.

Much misunderstanding is due to the failure to appreciate that the original was poetry and not prose, and oriental poetry at that— rich in figures of speech. It has been summarized as "flaming colour, superlative utterances, and overwhelming audacity," and all this was readily acceptable to the Eastern reader.

Like Esther, there is no mention of God's name in the Song, yet it is read or sung at the Passover Feast by the Jews.

Tradition maintains that Solomon was the author. The key word is "love" and the theme: "The Soul's Supreme Experience." That experience is intimate fellowship with the object of affection. Different views are held as to Solomon's purpose and intention. Some say the poem speaks of Solomon's marriage to Pharoah's daughter; others that any couple could have been in Solomon's mind; yet more think that this is the love of God for His chosen people or Christ for His Church.

The book has always been a favorite with the greatly-used saints of God: D. L. Moody, Charles Haddon Spurgeon, Hudson Taylor, and many others. Far from being mystics these were practical Christian men, founding colleges and orphanages, and yet they were influenced by a love poem!

The book is difficult to give in outline form unless the various settings are noted:

    I. THE PALACE GARDEN (1–3:5)
        The Bride Finds Her Lover
    II. THE HOLY CITY (3:6–5:1)
        The Marriage Procession and Banquet
    III. THE ROYAL RESIDENCE (5:2–6:9)
        The Bridegroom Lost and Found
    IV. THE PRIVATE PARK (6:10–8:4)
        The Friends' Admiration of the Bride
    V. THE RUSTIC HOME (8:5-14)
        The Bride's Surrender and Devotion

The "famous" chapter comes in the first section. The scene is set in the palace garden where the bride finds her lover. This is one of the few passages from the poem that can be read in public from the pulpit and it is the one from which most quotations are made.

Every season of the year has its particular charm and attraction: winter's tracery, spring's bursting buds, summer's glow, and autumn's mellowness. Summer and winter however summarize the main division of the year. Because of winter's ill effects—ailments and illnesses, we choose to eulogize summer. So it is in the spiritual realm.

When Jesus Christ is received into the soul as Saviour it is like the beginning of summertime. That is the atmosphere of this "famous chapter" which can be divided as follows:

> I.   FLOWERS FOR FAIRNESS (verses 1, 2)
> II. FRUIT FOR FELLOWSHIP (verses 3-7)
> III. FLOODS FOR FRESHNESS (verses 8-15)
> IV. FOOD FOR FULLNESS (verses 16, 17)

I. FLOWERS FOR FAIRNESS (verses 1, 2)

Flowers have always been a symbol of beauty and grace, form and fairness. In Palestine the spring brings in a glorious display of wild flowers, blooming for a few short weeks. They speak eloquently of earth's fairness, beauty, color and fragrant life.

The Lord Jesus Christ is likened to two flowers in this first subsection and the fairness of His Person is compared with them. It is of some conjecture what flowers in Palestine were really meant by Solomon. The "rose" may have been a sweet-scented narcissus, a wild flower of the plains. A modern Jewish commentary states: "The narcissus is plentiful in Palestine and beloved by the natives." The "lily of the valley" is another common flower in that part of the world, not, as we would imagine, white, but red, alluding here to the color of the lips. On the other hand it was a common word for "flower" and could be applied to any brilliantly colored flower, especially to the scarlet anemone.

Traditionally this has always been figurative of our Lord, the words being spoken by the Bridegroom Himself. Some commentators of recent years however say that it is spoken by the Bride, the Shulamite, about herself, showing her peasant, lowly upbringing. Such an opinion is based largely on wrong sentiment. These modern Bible critics affirm that it would be wrong for the Saviour to praise Himself. But who else could do it effectively and completely? Then, too, He descends to a very low level of comparison. The phrase "among thorns" and "among the daughters" infers the inferior worth of the other women of Jerusalem.

The older view is therefore preferable, that here Christ is presented as an object of beauty, admiration and delight. By comparing Scripture with Scripture (the only true method of Bible study) we know that this intepretation must be right, for our Lord compared Himself with the beauty and glory of the humble Palestinian lily which far outshone the glory of Solomon.

We do not think and sing and pray about the beauty of our Lord's Person as we ought to do and as our forefathers did. As we delight in flowers because of their beauty and scent so we should delight in "the altogether lovely One, the fairest of ten thousand," at the same time singing prayerfully—"Let the beauty of Jesus be seen in me."

II. FRUIT FOR FELLOWSHIP (verses 3-7)

This section, because of the pronouns used, is emphatically spoken by the woman about her lover. She is using fruit in a figurative sense to describe her fellowship with her beloved.

As with the flowers, so with the fruit. The apple here might well be the apricot, a tree that gave much shade as well as sweet fruit. Or some think it could be the citron, pomegranate or orange.

One or two terms need explanation before the sense of the passage can be gained. In verse 5 "banqueting house" means literally a house of wine, a small room or arbor in which travelers were rested and refreshed with light refreshment. "Banner" was a military standard around which the soldiers rallied. In verse 5 "flagons" were dainties or raisin cakes. It could be the name of a scent or stimulant. In verse 7 "roes" means gazelles, a small soft-eyed, graceful antelope. "Hinds" were female red deer. These two animals were used in Eastern poetry to represent female beauty, gracefulness and timidity.

What is represented here then? Fellowship between the Bridegroom and the Bride, between Christ and the Church. Note that they are sitting under the tree benefiting from the provision and the protection of the tree. The Church's enjoyment of her Lord comes from the efficacy and sufficiency of His salvation, the satisfying fellowship that He gives. The banqueting house stands for the ordinances of preaching and the Lord's Supper, the two means of grace and fellowship. The banner stands for the cross uplifted, rallying the forces of evangelism, showing the world that the Church upon earth is the Church militant. The banner is love. The cross emphasizes God's love for the world; the banner emphasizes our constraining love to evangelize and win the lost.

The final verse is most important. Great care must be taken to see that our communion with the Lord of the Church is not interrupted. "I charge you" or adjure you. It is an appeal to desist from attempts to turn the Church's affections away from the Lord. The older commentators see here a reference to grieving the Spirit. Denominationalism, organic church unity—these take our affections away from the person of the Lord.

III. Floods and Freshness (verses 8-15)

This subsection is ranked as the most beautiful in the whole book, at least from a literary standpoint. After the winter months the early spring rains have come. What a change from the heavy flooding of winter time. Continuing for six weeks they make the world fresh again.

The scene is this: the woman has been transferred from work in the fields to the vineyards in order that the Bridegroom might not find her. By force she has been taken to the royal court and confined in a building. She is confident that her lover will find her. He approaches the building and looks through the lattice but cannot see her. Pleading for a sound of her voice she sings a vineyard song in which she urges him to run until they can meet when the shadows flee away. It is, of course, figurative of how soon our communion and fellowship can be broken, and yet how diligently the Lord on His side seeks to restore the broken communion. Only little sins ("the little foxes that spoil the vines") have caused the breach in fellowship. That is why Satan tempts us to fall into little sins, for these are the first steps into backsliding and broken fellowship with Christ.

In verse 9 "shewing himself" (Hebrew "peereth") is a reference to the Shekinah glory gleaming through the fingers of the priest as he blessed the people. "To sparkle" means an ardent gleam in the eyes. So Christ looks at a backsliding believer. "The cleft of the rock" reminds us that doves nested in the clefts of rocks in Palestine, reluctant to leave them when frightened. Here there is strong urging to leave such a hiding place.

IV. Food for Fullness (verses 16, 17)

This final section is the climax of the love song. Christ is in the midst of His people and one day He is coming again for them. He feeds among us, or as the Revised Version has it, He feeds His flock among the lilies. His food is the only fare that fills and satisfies.

"My beloved is mine"—in this phrase is sovereign grace, election, predestination. Here is a reminder that we have been bought, we are Christ's purchased possession. "I am his"—here is free will, choice, profession and confession.

One day, when the shadows flee away, blown by the evening breeze, Christ will come and then it will be finally and eternally true that "my beloved is mine and I am his." If the whole of this famous chapter is "Summertime in the Soul" then this final subsection is "The Darkness Before the Dawn." The sinner faces nothing but eternal darkness; the saint looks for the dawn of eternal day, and until that day dawns he has the daily experience of summertime in the soul.

THE GOSPEL ACCORDING TO ISAIAH

Isaiah 53

The prophet Isaiah's name means "Salvation is of Jehovah," so it is no wonder that the book of the Bible attributed to him has been called "The Fifth Gospel," and this "famous chapter," *The Gospel According to Isaiah*. The key word of the book is "salvation," a word used more by Isaiah than by anyone else in the Bible with the exception of the Psalmist.

The prophet's theme is, "The Unquenchable Love of God," and the following is a useful division of the contents:

     I. REMONSTRANCE (1-35)
        Protest to Jewish and Gentile Nations
     II. DELIVERANCE (36-39)
        Besieged Jerusalem Freed and Hezekiah Healed
     III. CONDOLENCE (40-66)
        Sympathy and Consolation for God's Suffering People

This "famous" chapter, coming in the third main division of the book, contains a portrait of a unique person about whom the prophet has composed four songs (The Servant Songs). This Suffering Servant has been variously interpreted and dismissed by the Bible critics, but it is sufficient to say that only Jesus Christ, by His life, sufferings and death, fits in with the detailed portrait given.

The divisions of the chapter are:

THE SAVIOUR'S—
     I. REPUDIATION (verses 1-3)
        A. *Disregard of the Doctrine* (verse 1)
        B. *Disappointment With the Demeanor* (verse 2)
        C. *Disdain for the Deliverer* (verse 3)
     II. HUMILIATION (verses 4-9)
        A. *Fact and Fallacy* (verse 4)
        B. *Disease and Remedy* (verse 5)
        C. *Guilt and Penalty* (verse 6)
        D. *Goodness and Severity* (verse 7)
        E. *Violence and Eternity* (verse 8)
        F. *Shame and Innocency* (verse 9)
     III. EXALTATION (verses 10-12)

A. *The Sanction of the Father* (verse 10)
B. *The Satisfaction of the Son* (verse 11)
C. *The Subjection of the World* (verse 12)

I. THE SAVIOUR'S REPUDIATION (verses 1-3)

In this section we see how sinful man is offered a Substitute or Sin-Bearer. But not all sinners will come to Him in repentance and faith and avail themselves of His forgiveness, pardon and salvation; they repudiate or refuse to recognize Him.

A. *Disregard of the doctrine* (verse 1). "Who hath believed our report?" asks Isaiah. "Report" is translated "hearing" or "doctrine" in the margin. It means literally: "That which they have heard from us." The doctrine propounded by Isaiah and the previous prophets, that God would send a Messiah, a Deliverer, has been disregarded. Since as Paul later tells us, "Faith cometh by hearing," these people have put themselves beyond God's salvation by their refusal to listen. By disregarding the doctrine they have disregarded the Deliverer and hence the deliverance!

In the same way they were disregarding the display of God's power: "To whom is the arm of the Lord revealed?" The prophet is asking: "And who has had any experience of God's great delivering power?" God's power always accompanies the faithful preaching of God's Word. Jesus' teaching ministry was accompanied by "mighty works," and the preaching of the apostles by "signs following." The prophet's congregation, by their unbelief in the message, their disregard of the Good News, was preventing a display of divine power.

B. *Disappointment With the demeanor* (verse 2). The prophet's portrait of the Deliverer did not come up to their expectations. The Suffering Servant's demeanor or bearing, His appearance and outward person was not sufficiently awesome or splendid for them. He was too humble and insignificant. Isaiah describes Him as "a tender plant" (a mere sprouting plant, a first shoot in Spring, a sapling rather than a majestic tree), "a root" (a new sprout from the root), and a growth that had taken place "in dry ground" (that is, no quick and startling growth had taken place because there was no moisture). With such economy of words Isaiah described the origin and unassuming appearance of Jesus Christ. He did not have any "form" (external glory) or "comeliness" (adornments or gems signifying royalty). There was no outstanding beauty, nothing out-of-the-ordinary, that made them desire Him at first sight. Let there be no misunderstanding at this point. The prophet is not implying that the Sin-Bearer was ugly or deformed; he is only stressing that He was an ordinary Person, a normal Man.

C. *Disdain for the Deliverer* (verse 3). This Person became an object of scorn and contempt for all classes of men. In His lifetime on earth He was called Jesus of Nazareth (and could anything good ever come out of Nazareth?). They "hid as it were their faces from him." Whenever they saw Him they covered their faces that they might not look at Him. They "esteemed" Him not; they looked upon Him as a mere nobody; He was beneath their notice, hardly worth bothering about.

II. THE SAVIOUR'S HUMILIATION (verses 4-9)

Again each verse provides a subsection:

A. *Fact and fallacy* (verse 4). The fact is emphasized by the word "surely" ("of certain truth"). The truth Isaiah is asserting is that Jehovah's Suffering Servant suffered on behalf of others, for their "griefs" and their "sorrows." He "bore" them, that is, lifted them off and placed them on Himself, enduring them. It is the same language that could be applied to a disease or sickness. The Saviour dealt not only with our sins but also with the suffering sin brings in its train. "Carry" has the sense of "being burdened with." "Griefs" may stand for bodily pain and "sorrows" for mental anguish. Those are the facts. But now comes a fallacy.

The *fallacy* is introduced by "yet." They thought this Man was suffering as He did because of His own wrongdoing and sin, for blasphemy against God and an idle boast to destroy the temple. For such outrageous sin the people thought Him divinely "stricken" and "afflicted" (struck down with disease and by a visitation of God in judgment). It never occured to them that He was innocent and He was suffering on their account.

B. *Disease and remedy* is in verse 5 (the key text of the Book of Isaiah). On the cross Jesus Christ was "wounded" (implying injury from a sharp weapon). "Chastisement" means correction inflicted by another, the "stripes" refer to cuts or weals like furrows across a field. All this was for man's "transgressions" and "iniquities" (his breaking through God's barriers, His commandments, and the willful crooked living of a fallen nature.)

The disease was sin; the remedy was substitution, Someone perfectly sinless taking the place of the condemned sinner. His sufferings and death were endured on our behalf and indeed in our place.

C. *Guilt and penalty* (verse 6). There is a joyous change in the narrative now. Some of those who fell into the fallacy of thinking that it was the Christ's sin that brought God's punishment upon Him are now prepared to confess that it was their sin and guilt. They see themselves as sheep who have gone astray. There is no finer description of sin. Sheep without a shepherd take to their paths (sin is wilfullness); they follow one another (sin is contagious); they cannot find their own way back home (the sinner is helpless to save himself). Isaiah's emphasis is upon the universal taint of sin—all have gone astray, all are guilty before God. The whole human race is tainted by the sin of Adam.

Since God is just then guilt must be punished. But since God is a God of love and loves the sinner (hating only his sin), He allows a Substitute—"the Lord laid on him the iniquity of us all." Paul says: "He was made sin for us." He did not become a sinner— He bore the sinner's guilt and penalty. Although innocent He bore the punishment of the guilty party that the guilty might go free as though innocent.

D. *Goodness and severity* (verse 7). Again the figure of speech is a pastoral one. This time the sheep is a sacrificial one. It is being shorn and prepared for the altar of sacrifice. Such a sacrificial lamb was carefully chosen for it had to be a lamb without blemish. The first note in this verse then is goodness. Only God's Son was

> . . . good enough
> To pay the price of sin.

But notice the severity of the punishment: slaughter! Death by the hand of another. In spite of the severity the Servant was willing to submit, and silently submitted to it. He did not revile when reviled; He did not cry out against the injustice of it all. He submitted quietly to the Father's will as the sheep submits to the shearer.

E. *Violence and eternity* (verse 8). The violence is expressed in two phrases: "taken from" and "cut off out of." These words are equivalent to the modern expression "manhandling." The soldiers had a real "rough" house." They laid hands violently on our Lord before His execution, and His death was a violent one. The phrases also imply that His death was premature; He died in the prime of life.

But that was not the end. "Who shall declare his generation"? There are several possible interpretations of that question. It may mean: "Who can describe the wickedness of the generation or race who crucified Christ?" It might mean: "Who can tell how many will live as a result of His death?" As a result of Calvary there has arisen a new generation, born-again men and women, a "new Israel." These are a people who will never die but will endure throughout all eternity (and the same thought is carried on in subsection A of division III).

F. *Shame and innocency* (verse 9). "His grave was with the wicked" does not mean that He was buried with fellow criminals, for His grave was that of Joseph of Arimathea. It was with "the rich in his death." No, it means that they crucified our Lord between two thieves and murderers in order to emphasize the shameful nature of His alleged crime. A possible alternative rendering is: "They appointed it that He should be killed and buried with the wicked." That was *their* appointment, but divine appointment or overruling meant a change of burying-place. As His execution was with wicked men so His burial would have been with them if God had not intervened.

The shame of dying amidst thieves is matched by a description of His innocency: He did no violence and He never spoke deceitfully. He was as harmless as a dove.

III. THE SAVIOUR'S EXALTATION (verses 10-12)

After such humiliation on man's behalf God exalted His Son to the highest degree.

A. *The sanction of the Father* (verse 10). By the words "it pleased the Lord to bruise him" we must not think that God took pleasure in seeing His Son suffer. It means that God allowed or permitted Him to suffer voluntarily. God gave His consent, sanctioned it. The cross being foreordained before the foundation of the world leads us to believe that in eternity past God asked: "Who will go for us?" and Christ answered: "I will go." The Father's sanction or permission was given.

B. *The satisfaction of the Son* (verse 11). "Travail" here should not make us think primarily of childbirth. It is the Hebrew word for excessive toil resulting in physical exhaustion. It reminds us that the toll of the cross was physical, mental and spiritual; our Lord suffering in body, mind and spirit. Some people refer to Calvary as Christ's "finished work." *Work* it certainly was. He exhausted all His powers to redeem mankind. As He surveyed the result of that toil, looking forward into eternity, He was satisfied.

C. *The subjection of the world* (verse 12). This last verse of the chapter is one of triumph and victory. The crucified Saviour is to be treated in royal fashion like a Prince or returning Conqueror. On the cross the Saviour conquered death and Satan as well as sin. He triumphed over the evil one and man's last enemy, death. Now the cross is our guarantee that one day the world will be subject to the returning King when He comes in majesty and power and great glory. He will reign from shore to shore and sea to sea.

With what a daring thought Isaiah closes. This ultimate triumph is all because Christ interceded for others. The closing ministry of the Lord upon earth (interceding for His executioners for "they know not what they do") is the commencement of His ascended ministry in glory ("He ever liveth to make intercession"). His exaltation outweighs His humiliation; tragedy has been turned into triumph. One day He will come again for His own, His Bride, the Church, the "spoils" of Calvary. Such is the glorious message of the New Testament; such was the Gospel proclaimed by Isaiah the prophet centuries before Calvary!

THE POTTER AND THE CLAY

Jeremiah 18

The prophet Jeremiah has been called the "prophet of the broken-hearted." In his life of suffering we see a man who was a type of the Man of Sorrows. Although he was called to deliver messages of stern judgment, his underlying theme was, "The Tenderness of Divine Love." The key word of the book is "backsliding" and the key verse 3:22. The book can be given in the following outline form:

    I.   JEREMIAH'S CALL AND CONSECRATION (1)
   II.   PROPHETIC ORACLES (2—24)
  III.   HISTORICAL NARRATIVES (25—35)
  IV.   NATIONAL EVENTS (36—45)
   V.   INTERNATIONAL PROPHECIES (46—51)
  VI.   JEREMIAH'S COMMENTARY AND CONCLUSION (52)

The "famous" chapter then comes within Section II, the prophetic oracles delivered by Jeremiah to Judah and Israel, the "word of the Lord" calling them to repentance and to return to the Lord God.

The chapter divides into the following sections:

    I.   THE ILLUSTRATION AND APPLICATION (verses 1-10)
   II.   THE DECLARATION AND INTERROGATION (verses 11-17)
  III.   THE MACHINATION AND VINDICATION (verses 18-23)

I. THE ILLUSTRATION AND APPLICATION (verses 1-10)

This first division of the chapter is one of the several "acted parables" in the Book of Jeremiah. It is an illustration of the ways of God using the familiar scene at that time of a potter working his clay upon the wheel. The "wheels" means literally "the two stones," upper and lower. It does not matter that pottery-making has been modernized and that electrically-driven wheels have replaced the old hand-turned or foot-peddled ones. The important factors are the potter and the clay and these have remained to this day.

Here then we have the divine Potter, using human clay and producing a finished vessel. The first product, however, was marred in the making. Perhaps an air bubble, or a small piece of grit were in the clay, or maybe the texture was not quite right. At any rate, the first vessel was not cast aside, thrown to the scrap heap; it was squashed on the wheel and then remade. So it was with God's people of old and so it is all too frequently with God's people today. Because of idolatry, selfish desires or some other sin we cannot be used for God's purposes and need spiritual remolding.

Some characteristics of the potter must be noted and then applied to the divine Potter. First, he is *thorough*. In Jeremiah's day pottery was largely domestic. Tough utensils for cooking purposes had to be made well and strong. So in creation God made man "fearfully and wonderfully." The dissecting room or a film like *Dust or Destiny* (Moody Institute of Science) reveal the intricacies of the human body with its ball-and-socket joints, its system of muscles and nerves. So our minds, personalities and characters go to make up this complex being called man. As the hymn writer put it:

> His sovereign power, without our aid,
> Made us of clay, and formed us men.

The potter is *careful*. In kneading his clay he feels for hard stones, sharp pieces of flint. The right amount of water must be added. As the wheel turns and the hand goes inside the clay to shape the vessel there must be no bruising. Thus God is careful with the beings He has created. He does not leave us to some substitute workman to feed and clothe and provide for us.

How *patient* is the potter. Early pottery was a laborious process. Before the invention of the "wheels" pots and pans were built up ring of clay upon ring of clay, a tiresome and tedious process requiring much patience. God is always unhurried in His work—

> The mills of God grind slowly.

Patiently He works and waits, His purpose to present us "faultless." No wonder the Apostle Paul refers to "the God of patience" (Romans 15:5).

This then is what Jeremiah learned of God in the potter's house. Through watching the human potter he began to comprehend God's ways and purposes for His people, the children of Israel. It was a vivid lesson in divine sovereignty. The prophet learned much from the clay as well as from the potter.

Clay is a humble material, a common substance. So is all mankind, created out of the dust of the earth. According to the dictionary clay is "stiff and tenacious." Are we not all willful and lovers of our own way? Did not God frequently call His children "stiff-necked"? There are infinite possibilities in clay as we see from looking around a china shop and noting the different shapes and sizes on all the shelves. But how hard the divine potter must find it, working with such sinful, rebellious, unlovely clay! So Jeremiah saw his nation had been in God's sight. They had not willingly and unquestioningly submitted to the sovereignty of the Potter. They had not understood the absolute right of the Potter over the clay. They had not lain inert,

without "wish and with no right" (Dr. G. Campbell Morgan) on the
wheel, ready for the Potter to have His own way with them. And so
Jeremiah had to learn a second lesson, not only the sovereignty of
God, but divine severity—"he made it again." The rebellious clay, the
marred clay, had to be flattened and remolded.

A remade vessel! Jeremiah points out that it was "his" work on
wheels, the potter's, God's work. He would have the finished work as
He had planned, even though it meant remaking and remolding.
How Christians need this remaking! At creation we were made the
first time. At conversion we were recreated. But often after conversion we need a work of the Holy Spirit in our lives refashioning
us, making us more Christlike. We need to pray:

> Have Thine own way, Lord!
> Have Thine own way!
> Thou art the Potter, I am the clay.
> Mould me and make me
> After Thy will,
> While I am waiting,
> Yielded and still.

Jeremiah saw all this in the potter's house, and he applied it to
God's people for God said to Jeremiah—"Cannot I do with you as this
potter"? (verse 6). In verses 6 to 10 Almighty God tells His prophet
that if a nation does evil then inevitably He will repent of the good
wherewith He promised He would benefit it. "Righteousness exalteth a
nation" but "sin is a reproach"!

In the Book of Jeremiah there is God's message to the nations,
His word to the community of His people, and what He has to say to
the believing individual. Here in this section of the chapter we have
God's message to the nations. A nation has been defined as "a body
of people made one by their history." Israel had not only been made
one by their history, but by their religion and by their God. Theirs
was more than common blood, common speech, common traditions,
common country—they had "one Lord, one faith, one baptism—one God
and Father." But Jeremiah's call and commission was to be a prophet
to "the nations" (1:5) not just to God's people. The scope of his
ministry was wide, yet unlike the much-traveled Christian ministers
of this twentieth century, Jeremiah never visited other countries but
spent his time at home among his own people. How could he influence other nations without going to them? By influencing his own
people with what we now call "the missionary spirit," by showing
them that they had a responsibility to the Gentiles. The message of
God's people to the surrounding nations must be that their fate and
future were bound up with God's nation. They must learn allegiance
to the One true God. If they refused to listen and learn then God
would pluck them up and destroy them.

So today our Christian faith must always be put in a world context. "No man liveth unto himself" is true of nations as well as individuals. With the speed of travel in our time the world has "grown smaller." The nation whose God is the Lord must take the present opportunity and modern facilities and influence others for the truth. Time is short for such a witness, for the nations of the world are steadily becoming more and more debased and degraded. Religion is held in contempt and sin is countenanced. God will turn His hand against this ungodliness as He did long ago with Nineveh when they went back upon their repentance.

II. THE DECLARATION AND INTERROGATION (verses 11-17)

Having seen what God wanted him to see, Jeremiah now has to speak what God wants him to speak. So many Christians see, have a vision of the world's need, come to an understanding of God's Word, and then fail to speak on God's behalf. "Let the redeemed of the Lord say so"!

The application of the illustration provided by the potter has now to be declared to God's children. They must be told that exile is the new condition which is going to remold their life and faith. But first they must cease to be rebellious and become as responsive and as yielding as the potter's clay.

God has designed and determined the future of His people. It will appear evil to them, but He is "cruel only to be kind." Good always comes out of evil in the purposes of God, Calvary being the supreme example. But if His people will repent and reform, then in His graciousness He will shorten the evil days. The criticism that Christianity is negative and not positive is challenged here. It is not enough for God's people to refrain from doing evil, they must resolve to do good. Christianity is not a long list of "Thou shalt nots," it is a positive doing good.

The people are obstinate however and decide to continue living willfully sinful lives, following their own devices, living free from the constraint of the divine law. Probably, like modern society, they called this liberty; in reality it was licence.

There follows a series of divine interrogations. They may be listed as follows:

First, God asks them if they have compared their attitude with that of the heathen (verse 13). Even the surrounding heathenish nations (such as Nineveh for example) when warned, turned from their evil ways and repented. By contrast God's own people have defied God in refusing to repent. How sad it is when God speaks to His own people and they refuse to obey His voice, whereas the sinner responds gladly and quickly. Surely revival tarries for the Church of God today, because God's people refuse to obey the necessary conditions: "If my people, which are called by name, shall humble themselves, and pray, and seek my face, and turn from their wicked ways; then will I hear from heaven, and will forgive their sin, and will heal their land" (II Chronicles 7:14).

Second, God asked them if they were really willing to leave certainty for uncertainty (verses 14,15). To persist in evil and put themselves within the circle of divine judgment, exile in a foreign land, was forsaking a life of certain provision and protection for one of grave uncertainty. It was like giving up clear, crystal rivers for a drink out of "a dirty puddle" (Matthew Henry). It was like a traveler knowingly forsaking the meadow path for a rough, rocky road. Israel by taking to idol worship had done just that. God's people had turned their back on living water and taken to broken cisterns; they had left the ancient paths and were walking on a disused, uncared-for road.

The result was a lack of positive and effectual testimony. Those round about derided them and jeered at them (verse 16). It is always so. The so-called Christian, the nominal church member with no vital spiritual life, the one who is not separated from the world, this person is always a laughingstock to the man of the world. He comments: "You have just enough religion to make you miserable." It is the out-and-out Christian who wins the admiration of the worldling.

Having turned their backs on God there was but one attitude He could adopt toward them—He must turn His back upon them (verse 17). In Scripture the countenance stands for favor and the back for displeasure. Having forsaken God and His commandments they would find themselves God-forsaken in time of trouble. There is perhaps no more tragic passage of Scripture in the Old Testament, and there is certainly no more tragic experience for the believer.

III. THE MACHINATION AND VINDICATION (verses 18-23)

Having concluded speaking on God's behalf, which is now Jeremiah's *seventh* message delivered to God's people, certain reactions follow.

First, certain people, confident that Jeremiah's solemn message would not appeal to the people, plotted against the prophet. Their machination or intrigue has a two-fold interpretation. "Let us not give heed to any of his words" (verse 18) may mean: "Let us ignore his predictions and exhortations." That is a prevalent plot against preachers of the Gospel by nominal Christians. The attitude seems to be, "He is paid to talk like that. It's his job. We needn't take him too seriously." And so the spiritual life is not deepened and we are no nearer revival. The words may be interpreted (noting that the Septuagint omits the negative): "Let us watch the prophet's utterances closely and secure treasonable evidence against him." So the enemies of our Lord sought to trap Him from His speech. So the "heresy-hunters" of today listen to ministers of the Gospel, more concerned with "the letter" than "the spirit," more enamored with the so-called "educated ministry" than that of rough Galilean fishermen, wincing at grammatical errors rather than praying that sinners shall be converted by one "unlettered and unlearned."

Jeremiah's enemies wanted prophets of their own choosing, not one of God's calling and commissioning. They wanted ones who would speak "smooth" things, who spoke flattery and tickled their "itching ears." So it is today and will become more so during the "last days." Men will not be able to endure sound doctrine as the time approaches for the return of the Lord Jesus Christ in glory.

They agree to "smite (Jeremiah) with the tongue" or "blast his reputation" as Matthew Henry puts it. It has ever been so. God's prophetic servants have always been given an ill name, their characters being misrepresented. But "it is the way the Master went, should not the servant tread it still?" It is against this fury of the tongue that Jeremiah asks to be vindicated (verse 19). Like most preachers of God's Word Jeremiah is a sensitive man; he feels deeply all the criticism because he knows that none of it is true. Only those who have suffered in this way,

> "For truth, and righteousness and Thee"—

can fully understand. And only by understanding Jeremiah's true feelings can we understand his cry to God for vindication (verses 19-23). Many have thought these words too vehement and vindictive for Jeremiah. The previous provocation must be borne in mind. It is all untrue; it is more than his sensitive soul can bear; it is God's cause and not himself that is his concern. Because he is scorned then scorn is being poured out upon God and His cause. Jeremiah's cry is not for mere self-vindication but vindication of the God Himself and His cause.

The great lesson of Jeremiah to us is this: in his predicament he prayed. The temptation when persecuted is to "hit back," to answer charges with countercharges, to defend our position and action face to face with our accusers. It does no good. It is better to talk to God than to talk to man. "Vengeance is mine, I will repay" says God.

> Do thy friends despise, forsake thee?—
> Take it to the Lord in prayer.

If that is what we must do when friends turn against us, how much more ought we to do it when our enemies are against us!

> O what peace we often forfeit,
> O what needless pain we bear,
> All because we do not carry
> Everything to God in prayer!

Jeremiah "took it to the Lord in prayer." He knew that men were not listening to his preaching but he knew that God would listen to his praying!

In his prayer he reminds God of His righteousness and justice. It does not matter to Jeremiah that he cannot defend himself and devastate his opponents with arguments in his own favor. "The Judge of all the earth" will do right. He can leave everything to the One who does not allow evil to triumph finally over good, and injustice over justice. Personal safety, character—all could be left in the hands of God. He would vindicate His prophet, Himself and His cause.

A SONG OF SORROW

Lamentations 1

The theme of the Book of Lamentations is "The Constancy of Divine Love" (key word "destruction," key verses 3:22 and 23). The traditional writer is Jeremiah, "the weeping prophet," one whose message in the Book of Jeremiah is woe and calamity. In Lamentations he bewails the sins of God's people that have resulted in the fall of Jerusalem.

Five poems constitute the Book of Lamentations, each one in acrostic form in the Hebrew, the twenty-two verses beginning with a consecutive letter of the Hebrew alphabet. Chapter three has sixty-six verses and each group of three verses begins with the same letter. This arrangement might have been intentional for memory purposes or deliberate for liturgical purposes in worship. It does help to give the impression of short sobs, expressing the deep grief felt by the author for the destruction and desolation of the Holy City.

The following is a simple outline of the book:

I. DESCRIPTION AND REFLECTION (1)
   The Conditions in Jerusalem
II. DESOLATION AND EXPLANATION (2)
   The Catastrophe in Jerusalem
III. RESIGNATION AND CONSOLATION (3)
   The Chastisement of Jerusalem
IV. RECOLLECTION AND DENUNCIATION (4)
   The Contrast in Jerusalem
V. RETRIBUTION AND SUPPLICATION (5)
   The Consequences in Jerusalem

Chapter one, the first of the five "songs of sorrow" is undoubtedly the most well-known and famous of the entire book. Here Jeremiah the man, the prophet of God, is wonderfully revealed. Here we have the great heart-cry so often applied to those who seem indifferent to the Calvary love of Christ—"Is it nothing to you, all ye that pass by"?

This first "song of sorrow" may be divided into two sections:

I. DESCRIPTION (verses 1-11)
   The Prophet Laments the Condition of the City
   A. *The Solitariness of the City* (verses 1-7)
   B. *The Sinfulness of the City* (verses 8-11)

II.   REFLECTION (verses 12-22)

The People Lament the Cause of the Condition

    A.   *The Passers-by* (verse 12)

    B.   *The Surrounding Nations* (verse 18)

    C.   *The Lord* (verse 20)

I.   DESCRIPTION (verses 1-11)

This section begins with the word "how," a characteristic opening word for an elegy or song of sorrow such as this. The word actually gives the title to the whole book in the Hebrew Bible. It is a word of exclamation and infers that what follows defies true description. The weeping prophet does his best by describing the solitariness and the sinfulness of the city.

A. *The Solitariness of the City* is described in verses 1 to 7. As a capital city and as a center of worship Jerusalem was usually a very crowded place. Its present emptiness, desolation and solitariness is therefore a most sad sight. Suggestive metaphors are used by Jeremiah to bring home this sorry state to his hearers. Jerusalem is like a widow, a typical Scriptural image for loneliness and misery. But note the tiny word "as"—telling us that the state was not permanent but temporary. Bereft of husband and children the Holy City is desolate indeed.

The next picture is of unfaithful friends. Jerusalem has been deserted by her friends, surrounding nations to whom she looked for help. None come to buy and sell, none travel to pay tribute and taxes.

It is as if night has descended on the city perpetually. Night— the time of stillness when the lonely seem most lonely, and slight sounds are frightening.

Instead of her friends and lovers rallying to her help they are forming a confederacy to bring about her destruction.

Even the streets *leading* to the city as well as those within the city are empty and deserted for none wish to visit her. The "gates," that is the great spaces around the city gates, the usual places of concourse, the places where buying and selling takes place, the places where arrival and departure takes place, and where the judicial courts are set up—these too are desolate.

The temple is devoid of worshipers and so the priests sit and sigh, while single women grieve because there are no prospective husbands around!

The very children (always a concern of the sensitive prophet) of the city have been taken captive and their cries and chatter no longer are heard in the street.

No longer is the splendor of the royal court an attraction to tourists for the king and his princes have fled the city or have been taken captive.

What a contrast is all this with Jerusalem's former condition!

In the past Jerusalem was prosperous and happy. The former glory only serves to pinpoint or highlight the present departure of glory. And it is all part of God's punishment—"the Lord hath afflicted her" (verse 5), and His reason for doing so the prophet is going to develop in the next section—"for the multitude of her transgressions" (verse 5). But first we must ask: "What has this picture of Jerusalem's solitariness to teach us today?" When the believer loses his joy and knows only sorrow; when the Church becomes empty and people do not crowd its doors to hear its ministry; when the songs of pastors, ministers, teachers and evangelists are turned into sighs; when the very Holy Spirit of God seems to have departed from the Church—what is wrong? What can be done to put matters right? What should our attitude be?

First, like Jeremiah we must learn to weep. Jeremiah wept and Jesus wept—why should we not weep? We must learn to become more tenderhearted, less obstinate and hardhearted. As Jesus cried over Jerusalem so we cry over the condition of the Church today. Then, too, we must become less complacent. We have fallen into ways of glossing over the true state of affairs. Jeremiah's picture of the desolation of Jerusalem is a terrible one, but it is no more terrible than the true state of the Church of today. Appalling statistics regarding church attendance, lack of conversions, the loss of Sunday school scholars, our lack to evangelize the masses—these must not be whitewashed over; we must see and state the situation as it really is, as Jeremiah did.

B. *The Sinfulness of the City* is described in verses 8 to 11. Here Jeremiah develops his contention that Jerusalem's sad condition is due to her sin (verse 5). It is an inexorable spiritual law that sin brings suffering in its train; thus when there is suffering we can look back to discover the sin that brought it upon us. Having described the suffering, Jeremiah now describes the sin that brought the suffering upon Jerusalem. The "multitude of her transgressions" (verse 5) now becomes "Jerusalem hath grievously sinned" (verse 8). Her suffering then is not undeserved; she has brought it upon herself. The sin of Jerusalem is so great that it makes her appear a loose woman of the streets in the prophet's eyes. It is as if Jerusalem has been caught in the very act of adultery and now everyone only wants to shun and avoid her. Jerusalem, the Holy City, let us note, is considered unclean!

The true nature of her sin is given in verse 9—"she remembereth not her last end," that is, she has not carefully considered the consequences of her actions. Time and time again God gave a warning but the warnings went unheeded, and now she is seeing the performance of another spiritual law: "Whatsoever a man soweth, that shall he also reap."

How often we sin and do not look into the future to see the consequences before committing the sin. "Just one drink" or "Just one cigarette" people say, forgetting that every hardened alcoholic or nicotine addict began with "just one glass" or "just one puff." The so-called tiniest sin has far-reaching consequences. One idle word of gossip can blast a person's reputation and bring untold sorrow into a family. Such instances could be multiplied. And how often it is because we have refused to listen to God's warnings. He has given us His own Word; He has called and commissioned His servants, preachers and Bible teachers—but we have turned deaf ears. The Christian Church is weak and ineffective today because God's warnings have gone unheeded. He has told us as He told our forefathers that the secret of power is prayer, and yet the prayer meeting is neglected. We have been told repeatedly that it is no use relying on organization, men and methods—"Not by might, nor by power, but by my Spirit, saith the Lord of hosts" (Zechariah 4:6)—yet we refuse to be "filled with the Spirit." Again and again we have been told that the family to whom no children are born dies out and yet we are content to sit in our pews and see the same old familiar faces each service, instead of going out into "the highways and byways" compelling men and women to come under the sound of the Gospel and be saved. We are, therefore, reaping the consequences of our sinful neglect of God's Word.

Under Jeremiah's faithful ministry the people saw this and began to cry aloud to God for themselves. They break in upon the prophet's lament (verse 11) with what has been called "a panting cry of distress and prayer." "See, O Lord, and consider; for I am become vile." What a cry to God! What language! We are afraid of it in these days. When denominational hymnbooks are revised the lines omitted are such as these:

> "Where every prospect pleases
> *And only man is vile*"!

or:

> "What guilty, daring *worms*"!

or:

> "Vile and full of sin"!

Modern man, cultured, educated, respectable, will not humble himself and admit his *vileness*. Jerusalem in Jeremiah's day was prepared to do just that; revival will come to the "New Jerusalem," the Church of God, when she too is prepared to humble herself and admit her sinfulness.

II. REFLECTION (verses 12-22)

The people now lament like Jeremiah the cause of their condition.

This lament is addressed to three different audiences: the passers-by, the surrounding nations, and the Lord God.

A. *The Passers-by* (verse 12). Beginning with the well-known and oft-quoted words, "Is it nothing to you, all ye that pass by?" the people express their sorrow at the calamities that have befallen them under four separate pictures: fire, a net, a yoke, and sickness. Some say that God literally set fire to the temple in Jerusalem so that the heathen might not boast that they had destroyed it. Perhaps the better explanation is that they felt fevered with heat, dried up because of the fierceness of God's anger. It was as if they were caught in a net from which they could not extricate themselves, the stratagems of the enemy were so cunning and the binding power of sin so secure. Struggle as they may they could not escape the consequences of their sinning. So too their transgressions were like a yoke on the neck, bowing down the people, binding them together in slavery and servitude to Satan. So too they felt faint all the day and had not the strength to stand upright. Sin is, after all, a disease, a sickness of the soul.

B. *The Surrounding nations.* This lament begins in verse 18: "Hear, I pray you, all people." This surely is proof that upon reflection the inhabitants of Jerusalem are sincere in their repentance. It is more difficult to acknowledge wrongdoing to outsiders than to members of the family. Jerusalem was willing to confess her sinfulness to the heathenish nations round about her. Is it not time the Church confessed her sin not only within her walls but to the world without, those whom we have sinned against by denying them the message of eternal life? By our lack of evangelism we have deprived them of the Gospel.

C. *The Lord* (verse 20). "Behold, O Lord." They should, of course, have begun there, and then, having got right with God, confessed to their neighbors and friends. In one of the Lancashire cotton mills was a notice: "If you get your threads tangled send for the foreman." One new girl at the mill got her threads badly tangled. She tried untangling them herself and made matters worse. Then she enlisted the help of a nearby friend. Still they were unsuccessful. At last the foreman was sent for. Immediately he said: "You have been trying to untangle your threads yourself." The girl replied: "I did my best." "No, you did not do your best," replied the foreman, "your best would have been sending for me." Jerusalem's best would have been addressing themselves to God first. He is the One upon whom we should cast our burdens, and to whom we should confess our sins. At last they did so and made a good job of it. They were honest; they did not try to excuse themselves or use roundabout terms. They called their sin "grievous rebellion" (verse 20), which is what sin is—rebellion against God and against His righteous laws (verse 18). This confession of sin was accompanied by sorrow and suffering for we must not expect to escape all the consequences of wrongdoing. Their innermost beings (Hebrew "bowels" and "heart"), their very souls were restless and upside down with distress. But they know that they are coming to a God who is just and compassionate and who will deal with them righteously and in love. They affirm that they have done with those who contributed so much to their downfall, the idolatrous and heathenish nations round about. They will enter into no coalition with them.

So it must be with the Christian and the Christian Church. It is the world that is our downfall. The ways of the world, the world's methods, the world's standards, the very spirit of the world—these we have brought into the Church. At the same time we have neglected to witness to the world of the saving power of Jesus Christ. True confession on the part of the Church will involve us in complete separation; we cannot be unequally yoked with the world. Only as we are distinct and separate as the people of God can we hope to win the admiration and respect of the world so that they will take note of our message. "Is it nothing to you, all ye that pass by?" Calvary will be as nothing to the world until the world sees that Calvary really means something to us.

THE VALLEY OF DEAD BONES

Ezekiel 37

Ezekiel came from higher "rank" of the priesthood than Jeremiah, being acquainted with nobility. He was married, but his wife died during the final siege of Jerusalem. A word artist and visionary, Ezekiel gives us pictures in his prophecy that are inspiring, charming, terrifying and at times very mysterious.

His theme is, "The Goodness and Severity of God," and "visions" is the key word (key text 12:27). God's goodness toward the repentant and His severity toward those who persist in sin is here set forth and illustrated. Ezekiel himself is "the prophet of the Iron Harp." His prophecy can be given in the following outline form:

    I. PREDICTIONS BEFORE THE SIEGE OF JERUSALEM (1-24)
        A. *The Prophet's Fidelity*
        B. *The People's Infidelity*
    II. PREDICTIONS DURING THE SIEGE (25-32)
        A. *The Judgment of the Nations*
        B. *The Justice of God*
   III. PREDICTIONS AFTER THE SIEGE (33-48)
        A. *The Temple Restored*
        B. *The Land Revived*

The "famous" chapter, "The Valley of Dead Bones" (37) is characteristic of the prophet and his prophesying. It gives an accurate picture of the situation prevailing at that time and Ezekiel's preaching is characteristic of his whole loyal and faithful ministry. It occurs in the third main division of the book, and in the first subsection in which Israel's restoration is described. An outline of this "famous" chapter can be given thus:

    I. REVIVAL (verses 1-14)
        A. *The Need* (1-3)
        B. *The Means* (4-14)
    II. REUNION (verses 15-28)
        A. *The Disunity* (15-17)
        B. *The Unity* (18-28)

I. REVIVAL (verses 1-14)

Ezekiel predicts a certain revival for his nation, the people of God. First he describes the need of such a revival and then he explains the means whereby this revival will come to pass.

A. *The Need* (verses 1-3). The "hand of the Lord" (a phrase Ezekiel uses) took the prophet out of the city to a valley where he saw a vision. In this valley, which was full of dry or dead bones, he saw the need for revival. These dead bones suggest an army slain in battle. The question and answer in verse 3 impress upon us the seeming hopelessness of the situation. Nothing but a stupendous divine act, an act of resurrection, can revive this valley of dead bones.

What a picture of the need for revival today. The Church is like an army slain in battle. We are like dead bones without breath or life, no ability to rise up, walk, run or fight. The Church is lifeless and powerless. All human efforts to revive the dying cause of the Church have failed—large-scale, city-wide campaigns, church-based and denominational missions. It needs the sovereign power of God to be exerted. Our cry must surely be: "Revive thy work in the midst of the years"! (Habakkuk 3:2). But this must first be revealed to the Church as it was to Ezekiel. Too many Church members are complacent, content with the present situation. They do not see the desperate plight of the Church and the dire need for revival. May the Holy Spirit of revival soon reveal this need.

B. *The Means* (verses 4-14). God graciously explains to His servant Ezekiel the means He can and will employ to revive His people. In two words the answer to the situation is: preaching and Pentecost.

First Ezekiel is commanded or commissioned to preach to the dry bones. They are to hear the word of the Lord. It is usually during a time of spiritual declension that preaching is at a low ebb. An anti-preaching campaign is usually most successful when the dying Church is trying worldly methods of revival. But then it is that God's servants must remain faithful, and the faithful few must pray more zealously for the preacher. Here too is an indication that today's emphasis upon doctrine as being a forerunner of revival is correct. Right doctrine must be declared and accepted before revival can come. We must have done with superficial Christianity and be prepared to reach and be taught the deep things of the Word of God.

The result of Ezekiel's preaching was that the bones in the valley came together. Then the muscles and sinews knit again. Finally the flesh once more covered the skeletons. How wonderful! But note (verse 8): "There was no breath in them." It was doctrine but no life. It was "dead orthodoxy." It was being evangelical but not evangelistic. A return to doctrinal preaching is good, but it is not enough. We may become Puritans once again in our beliefs, but if we lack the power and influence of the Puritans then we are no better.

The sequel to preaching was "Pentecost." God commanded Ezekiel to pray for the Spirit of God to give life to the bones. This the prophet did, that was his part; then God did His part and gave the Spirit of life to the bones and they lived again, they were revived!

In Ezekiel vision and voice frequently go together. What a sight this valley was, but what a sound there was to be heard as well! What a commotion when the dead bones began to shake as they were once more joined together. Then (verse 7) "there was a noise"—that is, a noise from heaven, the voice of God commanding and controlling as He did at creation.

Note that this vision depicted what God would do for "the whole house of Israel" (verse 11). It would be fine to see a one-church revival in these days, or even a one-denomination revival, but Oh, to see a revival among the whole of God's people everywhere, throughout the world! Nothing is impossible to the Spirit of God.

Finally we must remember that no revival is for the mere sake of man, that many might be gathered into the church and empty pews filled. The final result of a spiritual awakening is that God might be glorified—verse 13: "And ye shall know that I am the Lord."

We may sum up the abiding lessons in this first section of the chapter like this: vision, proclamation, intercession, demonstration. We get a vision of the need; we proclaim the Word of the Lord; we cry to Him in prayer, and He demonstrates that He is still the sovereign God who can rend the heavens and come down in revival power.

Duncan Campbell, describing the revival in the Hebrides in 1958, states: "It began in a desperate sense of need and in an overwhelming conviction that God alone could deal with the situation." That same sense of need was Ezekiel's; may it soon be ours.

II. REUNION (verses 15-28)

Revival always results in certain consequences. The Church of God becomes true to God's original intention for it. It becomes zealous, enthusiastic, soul-saving, holy, prayerful, and so on. One definite result of every revival is the unity promoted between Christians. In this second section of the chapter Ezekiel describes the disunity of God's people and then the resultant unity.

A. THE DISUNITY (verses 15-17). Like Jeremiah, Ezekiel now enacts a parable. From dead bones we now change to dry sticks. God commands the prophet to take two sticks. One represents the southern kingdom and the other the northern (Judah and Joseph being respectively their chief tribes). The two sticks are joined together to represent one united nation. On each stick the appropriate name was written, "For Joseph" and "For Judah."

The people then asked the prophet the meaning of this symbolic act for as Matthew Henry points out, they knew Ezekiel did not "play with sticks for his diversion, as children do." No, this was serious. Division is always serious. There is unity in the Godhead, and there is meant to be unity in the body, the Church of God. Because the prophet joined the sticks together in and by his hands, we must not fall into the trap of thinking that unity can be manufactured or organized. True unity is spiritual and comes from within of the Spirit of the Lord. This symbolic act was to show the fact of disunity and the fact of coming unity, not to show how unity could be obtained.

B. *The Unity* (verses 18-28). The people of God were willing to learn; they had put aside all fancy notions of their own, their pre-conceived ideas about unity; they asked the prophet to explain God's pattern and principle of unity to them. "Wilt thou not show us what thou meanest by these?" How important is the prophet's answer in the words of God Himself: "I will . . . make them one stick, and they shall be one in mine hand" (verse 19). So in the succeeding verses the divine personal pronoun is prominent. "I will" is used seven times from verse 20 to the end of the chapter. Unity is God's work, not man's. Man's attempts at unity are doomed to failure; God's will always succeed. The devil loves to see men striving after unity with their committees and world councils for he knows that is keeping them occupied and too busy to evangelize.

True unity is described in this section. Briefly it is this: mutual interests, mutual affections—perfect harmony and agreement in belief and in service. As two separate sticks they were useless, now as one, strengthening and supporting one another, they were useful, "accept-able to God . . . formidable to their enemies" (Matthew Henry). Modern attempts at unity put affection and service first. The cry is: "We must be tolerant of one another; we must get together and work together as a witness to the world." The ecumenical experts for-get that mutual interests, mutual appreciation and regard for the cardinal doctrines of the evangelical faith must come first and form the basis of living and working together. For instance, the unity de-scribed by Ezekiel resulted in separation from the heathen, from "idols" and "detestable things." False unity does not shun worldly compromise and contamination. The *Daily Mail*, July, 1964, published a para-graph of a unity ball organized by Christian churches in Wimbledon, London, at which beer and liquor were to be on sale. True unity among Christians presupposes separation from the world. It is of interest to note that where holiness of life and character is most pro-moted (Keswick Conventions, for instance) there is exhibited the ban-ner "All one in Christ Jesus"! No wonder God exclaims to Ezekiel: "And the heathen shall know that I the Lord do sanctify Israel" (verse 28). The Spirit that promotes unity is the *Holy* Spirit and so true unity also promotes true sanctification. It must be so for true unity is not merely unity among believers, but believers united to the Lord— "I will be their God and they shall be my people" (verse 27).

In the light of Ezekiel's vision, and in the light of world events and the seeming helplessness of the Church, surely our prayer must be:

> Blowing where Thou listest,
> Thou the Word assistest;
> Thou death's power resisteth,
> Come O Breath and breathe.

PRAYER IS THE SECRET OF POWER

Daniel 6

The first half of the Book of Daniel is narration and the second half is revelation; the first part is history and the second prophecy. The reigns of Nebuchadnezzar, Belshazzar and Darius are recorded, also dreams are described and interpretations given. It is in fact, "a book of revealed secrets." The theme is "The Universal Sovereignty of God" and the key word is "dominion." The key text is 2:22.

Written in exile for the exiles *and* unborn succeeding generations of God's people the book shows how God's supreme purpose is worked out in history. God's power and wisdom in government is illustrated.

The book contains a great character study of Daniel himself. We see him primarily as a man of prayer. Chapter 9 is almost as famous and well-known as the one we have chosen for this study, chapter 6. The portrait of a man at prayer is always the truest portrait of the real person. A Puritan preacher once said that if a Christian's prayer life were revealed we should know all we needed to know about him! Dr. Alexander Whyte describes Daniel as "a great proficient both in penitential and in intercessory prayer . . . and he came to that great proficiency just as a great proficiency is come to in any other science or art: that is to say, by constant, and unremitting, and enterprising practice . . . it is like all the other arts that you have ever mastered; it must be early begun and assiduously practiced, else you will be but a bungler at it all your days. You must also have special and extraordinary seasons of prayer, as Daniel had, over and above his daily habit of prayer."

An outline of the Book of Daniel can be given in this form:

    I. HISTORY (1-6)
        Events in Godless Kingdoms—Current Events (Daniel and the Kingdom of Babylon)
    II. PROPHECY (7–12)
        Visions of God's Kingdom—Vision of the Future (Daniel and the Kingdom of God)

Our "famous" chapter comes within the historical section of the book and deals with the reign of King Darius. Darius was a Mede who succeeded to the throne after the death of Belshazzar and reigned over the Chaldeans. This "famous" chapter can be given the following outline:

I. DANIEL'S DANGER (verses 1-17)
   A. *Material Prosperity* (verses 1-3)
   B. *Moral Integrity* (verses 4, 5)
   C. *Malicious Conspiracy* (verses 6-9)
   D. *Magnificent Testimony* (verses 10, 11)
   E. *Monstrous Urgency* (verses 12-15)
   F. *Masterful Finality* (verses 16, 17)
II. DANIEL'S DELIVERANCE (verses 18-28)
   A. *Mental Anxiety* (verse 18)
   B. *Manifest Innocency* (verses 19-22)
   C. *Methodical Severity* (verses 23, 24)
   D. *Majestic Authority* (verses 25-27)
   E. *Material Prosperity* (verse 28)

I. DANIEL'S DANGER (verses 1-17)

A. *Material Prosperity* (verses 1-3). It was a common Jewish belief that material prosperity went side by side with spiritual prosperity. The divine promise to Joshua (1:8) was: "This book of the law shall not depart out of thy mouth; but thou shalt meditate therein day and night, that thou mayest observe to do according to all that is written therein: for then thou shalt make thy way prosperous, and then thou shalt have good success." Again and again in the Old Testament, especially in the Book of Psalms, do we find that obedience to the Word of the Lord resulted in the Lord prospering His believing child. This has also been the testimony of saints through the ages, especially regarding tithing. On the other hand it must be noted that many believers have been equally faithful and obedient, and yet have known no material prosperity. Daniel was obviously in the first class. He was prosperous in that he received preferment or promotion. He became prime minister for King Darius. Now the dominion of Darius was large. Divided into districts he had 120 princes seeing to administration. Of these 120 three were particularly eminent, and of these three Daniel was elected chief. It must be remembered that Daniel was now between seventy and eighty years of age for he had been in exile seventy years. What a faithful and consistent witness and testimony to God he had exercised over the years! Often those who receive preferment in the political realm compromise their Christian principles as they climb the "social ladder." Not so Daniel.

B. *Moral Integrity* (verses 4, 5). It is often said that public servants live "glass-house" lives. They are surrounded by spectators and critics. They are followed about by reporters and newsreel men. They are watched at work and at play, at home and abroad. Thus was Daniel watched, yet "no error or fault was found in him," and it was not for want of looking for they "sought to find occasion against Daniel." What they were looking for was something "against the kingdom," that is, something wrong with his administration, some shady trick, some piece of "graft," some underhanded piece of business, but Daniel never blundered in this way; he was the essence of discretion in all things. He was conscientious and walked circumspectly. He never did anything "unseemly." Would that Christians, humble church-members as well as those in more conspicuous positions in the Church, were as morally beyond rebuke today!

C. *Malicious Conspiracy* (verses 6-9). Not being able to find fault with Daniel's morals they conspired together to "frame" him. As he had done nothing that contravened any existing law, they must bring in a new law that Daniel will break! Let us put it in a modern form: They asked King Darius to make church prayer meetings unlawful for one month. Anyone found attending would be executed. Now prayer meetings are sadly neglected today in any case, but what would they be like under such a law? Well, that was how they tried to trap Daniel. Knowing that the king could not revoke a law to which he had put his seal they knew that they had Daniel in their power if he continued to pray to his God instead of petitioning King Darius.

D. *Magnificent Testimony* (verses 10, 11). As prime minister Daniel could have remonstrated with the king for not consulting him about the new decree, but there is a quicker and surer way of overcoming officialdom—upwards! Daniel went home and told his troubles to his heavenly Father.

Notice first Daniel's *practice* of prayer—he prayed every day three times, morning, noon and night. Does not that shame us? The psalmist also declared: "Evening, and morning, and at noon will I pray" (55:17). It is suggested that he learned the habit from the camel who knelt in the morning for his load to be put on; he knelt at midday for feeding and for readjustment of the load; while he knelt at night for the load to be removed. What lightness of load we should experience if we followed Daniel's practice!

Next we note Daniel's *posture* at prayer—on his knees. It is said that Anglicans pray kneeling, the Salvation Army standing, while the rest of us adopt the nonconformist slouch! Admittedly it is the posture of the heart that matters most, but in private devotions kneeling can be helpful as it suggests humility, reverence, submission, supplication.

Notice, too, the *publicity* of his praying—with his windows open. Many commentators have misled us here. We have been told that Daniel opened his windows toward Jerusalem that he might direct his thoughts to the temple there. Surely his windows were open that his enemies might hear him pray and look in and see his testimony! His was not the ostentatious prayer of the Pharisee for he could have done that at the street corner like them.

There is an interesting legend that Daniel's enemies bought the house across the road from Daniel. There they watched him day in and day out. Noticing his daily habit of prayer, they knew what to do to trap him. Daniel also knew they were there, peeping through the curtains, so he opened his window wide that they might hear him praying—for himself and for them! What a testimony! How it condemns our trepidation in the barrack room or in the boarding house.

Lastly we note the *pattern* of his prayer—"praying and making supplication," that is, it was praise and prayer, thanksgiving as well as supplication. For the real pattern of true prayer we need also to study chapter 9:3-19. There we have confession, adoration, thanksgiving, supplication, intercession—every aspect of prayer that there is. But our famous chapter gives the minimum essentials—praise and prayer must always go hand in hand. We have always something to thank God for as well as ask God for.

"Prayer is the Secret of Power." The secret is no longer a secret for God has revealed it to us through His Word; the power is always available but we neglect the one means of obtaining it.

E. *Monstrous Urgency* (verses 12-15). Daniel's enemies lose no time. Leaving Daniel before the "Amen" they hurry to the king to report what they have seen and heard. The new law has been broken. They want to make sure that the king is going to uphold tradition and refuse to revoke what he has signed and sealed. The king argues, cajoles, "bullies," reasons, but dares not refuse. Daniel must die. The men again "assemble" in the king's presence. The word means "they came tumultuously together," that is, they rushed into his presence clamoring for Daniel's blood. There was, of course, no need for such haste—Daniel was still praying, not running away. And if they waited until the next day he would be found either in the morning, at noon, or in the evening!

F. *Masterful Finality* (verses 16, 17). Their masterstroke is now delivered. Daniel's fate is certain for he is placed in a den of lions. To make "assurance doubly sure," and to finalize the whole matter, the king uses the same seal that ratified the decree to seal the stone laid across the den's mouth; the seal of these treacherous men is then added to his own. Nothing can save Daniel now, he is finished, done for! We shall see.

II. Daniel's Deliverance (verses 18-28)

A. *Mental Anxiety* (verse 18). Although King Darius told Daniel that his God would deliver him, it seemed a forlorn hope. All night long Darius kept thinking of Daniel in that den. He could neither sleep nor eat for anxiety. Like most people whose mind is overanxious or overactive the king "slept not a wink all night." Neither could he enjoy entertainment.

B. *Manifest Innocency* (verses 19-22). Arising with the crack of dawn the king ran to the den and called out to Daniel. Daniel answered that he was alive and that God had preserved him. This proved his innocency and integrity.

Spurgeon comments on this verse: "What a splendid night he must have spent with those lions . . . he must have had a glorious night. What with the lions, and with angels all night to keep him company." The angel of the Lord "stopped" the lions' mouths. He muzzled them. How we are not told. Perhaps the easiest explanation is that the shining light of this angelic being was like a flaming fire surrounding Daniel. The lions dared not penetrate such a blaze of divine glory. So the Christian may be persecuted, wrongly accused, slandered, elbowed out of the way, envied, and so forth, but if innocent then God will vindicate and preserve as He did Daniel, Job and others of His servants.

C. *Methodical Severity* (verses 23, 24). As Darius had been just in keeping the new decree, so now he is equally just in making the punishment fit the crime. The enemies of Daniel, and their families, are thrown to the same lions. Having seen them docile and harmless, what a shock to hear their roaring and raving as the den's mouth opened and they are thrown in! Darius was now obeying a higher law than one of his own, he was fulfilling God's law which declared false accusers should be put to death, the children suffering for the father's sin.

D. *Majestic Authority* (verses 25-27). Darius' true character comes out in this section. The best way to make amends for dishonoring one of God's servants is not only to restore that man to honor but to honor God Himself. The king makes another new decree, this time that the One, true and living God shall be worshiped in the future. Great tribute is paid to God's attributes and activity. He is living and steadfast; He has an unconquerable kingdom, and He is able to deliver and work miracles.

E. *Material Prosperity* (verse 28). The chapter comes full circle by emphasizing Daniel's restoration to material prosperity and position of honor. In the economy of God great good always comes out of great evil, even though we may not see it at the time. More than that, the rest of the book reveals another spiritual law—Daniel prospers now more than ever before. Trial, affliction, persecution—these are educative; they leave us better men and women; we are more spiritual because of having passed through the refining fires.

THE VALLEY OF DISCIPLINE

Hosea 2

"The Sin of Spiritual Adultery" is the theme of the Book of Hosea. "Return" is the key word by which to remember the book's message and the key text that sums it all up is found in 6:1.

At first sight there seems to be little order in this book, but after serious study the book can be given the following outline:

    I. THE PROPHET'S FAMILY (1-3)
       A. *His Home* (1:1-9)
       B. *His Children* (1:10–2:1)
       C. *His Wife* (2:2–23)
       D. *His Love* (3)
    II. THE FAMILY OF GOD (4–14)
       A. *Their Sin* (4:1–8:14)
       B. *Their Judgment* (9–11:11)
       C. *Their Restoration* (11:12–14)

Hosea lived and ministered during the reign of the northern kingdom of Israel and was fully aware of its rottenness, its public and private vices. His name means "help" or "salvation," and the word "return" (used fifteen times in the book) is his appeal to the backslider. Hosea himself knows great sorrow, for his wife has proved herself unfaithful. This poignant experience he uses as a lesson or illustration to God's people.

Our "famous" chapter, two, comes within the first main division of the book, and forms subdivisions two and three, the prophet's children and wife, their guilt, suffering and apostasy. A convenient outline of the chapter is this:

    I. THE PROPHET'S ANGER (verses 1-5)
       A. *Blatant Immorality*
       B. *Spiritual Impoverishment*
    II. THE LORD'S CHASTISEMENT (verses 6-13)
       A. *Difficulties*
       B. *Disappointments*
       C. *Deprivation*
       D. *Dishonor*
       E. *Depression*
    III. THE PEOPLE'S REPENTANCE (verses 14-23)

A. *Spiritual Restoration*
B. *Material Restoration*

Our title for this well-known chapter, *The Valley of Discipline* is taken from verse 15—"The valley of Achor for a door of hope." The name Achor means literally "troubling." The prophet is undergoing great personal sorrow and suffering on account of the unfaithfulness of his wife. God uses this suffering as a salutary lesson to His people. Suffering is divinely-imposed discipline, but one result of the stern discipline will be greater hope for a brighter future.

I. THE PROPHET'S ANGER (verses 1-5)

Is it right for a prophet of the Lord to be angry? The Bible speaks of the "wrath" of God. The New Testament records the "righteous indignation" of our Saviour. Hosea has good reason to be angry, for here in this section is blatant immorality and spiritual impoverishment.

A. *Blatant immorality.* The phrase "out of her sight" (verse 2, the Revised Version says "From her face") suggests the shameless character of the immorality of Hosea's wife. The word "plead" is better translated "reprove" or "rebuke." Gomer, Hosea's wife, has committed such blatant adultery that according to Hosea she has made null the marriage-relationship. Her children are thus rendered fatherless on account of a faithless mother, the sins of the parent being visited upon the children. All this is an illustration of Israel's—

B. *Spiritual impoverishment.* As Gomer has committed adultery, so Israel has committed apostasy, spiritual adultery. She has been unfaithful to God who has been as a Husband as well as a Father to His people. Israel has gone a-whoring after other gods, and attributed to them gifts which were really God-given. The "stripping naked" of the adulteress is symbolic of the stripping of the vegetation of the land and the taking away from Israel many spiritual blessings.

According to a modern Jewish commentary this first section of the chapter is full of "sudden transitions and ejaculations." This is to make vivid and graphic the anger of the prophet. The aim is to bring Israel to her senses and to the point of repentance. In God's name Hosea charges them with violating a covenant as sacred as matrimony. As a result God is prepared to seek a divorce from His people.

How this message is needed today! The twentieth century has been called the century of "the angry young men." It is high time the prophets of the Lord became angry over the spiritual adultery, the blatant idolatry of the nations, the Western powers with their forsaking of God, His Word, His Day, His Church, and their whoring after mammon, the god of materialism. Instead we offer our excuses. We are like the young man who murdered his parents and then besought the judge to be merciful because he was dealing with an orphan! We are without excuse. The Gospel has been faithfully presented for too long. We have religious instruction in our schools. There are religious programs on the radio and television. The Bible is still the world's best seller and can be bought cheaply in chain stores as well as in Bible book stores. Our spiritual adultery is worse than that of the heathen in his darkness who bows down to wood and stone.

II. THE LORD'S CHASTISEMENT (verses 6-13)

The divine personal pronoun figures prominently in this section, being used eight times. The Lord threatens to chastise His people in various ways: difficulties, disappointments, deprivation, dishonor and depression.

A. *Difficulties.* Verses 6 and 7 describe the difficulties that will confront Israel. Their political policies will come to nothing; no progress will be made with treaties with foreign powers. A "hedge" or "wall" will obstruct their path, saying "No further." She shall look for help in vain, or if it is offered it will be uselesss assistance.

B. *Disappointments.* In verse 8 we are told that the necessary comforts of life will disappoint them. Corn and oil, given them for their pleasure and delight will no longer satisfy them. Money will not buy what it once bought for they have abused God's plenteous gifts in the past.

C. *Deprivation.* Disappointment will then turn to deprivation. In verse 9 we see that the corn and wine and other divine provisions will be taken away. They will be "recovered" (that is a legal term), the recovery of goods rightfully belonging to a landlord from a tenant. God has an "incontestable right" (Matthew Henry) and "title" to all the creature comforts He gives us and we are accountable to Him as stewards. If we prove unfaithful then He can reclaim them at will.

D. *Dishonor.* Verse 10 promises to bring to light of day and exhibit before others in public all that Israel has done. The exceeding sinfulness of her sin will be revealed and she will be dishonored before all. Her friends and enemies will despise her and not venture to depend on her. She will not be considered worthy of friendship.

E. *Depression.* Verses 11 to 13 describe the depression that will follow in the wake of exposed sin and shame. They will be utterly depressed and miserable. No laughter will be heard from her lips and no smile will be seen upon her face. There will be no rejoicing in the heart. The very occasions of joy, the feast-days, will be taken away. Religious and spiritual joy as well as carnal and worldly joy will be removed.

What chastisement! We must surely interpret it in the light of the New Testament teaching in Hebrews: "Now no chastening for the present seemeth to be joyous, but grievous: nevertheless afterward it yieldeth the peaceable fruit of righteousness unto them which are exercised thereby" (12:11). Divine chastisement is educative and refining. It is God working out our future blessing. Remembering this we can agree with the exhortation: "My son, despise not thou the chastening of the Lord, nor faint when thou art rebuked of him: For whom the Lord loveth he chasteneth" (12:5,6). Yes, it is also proof of our sonship—"But if ye be without chastisement, whereof all are partakers, then are ye bastards, and not sons" (12:8).

III. THE PEOPLE'S REPENTANCE (verses 14-23)

The artist Turner once invited novelist Charles Kingsley to his studio to see a canvas he had painted of a storm at sea. Filled with admiration Kingsley asked how it was so realistic. Turner explained: "I went to Holland and engaged a fisherman to take me out in a storm. I was bound to the mast so that I would be able to see everything in safety. The tempest blew itself into me until I seemed to become part of the storm itself. When it was over I came back and was able to depict all its fury on canvas." So it is with the Lord's chastening. It is the storm that results in our coming through enriched spiritually. It is not in the so-called "school of comfort" that we learn God's ways and purposes, but in His "school of chastening." So it was with Hosea the prophet, and so it was with the people of God, Israel.

The valley of Achor or "troubling" was the valley of discipline for God's children. In that valley she learned more than on a hilltop. There she learned to sing again as she learned to sing in the wilderness when coming up out of Egypt. The valley of Achor was the place where Achan was punished for his theft and greed. It was also the valley through which lay the pathway that led to the land of promise. Chastisement is both a punishment for our sin and a promise of renewed blessing to come.

Here in this section then we have spiritual and material restoration:

A. *Spiritual restoration* (verses 14-17; 19-21). In place of chastisement will come comfort and consolation. The names of the idolatrous gods will not be mentioned again—God not only forgives but forgets! Once again God will be a husband to them, Creator, Protector and Husband. Having threatened to divorce His people He will in fact ratify His betrothal to them *forever*. He will reveal Himself to them in a new way and they shall know Him, more fully and clearly than before. He will teach them how to know Him. He will also hear them when they cry to Him in prayer. He will show them mercy and will call them "my people" as they shall call Him "my God."

B. *Material restoration* (verses 18, 22, 23). As we saw in Daniel 6, spiritual and material prosperity went side by side for these ancient people. God promises a covenant between Himself and the birds of the air and beasts of the field. Hosea's contention is that God is behind all the forces of nature and can use them for the discipline of

His people, for their bane or blessing. In our scientific age of "rain-makers" and so forth, we tend to forget this Scriptural attitude that God brings prosperity to mankind or withholds His gifts. This is yet another way in which God speaks to mankind. So here God promises that natural laws and spiritual laws will be inter-working for His people's benefit. He promises that He will permit no famine or disaster due to inferior creatures bringing disease or disaster to their crops. In verses 22 and 23 He promises material benefits and products of the earth in abundance for the support of themselves and their families.

How more ready we would be to endure our chastisement, and how more willing we would be to repent of our sin, if only we looked to the gracious and glorious future God promises to the repentant. Let Dr. G. Campbell Morgan have the last word. In his *Voices of Twelve Hebrew Prophets* he sums up Hosea and his message by three words: "sin, judgment, love." Concerning sin Hosea teaches us that "deeper down than any of the sins . . is that of infidelity to love." There, "sin always results in judgment" teaches the prophet. "Punishment is inevitable," it is "included in the course of sin." But "God never abandons man at that point." The dominant note of Hosea is "the appeal of the love of God." Sin both hurts God and destroys the sinner, but the love of God redeems the sinner and reclaims the backslider.

THE VALLEY OF DECISION

Joel 3

The prophet Joel has been called "the prophet of religious revival." The key word is "visitation" (key text 2:25) and his theme is, "Repentance, the Foundation Condition of Revival." His name was a common one (meaning: Jehovah is God), his style of writing elegant, and his preaching eloquent. He emphasized the nearness of the Day of the Lord, a day of divine activity and government in human affairs. An outline of the book can be given in this form:

SUPERSCRIPTION (1:1)
  I. NATIONAL CALAMITY (1:2–2:11)
      A. *The Plague of Locusts*
      B. *The Priests' Lament*
      C. *The Day of the Lord*
  II. CELESTIAL DIPLOMACY (2:12–32)
      A. *The Repentance of the Jews*
      B. *The Response of the Almighty*
      C. *The Promise of the Spirit*
  III. SPIRITUAL PROSPERITY (3)
      A. *The Judgment of the Gentiles*
      B. *The Valley of Decision*
      C. *The Blessing of Believers*

It will thus be seen that chapter 3 stands alone, forming the third main division of the book.

The prophet now depicts the ultimate spiritual prosperity of God's people. Celestial diplomacy, a direct intervention of the sovereign God in the days of national calamity results in a great spiritual revival. An outline of the chapter can be given in the same form as for Division III of the book, with the additional subsections:

  I. THE JUDGMENT OF THE GENTILES (verses 1-13)
      A. *The Investigation* (verses 1-3)
      B. *The Accusation* (verses 4-8)
      C. *The Execution* (verses 9-13)
  II. THE VALLEY OF DECISION (verses 14-17)
      A. *Prospect and Portents* (verses 14, 15)
      B. *Security and Sanctity* (verses 16, 17)
  III. THE BLESSING OF BELIEVERS (verses 18-21)

147

A. *Fertility* (verse 18)
B. *Fatality* (verse 19)
C. *Futurity* (verses 20, 21)

I. THE JUDGMENT OF THE GENTILES (verses 1-13)

Joel proclaims that certain nations are singled out for judgment. It is one of the characteristics of these Old Testament prophets that they felt honor-bound to express themselves about surrounding nations, their idolatrous nature and their impending judgment and doom. Thus Joel singles out the people of Tyre, Sidon, Philistia, Edom and Egypt. The first three were guilty of stealing the temple treasures and selling the Jews into slavery. The second were guilty of shedding the innocent blood of God's people. Joel vividly describes the Investigation, Accusation and Execution in this passage.

A. *The Investigation* (verses 1-3) takes place in "the valley of Jehoshaphat," Jehoshaphat meaning "the Lord will Judge." There (probably the valley of Hinnom to the west of the Holy City, for there is no other Biblical mention of any valley of Jehoshaphat), the prophet declared God would "enter into judgment" with the Gentile nations. The Authorized Version has "plead with them there," but the Hebrew means judge or pronounce sentence for or against. All their deeds of violence, their persecution, their spirit of ungodliness, contempt and reproach of the people of God is to be listed, noted, investigated before sentence is passed. Nothing will escape the all-seeing eye of the Almighty, Omniscient God. So in our time Almighty God is noting the deeds of those who oppose His Church—the Communists of Russia and China, the Roman Catholics in Spain and elsewhere. The day of reckoning will surely come. Even in this section that deals with judgment, however, we have an indication of future prosperity. The phrase in verse 1, "bring back the captivity," could apply not only to prisoners of war being repatriated but to relief from illness. We speak today about an invalid "taking a turn for better or for worse." Whichever interpretation of the phrase is favored the idea is of restoration to prosperity.

B. *The Accusation* (verses 4-8) that follows is detailed by contrast with the general one given in the preceding three verses—the scattering of God's people, the division of their land, and the selling of young people for base purposes. Tyre, Sidon and Philistia are now accused of definite cruelty and robbery. These people are named and accused not of wickedness against God's people as much as against God Himself. It is *His* silver and gold they have stolen, not merely the temple treasures, the valuable utensils of the House of God. It is *His* children who have been abducted, not just young people of the city of Jerusalem. All sin, in the last analysis, is sin against God, His holiness and His righteous laws.

C. *The Execution* is described in verses 9-13. The sentence of

God upon the Gentile nations is to be executed by His "mighty ones." From Psalm 103:20 it may be inferred that this means the heavenly hosts. The heathen nations are not only challenged but summoned to attend the assize of God and receive execution of His sentence. Reliance upon material weapons will be ineffectual; they will be insufficient in number. Farming implements will have to be refashioned into weapons of war but all to no avail. Material might and power can never match the superior forces of Almighty God.

The execution of the sentence is also in farming terminology. Just as the reaper cuts down the corn with his scythe so the Lord's enemies will be cut down by the sword. This verse (13) is further evidence that "the mighty ones" are the angels of God, for Jesus taught that "the harvest is the end of the world; and reapers are the angels" (Matthew 13:39). The enemies of Israel have sought to destroy God's people; they have sold their children into slavery. Now they themselves will suffer in the same way—their ultimate fate will be destruction. A Jewish proverbial saying is that "the Jews have always been a people standing at the grave of their persecutors."

II. THE VALLEY OF DECISION (verses 14-17)

This is probably a nickname, a local name for the valley of Jehoshaphat. "Decision" means "verdict." The "valley of threshing" may be a possible alternative reading, and would be more in keeping with the harvest metaphor of the previous section. In this section we have two further subdivisions:

A. *Prospect and Portents* are in verses 14 and 15. The prospect, the immediate future developments for multitudes of people, was the final Day of the Lord, a day of judgment and retribution. The repetition of "multitudes" suggests not only vast numbers but vociferous noise. The great multitude brought together at the last great judgment (both the dead and living, for Christ will come to judge "the quick and the dead") will be making a tremendous, clamorous noise. Fear, terror, uncertainty, anticipation—all these will find vocal expression and the air will be filled with the sound of multitudes mingling their shrieks of anguish. The day will be accompanied by portents or signs in the sky. Sun, moon and stars will become dimmed, perhaps because some of the heathen peoples being judged have worshiped them; perhaps because the glorious appearance of the Judge will outshine them.

B. *Security and Sanctity* is in verse 16 and 17. Jerusalem protected from ε   ck and defilement is the next divine promise. God Himself is going to be His people's "hope" and "strength" or "refuge" and "stronghold."

The presence of the Lord also insures sanctity. After the judgment has been pronounced and the sentence executed, then Jerusalem (the Church) will be "without spot or wrinkle or any such thing." "Then shall Jerusalem be holy" (verse 17) is literally "Then shall Jerusalem be holiness," that is, the quality or virtue itself! One day we shall see Him, be with Him, and be *like* Him, completely sanctified.

That Joel is predicting far into the future, perhaps to the final glorification of Jerusalem after the return of Christ, seems obvious from his statement that "no strangers shall pass through her any more." He sees Jerusalem as the future religious metropolis of the world, a place to which all nations will flow.

III. THE BLESSING OF BELIEVERS (verses 18-21)

This final section of the book and chapter brings the whole prophecy full circle. Calamity now becomes prosperity because of divine diplomacy. Believers and churches who have been experiencing spiritual barrenness will be blessed in abundance. Revival may tarry, but one day it will come. The description of this ultimate blessing is one that emphasizes fertility, fatality and futurity.

A. *Fertility*, in verse 18 is placed first because it emphasizes fulfilled prophecy and the result of God's retribution. In the divine economy restitution always follows retribution. His people are now to be as prosperous as they were once destitute. Hyperbole follows upon hyperbole in this verse, resulting in a tremendous picture of abundance and plenty. What a result of the outpouring of God's Holy Spirit! Oh, that we might experience just such another outpouring, and so enjoy not only the immediate results, large numbers of conversions, but the ultimate results as well, fertility, the "possession of our possessions."

B. *Fatality* is in verse 19. The final calamity mentioned in this verse appears as an afterthought by the prophet, as if he has previously overlooked the doom and destruction of Israel's historic foes, Egypt and Edom. Surely this note of denunciation is brought in at this point to heighten the effect of the previous verse and to emphasize the final note of the continuing nature of the prosperity.

C. *Futurity* (verses 20, 21). By contrast with the destruction of the enemy Israel is going to live forever and ever. For generation after generation, succeeding families will enjoy the blessings promised here to believers. And all this is certain for the future because "the Lord dwelleth in Zion."

The prophet Joel, this prophet of religious revival, has thus begun by recording history, by describing a plague of locusts, but he has taken us through the centuries to the end of time, interpreting history and making us aware of the imminence of the final judgment, a time of terror for the unbeliever but the continuation of blessing for the believer. The historical setting and national situation is forever changing, but the truths Joel proclaimed are as eternal and as fresh as ever. Revival is a divine foretaste of the Church's eternal prosperity in heaven.

A BASKET OF SUMMER FRUIT

Amos 8

Amos (the name being in Hebrew, "to carry a burden") may have been a hunchback or had an impediment in his speech. God's call came to him during days of Israel's material prosperity but moral poverty. He tells much the same story as Joel and Hosea: prevailing sins of avarice, immorality, profanity and blasphemy. The prophet thus predicts the judgment of God upon the nation and "punishment" is the key word of the book. The prophet's theme is, "The Patience of God in Punishment" and the key text is 4:12.

In the book are five visions granted to Amos, visions of grasshoppers, fire, a plumbline, a basket of summer fruit and God standing on the altar. Our "famous chapter" is the prophet's vision of *A Basket of Summer Fruit*. First, however, let us divide up the Book of Amos as follows:

PROLOGUE (1:1)
    A. *The Prophet and His Times*
  I. EIGHT EXPOSURES (1:2–2)
    A. *The Sinful Nations*
  II. THREE DISCOURSES (3–6)
    A. *The Severe Judgments*
III. FIVE VISIONS (7–9:10)
    A. *The Sensational Predictions*
EPILOGUE (9:11-15)
    A. *The People and Their Turning*

This "famous" chapter then comes within Section III, and is one of the sensational five visions that illustrates the divine plan for His people. All these visions predict a divine judgment that is "inevitable," "imminent" and "inescapable" (*The New Bible Commentary*, I.V.F.). In Chaper 8 and *The Basket of Summer Fruit* Amos emphasizes the imminence of divine judgment. Israel is like overripe summer fruit, ready to decay. The chapter can be divided as follows:

  I. IMMINENT JUDGMENT (verses 1-3)
  II. INCONVENIENT RELIGION (verses 4-6)
 III. INESCAPABLE DANGERS (verses 7-10)
 IV. INCAPABLE WORSHIPERS (verses 11-14)

I. IMMINENT JUDGMENT (verses 1-3)
In these verses in the Hebrew there is a play on words. The word

151

for "summer fruit" suggests "the end." Summer fruit is really autumn
fruit, that is, fruit ripe in the "fall" of the year. This suggests to the
prophet the "fall" of Israel. Again and again divine judgment has
been postponed. Now it is imminent and inevitable; God will delay no
longer: "I will not again pass by them" (verse 2). The prophet's
graphic description of this judgment is of dead bodies, unburied, with
a horrified silence hanging like a pall over the scene.

It is important to note that God asked His servant Amos the
question: "What seest thou?" Do we always see what God wants us
to see? Do we not sometimes shut our eyes to reality, the true state
of the Church, the state of the world. In these days He would have
us see the overripeness, the rottenness of the Church, unspiritual,
worldly, disobedient, nonmissionary, nonevangelistic. Such a condition deserves the judgment of God upon it! "Judgment will begin at
the house of God." Overripe fruit will not keep; it soon becomes
"mushy" and "pulpy," and has to be thrown away. If this seems
harsh treatment for the Church then the messages to the seven
churches of Asia in Revelation need to be studied very carefully.

Even when we see the Church as she is, as God sees her, how
strangely silent we are. How few voices are raised in prayer or in
protest about the prevailing sins of God's people today! We need
Christian "angry young men," successors to Amos, men with a burden, men able to plead with their fellow church members and able
to plead with God.

II. INCONVENIENT RELIGION (verses 4-6)

God's people in the time of Amos were so eager to increase their
wealth that they did not stop at exploiting the poor or even stooping
to fraudulent means. True, they kept the Sabbath and special feast
days, but they wished with all their hearts that such days would
soon pass so that they could get on with their plans for getting rich
quick. Their religion had become inconvenient! Business had to be
suspended while they observed the holy days.

What a picture of twentieth-century business and commerce—
even among Christians. Sunday has become an inconvenient day for
many. We now have a shorter working week and greater leisure hours,
but still we try to steal Sunday, the Lord's Day, from the Lord. It
holds up business and making money. That is why so many are now
"oncers" instead of "twicers" in church on Sunday. We "get by" with
the least possible time devoted to God and His worship. One service
a Sunday, and the earlier the better, is the aim of many church-goers.
There is still a "form of Godliness" but no "power." Church-going is
still maintained for it gives an air of respectability, but that is as far
as it goes. It must not interfere with getting, getting-on, or getting-up.
How hard is heaven going to be for such people, for in heaven there is
no Monday, Tuesday, Wednesday, Thursday, Friday or Saturday—

only one long Sunday! If Sunday is not the happiest day of the week for Christians on earth then it will be a miserable existence in heaven! How the Lord's Day has been encroached on bit by bit in recent years. Even Christians nowadays do things on Sunday they would not have dared to do before the Second World War. Sunday "joy rides" in the car, buying non-essentials in the stores, gardening, school homework or college study, these are but a few examples. It all brings judgment in its train. To dishonor God's Day is to dishonor God.

III. INESCAPABLE DANGERS (verses 7-10)

Earthquake and eclipse are the two grave dangers described by Amos. A terrible earthquake is here predicted. Not one or a series of slight earth tremors, but an earthquake of long duration comparable with the flood waters of the Nile which take about one month to rise and a second month to go down.

It has been calculated that a total eclipse of the sun occurred on June 15, 763 B.C. This might well have been during the life and ministry of Amos and he looked upon it as a divine portent.

These inescapable dangers, the earthquake and the eclipse, speak of uncertainty and darkness. Such will be the condition of the Church when God brings judgment to bear upon it. Even now we are beginning to see something of the uncertainty. Men and women in the Church, uncertain of what they believe, are gullible in the hands of the door-to-door visitors of the cults because they do not know the Scriptures and cannot answer their false arguments with the sure Word of God. What a darkness is enveloping the Church today. Spiritual darkness! Church members' eyes blinded by Satan so that they can neither see the glories of the Lord of the Church, nor the sinful condition of the world around. Toward the end of the age, and before the Lord returns in all His glory for the Church, these conditions will get worse and worse. False preachers and prophets will creep into the Church and teach untruths. The Church will enter into a confederacy with Rome. Organized union will result in visible enlarged numbers, but God has always had His purposes served by an elect remnant. "Peace and safety" will be the cry, but sudden destruction will come. Let us take heed, noting the signs of the times, the fulfillment of prophecy and the coming of the Lord.

IV. INCAPABLE WORSHIPERS (verses 11-14)

Parallel with earthquake and eclipse in the last section are hunger and thirst in this last section of the chapter. The prophet's most startling statement is surely: "They shall run to and fro to seek the word of the Lord, and shall not find it." The fault will not only be with the preachers but with the hearers. In the last days it will be difficult to find a gospel preacher, but worse than that, when a man is preaching the Gospel there will be people who will not perceive it, hear it, and accept it. The capacity for hearing will have been removed! And

remember, this is not said of men of the world, who have never wanted
to hear the Gospel in any case; this is said of those within the family
of God!

What a picture Amos gives us. Men and women are running to
and fro, from one end of the country to the other, yearning for a
comforting message from God and not able to find it or hear it. They
"wander" (literally "totter") like drunken men, like men weak from
want of water and food, but all to no avail. Having during their early
lifetime spurned the Word of God, going after pleasure and thrills, they
now desire the Word but are too weak from spiritual hunger and thirst
to benefit from it.

God's people before the time of Amos had known critical days of
famine in the land, and in captivity. Now they are going to experience
spiritual famine and find it the worse of the two. The idols to which
they have turned in their rebellion against God will be unable to help
them at such a time. So our generation has yet to learn that the god
of materialism which so many worship will not be able to help them
when in need of spiritual sustenance.

As the basket of summer fruit was ripe for Amos, is not the time
ripe now for the Church of God to repent before it is too late? Before
we are entirely spiritually insensible, now is the time to cry to God
for an awakening. While the world totters from crisis to crisis, from
searching after new pleasures and the latest thrill, now is the time to
beseech God to "rend the heavens and come down." If He does not
come in revival power then He will come in judgment. There is no
other alternative—it is revival or judgment!

POSSESSING OUR POSSESSIONS

Obadiah

This "famous" chapter is a complete Old Testament book. The key word is "restitution" and the prophet's theme: "Living the Victorious Life." Divine punishment, predicted by Amos, is here followed by divine restitution. The abiding lesson and title of this famous chapter is similar to the abiding lesson of the Book of Joshua— *Possessing our Possessions.*

The shortest book in the Old Testament, Obadiah has been described as "a single chapter with a single theme." The brevity of the book must not detract from the importance of the spiritual theme.

Of Obadiah the prophet we know very little, except that his name means "Servant of Jehovah" or "One that serves God." It was a very common name among God's ancient people and several Obadiahs are mentioned in the Old Testament.

An outline of this one chapter book can be given in the following form (and it will, of course, be the same outline for book as for chapter, unlike our previous studies):

     I.   THE DOOM OF SINNERS (verses 1-9)
         A. *Pomposity* (verses 1-5)
         B. *Treachery* (verses 6, 7)
         C. *Timidity* (verses 8, 9)
    II.   THE DESCRIPTION OF SIN (verses 10-14)
         A. *Belligerent* (verse 10)
         B. *Indifferent* (verses 11, 12)
         C. *Avaricious* (verses 13, 14)
   III.   THE DAY OF JUDGMENT (verses 15-21)
         A. *Retribution* (verses 15, 16)
         B. *Restoration* (verses 17, 18)
         C. *Recovery* (verses 19-21)

I. THE DOOM OF SINNERS (verses 1-9)

The doom of Edom is pronounced in the first verse. Nowhere else in Scripture is the antagonism between Jacob and Esau brought into such a clear light as in Obadiah. This antagonism runs right through the Scriptures from Genesis to Jesus before Herod (Herod being an Edomite and Jesus a descendant of Jacob according to the flesh). The principles of this ancient antagonism still apply today. The two ideals and conceptions of life of Edom and Judah divide people today.

Obadiah the prophet then begins with Edom, revealing for us her doom due to sin, and the doom for sinners of Edomite character throughout the ages.

A. First, there was the sin of *pride* or *pomposity* as it is rightly termed in our outline (verses 1-5). Pride is condemned again and again in God's Word. It has always been considered one of the seven deadly sins. "Pride goeth before destruction" declares the wise preacher in Proverbs 16:18. In Obadiah, verse 1, God declares that Edom will be destroyed in battle and the reason is her pomposity. Edom has believed herself to be impregnable with rock-like fortresses. She has exalted herself like the soaring eagle, flying high over her neighbors, believing her nest to be among the very stars of the heavens. Feeling overconfident, she has declared that no one will be able to raze her to the ground. But all this pride and pomposity was a deception, a self-deception in the heart and mind.

How sinners deceive themselves with their self-sufficiency and self-complacency. What a false sense of security we give ourselves! We rely upon our education or upbringing; we depend upon possessions or position. But God "resisteth the proud." We must humble ourselves before the Lord for salvation and so we must become broken and low before Him for daily sanctification.

B. *Treachery* (verses 6, 7) was also one of Edom's sins to be punished. Divine doom is pronounced upon Edom's deceitful ways. And note how the punishment fits the cry—treacherous enemies bring treacherous Edom to her doom.

Living in a commanding position on a number of important trade routes, Edom had acquired great wealth and this they hid in secret places. When they relied on so-called allies these deserted them treacherously at the last moment. Friendship with these confederates was the undoing of the Edomites. Their hidden treasures now became the spoil of a treacherous foe.

How true this all is of men of the world. They put their confidence in men and schemes and find both to fail. In business and in politics men find that they are "let down" when least they expect it and by whom they least expect. Contracts, treaties, bargains, promises, handshakes, all are broken with equanimity.

C. Next the prophet speaks about *timidity* (verses 8, 9). Edom had been famous for great statesmen, counsellors, officials of government. They were men of great experience, but now they have become like fools; they have no understanding of the situation that prevails. Their soldiers too, once men of spirit and courage, have become weak-kneed, "dismayed," cowardly, timid, afraid. So in our time we have international crisis after crisis because the statesmen, politicians, heads of the armed forces, have become afraid. Everyone is afraid of "going too far"; all are afraid that the very next crisis will cause someone to "push the button" and so instigate nuclear war. It is vain to "trust in chariots and horses," or in A-bombs and H-bombs, Polaris missiles, nuclear submarines or some other form of "ultimate" weapon. The doom of sinners is certain. Edom's doom was certain—God had pronounced it. The doom of the world in which we live is certain, God's Word has said so.

II. THE DESCRIPTION OF SIN (verses 10-14)

In this second section Obadiah the prophet describes the sin of the Edomites that has caused God to pronounce doom upon them.

A. First, they were *belligerent* (verse 10). God had noted them as "violent." They were violent men, a belligerent race. And their condemnation was the worst because they had acted in this violent manner toward their brethren, the people of God, Judah. God hates violence. He commends the peacemakers and promises them blessing.

B. Next, they were *indifferent* (verses 11, 12). Indifference, apathy, aloofness, there are the characteristics of the man of the world, the "I'm all right Jack" godless person. "In the day that thou stoodest on the other side" means literally, "In the day that thou didst stand aloof." Edom was quite content to stand as a spectator on the side line. They preferred to let others do the fighting and not to interfere or join in as allies. Their "callous aloofness" was as hard to forgive as their "active belligerency." One of the signs of the times today, on both sides of the Atlantic, is the way scores of men and women, all able-bodied, will stand by and watch a gang of thugs "beat up" a boy or a woman and do nothing to help. Police can grapple with delinquents and be outnumbered but so-called responsible bystanders do not go to their assistance—they do not want to "get involved" as they put it. Such is the callousness of our so-called cultured society.

C. Finally the Edomites were *avaricious* (verses 13,14). Although they had not joined in the fighting; although they had not lent their aid where it was necessary, they were still eager to share in the spoil. When Jerusalem was sacked the Edomites looked on with gloating pleasure, laughing derisively until the opportunity came to enter like jackals or vultures to spoil and loot. Matthew Henry sums it up in the following words. "Though they did not help to conquer them, they helped to plunder them."

What can we say of today's avarice, the awful spirit of greed, covetousness, and materialism that has thousands in its grip. "Something for nothing" is the cry of millions. Competitions in daily newspapers that are nothing less than a gamble; Premium Bonds; Bingo halls; football pools; sweepstakes—these and many more could be cited to illustrate the greed of the godless of this materialistic age.

III. THE DAY OF JUDGMENT (verses 15-21)

There is to be a day of final reckoning, the Day of the Lord, the day of judgment. This day that will "put in the dock" the nations who have oppressed Judah, will deal with Edom. As Edom became delirious with joy at the overthrow of Jerusalem, so now Judah will be drunk with joy at Edom's destruction.

A. This day will be then a day of *retribution* (verses 15, 16). Edom may expect worse to happen to her than happened to Judah. The very dregs of God's cup of wrath are reserved for the Edomites. They will have to drink it to the very bottom. They will be exterminated so that they will be as if they had not been. Divine retribution is very thorough. There shall be neither "remains nor any remembrance of them" (Matthew Henry). So at the "last day" all the enemies of the Lord and the Lord's people will perish off the face of the earth.

B. It will be a day of *restoration* (verses 17, 18) for Judah. The people of God shall possess their possessions. The word "possessions" has behind it the idea of an inheritance, a treasured possession giving constant delight. "Deliverance" and "holiness" are the twin possessions promised here to God's people, the second an outcome of the first. Now we sing "More holiness give me"; then we shall sing: "More blessed and holy, more Saviour, *like Thee*." All the riches of our inheritance in Christ shall be ours. Until then we have but a foretaste; then we shall possess all!

C. Finally it will be a day of *recovery* (verses 19-21). God's people will recover all lost land, they will reconquer territory taken from them, they will recapture their broken unity. The full extent of Judah's "possessions" is given in this section, and a glance at a map will reveal the great extent of land that will be recovered for them.

Finally the prophet finishes with a great affirmation: "the kingdom shall be the Lord's." This is the declaration that cannot be heard too frequently today. It turns our eyes away from the prevailing godlessness of a materialistic world to a sovereign God who rules the world. The gloom and darkness fade away in the light of these words. He reigns over all. The world and its future is not in the hands of evil men in high places. *He* "holds the whole world in *His* hand."

ON RESIGNING

Jonah 1

The theme of the Book of Jonah is, "The Importance of Missionary Enterprise" and not how Jonah was swallowed by a whale! The miracle of Jonah's salvation from inside the big fish is overshadowed by the miracle of the wholesale repentance of the city of Nineveh. To Nineveh Jonah was commissioned by God to go and preach (key word "commission"). The prophet went against the commission and fled in the opposite direction. God punished His servant Jonah and recommissioned him and sent him back to Nineveh. The divine message was delivered, the city repented, and judgment was averted. This second commission provides the key verse of the book (3:1, 2): "And the word of the Lord came unto Jonah the second time, saying, Arise, go unto Nineveh, that great city, and preach unto it the preaching that I bid thee."

Unlike the other minor prophets this book contains no prophetic "vision" or "burden." It is rather an account of the prophet's life, or a series of outstanding incidents in that life. And in the famous first chapter we have the account of the prophet's "resignation of his office" (G. Campbell Morgan). But first, an outline of the whole Book of Jonah can be given in the following form:

    I.   THE COMMISSION (1–3:2)
         A. *Call and Answer*
         B. *Flight and Danger*
         C. *Punishment and Prayer*
    II. THE CONSEQUENCES (3:3-10)
         A. *The Prophetic Preaching*
         B. *The Royal Edict*
         C. *The Averted Judgment*
    III. THE COMPLAINT (4)
         A. *Jonah's Repining*
         B. *Jehovah's Reproof*

The "famous" chapter thus forms part of the first main division of the book and can be given in this outline form:

    I.   THE DIVINE COMMISSION (verses 1, 2)
    II. THE PROPHET'S REACTION (verse 3)
    III. THE DIVINE PUNISHMENT (verses 4-16)

     A. *The Storm* (verses 4, 5a)
     B. *The Sleeper* (verses 5b, 6)
     C. *The Sailors* (verse 7)
     D. *The Situation* (verses 8-11)
     E. *The Solution* (verses 12-15)
     F. *The Sacrifice* (verse 16)
  IV. THE PROPHET'S PRESERVATION (verse 17)

It has been said that God called Jonah to go east but he "went west"! The result was that his testimony "went west" also, as is always the case when the believer goes against the will of the Lord. Let us look in more detail at—

I. THE DIVINE COMMISSION (verses 1, 2)

The commission was given to Jonah, meaning "dove." Jonah was the son of Amittai, meaning "my truth." "God's prophets," says Matthew Henry, should be "sons of truth" and "harmless as doves." To this man came God's word, an audible, authoritative word, a word of commission. Jonah was commissioned to go and preach to Nineveh, the capital of Assyria. The Assyrians were the bitterest enemies of Israel, and yet God was concerned for their spiritual welfare. He loved the Assyrians in spite of hating their sinful ways. How often we find when God speaks to us that He wants us to testify to a most unlikely (and perhaps unlovely) person!

Nineveh was "a great city." It was great in size; it occupied a great place in the heart and purposes of God. It was also great in wickedness. The word used here implies moral sinfulness rather than mere idolatry. In chapter 3 the word "violence" is used.

"Arise" implies "quickly" for the King's business requires haste. Time is always short for carrying the message of repentance and salvation and there must be no delay on the messenger's part. He who hears the call must immediately go.

The sins of the Assyrians "rose up" before God; Jonah "rose up" to run away from God. That was—

II. THE PROPHET'S REACTION (verse 3)

Was it fear that resulted in flight? Was it prejudice? Was it a sense of weakness? Was it inadequacy? Was Jonah running away in the opposite direction from the Assyrians? The Word says that he was running away from the presence of God, as if he could, for God is omnipresent! Dr. G. Campbell Morgan comments that Jonah "determined not to continue longer in that (the prophetic) office." His resignation was not due to ignorance but to knowledge. He was not ignorant of the sins and the wicked ways of the people of Nineveh, he knew them only too well. He knew also his God and the compassion of the divine heart for sinners.

How easy it is to resign in Christian service! And for what silly and paltry reasons people do resign. Some do it as a threat when they cannot get their own way. Others do it out of pique; others out of spite; others when in a huff. Sometimes a man is asked to "reconsider his resignation." Why should he be? If he has resigned as before the Lord, having taken the matter to the Lord in prayer, then he is acting as God has guided him. We should never ask men or women to reconsider resignations. Only God can do that, as He did in the case of Jonah the prophet—He recommissioned him.

Well, Jonah resigned. The only point in his favor at the moment is that he had the decency to "pay his fare"—he did not become a stowaway.

He fled to Tarshish. Tarshish was chosen because it was in the opposite direction from Nineveh. Because, perhaps it was a long way away and the further he could go from Nineveh the safer he felt. Maybe he had friends or relatives there. The ship was awaiting him, the tide was right, it all seemed most "providential," "the ready way is not always the right way" (Matthew Henry).

III. THE DIVINE PUNISHMENT (verses 4-16)

How easy it is to shirk Christian duty. How simple it seems to evade Christian testimony—but God knows, and He soon shows us that we cannot escape from the presence of the Lord. If Jonah were going to Tarshish then the Lord was going to follow him there.

A. *The Storm* (verses 4, 5a). It was no natural occurence— "the Lord sent (literally 'hurled') a great wind into the sea"—it was supernatural. The ship was in danger of being broken in pieces. The crew had seen nothing like it before and was terrified. Being of mixed nationalities they all called on their own particular deity. They were being superstitious rather than religious. Then they began throwing the ship's tackle, the cargo, and perhaps the passengers' luggage into the sea to "lighten" it. The word may mean "to make matters easier for them"—to give them more room to see to the running of the ship in such a storm.

B. *The Sleeper* (verses 5b, 6). Jonah was "down below" in his "cabin" fast asleep. Amazing that a man so completely out of the will of the Lord should be so calm and composed. (As Jonah was later three days in the fish's belly, a type of the Resurrection of Jesus Christ, so perhaps here we have a parallel with Jesus asleep in the boat during the storm.)

To Jonah the sleeper comes the captain of the ship. Jonah must have made some sort of testimony for he is recognized as a man of God and is asked to pray for the safety of the ship and all on board.

C. *The Sailors* (verse 7). We are not told if Jonah did pray for the ship's company. We may presume he did, for next there follows a conversation between Jonah and the crew. These sailors in their superstitious way cast lots to see who was the cause of the trouble. An ancient tradition says that the storm only affected this particular ship and other ships could be seen passing in safety. This made the crew realize that aboard must be someone causing divine displeasure. Not prepared to condemn Jonah on the lot alone, they ask him to confess if he is the cause of their peril.

D. *The Situation* (verses 8-11). They try to discover something about Jonah to see why he has caused this storm. They question him as to his occupation, his birthplace, and so on. Jonah answers but one of their questions—he tells them to what race he belongs and then adds a testimony as to his religious faith. This made the sailors afraid, for in his testimony Jonah stressed the might and power of God. He must also have told them his reason for being on the ship, and they are horrified that he should be trying to escape the presence of such a powerful God. If only Christians today were as outspoken in their testimony that it made people afraid! If only we spoke of our God as One who is all-powerful and holy, then sinners might be brought to repentance. And if only we realized, when we are so lackadaisical in service, how bad a witness this is to the unsaved. "Fancy you being here," these sailors said in effect to Jonah. "Fancy you being here," the non-Christian says to worldly Christians today when they find us in doubtful places of pleasure and amusement.

Although the sailors now had their answer, the storm still became more severe. They did not know what to do with the culprit, and so they ask Jonah for his advice.

E. *The Solution* (verses 12-15). "Throw me into the sea," says Jonah. The sailors are reluctant and try to row for the shore, but the storm becomes worse and worse. Because God had sent the storm they prayed to God, although He was not their god. They prayed that they might not suffer and be condemned because of Jonah's death (surely here is another New Testament parallel—Pilate washed his hands of our Lord's innocent blood).

Jonah is cast overboard. But note first his willingness to be thrown out of the ship. When things go wrong in the church—when we see little blessing—when there is a dearth of conversions—we usually say: "What is the cause? It must be our methods or our organization or our lack of finance." What we ought to say is, "I'm the trouble. I'm the Jonah on board. It must be my prayerlessness, my neglect of God's Word, my lack of giving, my resentment toward another Christian that is holding up the blessing." Like the disciples at the supper table we should ask, "Lord, is it I?"

F. *The Sacrifice* (verse 16). After Jonah was thrown overboard the sailors made a sacrifice and promised to make further ones in the future when they got safe to land. Some take it to mean that they were converted to God.

IV. THE PROPHET'S PRESERVATION (verse 17)

Jonah's life is saved by a miracle. A miraculous storm brought danger; the prophet is miraculously preserved from the danger of drowning when thrown overboard. Notice that only "a great fish" is mentioned here, not a whale, although there is on record the story of a sailor who was swallowed by a sperm whale and was coughed up on dry land after three days. This "great fish" is one of the four "prepared" things in the Book of Jonah. In Genesis whales are specifically mentioned, and Jesus spoke of Jonah and a whale in Matthew 12:40. This particular fish was prepared in several senses: it may have been especially created by God for this purpose; it may mean that it was swimming close by the ship, the very spot where Jonah would enter the sea; it was prepared in the sense that it only swallowed Jonah whole and did not devour him—Jonah was alive and well three days later. This was miraculous preparation and miraculous preservation. What a warning and what an encouragement it should be to us not to step outside the circle of God's will; to go where He sends, to speak what He says, and to do what He bids. There must be no willful resignation, and there can be no retirement in the Lord's army. We must be faithful "even unto death."

THE KING'S BIRTHPLACE

Micah 5

Micah means "Who is like unto Jehovah?" and the prophet was a contemporary of Isaiah and Hosea. His preaching on the theme, "The Divine Requirements," was forceful, vivid and bold. The key word of the prophecy is "censure" and Micah passes censure upon authority in scathing words, denouncing the corrupt priests, the false princes, the money-grabbing prophets of his time. The key text is 6:8.

In the New Testament Micah is quoted by the Wise Men visiting the babe in the manger, and by our Lord when sending out the twelve disciples.

A concise outline of Micah is:

     I.   GENERAL CONDEMNATION (1, 2)
    II. PARTICULAR RESTORATION (3–5)
  III. DIVINE DENUNCIATION (6, 7)

Our "famous" chapter, the fifth, *The King's Birthplace,* comes within the central section of the book which sets forth the blessings of Israel in the future, the coming of God's Deliverer or Messiah, her ultimate triumph after trial.

The chapter in outline form* is:

     I.   THE COMING OF CHRIST (verses 1-3)
    II. THE KINGDOM OF CHRIST (verses 4-7)
  III. THE CONQUEST OF CHRIST (verses 8-15)

I. THE COMING OF CHRIST (verses 1-3)

It has always been acknowledged that one of the finest proofs of the divine inspiration of the Bible is fulfilled prophecy. There is no better example of fulfilled prophecy than the advent of the Saviour.

In order to hearten the people of his day Micah prophesied the coming from Bethlehem (the house of David) of a Messianic King who would deliver them and restore the kingdom. The reason for this heartening prophecy is in verse 1 of the chapter, a graphic description of Jerusalem and God's people besieged and beleaguered. Assyria is gathering her forces against God's people and with great arrogance is insulting her ruler. This was taken as an insult to Israel's greater King, the coming Messiah, which leads naturally to a foretelling of His advent.

At last the secret is out! The Messiah's birthplace is specifically

* These three divisions follow the chapter headings given in the Authorized or King James version of the Bible.

mentioned, Bethlehem-Ephratah. The family of David were Ephra-thites of Bethlehem in Judah, and Bethlehem is called Ephrath in Genesis 48:7. The allusion would be unmistakable to Micah's hearers. The place is "little," that is, so small that one would hardly expect to find it numbered or listed with more likely places—it was almost "off the map" as we sometimes say.

The Christ was to "come forth" from little Bethlehem "unto me," that is, to fulfill My (God's) plans and purposes. The Messiah's "goings forth have been of old, from everlasting"—the Christ who came to earth previously existed in heaven, being eternally coexistent with the Father. It is interesting to note that in the Jewish *Talmud* the Messiah is one of the seven things already existing when the world was brought into being. His birthplace being Bethlehem also illus-trates the pastoral nature of His ministry, the true Shepherd of His sheep (see later verse 4).

In verse 3 we see something of the trials and tribulation through which Israel must pass before the advent of the Messiah. But at last all will be incorporated into the true commonwealth of Israel, and all will be brethren.

II. THE KINGDOM OF CHRIST (verses 4-7)

The Jews of our Lord's day, and many even to this day, believed that the Messiah, God's Deliverer of His people, would set up and establish a material kingdom, overthrowing by force of arms the oppressor. Thus when standing before Pilate Jesus referred to His kingdom as "not of this world." The kingdom of heaven is spiritual not material, of eternity rather than time. It is easy to see how the Jews, whose spiritual eyesight Satan has blinded so that they cannot see that Jesus of Nazareth was the true Messiah, have been blinded to the true nature of the kingdom.

In this section the kingdom is described in detail. First, however, some details of the Deliverer are added. "Carefulness, confidence and strength" (I.V.F. commentary) are implied in the phrase "He shall stand." If that is so then "feed" may stand for wisdom, care and love. How similar this pastoral allusion is to Psalm 23—the Shepherd who leads His sheep by quiet waters and through fields of tender grass. The fame of such a Shepherd will spread to every corner of the earth, and His power will extend to the same extent.

Just as King Hezekiah was delivered from the clutches of Senna-cherib, so the Church, the true Israel, will be delivered from Satan and the powers of darkness. The gates of hell shall not be able to stand against the witness and testimony of the Church. Seven shep-herds (seven the number of completion) and eight principal or princes among men (eight being the number of certainty—twice four, four points of the compass, four corners of the earth, etc.) will God provide for the safety of the Church in perilous times.

The persecutors of the Church will themselves be brought low and Satan himself shall be finished forever. We may be but a "remnant" (verse 7) a small company of God's people in the midst of many great people, but our influence will be as refreshing and as regenerating as dew and rain upon vegetation. And like the dew and the rain the Church's influence will be from heaven, from God, and not from man.

III. THE CONQUEST OF CHRIST (verses 8-15)

This wonderful, triumphant section of the chapter describes the conquest of Christ over the worldly, material, superstitious sources of confidence in which His people so often put their trust. For Micah's generation these were: horses and chariots (the most powerful form of military armament at that time); cities and strongholds (that is fortified, walled towns); witchcrafts and soothsayers, (superstitious sources of supposed help); graven images and groves (idols manufactured by hand and natural objects such as trees and stones)—all these were to be destroyed, but that would not leave God's people defenseless, for He would defend them.

What a condemnation of the Christian Church! How we depend upon material methods, human organization and so on. Unless we can "gear" our work to some sort of visual/audio aid, unless we can form a committee, unless we can budget and organize a stewardship campaign we feel the work of the Church will not prosper. Micah's brother prophet Zechariah cries out: "Not by might, nor by power, but by my Spirit, saith the Lord of Hosts" (4:6). Jesus Christ and the Spirit of God are mightier than all up-to-date methods and efficient committees. The day must surely come when we yield up our reliance upon these things or else the Lord God will take them away. The emphasis of Micah is that God is not only stronger than the things in which man places his confidence, but He is superior, He is holier. He is a *personal* God, these inferior things upon which we rely are impersonal. At the present time the churches of Britain are struggling to maintain themselves. Losses by death and removal to other districts are barely made up by conversions and additions to the membership. Almost every night of the week some small organization of the church is meeting in some small hall, barely existing. The experts have been called in. Advice has been given. Books and pamphlets have been read and digested and discussed and the methods advocated applied to the situation. Still the drift goes on. Is it not time we took to heart the picture Micah presents of the conquest of Christ! Forsaking our reliance upon material aids and coming to the position of the early New Testament Church, who had none of them, we might well become a spiritual Church, and filled with the Spirit of Pentecost go on to reach the unsaved masses in the power of Christ.

WARS AND RUMORS OF WARS

Nahum 2

Nahum is reminiscent of Jonah, for the message of the prophet Nahum was directed against the same city one hundred years later. Perhaps an abbreviation of Nehemiah, Nahum means "Full of Comfort" and yet the theme of his prophecy was "The Wrath of God." "Doom" is the key word and the key text is 1:3.

Nineveh was almost impregnable at the time of Nahum, but by the second century after Christ nothing remained of it. Such was the judgment of God upon a once repentant city now unrepentant. Nineveh had repented of her repentance! Divine wrath follows upon Nineveh's change of heart and the prophet uses seven different words to describe this aspect of the divine character that is hardly ever preached about today.

The following is an outline of the book.

    I.   Divine Judgment Declared (1)
   II.   Divine Judgment Described (2)
  III.   Divine Judgment Defended (3)

Our "famous" chapter is therefore the middle section or pivot point of the whole book. The divine judgment upon sinful Nineveh is described in detail and can be given in this form:

    I.   The Siege of the City (verses 1-6)
   II.   The Sack of the City (verses 7-10)
  III.   The Scuttle of the City (verses 11-13)

The vice of Nineveh demanded the vengeance of God. So the demoralizing of cities, countries and empires has always been dealt with by Almighty God. Men and nations who persist in evil, people and governments who persist in vice or oppression, must ultimately come under the judgment of God. Proud empires in the past have passed away because at the heart they have become morally rotten. God has allowed them to be defeated in battle, sometimes by a much smaller foe, because of their moral corruption. History is one long account of wars and rumors of wars, "man's inhumanity to man," because of national corruption. Such is the story of Nineveh.

I. The Siege of the City (verses 1-6)

The first verse of the chapter is called by Matthew Henry "an alarm of war sent to Nineveh." The Assyrians are besieging the city and the Ninevites must prepare for the worst. Their instructions are three-fold: "keep the munition," that is "Guard the defenses," look after the watchtowers and armories; "watch the way," or "Set a guard on all the city's approaches"; and "make thy loins strong," that is, "Be brave, have courage." The loins for these ancient people were the center of physical and moral strength as the heart was the seat of the emotions. The result of obeying these instructions would be that *all* their powers, mental, moral and material would be harnessed for stout resistance—but it would all be in vain, Nineveh would be destroyed. Nahum's instructions to Nineveh have all been given with sarcastic mockery for he knows that the judgment of God is upon the city for her wickedness.

The reason for Nineveh's coming defeat is given in verse 2: pride! The "excellency" or pride of Jacob and Israel has been dealt with, so now the pride of Nineveh.

Now follows a description in detail of the terrors of the siege. Here is a battle scene of loud noise and garish colors, red shields and cloaks, chariots carrying lighted torches in the early morning half-light, and the rumbling of the chariots' wheels can almost be heard, accompanied by the shouting of the soldiers. The red shield is sometimes said to mean "No quarter will be given." Red has always been a military color, until the introduction of khaki, and probably it best describes the bloody nature of war. The shaking of the fir trees may mean the wooden shafts of the spears, made in that time of cypress wood.

The scene is now within the city itself. The chariots are rumbling along the built-up suburbs. There are so many that they jostle one another, getting in each other's way. Now the sun has risen and, shining on the chariots, they glint like huge torches.

The defenders in their haste to man the defenses fall over one another.

The enemy manage to open the sluice gates that drain the moats, so enabling them to crowd into the city to attack it. Finally the palace is "dissolved," that is, utterly cut off, surrounded. This may be a carrying-on of the result of the open sluice gates. The water from the moat floods into the city and surrounds the palace building, then, rising like a flood, carries it away.

Such then is the vivid and graphic account of the siege of Nineveh. How descriptive it is of the judgment of God upon sin, especially the sin of pride. God abhors pride and brings low the proud man or church or Christian institution. No wonder Dr. G. Campbell Morgan used to comment that "it is impossible to read this prophecy of Nahum without an almost frightening sense of awe." Nineveh was to be blotted out as a city and as a people. When a people become proud and set themselves up against God, then the wrath of God is aroused and He must punish and bring low. Pride is manifest in self-satisfaction, self-sufficiency, self-confidence—such was Nineveh, and such is the sin of the twentieth-century church with its reliance upon man, movements, organization—anything but upon the spirit of God.

The Assyrians have been described as a "savage and barbaric people, with a low moral standard . . . living in vulgar luxury." Such is the moral tendency of nations today and God will not allow it. In His own time and way He will bring low and utterly cast down those who are proud.

II. The Sack of the City (verses 7-10)

For a long while Nineveh has been a wealthy city. From many trade routes goods and gold have poured into the city as water into a reservoir. Now it is to be taken away—the city is to be sacked.

The queen, Huzzab (some commentators say she was looked upon as a female god), is led away with her attendants. She is treated with disrespect, stripped of all her ornaments and conducted out of the city with none of the usual courtesy and dignity accorded to royalty. Her attendants beat their breasts as a sign of their deep inward grief over such humiliation.

With the removal of the queen the people stampede, panic-stricken. They are compared with a huge tank of water pouring away when the sluice gate is opened, thus carrying on the picture of the enemy's torrential entry into the city. Here then is two-way traffic: the flood of the invaders followed by the flood of the retreating inhabitants of Nineveh. All calls, commands and appeals to stand firm are disregarded. Frenzied flight is the order of the day.

The besiegers now begin to sack the city. The stores of gold and silver become the spoil of the Assyrians. Articles of furniture are taken as well as the more convenient articles of jewelry. "The accumulated wealth of centuries is looted" (I.V.F. commentary). A few survivors, terrified and afraid, look upon the city "empty, and void, and waste." The Hebrew has been reproduced in two alliterative ways: void, vacuity and vacant, or blasted, blank and bare. The sacking of the city is complete.

What a lesson to an affluent society who puts such emphasis and importance upon money, riches and raiment, luxuries and "lolly." The love of money is the root of all evil. Here lies the secret of their pride —they have put their trust in wealth, in material advantages so-called. Now God has removed it and there is nothing left. Being driven from the city they have not been able to take it with them, any more than one who dies is able to take his money with him! How much better to have treasure in heaven, for "where the heart is, there is our treasure also." Neither moth nor rust can trouble our heavenly riches, they are safe there, deposited with Christ.

III. The Scuttle of the City (verses 11-13)

"Scuttle" is usually used of a ship, but from the dictionary it is legitimate to use it of walls and buildings and even situations. It can be used (Oxford Dictionary) of abandoning one's post in the face of danger. It may also be used of retreating in an undignified way.

In this final section then we see the city deserted and desolate. Like a lions' den forsaken by the lions, Nineveh is a thing of the past. Lions speak of royalty, the lion being a king among beasts. Once Nineveh was a royal city, a strong city, fearless and courageous. But she was also proud like the lion, and bloodthirsty and cruel. No longer will she be able to prey upon surrounding smaller nations for she is empty, abandoned. The city is silent—not a footstep is to be heard.

The key to this scuttling of the city is in verse 13—"Behold, I am against thee." Although the Assyrians were the instrument, it is God who has done this thing to Nineveh. The Assyrians were only the tool in God's hand. Founded upon force and cruelty Nineveh was dealt with in a divine way. God had destroyed her weapons of war and taken away her "messengers," her officials who exacted the tribute money that made her rich. Nineveh is deserted and lifeless, devoid of royalty and riches.

The scuttling was so efficient that "no second blow" (Dr. W. E. Orchard) was necessary. The swift decay of such former glory must remain a lesson to us. It must be a lesson to the nations of the world, proud of their materialism. It must be a lesson to the Church, proud of its scholasticism. It must be a lesson to the Christian, perhaps proud of his independence, the pride of neglect of God, His Word, His Church, His Day. Sometimes by our neglect of God we are, like Nineveh, repenting of our repentance; we are living as if we regret that we were ever converted! What other explanation can there be of the Christian's worldliness? If we are turning back to sins and pleasures, the past and companions that we once abandoned for Christ's sake, then we are repenting of our repentance and God is a God of wrath and conducts holy war against all such. "He will pursue his enemies into darkness."

FROM FEAR TO FAITH

Habakkuk 3*

The important theme of the Book of Habakkuk is, "Living the Life of Faith." "Justice" is the key word and the key text is 2:4 ("the just shall live by his faith").

A book with great literary appeal, Habakkuk is in dramatic form with conversations between God and the prophet, ending with a hymn and doxology that are still sung at the public worship in Jewish synagogues.

Habakkuk means "The Embraced One." Contemporary with Jeremiah, Habakkuk has been called "The Grandfather of the Reformation" in view of the key verse of the book. Beset by two spiritual problems, the troubled prophet retired to his watchtower and communes with God. He was living in times of violence and iniquity, contention and apostasy, and yet God seemed to be doing nothing! He did not even seem to be a prayer-answering God for Habakkuk had not learned that delays are not denials, and that "No" is as much an answer as "Yes." These two problems then we can call "The Problem of the Seeming Triumph of Evil" and "The Problem of Unanswered Prayer."

An outline of the book is this:

    I.   THE PROPHET'S PROBLEM (1)
        A. *God's Explanation*
        B. *Habakkuk's Affirmation*
   II.   THE PROPHET'S PROMISE (2)
  III.   THE PROPHET'S PRAYER (3)
        A. *Prelude*
        B. *Postlude*

This "famous" chapter then is the last main section of the book and can be given the following outline form:

    I.   SUPERSCRIPTION (verse 1)
   II.   THE PRELUDE TO THE PRAYER (verses 2-15)
        A. *The Pre-Eminence of Revival*
        B. *The Majesty of God*

* Much of the material for this chapter is taken from the author's book, *Faith's Glorious Achievement,* Three Studies in the Book of Habakkuk (Marshall, Morgan and Scott, London).

We entitle this chapter *From Fear to Faith*, for the prophet has now had a satisfactory answer to his two spiritual problems. He is no longer afraid of circumstances, of the future, of the triumph of evil; his faith is on a sure foundation. Problems and events are now seen within the sovereignty of God. What happens all around him he sees is part of the divine plan. History is seen as *His*-story. Habakkuk notes with A. C. Ainger centuries later: "God is working His purpose out as year succeeds to year." The prophet's discovery must be ours if in these troublous times in which we live we would live a life of faith, not fear.

I. SUPERSCRIPTION (verse 1)

"A prayer of Habakkuk the prophet." The man whose problem was once unanswered prayer is now seen to be a man of prevailing prayer. This chapter brings us around full circle.

"Shigionoth," the plural form of "Shiggaion," is the superscription of Psalm 7. Derived from a Hebrew word meaning "to wander," "ramble" or "stray," it describes the kind of music which accompanied Habakkuk's prayer. Dr. Martyn Lloyd-Jones describes it as "a prayer accompanied with music, neither mournful, nor joyful, but expressive of profound and strong emotion." This prayer then is almost a lyrical song because the prophet has found the solution to his problems. It is a great climax of communion, not an abstract meditation upon a certain situation.

At this point it is worth noting another musical term which will occur in verses 3, 9 and 13—"Selah," a word which need not be read aloud in the public reading of the Scriptures. This is the only occasion on which it is used outside the Book of Psalms. Some affirm that it means "Pay attention to this" or "Note this well." Jewish commentators accept it as a musical term, or a direction to the musicians to play louder, or to play alone as an interlude.

This prayer of the prophet was "upon" Shigionoth, that is, in the manner of a lyrical rhapsody, thus emphasizing the fervor as well as the faith of the prophet.

The prayer has pattern in it like so many Biblical prayers (Daniel, chapter 9, our Lord's prayer in Matthew 6 or Luke 11). In Habakkuk's prayer there is humiliation of self, exultation of God, confession of sin, intercession for others, adoration of the divine attributes and resignation to the divine will.

I. The Prelude to the Prayer (verses 2-15)

The prelude begins with a petition which we will call—

A. *The Pre-eminence of Revival.* Note that this is the only petition in the whole prayer! How fond we are of making our selfish needs known to God, saying, "Do this, give us that . . ." Many a church prayer meeting would become lively and fervent if those attending would follow the prophet's example and pray for one thing only. If we still want to talk then let us talk about God like Habakkuk and not about ourselves!

What a request! Since this is the only petition in the prayer it must be studied thoughtfully. "O Lord, revive thy work in the midst of the years." Is revival as pre-eminent in our thinking and praying as it ought to be? How many people pray for revival in a church prayer meeting? Many pray for evangelism and evangelistic enterprises. True it is that evangelism is the commission of the Risen Lord to the Church. Every day we are meant to be spreading the Gospel; on the other hand evangelism has largely failed to reach those "without the camp." Now revival depends on the sovereignty of God—He can send an awakening at His pleasure. When it comes it makes evangelism easier. It makes evangelism far less expensive. In revival there is no need for expensive publicity for God does it all, bringing people under the sound of the Gospel by the direct agency of His Holy Spirit.

We can organize evangelism. We can arrange for the Gospel to be preached on the next Lord's Day, or for a sustained mission in a neutral hall. But we cannot organize or arrange revival; we can only beseech the Sovereign God to send it when He wills. It is in times and situations when all else seems to have failed that we can expect God to pour out of His Spirit upon us in revival blessing.

Habakkuk saw that the only answer to the situation of his time was revival, the revival of God's own work. The terrible conditions prevailing threatened to engulf the prophet and his people. Suffering and calamity were on every hand. It was time for God to step in and do something. That is sometimes the beginning of revival—when we are prepared to confess our helplessness and tell God that our sole hope is in Him. In evangelism we pray, "Lord, prosper *my* work," or "Lord, bless Billy Graham"; in revival we pray, "Lord, revive *thy* work."

"Revive" here means "recover, repair, restore." Revival is thus a re-emphasis, a rediscovery or recovery of something no longer present. It is a revival of true religion, a re-emphasis of the "faith once delivered." Revival depends upon right doctrine and God has never yet been pleased to send a spiritual awakening through or upon one who minimizes the authority and inspiration of the Bible.

"Lord, revive *thy* work"—and since "we are his workmanship" then revival must begin with the individual believer. Habakkuk is a revived prophet praying for revival. There must be a revival *in* the Church before the Church can be used to bring revival *to* the world.

Passing from petition to adoration Habakkuk now describes—

B. *The Majesty of God.* The prophet appeals to God's majestic manifestation to His people when He gave the commandments to Moses on Sinai as a ground for praying for a further manifestation in revival blessing. God's glory for Habakkuk is unsurpassed. Surely the prophet takes this particular incident because it is connected with the Decalogue. Revival is not only dependent upon doctrine but upon obedience, our turning from waywardness and willfulness (II Chronicles 7:14).

C. *The Might of God.* Here is destruction and universal consternation. The God of revival is the God who controls nature, dividing the sea and arresting the course of the sun and moon. The children of Israel were powerless to cross the Red Sea but God made a way of escape. The Church today is "engulfed in the land, the wilderness (has) shut (us) in" (Exodus 14:3). Only the Lord's miraculous power can release us.

D. *The Mercy of God.* All God's mighty acts had mercy as their ultimate aim—the salvation of His people. In verses 13 to 15 are allusions to saving and delivering acts of God in the past, but "the mercy of the Lord is from everlasting to everlasting" and He has the spiritual welfare of His people at heart today.

III. THE POSTLUDE TO THE PRAYER (verses 16-18)

Habakkuk now addresses God in a spirit of resignation—

A. *The Resignation of Habakkuk.* "That I might rest in the day of trouble" (verse 16). Here is vivid language for a spiritual experience that came to the prophet, comparable with the convulsion in nature that he has been describing previously. Almost on the verge of collapse Habakkuk suddenly sees that his attitude is to be one of resignation, "resting" or "waiting calmly." Just as relaxation plays a part in the cure of certain mental and physical diseases, so resignation to the will of God plays an important part in the cure of spiritual sickness. We must not fight against God and His will but resign ourselves to Him, saying—

> Thy way, not mine, O Lord,
> However dark it be.

B. *The Rejoicing of Habakkuk.* "I will rejoice in the Lord." While we may only rejoice when things are going right Habakkuk learned, like Paul, "to rejoice in the Lord, always," amidst the devastation of war, famine and crop failure, and untold hardships. As Matthew Henry comments: "When all is gone his God is not gone." The prophet's secret is that he is rejoicing in the "God of my *salvation.*" True joy is not dependent upon circumstances, comforts, *things,* but upon the unchanging Lord and His eternal salvation which none can take away from us.

C. *The Recovery of Habakkuk.* Once a man bowed down by problems and difficulties Habakkuk has now recovered his spiritual equilibrium. He is again able to live the life of faith with poise. He uses vivid language to describe his recovery. Hinds were noted for their fleetness of foot. The prophet no longer dawdles along the King's highway, he is fleet of foot and travels with freshness. He can "outrun his troubles" (Matthew Henry).

"High places" may refer to the mountain haunts of the hinds or it might mean a highroad along which the prophet now marches triumphantly. Either concentrates upon the lifting up of the prophet to higher ground, morally and spiritually, away from his problems and nearer to his God.

Thus we leave the prophet Habakkuk: fully recovered, rejoicing in the God of his salvation. He has prayed and prayer is no longer a problem. He takes his troubles to God and resigns himself to await God's time and fulfillment of purposes. He knows that ultimately evil will not triumph over good.

IV. SUBSCRIPTION (verse 19)

The last sentence of the book is: "To the chief singer on my stringed instrument." Temple singing was antiphonal or responsive in character. The priests led and the congregation answered, accompanied by the Levites with their musical instruments. The Revised margin gives "Neginoth" for "stringed instruments." Coming from a word meaning "to touch," it was used for stringed instruments in general and not one (such as a harp) in particular. This superscription gave directions about the meter, and this subscription about the music.

Dr. G. Campbell Morgan once delivered a lecture called *The Music of Life.* He gave the lecture more than seventy times. In it he likens the life of man to an oratorio, beginning with infancy (Dolce) and ending with old age (Lento). The progress of Habakkuk from fear to faith has reversed the terms. Beginning slowly and heavily he has ended lightly and sweetly. There is now no discord between himself and God. Such is the true music of life, and only those living the life of faith can hear it, experience it and appreciate it.

DIVINE WRATH

Zephaniah 1

The Book of Zephaniah has been a battleground for the critics for decades. Zephaniah's words, expressions, terms and so on have been questioned and rejected. Suffice it to say that the conservative evangelical scholar can answer the liberal higher critic on all points and maintain the inspiration of Zephaniah.

Meaning "Hidden of God" (perhaps a reference to himself in 2:3), Zephaniah's theme is, "God's Intervention in History." Probably the great-great-grandson of King Hezekiah, he prophesied during the reign of Josiah, during days of religious revival. As he does not mention this revival we may assume that he was ministering to a tragic minority untouched by the revival. His message is one of stern denunciation (key text 3:17) and the key word is "jealousy." This is not the all too common emotion that transforms a heart or home into a hell on earth. This jealousy is the natural outcome of divine love, a love that will brook no rival. God expects His people to live in accordance with His will.

The following is a convenient outline of the prophecy:

    I.   THE PROPHET'S REBUKE (1)
   II.   THE PEOPLE'S REPENTANCE (2:1–3:7)
  III.   THE LORD'S RESTORATION (3:8–20)

Our "famous" chapter is the first main division of the book— "The Prophet's Rebuke" and can be subdivided as follows:

    I.   THE MAN (verse 1)
   II.   THE MESSAGE (verses 2-18)
       A. *Idolatry* (verses 2-5)
       B. *Indifference* (verse 6)
       C. *Intrigue* (verses 7, 8)
       D. *Irresponsibility* (verses 9-11)
       E. *Inertia* (verses 12, 13)
       F. *Iniquity* (verses 14-18)

We are living in days of much superficial religion. Superficial evangelism has resulted in superficial conversions. There is much superficial talk about "revival." It may be that the revival in King Josiah's reign appeared superficial to the prophet Zephaniah and so he delivers a necessary rebuke. What kind of man was this who dared to rebuke others?

I. THE MAN (verse 1)

Verse 1 is the superscription to the book as verse 20 of chapter 3 is the subscription.

The pedigree of this man whose message is marked by a sterner note of denunciation than his contemporaries is given in the superscription. Something which is unusual in the Old Testament is done —we are taken back four generations. The last ancestor named is Hezekiah, whom many affirm to be the king by that name. This would mean that Zephaniah was of royal blood and thus became the forerunner of others throughout the generations who have spoken against their own class of the nobility and royalty.

Then, too, Zephaniah has been described as the first of the Old Testament prophets to have a mind and message dominated entirely by eschatology (the doctrine of the Last Things). Certainly no other prophet has given us a more realistic picture, with so many detailed descriptions, of "the day of the Lord."

This man is therefore shrouded in mystery. We know nothing else about him from the Bible; all that we have is in the superscription of this book. Perhaps God has intended it so, for when the man, the messenger, is hidden, then we concentrate on and listen to the message. That is why the gospel preacher always prays, "Lord, hide me behind the cross; let Jesus only be seen." So Zephaniah, "hidden of Jehovah," withdrew into near-anonymity that his message might be the clearer for succeeding generations.

II. THE MESSAGE (verses 2-18)

Zephaniah's message was similar in content to his predecessors and contemporaries. A summary can be given in this concise form: God is the God of the universe. He is holy and righteous. He expects His people to live in accordance with His will. Rebellion must be punished (and will be punished) by direct divine intervention in human affairs.

Isaiah's sublimity and Hosea's eloquence do not rival Zephaniah's stern denunciation of the sinfulness of his generation. No wonder this prophecy inspired the old medieval hymn *Dies Irae* by Thomas of Celano (c. 1250)—"Day of wrath, on that day the world shall dissolve in ashes." No wonder we are constrained to entitle this "famous chapter" *Divine Wrath*. How this prophet and his stern message are needed in this twentieth century of superficial Christianity with the selfsame sins prevalent today as in the prophet's day. These sins Zephaniah rebukes in his message.

A. *Idolatry* (verses 2-5). Four different kinds of idolaters are listed in this section and terrible judgments from the Lord pronounced upon them. It is easy to find modern counterparts of the false worshipers. There are the Baal worshipers (verse 4). Baal means "Lord," "master" or "possessor." He was a Canaanite and Phoenician god represented by the sun. His female counterpart was Ashtoreth and was represented by the moon. Baal worship then was nature worship, and one commentary (Jamieson, Fausset & Brown) suggests that Baal worship corresponds with our scientific exaltation of nature, the elevation of scientific discoveries to the position of deity. Ultimate weapons, artificial satellites, moon rockets, man-controlled space craft—these are all tending to deify man. Almighty God who made the laws that permit these experiments and inventions is forgotten.

Then there were the "Chemarim" (verse 4) of Zephaniah's day. The derivation of the word is doubtful but many scholars suggest that in a verbal form it could mean "to be black." This may be a reference to the priests, clad in black, or with blackened faces because of their tending the altar fires. These were the priests of Moloch, a god of the Ammorites, a god to whom people sacrificed their own children. Our modern counterpart is surely the parents who sacrifice their children to the spirit of the age in which we live, allowing them freedom with no exercise of restraint. The phrase "to pass through the fire" was used of Moloch-worshipers. What fires our children and teen-agers are passing through today, fires of temptation—and no one can play with fire without being singed. Mothers who sacrificed to Moloch did so with tears and sobs, while flutes and drums played to drown the shrieks of the victims. How like our crescendo of sound, our modern "pop" music, each "group" louder than the next, a cacophony of sound that does not entirely hide the cries of those who have succumbed to the New Morality and found it to be the old immorality!

Then the prophet rebuked the worshipers of the "host of heaven upon the housetops" (verse 5). They were using their flat roofs as platforms for observing the moon and stars and burning incense to them. Astronomy, remember, is a science—the scientific study of heavenly bodies; astrology, by contrast, is superstition—the study of occult influence of stars on human beings and affairs. Today, otherwise intelligent people consult their papers and magazines to see "what the stars say" about their lives. This is idolatry, or rather *lunacy*, a word derived from the Latin *luna*, the moon!

Finally there were those who worshiped by "swearing to the Lord and Malcham." The margin was "to" and not "by." Malcham is another form of Moloch. These are those who profess with their mouths loyalty to God, but by their lives allegiance to an idol. These are those who want to "run with the hare and the hounds," who "want the best of both worlds." Like the Thessalonians they must turn "to God from idols to serve the living and true God."

B. *Indifference* (verse 6). The prophet now addresses two classes —the backslider and the unbeliever. There were those "that are turned back from the Lord" (corresponding with those that "did run well"— Galatians 5:7) and there were those who had not "sought the Lord, nor enquired for Him." Both classes were indifferent to the earnest and eloquent appeals of the prophet. His message did not seem to concern them. Thus today's society is characterized by the spirit of indifference to divine things, to the Lord's Word and His day.

C. *Intrigue* (verses 7, 8). A Jewish commentator uses the modern term "assimilationists" for those mentioned in verse 8, those "clothed with strange apparel." "Strange" means "foreign." They were wearing imported foreign clothes, surrendering their own distinctive national dress in order to make themselves more at one with neighboring countries. They were trying to ingratiate themselves, curry favor with, carry on an intrigue with these enemies of God—their aim being to bring foreign flavor into the worship of Jehovah. Such is the danger of church unity today. If we are not careful we shall be wearing the "strange clothes" of Rome. Some church leaders seem prepared to do this in order to give a semblance of ecclesiastical unity to the world.

D. *Irresponsibility* (verses 9-11). The prophet now speaks of those who "leap on the threshold" or "leap *over* the threshold," a reference to the sacredness of the domestic threshold of that time. The doorstep was the place of sacrifice. Excavations have revealed both human and animal sacrifices that had taken place upon the threshold of Palestinian houses. In a spirit of irresponsibility, house-breakers jumped over the threshold to ransack the house. They jumped over the threshold to avoid contact with the gods or to show their contempt for these deities. This had become proverbial in the time of Zephaniah and was used to describe any irresponsible "breaking and entering." Today we live in just such irresponsible days. Thugs hold human life very cheap and have no regard for property. They "slug" the lonely old lady in her village shop or the night watchman in his warehouse. With equal calmness they gun down the bank clerk.

E. *Inertia* (verses 12, 13). This crippling spirit is rebuked next by Zephaniah. He sees a certain class of people who are "settled on their lees" (verse 12). "Settled" means "solidified" or "congealed" and "lees" is "sediment." The prophet is using the picture of winemaking. After fermentation the good wine is poured off, leaving a sediment behind. If this sediment is allowed to remain then the wine would be syrupy and sickly. This was another proverbial saying indicative of a state of sloth, indifference and "the muddy mind" (G. A. Smith). Zephaniah applies it to the people of God who had become smug and complacent in their spiritual lives. Inertia, lack of effort, no power to act, was the mark of these people. "Enthusiasm," wrote Arthur James Balfour, "moves the world." Yes, and it moves the Church! The first two letters of Gospel spell "Go." But the sin of inertia has gripped the Church. The twentieth-century church is not enthusiastic in the field of evangelism or missionary enterprise.

F. *Iniquity* (verses 14-18) is also rebuked by the prophet. Various forms of sin have been rebuked by Zephaniah and he has specified them one by one. Now he used a word that embraces them all—"They have sinned against the Lord" (verse 17). The word is chā-tā" in the Hebrew, meaning "to miss" and thus to sin. The New Testament equivalent is *"come short* of the glory of God" (Romans 3:23). Twice later in this prophecy Zephaniah uses a word for sin which our translators have rendered by the word iniquity. The word must be used of the Church and the people of God today. We are "missing the mark"; we do not "love the Lord (our) God with all (our) heart, and with all (our) soul, and with all (our) mind . . . and (our) neighbor as (ourself)." While there is idolatry, indifference, intrigue, irresponsibility and inertia in our midst we are guilty of gross iniquity.

God, being righteous, must punish such sinful ways. Zephaniah paints in glowing colors "the day of the Lord" in this chapter. Dr. H. H. Rowley in *The Relevance of the Apocalyptic* points out that Zephaniah is not propounding a new idea when he speaks of this day of universal judgment; he is "merely gathering up into one great climax the many judgments the other prophets had foretold." Zephaniah emphasizes the rapidity of the approach of this judgment, and the impossibility of escape by the sinner. There is no escape from the wrath of God either by flight or concealment. Truly the prophet's message is a terrible one, and yet one that needs fearless telling forth by preachers today. Like Zephaniah and Paul we must preach "boldly . . . as (we) ought to speak" (Ephesians 6:20).

FALSE DISCONTENT

Haggai 2

"A small book of only two chapters by a little-known author who was born a slave." That just about sums up the minor prophecy, *Haggai*. The prophet's name means "Feast of Jehovah." Under Zerubbabel Haggai returned from captivity to his native land and became a prophet of the restored remnant of God's people. His task was to "hearten, rebuke, and instruct that feeble and divided remnant." Thus his heartening theme is, "Living in the Immediate Present" and his message is couched in plain, simple, businesslike, and at times curt language. "Consider" is the key word and again and again Haggai pulls his congregation up short with that word. The key text is 2:4.

When the prophet arrived in Jerusalem the work of rebuilding the temple had been at a standstill for about fifteen years. During a short ministry of four months Haggai delivered four sermons, urging the people of God to have done with idleness and indifference, depression and despondency and to be up and doing. Some were not working because they thought it was not the right psychological moment to begin; others refrained from working because the project did not seem spectacular enough; while a third section were wondering if they would get any personal renumeration out of it. All these attitudes are prevalent in Christian circles today—the Book of Haggai is as pertinent as the other minor prophets. Some were even not working because the future seemed uncertain!

Haggai sought to counteract these vain excuses in his prophecies, and the more so because he knew that although they were not working to build God's House, they *had* been busy building their own dwelling-places! No wonder it became a Hebrew proverb: "No Haggai —no Temple."

The following is an outline of this brief book:

    I.   First Sermon (1:1-11)
           A Word of Rebuke
    II. Interlude: The Work Begun (1:12-15)
    III. Second Sermon (2:1-9)
           A Word of Encouragement
    IV. Third Sermon (2:10-19)
           A Word of Explanation
    V.   Fourth Sermon (2:20-23)
           A Word of Promise

The "famous" Chapter under consideration therefore contains the last three sermons and deals with the various moods and attitudes of the people who threaten to prevent the accomplishment of the great work of rebuilding God's "house of prayer." The chief of these was *False Discontent*. Like a great many Christians these people thought too little of the work they were doing for God. The temptation is always that of belittling the Christian work we are doing by comparing it with something done by someone else, especially someone in the past, some notable, outstanding Christian personality.

We can divide up this chapter then in this way:

    I. Encouragement for—
        A. *Prince*
        B. *Priest*
        C. *People* (verses 1-9)
    II. Explanation About—
        A. *Defilement*
        B. *Disobedience*
        C. *Declaration* (verses 10-19)
    III. Promise of—
        A. *Power*
        B. *Preservation*
        C. *Preferment* (verses 20-23)

This chapter opens, and the first message is delivered, at a time when the crops have been poor and the people are despondent. Instead of it being a time of feasting and festivity, gladness and thanksgiving, it has become a time of retrospective comparison. The people are looking back to "the good old days." The prophet thus begins with a word of—

I. Encouragement (verses 1-9)

The sermon of encouragement is for prince, priest and people. Delivered in the seventh month, on the twenty-first of the month, this sermon coincided with the Feast of the Tabernacles.

A. *The Prince*. The prophet and preacher first addressed himself to Zerubbabel, son of Shealtiel, governor of Judah. To this man of royal blood Haggai says "Be strong" (verse 4). This word of encouragement is repeated for all three classes. In spite of their different stations in life and their different situations within the rebuilding project, they all need to be strong; they all need the same firm tenacity of purpose, the same consistency of character and conscientiousness in fulfilling their tasks. "Like Prince, like people" is the apt proverb at this point. If the ruler set the example then the people would be sure to follow. Then adds the prophet on behalf of his God: "For I am with you, saith the Lord of hosts." It is not human strength but divine that the prince can have. The companionship of God makes the most difficult of tasks seem easier and lighter.

B. *The Priest.* Joshua the high priest must also "be strong." If the prince, the earthly ruler, is to show an example of strength of character, then how much more must the religious ruler show spiritual strength. The same promise is for him—"For I am with you." If only the religious leaders of our day would see that spiritual strength must go hand in hand with political might or the force of arms. What a lead must be given to rulers and peoples by those who profess to serve the Church of the Living God!

C. *The People.* The same exhortation and promise is given to the people, but one extra word of encouragement as well—"and *work*"! The prince must direct operations, that is his responsibility; the priest must surround the project with prayer and care for the spiritual welfare of ruler and people, but the people themselves must work, carrying out the ruler's orders. There must be no excuses for idleness or slackness. His exhortation is not to talk, but work. At that time they were wasting time talking, holding an inquest on the greater glory of the first temple and the impoverished building they were now erecting. By comparison it seemed to be nothing. They were to have done with odious comparisons and time-wasting reminiscences and get to work, and work until the job was completed, for it is "this house," that is God's house, the house of prayer. God promises that the "glory of the latter house shall be greater than that of the former." The importance of the building is not its outward architectural beauty but its inward witness and ministry. "In this place will I give peace," promised God. Outward beauty only satisfies mind and eye; inward beauty will satisfy heart and soul and spirit. The deep-seated spiritual needs of men will be met within its walls. How true it is that in architecturally ugly mission halls, and in the plain "meeting houses" of the nonconformists, men's spiritual needs have been met as surely as in any lofty and stately cathedral.

Perhaps some were idle and critical because there seemed to be a lack of money and in their eyes materials seemed skimpy. At any rate Haggai emphasizes that "the silver and gold is mine, saith the Lord of hosts." "Can we afford it?" is all too frequently the question of Christian people. Missionary endeavor and evangelistic enterprises are restricted because God's people do not take their stewardship seriously and so release the necessary money for the forwarding of God's work. God is able to "shake the heavens" and "shake all nations" (frequently a figure of speech in Hebrew to denote great political or social changes) in order to enrich His house. He can touch the stoniest heart and open the most stubborn purse.

II. EXPLANATION (verses 10-19)

The message of explanation is about defilement, disobedience and declaration.

Two months have now elapsed and the work has been proceeding satisfactorily. But they are again asked to "consider" their ways in order that a renewal of love for God will result in a renewed zeal and zest for His house.

A. *Defilement.* God now instructs Haggai to interrogate the priests regarding their knowledge of the laws of cleanness and uncleanness. Perhaps during the years of exile they had forgotten these laws as some young Christians today forget others of God's laws when they go away from home to study at university or take up their profession. The divine laws regarding Sunday observance are usually the first to go by the board.

Haggai's object lesson to the priests (verses 12, 13) may be summed up in a sentence: "Uncleanness has a more infectious power than holiness." The prophet's contention is that something holy merely renders holy whatever it touches, but something unclean contaminates to a far greater extent, it contaminates not only one person, but everyone else whom that person touches. The transmitting power of impurity is greater than the transmitting power of holiness! The sinful person more easily taints the righteous person than the holy person the sinner! Thus the slothful, idle, apathetic workers were greatly infecting the zealous with their spirit of indifference; the zealous and enthusiastic ones were not infecting the idle.

In a certain factory where a deadly poison was used (cyanide of potassium) the chemical worked its way down through the floor into a grocer's shop below. Ultimately it permeated the stock and the goods had to be taken away and burned and the shop completely renovated. In that shop was soap, disinfectant, detergents, and so on, but they did not infect the small factory above; it was the poison that infected the shop. There are sins, unclean words and habits that infect others with whom we come into contact. How carefully we ought to live so that we neither infect nor become infected.

B. *Disobedience.* In verses 15, 16 the prophet reminds the people that before they started building they had been disobedient to God and had failed Him. They had delayed to build when the command to build had come. Verse 17 describes the punishment, the divine judgment upon them for their disobedience, and in spite of the hardships involved they were unprepared to obey Almighty God.

C. *Declaration.* Haggai explains the divine declaration regarding future prosperity. He prophesies that now they have ultimately begun to work their future is assured. A good harvest is promised; material benefits frequently accompanying spiritual blessings in the economy of God. Disobedience resulted in pollution and poverty; obedience will result in possession and prosperity which is the general theme of the fourth and last sermon by Haggai, delivered on the same day as the previous one.

III. PROMISE (verses 20-23)

Once more the prince and ruler of the people is addressed, and the theme of divine optimism remains. The prophet lists a process of events that speak of power, preservation and preferment.

A. *Power.* Once again the word "shake" is used. This time it is the present continuous tense. Haggai is reminding the people of what God is already doing for them before their very eyes in the "shaking" of the Persian Empire. Then Haggai turns to the future and gives the prince a vision of other heathen kingdoms that will totter and fall before the power of God. As the Inter-Varsity commentary points out, the "*I wills* are arresting—I will overthrow . . . I will destroy . . . I will take . . . I will make" (verses 22, 23). The power of the omnipotent God is going to be revealed on behalf of His people. But notice, God uses human instruments—this power will be exhibited through Zerubbabel.

B. *Preservation.* While all these heathen powers are destroyed, God's true throne for His people will be preserved. Zerubbabel as a true descendant of David will ascend the throne, being given a position of great authority. This is more than preservation, it is—

C. *Preferment.* Zerubbabel will be as "a signet," a valuable and precious ring, in the eyes of the Easterner a sign of precious possession and kingly authority. Zerubbabel will be raised to a position of noble succession and his people with him. All this promised blessing is a result of the prince, the priest and the people becoming obedient to the will of God and doing the work of God. This is true New Testament teaching, that when we seek first the kingdom of God then other things are added to us. If God is put in the life of a nation, then that nation flourishes, for "righteousness exalteth a nation." If God is put first in civic affairs then that town or city flourishes, for "righteousness exalteth a nation." If God is put first in civic affairs then that town or city flourishes as a community. God first in the life of the Church and that fellowship flourishes with spiritual blessing, in evangelism and in being built up. If God is placed first in the life of the individual then the individual flourishes; he has a vital and glowing testimony to give to others. There is no need for false discontent, a sighing for the "old days." The present and the future can be more glorious than the past as long as we are obedient to the commands and will of God. And the secret of it all is to give true honor and respect to the house of God, the house of prayer. We neglect that to our peril.

THE SECRET OF STRENGTH

Zechariah 4

The Book of Zechariah contains a visional account of the history of Israel up to the time of their complete restoration and has been called "the Apocalypse of the Old Testament." "Consummation" is thus the key word by which to remember the book's message and its abiding theme is, "The Keeping Power of God."

Haggai and Zechariah were contemporary and Zechariah's prophecy is complementary to Haggai's. Part of their commission was to be outspoken against idolatry and wickedness among God's people.

Zechariah ("One whom God remembers") saw ten visions and these all contribute to the central theme of the book and inspired God's people to take heart and have hope for a brighter future. The key text illustrates the keeping power of God: "He that toucheth you toucheth the apple of his eye" (2:8).

An outline of Zechariah is as follows:

    I.   God's People and God's Temple (1—8)
        A. *Visions*
        B. *Fasts*
        C. *Feasts*
   II.   God's King and God's Kingdom (9—14)
        A. *Restoration*
        B. *Rejection*
        C. *Victories*

This "famous" chapter, *The Secret of Strength,* comes in the first main section and contains the fifth vision granted to the prophet. The following is an outline of the chapter:

    I.   The Vision (verses 1-3)
        A. *The Candlestick*
        B. *The Olive Trees*
   II.   General Interpretation (verses 4-10)
        A. *Obstacles*
        B. *Resources*
  III.   Particular Explanation (verses 11-14)
        A. *Spirituality*
        B. *Continuity*

For centuries now the Christian Church has tried to recapture the strength of the Early Church, those believing people who "turned the world upside down." Scholasticism has been tried and literary counterblasts to atheism and modernism have been issued by the evangelical press—this has been an emphasis upon an appeal to *reason*. Organization has been resorted to and the Church and its societies have been "geared" to meet the times. Modern scientific aids, visual and audio, have been harnessed to the work of the Church. The current "hobbyhorse" is organized unity in the sense of uniformity—a world-wide Church, visibly united, to speak to a world divided about so many problems. But none of these schemes has proved successful; none of them has been a discovery of God's secret for strength. The failure has been a forgetting of the fact that "the weapons of our warfare are not carnal." We are engaged in a spiritual struggle and the secret of victory is reliance upon spiritual strength. In this fifth vision the prophet gives us "a representation of ideal Israel" (G. Campbell Morgan). This then is the pattern for the ideal new Israel, the Christian Church. "The principles apply to the Church equally with Israel" (Campbell Morgan). What is offered to Israel in this chapter is at the disposal of the Church today.

I. The Vision (verses 1-3)

It is important to note the manner in which this fifth vision was given to Zechariah—the interpreting angel roused him from sleep (or perhaps a prophetic trance) with the question, "What seest thou?" The prophet may have been so impressed by the previous vision that he went to sleep thinking about it. At any rate he is awakened in order to take note of the new vision. He saw two principal objects, a candlestick and two olive trees (taking the latter for our purposes as one visionary object).

A. *The Candlestick*. This was of gold, with a central bowl or receptacle for the supply of oil or fuel. It was a seven-branched candlestick, each branch a kind of feed-pipe, branching out from the central stem. This stood for the community of Israel (or the Church for us). It also stood for the divine presence, the "eyes of the Lord that run to and fro through the whole earth" watching over His people. A further reminder is that the people of God are to be a light to the entire earth. This function, however, could only be performed as the Church remained in communion and fellowship with God's Holy Spirit, the energy and illumination of the Church. Thus Zechariah further sees—

B. *The Olive Trees*. These stood one on either side of the candlestick and fed it continuously with oil. The importance of the olive trees is this: the lamp was supplied with fuel *without human labor*. There was no fetching and carrying, pouring and mopping-up. Besides that the supply of oil was *inexhaustible*—the supply never dried up, there was no shortage of fuel. How we imagine in Christian work that it all depends on us, what we say and do! We should be more ready to "Stand still and see the salvation of the Lord"—standing back seeing God at work.

II. GENERAL INTERPRETATION (verses 4-10)

In this section the interpreting angel tells the prophet of the overall significance of the vision. It is an illustration of a message to Zerubbabel, the builder of God's temple. And it concerned *obstacles* and *resources*.

A. *Obstacles.* There seemed to be so many drawbacks and set-backs, so many mountainous obstacles to be surmounted by the temple builders that human might and power seemed totally in-adequate for the task. These obstacles are hinted at here; they are listed more fully in the Book of Ezra. There were political obstacles and there were defeatist discouragers who looked upon the work as "the day of small things." These obstacles which appeared like huge mountains were to be leveled out and become as a plain.

B. *Resources.* Zerubbabel's resources were divine, not human, spiritual not material—"Not by might, nor by power, but by my Spirit." "Might" is the word for collective strength, that is, reliance upon armies and allies. "Power" stands for individual strength, outstanding individuals of great influence or with great wealth, learning and ex-perience. Neither of these is Zerubbabel to rely on but upon God's Spirit, the third Person of the Trinity. The Holy Spirit could give Zerubbabel guidance, energy, enthusiasm, insight, illumination, and much more. God promises Zerubbabel, and His Church today, un-limited strength, a continual anointing, a much-needed infilling, that His work might progress and glory be brought to His holy name. As the lamp in the vision provided continuous light, supplied by the olive trees, so God's Holy Spirit is available at all times. The tragedy of this generation is that we seem to expect an outpouring of the Spirit on *special* occasions. He is available all the time for our regular work and witness.

III. PARTICULAR EXPLANATION (verses 11-14)

After receiving the angel's general interpretation, the wider sig-nificance of the vision, Zechariah desired to know about one specific feature, the two olive trees. They stood for *spirituality* and *continuity*.

A. *Spirituality.* Oil in Scripture stands for the Holy Spirit. Again and again in the Old Testament the anointing oil used at the installa-tion of priests, stands for the communication of the Spirit of God. The same figure of speech is used of the coronation of kings. Outwardly and physically the Eastern oil enlivened and freshened the body; inwardly it stood for a plenitude of grace, a deep spirituality that accomplished things connected with God's glory.

The oil in the vision was "golden oil," that is, it may have looked golden as it lay in a golden bowl and flowed from golden pipes. Being *olive* oil, it naturally had a slightly golden look. Gold stands in

God's Word for purity and splendor. Thus "the two anointed ones," Joshua and Zerubbabel, representing the priestly and regal offices, were to be spirit-filled men, pure, full of divine splendor. So the Church of God today is to be a clean channel through which the Spirit of God can flow to accomplish His work of conviction and conversion.

> Jesus, fill now with Thy Spirit
> Hearts that full surrender know;
> That the streams of living water
> From our inner man may flow.
>
> Channels only, blessed Master,
> But with all Thy wondrous pow'r
> Flowing thro' us, Thou canst use us
> Ev'ry day and ev'ry hour.

B. *Continuity.* These two olive trees were, according to the Jews, growing and bearing fruit. That stands for the continuity of the witness, the continuing Church through the ages. "The lamps fed in this manner would never go out for lack of oil" (I.V.F. commentary). Many men have tried to stamp out the Church in history; many have predicted its downfall and destruction. It may have been driven underground in certain countries from time to time, but the Church of God can never be defeated while this vision and prophetic message remain in God's Word which is "eternally settled in the heavens." As blessings were communicated to Israel through Joshua and Zerubbabel so blessing is constantly communicated to the Church by the Spirit and by the Head of the Church even Jesus Christ—He is both Priest and King, Joshua and Zerubbabel.

How we must apply this individually. If we are to be "lights in the world," continually, constantly, then our lamps must be kept burning with the oil of the Holy Spirit. Men may see our zeal and admire us, our enthusiasm and envy us, but unless they feel our spirituality, through our close communion with the Comforter, they will not be convicted by righteous lives and loving lips.

THE UNCHANGING GOD

Malachi 3

"The Sin of External Observance Without Internal Experience" is the abiding theme of Malachi. The prophet is unknown for Malachi merely means "messenger." He leaves us in no doubt whatsoever as to the spiritual declension of his times ("Declension" is the key word; key text, 3:10). God's people have declined morally, socially and spiritually, being guilty of fraud and oppression, unscriptural marriages with unbelievers, and profane sacrifices.

Three times the prophet tells his people that they have robbed God in tithes and offerings. They were giving *some*, but not *all* that was required. They were carrying on the "externals" of religion but there was no true inner experience.

An outline of the book can be given in this form:

  I. RELIGIOUS DECLENSION (1:1–2:9)
    The Lord's Love
  II. SOCIAL DECLENSION (2:10-17)
    The People's License
  III. MORAL DECLENSION (3:1–4:6)
    The People's Lapse

Chapter 3, our "famous" chapter, forms the major part of the third and last division of the book. In it we see how the people have so lapsed morally that they are robbing God of His due. But if they remedy this great defect then great blessing and prosperity will follow, for God is an unchanging God and will fulfill His promises. He will send a Messiah. He will Himself minister to His people, urging them, judging them, and then blessing them. That is always His method for His nature, character and attributes are unchangeable.

The chapter can be divided in this way:

  I. DIVINE INTERVENTION (verses 1-6)
    A. *The Judge*
    B. *The Judgment*
  II. HUMAN INGRATITUDE (verses 7-12)
    A. *Tithes*
    B. *Offerings*
  III. SINFUL IMPATIENCE (verses 13-15)
    A. *Defiance*
    B. *Disregard*

IV. Sovereign Inscription (verses 16-18)
A. *Virtue*
B. *Vice*

I. Divine Intervention (verses 1-6)

"I will send" is better translated "I am sending." The implication is that God's intervention in human affairs is imminent. The day of judgment is near at hand and so the Judge is being sent.

A. *The Judge.* The Judge is described as "my messenger," the same word that is used for the title of the book—Malachi. It has been suggested that God meant Elijah, and our Lord quotes these words and identifies Elijah with the ministry of John the Baptist. The prophet Malachi is prophesying a revival of religion before the coming of the Messiah, and this occurred with John the Baptist.

Then Malachi goes on to prophesy the coming of the Christ— "and the Lord, whom ye seek, shall suddenly come to His temple." The Jews looked upon the coming Messiah as a King and a Judge Messiah. He is further described as "the messenger of the covenant," that is, the representative upon earth of the covenant-God and One who will deal with all who have broken the covenant. The covenant is the covenant of salvation through the blood. All who have not availed themselves of that divine redemption will be judged at the return of Christ to His temple.

B. *The Judgment.* Christ the Judge is coming to "purify rather than destroy" (I.V.F. commentary). His coming is like "refiner's fire" and "fuller's soap," a twin picture of the metal worker and the dry cleaner. From verse 5 it is seen that morality is to be judged as well as worship. Evildoers of all kinds will be exposed. The picture of the metalworker and the cleaner of clothes impresses upon us the care, skill, patience and thoroughness of the Judge. He will take time and trouble; He will pay due care and attention to detail; nothing will escape His notice; and as the dross is removed from the pure metal, and the stains from the clean cloth, so evil will be separated from righteousness. The process will begin with the priests, for "judgment must begin at the house of God," then the people will be dealt with.

Two graphic phrases are used of the judgment: "I will come near you to judgment" and "I will be a swift witness." "Near" is the divine answer to those who have been pouring scorn upon judgment, asking: "Where is the God of judgment?" "Swift" shows that He will *surely* come, and that God's time is not necessarily human time, and so the question "Where is the promise of his coming?" will be answered eventually, if not immediately. "Swift" is used in the sense of final overtake rather than immediate. Judgment will not be delayed for-ever.

The ratification of all this is in the declaration, "I am the Lord, I change not." God is an unchanging God. He may "wink" occasionally at our times of ignorance, but He is always righteous, holy and just, and He must eventually punish sin. He is always a God as good as His word.

II. HUMAN INGRATITUDE (verses 7-12)

In this section Malachi utters a strong call to his people to turn to the Lord in obedience to His commands and to observe His ordinances.

A. *Tithes.* The people have been robbing God by keeping back part of the tithes, giving Him but a portion and not all. "All the tithes" may suggest that the people have given up tithing altogether. That is especially true of certain sections of the Christian Church today. Christian work and witness is sorely restricted through lack of funds. Christian people do not honor the tithe as the Scriptural minimum of giving. "The tithe is the form of giving advocated in the Bible. All through the Old Testament, the principle of dedicating the tenth to God is taught. So much was it a part of the habits and customs of men of that day that in New Testament times it was taken for granted—something that simply was expected of men of integrity. Jesus expected it of men of God. He felt it was only when a man began to give above his tenth that he was showing real generosity" (Peter Marshall, *Mr. Jones, Meet the Master*). "Rob" is a forceful verb meaning "to take by force." To refrain from giving one's dues to God then is an act of violence against Him! No wonder He was sending His Judge to mete out justice!

B. *Offerings.* The above quotation from the late Rev. Peter Marshall includes the words: "only when a man began to give above his tenth" was he "showing real generosity." Some Christians are "sticklers" for tithing but they regard it as a maximum not a minimum. The tenth is required by law; under grace we then start giving. So under law they still had offerings after tithes were given. A Jewish commentary explains that here is meant the heave-offerings—a contribution to the priest as the tithe was a contribution to the Levites. The contribution to the Levite was one-tenth; that to the priest was estimated at one-fiftieth!

By giving both tithe and offerings the people could "prove" God, prove Him to be a God as good as His word. Give to God and He immediately blesses in abundant measure; it is as if the windows in heaven open and we have hardly enough room to contain all that He gives. The Hebrew can be interpreted: "He gives until there is no more need." And this is meant to be a witness to the heathen peoples round about: "All nations shall call you blessed." What a difference it would make to Christian giving today if we saw it as an act of witness to the non-Christian world. By giving to God He will prosper and bless us and the unbeliever will marvel at our giving and God's giving. If only the world could say of the Church as they say of certain philanthropic societies and charities—"How well they are supported and maintained financially." The Church's offerings should astound the world; instead of that most ministers would be ashamed to let the world know how little is given!

III. SINFUL IMPATIENCE (verses 13-15)

Malachi again reminds his hearers of their attitude toward God. It has been *defiance* and a *disregard* of His ordinances.

A. *Defiance.* The prophet repeats some of the defiant words that they have spoken. "Ye have said . . ." And their words have been "stout," that is "unyielding," "impatient," "insistent." Their defiant attitude has been: "Does real religious observance pay a dividend? Surely the wicked seem to prosper well enough without all these observances and ordinances!" The tense of the verb implies that they have split up into little defiant groups, discussing among themselves whether it is profitable to worship and serve God loyally.

B. *Disregard.* While they have been talking they have further disregarded worship and obedience to ordinances. They have, or a small faithful remnant have, "walked mournfully," that is, dressed in black, the sign of mourning. This remnant have fasted and sought God's face on account of His anger with His people, but the majority of them have failed to repent and have disregarded the very acts of spiritual worship that would have pleased God and turned His anger away from them.

III. SOVEREIGN INSCRIPTION (verses 16-18)

The final section of the chapter concentrates upon the faithful few, the remaining remnant that are true to God.

A. *Virtue.* They met together and spake together. Unmoved by the specious arguments of the unfaithful, the faithful continued to exhort one another and to seek God's face in prayer. They met in fellowship with the purpose of deepening that fellowship. And their names were "written before him," recorded in heaven because they "feared the Lord and thought upon his name." One day and "that day" here may mean "the day when I rise to take action" (G. A. Smith), the Day of Judgment. In that day the Lord will take this remnant to Himself as a peculiar treasure, a crown of jewels. They will be spared the judgment that will fall on the ungodly—spared as if they were the very sons and daughters of God, which indeed we are if we are saved by faith in the blood shed upon Calvary. The doctrine of the remnant runs right through the Old Testament and into the New. It is an encouraging doctrine for true Christians today as they look at the attempts to unite Christendom into one gigantic world Church, irrespective of creed or doctrine.

B. *Vice.* Jesus the Judge is coming to receive, recompense and reward the virtuous, the remnant who have continued faithful. But He is coming in judgment and with punishment for those still steeped in vice. He will "discern between the righteous and the wicked, between him that serveth God and him that serveth him not." If we do not serve God then we serve mammon; if we do not serve Christ then we serve Satan. We cannot serve two masters.

The final dealings of God with the wicked are set out in the next chapter and so lie outside the scope of this study of chapter three. Suffice it to say that the wicked shall be burned up like stubble while the godly shall be justified and healed. Virtue will be rewarded and vice will be punished.

> He will gather, He will gather
> The gems for His kingdom;
> All the pure ones, all the bright ones,
> His loved and His own.
>
> Like the stars of the morning,
> His bright crown adorning,
> They shall shine in their beauty,
> Bright gems for His crown.

CHRISTIAN CHARACTER—BEING
NOT DOING

Matthew 5

Matthew in his gospel presents Jesus Christ as King, portraying His "regality" (key word). The theme is, "The Coming of the Kingdom" (the phrase, "the kingdom of heaven" being used more than thirty times). In chapter 13 alone there are eight parables on the subject of the kingdom. At the close of the gospel we see written over the cross of Calvary: "This is Jesus the *King* of the Jews." Many Old Testament Scriptures are quoted to prove the point, the regality of Jesus of Nazareth. Dr. Graham Scroggie divides up Matthew's gospel into the person, purpose and passion of the King. We give a slightly more detailed outline of the gospel:

The King's—
  I.   BIRTH AND BAPTISM (1, 2)
  II. TESTING AND TEACHING (3-7)
  III. MIRACLES AND MINISTRY (8-20)
  IV. REJECTION AND RESURRECTION (21-28)

Our "famous" chapter is within the second main section, "Testing and Teaching," and forms part of our Lord's teaching ministry. The question is, to whom and for whom was this teaching (the Sermon on the Mount) given? There are several views held by a variety of scholars. Some say this famous sermon is Christian "socialism" and contains principles for everyday living for all the world, Christian and non-Christians, and that if applied to our social and international situation then the Golden Age would come and this earth of ours would be a fine place in which to live. This view became the "Social Gospel" of the Church which has persisted now for generations. Doing, not being, is the emphasis of the adherents of this particular interpretation.

Others interpret the sermon as legalism, an elaboration of the Mosaic law. The Beatitudes, however, deny this view for they go far beyond the requirements of the law of Moses.

For others dispensationalism has been the key by which to interpret the Sermon on the Mount. Holders of this view say that the sermon was for Jews of our Lord's time. They would not accept it and so it awaits the final establishment of the kingdom of God. It is not for this church age, but for the kingdom age, the millennium.

But we are specifically told that this sermon was for "disciples," and what our Lord urges in His sermon is again and again recommended to us in the New Testament epistles—it is for disciples of every age as Dr. Martyn Lloyd-Jones proves so satisfactorily in his commentary on the Sermon on the Mount.

In the sermon our Lord tells His disciples how they can live so that they will be seen as Christians wherever they go and whatever they do, although it is their Christian character, *being* that is of greater importance than *doing*.

An outline of the chapter is this:

I. SEEING AND SAYING (verses 1, 2)
II. BEING AND BLESSING (verses 3-12)
III. SALT AND LIGHT (verses 13-16)
IV. LAW AND GRACE (verses 17-48)
    A. *Letter and Spirit* (verses 17-20)
    B. *Murder and Contempt* (verses 21-26)
    C. *Marriage and Divorce* (verses 27-32)
    D. *Oaths and Perjury* (verses 33-37)
    E. *Retaliation and Self-denial* (verses 38-48)

I. SEEING AND SAYING (verses 1, 2)

"Seeing the multitude"—and how He saw them! Weymouth elsewhere translates "had compassion" as "He broke His heart over them"! If only Christians today saw the unsaved multitudes of London, New York, Moscow, Peking, Paris and other cities, towns and villages like that. No wonder our Lord withdrew to the mountain— such a sight of the sinful multitude drove Him to prayer. We must go to prayer before we go to the people in evangelism. While in the mount His disciples came to Him and He taught them. He had not long to live before the cross and He wanted, in the words of Paul to Timothy, "to teach others also."

He also "opened his mouth." What a lesson in elocution for preachers and those who pray in our prayer meetings! How shall the people hear unless we speak up? We must not forget the other side of the coin. There is the responsibility of hearing as well as speaking well. There are fifteen columns in a certain Concordance of words in Scripture for "hearing," but only six columns for "speaking." Some need to sit nearer the front in our large chapels; others need to move their seat away from a friend who distracts their attention.

II. BEING AND BLESSING (verses 3-12)

We study first the Beatitudes. Remember that they are the *Be*-attitudes and not the *Do*-attitudes. They sum up the kind of Christian character that results in the person being "blessed" or truly happy. There are various opinions as to whether we have seven, eight or nine beatitudes, seven being the perfect number, eight being a "divine octave" and nine being three times three, the number of the Trinity.

All Christians are meant to be like this "happy man." All believers in the Lord Jesus Christ are meant to manifest these characteristics—all of them, not some of them. They are all produced by an operation of the Holy Spirit upon the human heart.

The first characteristic is: "poor in spirit"—a fundamental characteristic (all others stem from this one). This is not, however, a commendation or recommendation to material poverty for the Christian. It is poor in *spirit*. Material poverty (which might well be the lot of the Christian) is no guarantee of spirituality. Neither does "poor in spirit" mean a retiring nature, and kind of Uriah Heep false humility. None of these *Be*-attitudes are *natural* attitudes, they are supernatural, spiritual attitudes. "Poor in spirit" is a consciousness of our nothingness before God, our complete and utter dependence upon Him for all things. It is reliance upon Him for all things necessary in the spiritual life. It is living by the motto: "He must increase and I must decrease."

Second: "they that mourn" (verse 4). Everything possible is done today to banish the spirit of mourning. Undertakers are now called funeral directors; death and burial are commercialized and made as "pleasant" as possible. But "mourn" here has nothing to do with physical bereavement and sorrow. This is spiritual mourning— a continual cry, "O wretched man that I am." It results from daily self-examination of the things of the spirit and a realization of our spiritual poverty. It means also a mourning over the sins of others as we listen to news bulletins and read the newspapers. The Saviour "wept" and "groaned in the spirit" over Jerusalem. Doing that we become blessed of God for it brings us into His presence with repentance and so we find peace through Jesus our Saviour. Serious, solemn, sober-minded we might be, but not miserable, moody or morbid Christians.

Third: "the meek" (verse 5). Not flabby milksops, spineless Christians, but a complete absence of pride, no reliance upon the cult of the personality like film stars; none of their self-assertion or personal aggressiveness in dress. The meek man does not worry what others think of him; he is only too amazed that God thinks sufficiently of him and deigns to save him. Ceasing to worry about his position or reputation he will one day inherit the kingdom and reign with Christ.

Fourth: "hunger and thirst after righteousness" (verse 6). Not hunger and thirst after the blessedness, the promised happiness, but after righteousness. This word underlines the correctness of our interpretation, that these "attitudes" are spiritual and not natural, for we have no natural righteousness (that is as "filthy rags"). This is a thirst after being in a right relationship with a righteous God, a desire to be rid of every sin and barrier that would prevent such a relationship. How few Christians have such a hunger and a desire! So few have any sort of spiritual appetite for God's Word, God's house, God's day. It means, of course, that we engage in nothing worldly that will blunt the spiritual appetite.

Fifth: "merciful" (verse 7). This is a term that is applied to God Himself. It is far more than the human attribute of pity or showing mercy. On God's part it is active kindness toward those legally in His power, illustrated by the text: "God was in Christ reconciling the world unto himself" (II Corinthians 5:19). What an ideal of mercy we have to attain to therefore!

Sixth: "the pure in heart" (verse 8). The world sometimes glibly states: "To the pure all things are pure," or "Evil be to him who evil thinks," thus relating purity to the mind. In this beatitude it is related to the heart, "the essntial being" (I.V.F. commentary). Such purity can only be obtained by receiving the new birth. The result is seeing God now, by faith, and then one day, in glory, face to face.

Seventh: "peacemakers" (verse 9). This does not mean "peace at any price," or "anything for a quiet life." It means an active interest in bringing people into a peaceful relationship with God— "Peace with God through the blood of the cross."

Eighth: "persecuted" (verse 10). This is not so much *what we are*, but *what is being done to us by others*. The more we become like Jesus the more we shall be persecuted, either in mild form (those of us in the western world) or in the more severe forms of the Communist or Catholic countries. But this is our final proof that we are citizens of the eternal kingdom of God.

Ninth: "revile" (verse 11). Perhaps this is another form of the persecution spoken of in the previous verse. Well, if persecution takes that form then, like our Saviour, we do not revile again, we do not even resent it, we rather rejoice in it for we are following in a glorious train and going the way the Master went.

III. SALT AND LIGHT (verses 13-16)

After dealing with the individual's Christian character the Lord now reminds His followers that they cannot and must not live in isolation. Although no longer "of" the world we are nevertheless "in" the world. And it is a bad, contaminated, sinful world. It is a world that is steadily getting worse and not better. Christians then are to be like salt in society.

This metaphor of salt has frequently been misunderstood. Because we see salt on our tables in a refined form and use it to give certain foods flavor, we apply it like that to the Christian in a sinful world. But we do not want to bring out the flavor of the world. Salt is a disinfectant and a preservative. In the early days of medicine it was rubbed into open wounds to prevent their becoming infected. Meat and other kinds of food is "salted down," preserved for future use in salt.

Christians then are like an antiseptic in society, a preservative. We prevent society from becoming one hundred per cent rotten. We stop the complete decay of society through sin. In the non-Christian home, office, shop, factory, mine, wherever the Christian is placed, he flavors society with Christ and Christian principles, helping to prevent blasphemy, smutty stories, swearing, and all the rest.

The world is spiritually dark because of sin. Christians must be like light. As Christ is the Light of the World, so His followers are lights in the world. No one else can lighten the world's darkness, not the politician, the educationalist, the scientist, the philosopher—what a responsibility is placed upon the Christian then to be a lightbearer for Jesus.

What does light do? It exposes the darkness. Switch on the electric light in a dark room—the darkness has gone! Next, the light reveals things hidden in the darkness. Third, the light shows the way out of darkness. So the Christian does all that for the unbeliever in his darkness. And so the Christian Church becomes like a city on a hilltop—conspicuous for all to see, not useless like a candle hidden in an earthenware jar and placed under a bed.

IV. LAW AND GRACE (verses 17-48)

In this last and longest section the Lord turns from describing the individual Christian's character and defines the method by which we can reach His high standard. We do this by keeping His laws which are in harmony, which are a completion, a fulfillment of the Old Testament Scriptures.

A. *Letter and Spirit* (verses 17-20). Those who say that the Christian is no longer under the law but under grace and so need not tithe need to read and reread this section. Not one "jot or tittle" of the Old Testament commands shall be altered while time is and the world remains. God's laws are absolute and cannot be changed or modified. Our Lord therefore came not to change but to obey. He carried God's laws out to the very letter and then carried over the spirit of them into other spheres. How different from the Pharisees who kept the laws and then added a few "tittles of tradition" to make them burdensome, and in keeping law and tradition thought they were earning special merit with God. The Christian is obliged to keep the law, but it earns him no merit as regards eternal salvation. He is saved by grace, not by lawkeeping. The law is only a schoolmaster, a pointer to Christ. Lawkeeping is not merely refraining from murder, Sabbath-keeping, tithing—that is the letter of the law; it is keeping also the spirit of the law which our Lord exemplifies in the next section.

B. *Murder and Contempt* (verses 21-26). The law states, "Thou shalt not kill." Keeping the law to the letter means that we do not commit murder. Behind the act of murder is a motive. The motive may be hatred, jealousy, greed, and so forth. Thus we may murder in our minds without committing outwardly the act of physical murder. Resentment in the heart, a feeling of "I wish you were dead," is breaking the spirit of the law. The real sin is committed in the heart before the outward act takes place. The man who calls his brother "Raca" or "vain fellow" or "fool" is potentially a murderer for he is already killing in his mind. A feeling of contempt for others, especially others of the household of faith, is breaking the divine law. Contempt in one's mind leads to talk and criticism. Criticism is frequently the murdering of another's reputation.

The Old Testament commandments were all negatives (apart from the fourth commandment which begins with "Remember"). Jesus here emphasizes that the laws of the kingdom have a positive side. Gifts must be brought to the altar only after human relationships are right.

C. MARRIAGE AND DIVORCE (verses 27-32). The commandment says: "Thou shalt not commit adultery." Jesus emphasizes that adultery is more than the outward act; it can take place in the mind; we can be unfaithful in thought (that is why modern plays, posters, films, magazine covers, and so on are so dangerous—they are suggestive). Then Jesus spoke of another form of adultery that is all too common in the twentieth century, the marriage of a person with a divorced person, while the divorcèe is still living. At this point we must be very careful to distinguish between the law of Moses regarding divorce and that which the Pharisees added to it, and finally the true meaning of our Lord's words. Moses decreed that adultery was not grounds for divorce—the sentence for adultery was *death* not divorce! Divorce in Moses' time was permissible only if in marriage a man found a moral or physical defect in his wife. The divorced wife was then given a bill of divorcement to prove that it was *not* unfaithfulness. It was similar to our annulment. The same man and woman were then not free to re-marry. The emphasis was always upon the sacredness, the sanctity of marriage; it was not something to be walked into and out of lightly. But the Pharisees had their own interpretation of "uncleanness," and so they permitted divorce on many grounds. Our Lord gave but one ground for divorce and this has been greatly misunderstood—"fornication." Any good English dictionary will show the difference between adultery and fornication. Adultery is illegitimate sex relationships by married persons; fornication is illegitimate sex relationships by unmarried people. Now we must understand the differences between Eastern and Western marriage customs. "Wife" is a word that is used in the Bible of a woman who is married and also a woman who is "betrothed." In the East a betrothal is as serious as marriage itself, and as legally binding. Joseph, for example, was betrothed to Mary. When the angel assured Joseph that Mary had not committed fornication, that she had not had illegitimate sex relation-

ships during the betrothal period, then he did not "put her away priv-
ily." Our Lord's use of "divorce" then was a legal end to a betrothal
period for premarital unchasity, not the divorce of a married person
for unfaithfulness. It is significant that in Mark's gospel (believed
to be the first gospel to be written) our Lord does not mention any
ground whatsoever for divorce. And today we live in times when
"incompatibility of temperament" is offered as suitable grounds for
divorce!

D. *Oaths and Perjury* (verses 33-37). God's Name is not to be
taken in vain. The holy Name was not to be used to back up a statement, to give it added authenticity. The Pharisees interpreted the third
commandment as meaning: although a man must not use God's Name,
or the name of the temple, he could use the gold of the temple. It is on
our Lord's answer to this interpretation that the Quakers and others
base their refusal to take the oath in a court of law. "Swear not at
all," said Christ. But our Lord Himself took the oath when on trial
before the cross. Paul took the oath. Our Lord is not here referring
to courts of law but to ordinary speech and conversation. We are not
to take the name of God on our lips to "back up" what we are saying.
Christians should be particularly careful in using such expressions as
"By Jove" and "For goodness' (for God's) sake." Often these slang
expressions are corruptions of the divine Name. As men of God our
word should be known as our bond, and our Yes as Yes and our No as
No. We should speak always as in the presence of God, so the non-
Christians would be able to trust all that we say.

E. *Retaliation and Self-denial* (verses 38-48). The spirit of revenge and retribution is prevalent within us all. We dislike being
wronged and slighted without seeking to avenge ourselves. The Old
Testament law declared "an eye for an eye" and "a tooth for a tooth."
It was legislation aimed at controlling excess. Shakespeare illustrates
it beautifully with Shylock and his "pound of flesh"—not an ounce more
was he to take. The spirit of the law of Moses was that when revenge
was taken it must be fair revenge. Our Lord here is not speaking to
the nations of the world, giving them principles for armament or dis-
armament, He is speaking to the individual believer. When wronged
we do not seek retaliation. We become willing to be doormats,
trampled under foot in order that the spirit of Christ in us might be
manifest. Far too many Christians are concerned about their so-
called personal insults and injuries. We do not "hit back," we endure
it for Christ's sake who was spat upon and insulted to the last degree.

Then the Saviour says that the Christian is not a man who
insists upon his rights. If a man is sued in court for his inner garment
then he relinquishes willingly his outer coat also. Required to carry
baggage for a mile by a government official, the Christian of his own
free will carries it a second mile. We do not stop at the law's exact
demand.

To sum it all up our Lord urges that we love our enemies. Then we shall be truly Godlike, for He loves the rebel—unreconciled sinners at enmity with Himself. Our attitude toward others does not depend on what they are, but upon what we are by God's grace, and upon what they might become by that same grace. How much easier it is to be "nice" to "nice" people, but the Christian is one who can love the unlovely. As we do this we become more and more spiritually mature, even as our Father in heaven is perfect. The Christian is thus a unique person for he is in a unique relationship with God.

CHRIST'S SOCIAL GOSPEL

Mark 10

Mark portrays Jesus as Servant, emphasizing His humility. He does not begin with our Lord's birth and genealogy for this is a vivid, active gospel; it is the Servant at work, ministering to others not being ministered to. And the Servant's greatest work or service was on the cross of Calvary. The key text of the book comes within the verses of this "famous" chapter (10:45). The key word is "humility" and the theme, "The Suffering Servant."

An outline of Mark's gospel can be given in this form:

THE SERVANT'S—
    I. PREPARATION OF SELF (1:1-13)
        Baptism and Temptation (Water and Wilderness)
   II. MINISTRY TO FELLOWMEN (1:14–10)
        The Galilean Ministry
  III. SACRIFICE FOR MANKIND (11-16)
        Journey to Jerusalem (Cross and Consummation)

Chapter 10 then is the final chapter in Section II, Christ's ministry to His fellow men, and we entitle it *Christ's Social Gospel*.

For too long a time evangelicals have been afraid of what is called "the social gospel." Because certain theologians and preachers of the past (and there are still a great many today) have maintained that social work, the betterment of mankind's living conditions, is the be-all and end-all of Christianity; because these same men and women have implied that man can be saved by engaging in such social work, instead of by faith in the blood of Christ, evangelicals have gone to the other extreme and have largely forgotten the social implications of the Gospel. The result has been the dulling of what used to be called "the Nonconformist Conscience," and the lack of preachers and prophets with a flaming zeal for social righteousness. The New Testament emphasis is that the Gospel ought to permeate every aspect of the believer's life. Salvation is not of works, but by faith. After salvation, however, the believer must see that his influence is brought to bear upon all the social evils of the time. This has always been an outcome of evangelical revivals.

Here then in this "famous" chapter we have our Lord dealing with some of the great social questions of his time, such as divorce; and with some of the great people of His time, a rich young ruler. Here he is concerned with the children and with the blind.

Our outline for the chapter is this:

    I.   Marriage not Divorce (verses 1-12)
   II.   Blessing not Christening (verses 13-16)
  III.   Faith not Works (verses 17-31)
  IV.   Humility not Prominence (verses 32-45)
   V.   Sight not Blindness (verses 46-52)

We begin with a link with our previous "famous chapter," Matthew 5:

I. Marriage not Divorce (verses 1-12)

When studying Matthew 5 we saw that society in the time of Jesus had found easy excuses for divorce. Here (verse 12) we see that women were separating themselves from their husbands and not even the law of Moses had allowed for that. What Jesus does is to go back beyond the law given to Moses to God's original intention, that is, that the marriage union was sacred, God-ordained, and therefore unbreakable. Since sexual relationship constitutes marriage (a man and woman becoming "one flesh") and not a civic or church ceremony, it is clear that a man and woman belong to one another after sexual union whether that union occurs before or after wedlock. For this reason there can be no second marriage while the first partner is alive for that would be adultery.

The Roman Church and, in the main, the Anglican Church knows where it stands regarding marriage, divorce and remarriage. In nonconformity it is a case of "every man for himself." Some ministers will remarry the so-called "non-guilty party," others will not. The issue is quite clear here from the teaching of our Lord Himself. We dare not preach a message of reconciliation on Sundays and then be prepared to condone separation between a man and woman on weekdays.

After marriage it seems to follow naturally that our Lord should deal with children:

II. Blessing Not Christening (verses 13-16)

Those of Baptist persuasion must, in love, agree to differ from their evangelical brethren who christen babies. But whether we "christen" or "dedicate" babies neither side can appeal to this particular passage for evidence or proof that their practice is right. Here is a simple and sublime incident which many have made complex and controversial.

The women who brought their children to Jesus are not defined as being privileged or poor. Perhaps they were ordinary women in the crowd who wanted a good, kind man, a Teacher, to put His hands on the head of their children and bless them (a common enough custom in those days, reminiscent of Jacob in Genesis 48:14). Some commentators maintain that Jesus was still in the house (verse 10) and these children merely came to Him to say "goodnight"). The disciples, perhaps from good and well-meaning motives, tried to prevent their Master being besieged. Obviously Jesus was "displeased" with them and their attempts (verse 14).

Now notice what happened and what was said. At a christening service a baby is pronounced to be a child of God and a member of God's kingdom. Jesus only said: "*Of* such is the kingdom of God." Then He proceeded to explain that any adult person who wanted to enter His kingdom must do so like a small child, on the basis of childlike trust. Some have said that these children were innocent and humble and that is how we inherit the kingdom. However most children are not innocent and humble, but sinful and precocious. Our Lord's emphasis is solely upon the child's ability to trust and be dependent on others. The word here is "young children," not babies. And while the Baptist can support his service of Infant Dedication or Presentation from Scripture (Mary and Joseph presenting Jesus in the temple, for example), he cannot justify it from this passage we are studying. It was an act of blessing; perhaps He spoke words of encouragement to them or prayed over them. We do not know. We only know that it was an act of blessing, not a baptism, christening, dedication or presentation as we know them in the Church today.

The way into the kingdom is further explained in the next section:

III. FAITH NOT WORKS (verses 17-31)

At first sight it seems that in reply to the rich young ruler's question our Lord denied His deity and His goodness! On closer consideration, however, it is obvious that Christ was trying to impress on this man the fact that He Himself was God and therefore absolute goodness was embodied in Him and He alone was the source of eternal life. The young man came with a question of morality; Jesus lifted it to the higher plane of theology.

The next difficulty is that in His reply our Lord seems to be emphasizing doing, lawkeeping, as a means to obtaining life eternal. Again the closer look clears the matter up. The Ten Commandments can be divided into two main groups; four have to do with our relationship to God and six with our relationship with our fellow men. Jesus ignored the first four and dealt with the last six: adultery, murder, theft, perjury, fraud, honor of one's parents. Why did He do this? Because the ungodly man cannot keep the first four. The sinner cannot honor God's Name. So this man had only been able to keep the laws that covered human relationships. This did not automatically give him eternal life. Jesus then went right to the heart of the matter and told him that eternal life was dependent upon a one hundred

per cent committal to Christ. This man loved his riches, his possessions. They were the barrier keeping him from faith in Christ. Jesus
was not saying that all men must give up their earthly wealth in order
to become a Christian. Ours may be another hindrance or stumbling-
block or barrier to belief. Whatever it is, when God the Holy Spirit
reveals it, it must be given up.

Turning to His disciples the Lord explains salvation further.
Notice the use of "trust" (verse 24). The Christian life is a life of
faith. Trusting in possessions or good works, however, is a man-made
plan of salvation and is as useless as trying to thread a camel train
through a needle's eye, or, as some think it to mean, trying to get a
camel to pass through the small pedestrians' gate in the city wall.
The crux of the whole issue is in verse 27. A salvation plan that orig-
inates with man and depends upon man's efforts is useless. We need
a divine plan, initiated and carried through by God Himself. Because
of human sin there had to be divine intervention. Trying to lift up
oneself to God's level by doing good works is like trying to lift up
oneself by one's own shoelaces. God has stooped down from heaven
in the person of Jesus Christ to lift us up to heaven. What is a human impossibility has become a divine reality.

Having spoken of His kingdom and the way of entrance into it,
it now naturally follows that certain disciples should be concerned
with their place in the kingdom:

IV. Humility Not Prominence (verses 32-45)

In verse 24 Jesus had to call His disciples children because they
did not fully understand the way of eternal life. Now we see their
lack of perception once more. In verses 32-34 Jesus describes and
foretells His sufferings and death. All that two of the disciples could
think about was their final position in the kingdom. Would they have
due prominence, one sitting on either side of the Lord in glory? How
great is the danger for us all of being preoccupied with petty, personal
problems when bigger and more important things are happening and
demand our attention!

The other disciples seemed to disagree but perhaps they were
annoyed because they also wanted places of prominence and failed to
"get in first" with their request!

In verse 38 our Lord spoke of His "cup" and "baptism." Obviously
He was not referring to His water baptism in Jordan, for His disciples
would also have already undergone that rite. "To drink the cup" was
a phrase standing for affliction or punishment (see Matthew 26:39, our
Lord's prayer in Gethsemane). In the same way baptism was often
used to express the same idea of *overwhelming* affliction, being im-
mersed in the flood waters of sorrow (see Psalm 69:2). Thus Jesus
here prophesied that His followers would share in the same kind of
tribulation or persecution as He was to endure—but as to the promi-

nence they sought, that was not His to give. Indeed they should not desire it for had He not said in His Sermon on the Mount that "the meek shall inherit the earth"? Now He says that he who would be greatest must first be the greatest servant of others. They must take note of His own supreme act of humility—He came not to be ministered unto but to minister.

Again there is a natural transition. Having declared the fact that the Christian's aim is to be the servant of all, He set them an example by dealing with a blind man:

V. SIGHT NOT BLINDNESS (verses 46-52)

Bartimaeus was well-known. There is a definite article in some ancient manuscripts—"*the* blind man," the blind man known to passers-by. He was a man with a reputation. Perhaps his disease was a disfiguring one and he was very conspicuous. At any rate he was a beggar and yet our Lord deigned to help him. There is an interesting conjecture that this importance of detail in Mark's account is given because Bartimaeus became a prominent member of the Christian community as one of the "eyewitnesses" of the events of the following weeks, the sufferings, death, and Resurrection. In an apocryphal book called "The Gospel of Nicodemus" Bartimaeus appears as a witness for the defense of Jesus at His trial.

What are the other interesting details peculiar to Mark's record? First, the cheering words of the bystanders (verse 49). Then, the fact that Bartimaeus calls Jesus "son of David"—the first time that title is used in this gospel. It was a Messianic title and so is prophetic here of our Lord's public presentation as God's Messiah on the cross. Again, he cast off his garment (verse 50), thus emphasizing his faith in a cure. This was the outer garment that would hinder his running to Jesus. At the prospect of sight he wanted nothing to encumber him. What a parallel with the way in which a man or woman should come to Jesus for salvation, flinging away the garments of our own righteousness. Finally, "leaping up" (verse 50) or "rose" reveals the man's abandon and joy.

Note how our Lord questions the man in the same words as He had previously used to the disciples in verses 36 and 51. How often the unbeliever shows more discernment than the believer!

The chapter ends on the note that has been emphasized throughout: faith (verse 53). "Thy faith has made thee whole." Christening, baptism, dedication—these are not saving rites—we are saved by faith alone. Riches do not help a man get right with God, frequently they are a hindrance. Commandment-keeping earns no merit with God. Faith alone can bring spiritual sight as it brought physical sight for Bartimaeus. Faith alone can result in the bestowal of God's gift of life eternal.

LOST AND FOUND

Luke 15

Jesus Christ is portrayed as Man in the gospel according to Luke, His "humanity" (key word) being emphasized. He is seen as "The pattern of Perfect Manhood" (the theme). It is a universal gospel, in outlook and scope. Luke begins by tracing the descent of Jesus from the first man, Adam. He is then proclaimed to be the Second Adam. The following is an outline of the gospel:

I. BIRTH AND CHILDHOOD (1, 2)
II. BAPTISM AND TESTING (3–4:13)
III. BAND OF DISCIPLES (4:14–21)
     Galilean and Jerusalem Ministries
IV. BETRAYAL AND RESULTS (22–24)

The key text of the gospel is 7:34, which words are a criticism of our Lord's mode of life and ministry. For Christians the words can be taken as great commendation.

Our "famous" chapter comes within Section III and comes within the context of further criticism of our Lord. An outline of this chapter is as follows:

THE INTRODUCTION (verses 1, 2)
A. *Conduct*
B. *Criticism*
I. THE ACTIVITY OF THE SON (verses 3-7)
A. *His Perseverance*
B. *His Tenderness*
II. THE INFLUENCE OF THE SPIRIT (verses 8-10)
A. *Earnestness*
B. *Diligence*
III. THE ATTITUDE OF THE FATHER (verses 11-32)
A. *Willingness*
B. *Generosity*
C. *Compassion*
D. *Accessibility*

Dr. G. Campbell Morgan in his commentary on the *Gospel According to Luke* says of the fifteenth chapter: "I suppose if we were selecting the great chapters of the Bible, it is certain that we should choose, among others, this fifteenth chapter of the gospel according to Luke. I think that would be done by the most superficial student of the Scriptures. It would be done by such because of its matchless pictorial beauty. Among all the things that our Lord said, none is more wonderful in its light and shade, its colour and its glory, than this. I think, also, that those who have given longest time to the study of it, would still feel it to be one of the greatest chapters, and that because in a very remarkable way in this chapter we have focussed the great fact for which the Bible stands, and the great truths revealed through the process of the literature."

We tend to divide the chapter into three parables, although Luke writes: "He spake *this* parable unto them." In the first two stories Jesus justifies His own conduct ("that He receiveth sinners and eateth with them"), and in the third He rebukes the criticism of His enemies. This conduct and criticism we see first in—

THE INTRODUCTION (verses 1, 2)

A. *Conduct.* Our Lord was allowing "publicans and sinners" (tax-collectors and "outsiders," Gentiles or non-Jews) to benefit from His teaching. He allowed them to come into close contact with Him. He "received" them, that is, gave them access to Him. Further, He accepted their invitation to eat with them.

B. *Criticism.* In the eyes of the Pharisees His conduct was a breach of decorum, a contravention of high society code of "purity." He should have gathered His garments about Him so as not to be contaminated. He should have them or Himself at a distance. He was too "hail-fellow-well-met" or "all things to all men."

Thus in these three familiar stories we must keep in mind the Scribes and Pharisees. The Lost Sheep and the Lost Coin reveal that our Lord's conduct in mixing with sinners was the right one, while in the Prodigal Son the younger son resembles the publicans and sinners and the elder son the murmuring Scribes and Pharisees. On a wider scale the younger son may also represent the Gentiles and the elder son the Jews.

All too frequently we make the mistake of looking on these three stories as being the basis of gospel addresses to the unsaved. In the first instance they were given to religious people! And since the lost sheep was originally in the flock, and the lost coin in the house, and the lost son in the father's home, the real emphasis is reclamation from backsliding and not salvation for sin.

The early Church Fathers saw in these three parables the Triune God and the special activity or influence or attitude of each divine Person. We shall not do better than study these stories under such headings as we have given in our chapter outline.

I. THE ACTIVITY OF THE SON (verses 3-7)

It is important to notice that the man in the parable is more than a shepherd, he is the owner of the sheep ("having a hundred sheep," verse 4). If he were merely a shepherd then he would be leaving his post and exposing ninety-nine other sheep to danger by looking for the lost one. "In the wilderness" does not imply a dangerous, desolated desert, but the ordinary pasture where the sheep had been led for their food. Being the owner of the flock we can safely assume that he made ample provision for the ninety-nine while he went looking for the lost one.

Looking at the activity of the shepherd (calling him that for the sake of convenience) we note first:

A. *His Perseverance.* This is summed up in the phrase "until he find it." He did not cease in his endeavors until he had both found and restored the wayward sheep. He could have led or driven it back to the fold but he "carried it"—he went to both time and trouble, not delegating the task to a servant but doing the dangerous work himself, diligently, perseveringly.

B. *His Tenderness.* We noticed that he carried it, but how? "He layeth it on his shoulders." The shoulders provided firmness, the sheep would feel safe. Straining forward through the darkness of the night, perhaps battling through wind and rain, the shoulders would provide protection, the sheep would be safe and warm. Isaiah says: "He shall carry them in his *bosom*" (40:11), nestling against the shepherd's chest, his clothes wrapped around him. Isaiah is prophesying salvation through Christ, that is, safety; our Lord in Luke 15 is describing salvation, its security. The saved one is borne up on His shoulders, eternally secure. We cannot be lost; once saved—always saved.

Here then is the activity of the Son, the Good Shepherd. He "endured the cross" as the shepherd of the parable endured the dark night, and it was "for the joy that was set before him" as the shepherd in the parable "rejoicing", brought his sheep home again. Joy is the emphasis in all three parts of this one parable, joy over three lost things found. Elizabeth Clephane sums up the shepherd's joy in her immortal descriptive hymn:

> But all thro' the mountains, thunder-riv'n,
>   And up from the rocky steep,
> There arose a glad cry to the gate of heaven,
>   "Rejoice! I have found My sheep!"
> And the angels echoed around the throne,
>   "Rejoice! for the Lord brings back His own!"

II. THE INFLUENCE OF THE SPIRIT (verses 8-10)

A small but significant change or two is made in this part of the parable. The central character is now a woman and not a man. A conscious, straying animal, now becomes an inanimate object, a silver coin or the missing piece of a bridal headdress. The sheep could bleat to attract attention to its lost condition; the coin could do nothing. But the common element to both stories is the fact that no efforts are spared to reclaim that which was lost.

Here then we have the influence of the Spirit of God through the Church. The Motherhood of God is always portrayed in Scripture by the Holy Spirit. In Genesis the Spirit "moved" or "brooded" over the waters. It is a feminine illustration. In God's Word the Church is also feminine—"the Bride." The woman in the story is characterized by earnestness and diligence, two traits of character that should mark the twentieth-century church.

A. *Earnestness.* She began by lighting a candle. She meant business! Her act speaks of the illuminating power of the Spirit of God, speaking to man in darkness through the Word of God, whether read, exhibited, proclaimed or preached.

B. *Diligence.* This woman swept the house clean, turning everything over, leaving no stone unturned, until she found her missing piece of silver. Perhaps the floor was ripped up and the furniture removed outside, we do not know; we only know that she searched "diligently" until she found it. So the Spirit of God diligently searches out the elect of God. So He seeks after the backslider until such a one is found and restored and enjoys again the joy of salvation.

III. THE ATTITUDE OF THE FATHER (verses 11-32)

Again there is a marked difference between this third and longest story and the previous two. The sheep strayed willfully; the coin was lost by neglect; the younger son was also willful. But note that the sheep and coin were both sought after; the boy had to return of his own free will. Some say that here we have a meeting between Arminian and Calvinist, that salvation depends on man's free will and that salvation is all of God's grace! These two doctrines are parallel lines and parallel lines only meet in eternity!

This so-called parable of the Prodigal Son is really the "parable of the Father" for it depicts the Father's longing, His love, His waiting, His watching.

It is possible to study the career of the younger son like this: home, sick of home, homesick, home again! Or it is possible to study it under these Scriptural divisions: "Give me," "Make me," "Began to be in want," "Began to be merry." Or to put it in fewer divisions: A man beside himself came to himself. Whichever divisions are used the Father must be considered pre-eminent and not the prodigal son.

Let us look then at the Father's—

A. *Willingness* in the face of the younger son's willfulness. Upon the suggestion of the son the father was willing to divide up his living. It was a Jewish custom to mete out the inheritance while still alive to save a lot of relatives "squabbling" over a will after death. The father then had to be maintained by his sons. Since such an action was irrevocable, if a son asked for his "share" it was synonymous with saying, "Father, I wish you were dead!"

This sacrifice on the part of the Father was spurned by the

younger son. Instead of taking his share of the responsibility of the upkeep of his father, he leaves home for a distant land, there to waste his money in high living, indulging his passions and appetites to the full. Then one of those "providential coincidences," as they have been called, happened. He was left destitute, hungry and friendless. He is soon "beside himself," that is, mentally disturbed. Eventually he "comes to himself" and thinks of the father's—

B. *Generosity.* By contrast with his own straitened circumstances the son remembers the servants at home, paid generously by his father, and provided for with shelter and food. His father always saw that there was "enough and to spare." Knowing the father's generosity he decides to go back and begins to rehearse his confession. He is willing to go back not as a son but as a slave. Only when the sinner is willing to become a bond-slave of Christ can he enter into his rightful inheritance and become heir to all the riches of heaven.

C. *Compassion.* Following the son's confession we see the father's compassion. The father did not leave home like the shepherd, but he was on the lookout, and as soon as his son appears on the horizon he runs to meet him.

There is no waiting by the father to see in what state or with what spirit the boy has returned home; he is taken in just as he is. The father does not first extract promises from the son that he will in future "go straight." It is enough that he has returned. The best robe must be put on him. *The,* not *a* best robe—the ceremonial robe kept for important occasions. A ring, perhaps a signet ring (the sign of honorable standing and official position) must be placed on his hand. Shoes must be put on his feet, for only a slave went about the house barefooted and he is back as a son, not as a servant. *The* fatted calf, the only one, the extra special one, must be killed for eating. A time of rejoicing and merriment must begin to celebrate the return.

How much more quickly we would return from the world and from spiritual backsliding if we but realized what the Father has in store for us! The blessings, comforts and joys of eternal salvation, a foretaste of the Father's home above.

The last attitude of the Father is revealed by the conduct of the elder son—

D. *Accessibility.* This son has been faithful and loyal. He has performed his duties about the farm. He has paid out for the upkeep of the father. But it has all been done grudgingly, under protest. He has become so sour and embittered that he cannot bring himself to call the returned prodigal "brother," only "this thy son," or more literally, "This your precious son." He is as selfish, self-righteous, critical, and harsh in judgment as the Pharisees of our Lord's time.

The father appeals to the elder son something like this: "You stayed at home; you have not been enjoying the pleasures of sin for a season, but remember that while in my home all my possessions and belongings have been available to you at all times. I have been accessible too, but you have denied yourself the right and privilege of making use of them or me." He was as much a prodigal at home as his brother was in a distant land—so the Pharisees, the critics of Christ. They were sons of Abraham. God's gifts could have been appropriated by them but they were too self-righteous, high and mighty, blind and complacent to avail themselves of God's offer.

There the parable ends. We are not told what we want to know. Did the elder son become reconciled to his young brother? Did the younger son remain at home, making up for his misdemeanor, becoming steadfast and faithful to the end? Both were free agents. Both had free will. Perhaps it is well that we do not know what became of them for we are left with this: we must press on with evangelism knowing that no one is past reclaiming. We must pray on for the backslider knowing that he has not gone too far. And we must take heed, "lest standing we fall." Looking at both sons we have to comment, "There but for the grace of God, go I." Thank God the Father remains ever the same and His attitude is well-expressed by Jude:

Now unto him that is able to keep you from falling, and to present you faultless before the presence of his glory with exceeding joy, To the only wise God our Saviour, be glory and majesty, dominion and power, both now and ever. Amen (verses 24, 25).

A SAFE AND SURE TRANQUILIZER

John 14

The gospel of John portrays Jesus Christ as Son of God, emphasizing His deity. The writer's theme (with the whole Christian Church in mind) is Jesus as God, "Believe and Live." John's proof of the divinity of our Lord is the imposing number of miracles.

John does not give us a biography in the accepted sense of the word, for there is little chronological order in the gospel. It is, in fact, a *gospel;* it is good news presented so that belief may be inspired in the hearers or readers.

The method John adopts is selection. He selects certain "signs" or miracles from among a great many. A "sign" in Scripture emphasizes the value of the thing done, and so John selects certain signs that reveal our Lord's power over nature, thus proving His deity.

In the same way he selects words as well as works, and so we have the great "I am's" of our Lord in this fourth gospel. An outline may be given as follows:

PROLOGUE (1:1-14)
      The Son's—
  I. FORERUNNER AND FOLLOWERS (1:15-51)
  II. PUBLIC MINISTRY TO THE WORLD (2–12)
  III. PRIVATE MINISTRY TO HIS OWN (13–17)
  IV. SUFFERING AND SACRIFICE (18–20)
EPILOGUE (21)

This "famous" chapter comes in the third main section of the gospel, among five chapters recording our Lord's discourses to His disciples and His high priestly prayer on their behalf.

The Passover has been observed and superseded. The Lord's Supper has been instituted, Judas having left. The conversation then becomes very intimate and deeply spiritual.

The attitude of the disciples, however, is one of unrest, anxiety, perplexity, indeed well-nigh despair. They have come to realize that Jesus is going to certain death, and they cannot understand it, nor how they will fare after that event. Today the world is strangely similar. Anxiety, dread, fear, perplexity, and despair hangs over the heads of the nations like a heavy pall. The crucifixion that seemed so catastrophic to these men is replaced by the threat of nuclear war in our time. Some resort to escapist pleasures, others to the pychiatrist.

Doctors and chemists report that tranquilizers and "pep pills" are purchased almost like candy.

Our Lord's dealings with His disciples in their plight reveals for all time the only safe and sure tranquilizer in the face of the unknown. We might divide the chapter into the following divisions:

I. CHRIST'S COMFORT (verses 1-15)
    A. *The Hope of Heaven* (verses 1-7)
    B. *The Glory of God* (verses 8-12)
    C. *The Power of Prayer* (verses 13-15)
II. GOD'S COMFORTER (verses 16-31)
    A. *The Gift of God* (verses 16-20)
    B. *The Teacher of Truth* (verses 21-26)
    C. *The Promise of Peace* (verses 27-31)

I. CHRIST'S COMFORT (verses 1-15)

Our Lord begins with words that have brought comfort to untold millions of mourners at funeral services. They speak of—

A. *The Hope of Heaven* (verses 1-7). A hope in Scripture is always a "certainty," it has none of the uncertain longing of our modern meaning of the word. And the grounds of a Scriptural hope are the nature of God Himself, His absolute faithfulness. Thus Jesus began by reminding His followers of their hope in God, their trust in His faithfulness. In the same way they could trust the Son for He too is divine.

As the Jewish temple of old had many courts and chambers so heaven for the Christian has many "mansions" or abiding places. We tend to limit heaven by our earthly conception of eternity, but heaven is where God is and He cannot be contained in a small compass. "Abiding places" should make us think of the infinite variety that there will be in heaven. "Mansions" is a word that was used for the "stations" or "arbors" providing rest and refreshment for weary travelers along a hot and dusty road. Heaven is a place of well-earned rest, although Scripture also reveals that it is a place of service.

An added attraction is that heaven is being prepared for us by our Lord Himself. He prepared the way there by dying, but now He is preparing the place itself. Who can imagine such preparations? Some complain that the Bible is not explicit enough about heaven, but what more do we need to be told, and what more could we want, than *His* preparations and *His* presence when we are there? To be with Him and to be like Him will be enough. Of course, if we are not enjoying His presence now, while on earth, then this concept of heaven will be unsatisfying. If we are looking for our pleasures in the world instead of in Christ then our concept of heaven will be a limited one.

Thomas was wondering about the way to heaven and what heaven was like (verse 5), so our Lord told him that He Himself was the way, the road between this world and the next, the path from the seen to the unseen, the bridge between the temporal and the eternal, and He alone was the road—there was no other way to the Father in heaven. Suddenly it must have dawned on the disciples. By looking at Jesus they could see God, which leads us to the next subsection—

B. *The Glory of God* (verses 8-12). Philip again takes up the questioning and desires to be shown the Father. His real desire is for a more tangible form of the future, and actual sight with physical eyesight of God. As Moses had a vision of the divine glory on the mountaintop so Philip wants a manifestation of divine glory. His desire is so real and deep that if it is satisfied then he will ask nothing more. Dr. G. Campbell Morgan comments that here Philip was expressing "the great cry of humanity." He was voicing the desire of human beings down the centuries, to see God with the naked eye and have done with the eye of faith. Dr. F. B. Meyer comments: "We think we see Him in nature, in history, in the progress of the Christian Church, in His Word, in transformed lives, but we still cry—'Show us the Father'." Such an attitude is natural but it is wrong. Jesus did not condemn Philip for the same desire, but He showed him that what he had been looking for and desiring was present. He Himself came to reveal the Father and the glory of God; He and the Father were one.

What proof have we? The same proof that Philip had—the works that Jesus did and is still doing today. "No man can do these miracles that thou doest, except God be with him" (John 3:2). Philip had been present when Christ exhibited His power over nature. He had been present when Jesus preached and "never man spake like this man." Philip had had daily proof of His deity. All that Jesus said and did was a result of His "oneness" with the Father. As our fellowship with Christ deepens then we shall see more and more of the Father and His glory. Not only so but we ourselves shall find that we are also doing "greater works." How is that possible? Only through—

C. *The Power of Prayer* (verses 13-15). In this subsection we note two limitations for successful praying. At first sight it looks as if we can ask anything and anything will be granted, like a small boy praying for a fine day when it is pouring "cats and dogs." The first condition is this: what we ask must be in line with God's will. Second, the motive behind our asking must be the furtherance of God's glory and not the mere gratification of our personal desires. A third requirement is (verse 15): obedience to His commands. Obedience is proof of our attachment to Him, evidence of our sincere love. Perhaps the lack of power in some of our prayer meetings is our hesitancy about commandment-keeping, our lack of conformity to His will. No wonder a great man of prayer once said: "We have not fully learned or obeyed the laws and conditions of prayer. Until they are apprehended and complied with, it is not possible for us to pray as we might."

Note how our Lord expected His followers to pray after He had left them. They could not possibly do His works without reliance upon the power of prayer.

II. GOD'S COMFORTER (verses 16-31)

Christ's comfort was balm to their souls in their anxiety and uncertainty, but there was more promised. When Christ returned to His Father's Home then God would give them another Comforter.

A. *The Gift of God* (verses 16-20). The word "another" is often overlooked. Christ was "one Comforter," now they were to have "another" Comforter. One of Spurgeon's sermons is entitled *The Two Paracletes* ("Paraclete" being the Greek for "Comforter"). The word really means advocate, or literally, "one called to the side of another for the purpose of counseling, supporting, or aiding him."

The disciples had had Christ as their Advocate. Now the Holy Spirit is to be their Advocate. This second Advocate will "abide with (them) for ever," that is "until the end of the age." Note how the Holy Spirit is "with" us and "in" us (verse 17)—fellowship or companionship and also actual indwelling. The world may not understand the doctrine of the third Person of the Trinity but for the Christian it is all-in-all; He is with us and in us, energizing us, influencing us, empowering us—He is our very life.

Verse 18 makes it quite clear that the definition of the Holy Spirit as "Jesus' other self" is a good one. He was going away, but in the person of the Holy Spirit He was going to visit them on occasions. It has been put like this: He is always with us yet comes again and again; He will come when we need Him most; He will come unasked but He likes to be asked; He will come when we expect Him and He will come on surprise visits. He will come as—

B. *The Teacher of Truth* (verses 21-26). The Holy Spirit has already been referred to as "the Spirit of truth" in verse 17. Now John records our Lord as saying that the Spirit's mission on earth is to be that of tutor, teaching and reminding, revealing and bringing to remembrance what had already been taught. Once more conditions are laid down by Jesus: obedience and love. The first is a result, a natural outcome of the second. That is why the world cannot have this special ministry of the Spirit for the world neither loves God nor is obedient to Him. A true believer, by contrast (verse 23), "keeps his words," that is, the gospel message in its entirety, not broken down into separate commands.

C. *The Promise of Peace* (verses 27-31). "Peace"! Who can define the word? Who can comprehend it? In a world of such unrest and tension as the world of the twentieth century, where is there peace? Peace! It means freedom from disturbance, outwardly as in the case of war, inwardly as in the case of anxiety. The word in Scripture means soundness, health, prosperity, well-being in general. What Jesus was doing was taking a word used in a farewell greeting, a term of benediction, and placing it on a higher level. "Peace be to you" was the common greeting of the market place. But Jesus makes a distinction: "*My peace*," He says. He is not giving one of the world's gifts to His people; this is a divine gift. This peace has to do with the heart and soul—it is a spiritual gift. So we are brought full circle. Here is the safe and sure tranquilizer the world needs in the face of possible disaster. This gift of peace was big enough to take the place of Himself as He left His disciples. "I go away," He said (verse 28), but He was compensating them. He was giving them a gift that would turn the sorrow of parting into joy; it would turn doubt into faith and trust; it would make the silences of the future eloquent; it would enable Himself to go from them and offer Himself as a sacrifice for the world. "Arise, let us go hence" became a shout of victory for He was going in the strength of the Spirit and that same Spirit would sustain Him and them.

THE CHURCH WE OUGHT TO BE

Acts 2

The Acts of the Apostles could be more correctly entitled, "The Acts of the *Holy Spirit* Through the Apostles." It is, however, an unfinished book, for the Holy Spirit is still working through the Church today. Thus the theme of the book is, "The Passion and Power of the Church" (key text, 1:8).

After the crushing blow of Calvary, to the early Christians there came the descent of the Spirit at Pentecost. This resulted in growth, power and expansion. No period of church history (even when the biggest revivals are studied) has such a story to tell as the twenty-eight chapters of the Acts of the Apostles. With all our modern, up-to-date methods, our "slick" publicity, our efficient organization, we are not seeing the growth and expansion of the Church of Christ that these early followers saw. Their secret is to be discovered in our "famous chapter," chapter 2.

First, an outline of the whole book can be given in this form:

THE CHURCH'S:
    I.   FORMATION (1–5)
   II.   PERSECUTION (6–9:31)
  III.   EVANGELIZATION (9:32–12:24)
         The Ministry of Peter
  IV.   COMMISSION (12:25–28)
         The Missionary Enterprise of Paul

The "famous" chapter (*The Church We Ought to Be*) then comes in the book's first section, which is an introduction to the scheme and scope of the whole book.

Our twentieth-century church situation is one of desperate plight. Living as we do in a world of delinquent youth and divorced couples; having lost much of our contact with the working people; membership of all denominations increasingly on the decline—what can we do? Wherein lies the solution? What is wrong with the Church?

Some look back longingly to the successes of the past, the Puritan era or the great spiritual awakenings. What we should really do is to go right back to New Testament times and rediscover the secret of the Church then. In the Acts of the Apostles we see the Church as God meant it to be, the Church as we ought to be today.

The chapter can be studied under the following outline:

I. THE FULFILLMENT OF PROPHECY (verses 1-13)
    A. *Obedience and Unanimity* (verse 1)
    B. *Symbolism and Phenomenon* (verses 2-4)
    C. *Cause and Effect* (verses 5-11)
    D. *Perplexity and Mockery* (verses 12,13)
II. THE FOOLISHNESS OF PREACHING (verses 14-40)
    A. *Text and Context* (verses 14-21)
    B. *Illustration and Application* (verses 22-40)
III. THE FOUNDATIONS OF PROSPERITY (verses 41-47)
    A. *Birth and Growth* (verses 41, 42)
    B. *Fear and Favor* (verses 43-47)

I. THE FULFILLMENT OF PROPHECY (verses 1-13)

Without encroaching on the next section, what is described in these opening verses of the chapter is a fulfillment of the prophecy that forms part of Peter's sermon. What exactly happened? And how did it happen? Well, it is obvious that certain conditions were fulfilled. First there was:

A. *Obedience and Unanimity* (verse 1). They had been commanded "not to depart from Jerusalem" (1:4). Now in obedience they were waiting with unanimity of mind and purpose for the Holy Spirit to come upon them. They could have been out in the streets, distributing tracts, holding open-air meetings, but they had been told to wait. Anything else would have been work in their own strength and had they not been told—"Without me ye can do nothing"? So they await the enduement and the empowerment of the Holy Spirit. It was not an organized prayer meeting, and they were not yet an organized church; they were ordinary believing people, obedient and at one with each other.

B. *Symbolism and Phenomenon* (verses 2-4). When the Spirit came He was accompanied by symbols or signs that had great value for that day and generation of people—wind, tongues, fire. *They* are not necessary today, but the visitation of the Spirit is. Note that *all* were filled with the Spirit, not just the leaders.

Now the Holy Spirit had been in the world since creation. The Spirit had helped cunning craftsmen to build the tabernacle according to God's design. But now occurs a new thing, a phenomenon never experienced before. The Spirit of God passed into these people filling them to overflowing. They were given new spiritual life, a new vision. They began to praise God; they spoke in foreign dialects and languages. Because they were transformed Jerusalem was transformed.

That is the experience the Church needs today. We must first be "filled with the Spirit" and be transformed so that we have a transforming effect upon society. It would be a shattering experience. We should never be the same again. In the past, during revivals, it has bent and broken men and women physically. Are we prepared for such an outpouring? Do we really desire it? Dare we pay the price? Or are we afraid of being labeled fanatics?

C. *Cause and Effect* (verses 5-11). God may be reverently called "an opportunist." He knew that at the Feast of Pentecost (the Old Testament Feast of Weeks) every male Jew was required to present himself in Jerusalem. This was the cause of the crowd in festive mood in the Holy City. The barley harvest was complete and so it was a kind of "Harvest Home" celebration. Jews from many districts were assembled for the occasion and suddenly they all heard the Gospel in their own dialect. Their intellects were arrested, their interest was aroused—this was the effect of Pentecost, but so far they were not spiritually enlightened.

D. *Perplexity and Mockery* (verses 12,13). They were compelled to ask for an explanation of all that they saw and heard—"What meaneth this?" they asked. The natural man can never understand spiritual phenomena, a mighty display of God's power. Thus they sought a natural explanation. They said that these Christians must be drunk with wine; they were incapable of controlling themselves. Thus perplexity turned to mockery. When an unregenerate man cannot understand something spiritual he frequently mocks at it. Dr. G. Campbell Morgan comments: "The criticism of the world that is of value is that criticism in which it says that the Church is drunk. Has anyone ever charged you with being drunk with your Christianity? We lack the flashing eye, the pulsating song, and the tremendous enthusiasm of an overwhelming conviction." Is it not true to say that one of the great hindrances to revival today is our love of things being done "decently and in order," "icily regular." We do not want to give offense or create a wrong impression and so we are overcareful how we act and speak. We must not become fanatical, throwing caution to the winds, but at the same time we must not hinder the Spirit of God by our dislike of emotion or spiritual excesses.

II. THE FOOLISHNESS OF PREACHING (verses 14-40)

Pentecost sets the seal upon the divine method, that it is by the foolishness of preaching that men are saved.

A. *Text and Context* (verses 14-21). One astounding effect of the coming of the Holy Spirit is the changed attitude of Peter. Peter had previously denied his Lord; now he is "standing up with the eleven" and lifting up his voice. He becomes their spokesman and God's mouthpiece. Teachers sat and heralds stood—Peter is a herald of God.

Like all good preachers he sets his text within its context. In order to answer the question "What meaneth this?" he replies, "This is that," that is, that which the prophet Joel prophesied hundreds of years before. Then he began, as preachers should do, where the congregation was; he put himself on good terms with them. They had accused the Christians of being drunk. Peter replies, in effect: "Impossible, for the taverns are not yet open"—"It is but the third hour of the day." And so he reminds them of an ancient prophecy that is being fulfilled before their very eyes, a prophecy which contained the text of his own sermon—"Whosoever shall call on the name of the Lord shall be saved."

B. *Illustration and Application* (verses 22-40). Peter's desire is to preach Christ. Like other preachers he knows something of the art of illustration and the science of applying truth in a personal way. He illustrates the truth of his message from "the patriarch David."

First, however, he traces the history of Jesus. His congregation knows of Jesus—His life and ministry, His sufferings and death. What they do not know about Him is that He wants to be their personal Saviour and Lord. Thus Peter preaches Christ, Christ as perfect Man, approved of God; a man who did mighty miracles in their midst. He preaches Christ crucified, dying a death predetermined by the Father in heaven, and yet a death for which they themselves were responsible. Finally he tells of Christ risen from the dead and ascended into heaven.

At this point Peter is interrupted. No one interrupts today because many are not preaching Christ crucified. When we play at preaching and preach social welfare and politics, peace and war, and so on, no one needs to interrupt for it does not convict of sin or disturb a slumbering conscience.

Peter was interrupted because the people were under deep conviction and cried out for simple instructions as to what they must do. Peter's advice (verse 38) was contrition and confession. Sin must be repented of and that must be followed by an outward and visible expression of the inward experience—baptism.

This is where most preachers would stop. The sermon has been preached; men have come under the convicting power of the Spirit; they have been counseled and converted—there surely is an end of the matter. That is where Peter began again!—"And with many other words did he testify and exhort" (verse 40). He kept on earnestly exhorting men to be saved, explaining the way of salvation to them. He placed the responsibility squarely on his congregation. God had done His part; Jesus had done His; now it is up to them to do theirs and respond to the Gospel. Either they continue going the way of the world, following their own generation with its hardness of heart and indifference to God, or else they become saved.

III. The Foundations of Prosperity (verses 41-47)

A. *Birth and Growth* (verses 41, 42). The result of the preaching was that 3,000 were saved, born again, baptized and received into the fellowship of the Church. For many today that is the end. Once having been given the "right hand of fellowship" into the church membership that is all that is seen of them. They are never to be seen or heard at a prayer meeting or Bible study. They remain stunted, un-developed "babes in Christ"—carnal Christians. Not so these Pente-costal converts! They had been converted under a doctrinal sermon (not one of the current "snippets" or ten-minute essays) and so they wanted more doctrine. They progressed from the milk to the meat of the Word, growing stronger each week, becoming rooted and grounded in the faith. Then they continued in fellowship. None of them were like the twentieth-century "lone wolf" or "spiritual gipsy." They did not ask, "Need a Christian belong to a church?" They saw that they needed the help and companionship of fellow-believers. They found that the deepest expression of such fellowship was around the Lord's Table, and so they continued in the "breaking of bread." Finally they knew that "the family that prays together stays together" and so they continued "in prayers" or "in *the* prayers" as is the more correct rendering, that is, special meetings for prayer, the prayer life of the Church being definite and systematic. This then is the foundation for real spiritual prosperity in a church. And it has a two-fold result:

B. *Fear and Favor* (verses 43-47). "Fear came upon every soul"! Today people do not fear the Church; they poke fun at it! They laugh at its weakness, its ineffectiveness, its out-of-dateness, saying that it is out-of-touch with life. At Pentecost there was some-thing about the Church that made men fear it; they looked upon it with reverence and awe; they saw it as a society of people in whom the power of God was manifest.

Fear turned to favor. Note, "favor with all the people." *The people!* It was generally the rulers of the people that were against the Church in early times, not the people themselves. So today, it is the Communist leaders that indoctrinate the people against religion. The people after Pentecost looked upon the Church with favor then. Why?—because they saw the genuineness of their faith, that they practiced "communism." Communism with a capital "C" has as its motto—"What's yours is mine"! Christian "communism" with a small "c" says: "What's mine is yours"! The world watched these people living together, worshiping together, growing in grace together, shar-ing together—and they saw that they did it "with gladness and single-ness of heart," that they were utterly sincere and genuine. No wonder the Church continued to grow daily, the Lord adding "such as were being saved." No one could point the finger and say, "The Church is full of hypocrites." Their lives tallied with their lips; what they preached they practiced. And above all they were an evangelizing center, they knew that the primary work of the Church was to pro-claim the Gospel that men and women might be saved from sin and from the spirit of the age. This is the kind of church we ought to be.

AFTER CONVERSION WHAT?

Romans 5

The key word of Romans is "righteousness," and the theme of the letter: "God's Moral Perfection." It was one of the Apostle Paul's letters as a pioneer missionary, the writing of an itinerant preacher. Paul wrote the letter from Corinth and it was carried to Rome by Phoebe, but little did she know that she was carrying what was to become centuries later, "The Handbook of Protestant Theology," or "The Gospel According to Paul." The letter can be given in outline form thus:

PROLOGUE (1:1-17)
THE RIGHTEOUSNESS OF GOD AND—
    I.   THE WORLD'S NEED (1:18—3:20)
   II. JUSTIFICATION (3:21—4:25)
  III. SALVATION (5:1—8:39)
  IV. HISTORY (9-11)
   V. CHRISTIAN LIVING (12—15:13)
EPILOGUE (15:14-16)

The "famous" fifth chapter comes in the third main section of the letter and is devotional rather than practical or doctrinal. It is part of Paul's own experience of God's dealings with him. Salvation for the apostle is a process. It can begin with a sudden experience, a turning point such as his own on the Damascus Road, but that is only the beginning. Paul was not like some present-day Christians who live on their conversion experience and when asked to give a testimony give a "stale" or "bottom drawer" testimony. Paul believed in "going on" and "growing up." Conversion must develop into daily sanctification. After the "wicket gate" experience a long pilgrimage lay ahead of Bunyan's Pilgrim before he reached the Celestial City. We therefore entitle this chapter—*After Conversion What?* And we shall study it under the following divisions:

    I.   THE CONSEQUENCES OF JUSTIFICATION (verses 1-5)
        A. *Tranquillity of Soul* (verse 1)
        B. *Facility of Access* (verse 2)
        C. *Hilarity at the Prospect* (verse 2)
        D. *Victory over Trouble* (verses 3-5)
   II. THE ADVANTAGES OF RECONCILIATION (verses 6-11)
        A. *Help for the Helpless* (verse 6)

B. *Life for the Lifeless* (verses 7, 8)
C. *Friendship for the Friendless* (verses 9, 10)
D. *Joy for the Joyless* (verse 11)

III. THE PRIVILEGES OF SANCTIFICATION (verses 12-21)
A. *The Persons: Adam and Christ*
B. *Their Act: Disobedience in the Garden*
Obedience on the Cross
C. *Those Affected: All mankind*
D. *The Effect of the act: Spiritual Death*
Spiritual Life

I. THE CONSEQUENCES OF JUSTIFICATION (verses 1-5)

"Therefore" takes us back to the previous chapter and the apostle's theme of justification. Therefore, as a result of being justified, certain consequences follow. Justification has been defined as "just-as-if-I-had-never-sinned." That results in—

A. *Tranquillity of Soul* (verse 1). The justified man is at peace with God. Peace is the opposite of war. The sinner is no longer at enmity with God; he has been reconciled. Peace is the opposite of turmoil; no longer is the sinner's mind and conscience a trouble to him. The saved man knows a great sense of relief at losing his sin with all its guilt and punishment. It is like a load lifted. Of course, feelings fluctuate, and so we rest not on feelings but on fact. When the initial feelings of conversion have worn off we rest on the sure Word of God and so have tranquillity of soul.

B. *Facility of Access* (verse 2). It was through faith that we were saved. It is again through faith that we have ease of access to God in prayer. We were not saved through any merits of our own, and no human merit is a means of approach to God. Christ leads the saved sinner by the hand and presents us to God the Father. He did that at conversion and so we are now in a state of grace and justification.

C. *Hilarity at the Prospect* (verse 2). True conversion results in true joy. There is joy in heaven over every sinner that is saved. There is joy in the human heart as well. This happiness is not merely over sins forgiven and hell escaped but the hope of heaven and seeing the glory of God.

D. *Victory over Trouble* (verses 3-5). We are saved but we are not in heaven yet! We are not *of* the world any longer but we remain *in* the world, and it is a world of trouble, trials and temptations, persecution and affliction. The Christian can glory and rejoice when things are going wrong as well as when things are going right. J. B. Phillips' rendering is: "We can be full of joy here and now even in our trials and troubles." Romans 8 supplies the secret: "All things work together for good to them that love God." Tribulation produces patience, ripeness of character, and a hope that never disappoints.

The final comment by the apostle in this section is that all these consequences are brought about by the Holy Spirit. This is the first mention of the Spirit in this letter. We see Him as One who produces Christian graces; One who diffuses love in the believer's heart.

II. THE ADVANTAGES OF RECONCILIATION (verses 6-11)

Here we have a great description of the love of Christ and the grace of God. In the last verse of the section Paul uses the word which is translated "atonement" in the Authorized or King James Version. It is the same word as is elsewhere translated "reconciliation," that is, being made *at one* with God. Paul describes the benefits or advantages of this new relationship, this new standing which the believer has with God.

A. *Help for the Helpless* (verse 6). "Without strength" means that we were so helpless we could do nothing at all. The same word is used of people stricken with paralysis. Morally and spiritually the sinner is crippled by sin and is absolutely helpless. But in "due time," at just the right moment of time God the Great Helper stepped in and did something on our behalf.

B. *Life for the Lifeless* (verses 7, 8). Who would think of dying for a bad man, but a morally good person is deserving of another's sacrifice. Christ's exhibition of love on the cross is unique for "while we were yet sinners, Christ died for us." By dying in our place He allowed us to live.

C. *Friendship for the Friendless* (verses 9, 10). He died while we were enemies of God that He might become our Friend. Thus the Friend of sinners becomes the "friend that sticketh closer than a brother." Now we can sing:

> I've found a Friend; oh such a Friend!
> He bled, He died to save me;
> And not alone the gift of life,
> But His own self He gave me.

D. *Joy for the Joyless* (verse 11). When we were without Christ we thought we were happy, but it was a transient happiness, a happiness that was dependent on what *happens,* on favorable circumstances and the like. Often our joy was hollow and shallow. But in Christ we have found a deep, abiding, eternal joy that is not dependent on circumstances for it is "joy in the Lord" and so we can "rejoice always" (which is the apostle's theme to the Philippians).

III. THE PRIVILEGES OF SANCTIFICATION (verses 12-21)

In this final section of the chapter the apostle reveals great insight into the full process of God's plan of salvation. The "therefore" of verse 1 is now replaced by the "wherefore" of verse 12. Paul is following a train of thought suggested by his writing of reconciliation. Now he goes deeper, explaining the process of salvation still further.

These verses are rightly acknowledged to be some of the greatest and some of the most difficult in the New Testament!

Brunner calls this section, "The history of death and the history of life." C. H. Dodd states that Paul is "debating a difficulty," but that has been counteracted by the comment: "No! he is singing a rhapsody!" His aim is to show that our sanctification, with all its attendant privileges, is dependent upon God's remedy for inborn sin—free grace! The best way to follow the line of the apostle's thought and argument is by a chart of the persons, their act, those affected by the act, and the effect of the act—

A. *The Persons.* Going back to the Genesis account of the fall of man and the entry of sin into the world, Paul names Adam as representative of the human race. Christ came as the Second Adam, and again He is representative. Adam was the head of the physical human race; Christ is Head of the new spiritual fellowship, the Church.

B. *Their Act.* Adam's noted act was one of disobedience. Told not to touch a certain tree in the Garden of Eden Adam, in defiance of the divine will, touched and thus disobeyed. By contrast Jesus Christ was "obedient unto death, even the death of the cross." By dying on Calvary Jesus was doing the Father's will—"Thy will, not mine, he done."

C. *Those Affected.* All mankind was affected by Adam's act of disobedience. Sin became hereditary for all the human race, so that "all have sinned"—"there is none righteous, no not one"—"all we like sheep have gone astray." Every baby born into the world has this taint and tendency to sin within its heart. The one exception is Jesus Christ. He was born of a virgin, who supernaturally conceived, that her son might escape the taint of original sin. The Holy Spirit by-passed man as a father. Now all mankind is affected by the unique birth and death of Jesus Christ. The cross is for all; the forgiveness and eternal life offered there is available for all and can be appropriated by all—on the basis of repentance and faith.

D. *The Effect of the Act.* There is an immediate and a remote effect. At the moment Adam and Eve became disobedient they died—spiritually; later on physical death entered the Garden. Today death is man's last enemy, but by faith in Christ salvation replaces spiritual death and ultimately bodily resurrection will replace physical death, upon the return of the Lord in glory.

That then is the argument of the apostle in outline. Within that framework is the apostle's discourse upon the law. Could there have been sin before the days of the Ten Commandments? Yes, for before the Decalogue the divine will had been made known regarding observance of the Sabbath, tithing, sacrifice, and the penalty for murder. The law was merely given to be a "schoolmaster" to humanity, pointing the way to Christ, or as J. B. Phillips puts it: "The law keeps slipping into the picture to point the vast extent of sin" (verse 20).

The chapter ends as it begins: verse 1—"through our Lord Jesus Christ"; verse 21—"through Jesus Christ our Lord." Justification is through Jesus Christ; sanctification is through Jesus Christ. He is "the author and finisher of our faith."

THE SUPERIORITY AND SUPREMACY
OF LOVE

I Corinthians 13

Writing to a Christian community in a Roman colony the Apostle Paul takes as his theme, "Co-operating in the Work of God" (key word, "Lordship"). Corinth had many so-called advantages: material wealth, architectural beauty, cultural opportunities—and yet it was a corrupt city, full of vice and excess. The Church had imbibed some of this wickedness and was marked by carnality, unspirituality and worldliness. Among its members was a lack of growth in grace. The outline of the first letter explains further the dire situation of the fellowship:

   I. INTRODUCTION (1:1-9)
      A. *Greetings*
      B. *Thanksgiving*
  II. DIVISIONS (1:10–4:21)
      A. *Cause and Cure*
 III. DISORDERS (5,6)
      A. *Moral and Legal*
  IV. DIFFICULTIES (7-14)
      A. *Marriage, Food and Worship*
   V. DOCTRINE (15)
      A. *Resurrection and Immortality*
  VI. INSTRUCTIONS (16)
      A. *Systematic Giving*
      B. *Sympathetic Recognition*

The "famous" chapter, thirteen, is in parenthesis; it occurs in the middle of an argument which the writer resumes immediately afterward. Paul has been writing about gifts, urging these Corinthians to seek only the best. The best is, of course, love, the theme of this chapter, well-known but little-practiced, read at most weddings (some of which end in divorce).

Love in this chapter is "not defined" says Dr. Graham Scroggie, "only displayed." Dr. G. Campbell Morgan affirmed: "It is almost irreverent to analyze it."

The Christians at Corinth could speak in tongues, prophesy, lay hands on the sick and preach, yet their hearts were cold and lacking in love. A Bible dictionary defines love as: "an earnest and anxious desire for, and an active and beneficent interest in, the well-being of the one loved." In *The Oxford Dictionary of Quotations* there are twelve columns of extracts on love culled from poems, sonnets, hymns, prose, plays, and so on. These, however, are about a natural affection, a purely human emotion or sentiment. Paul is writing about something vastly different—a love that is only possible in one whose life is dominated by the indwelling Christ, the Son of God, who Himself is Love.

Love is displayed in this "famous" chapter as:

    I.   LOVE IS ESSENTIAL—ITS SUPERIORITY (verses 1-3)
        A. *Eloquence* (verse 1)
        B. *Prophecy* (verse 2)
        C. *Knowledge* (verse 2)
        D. *Super-faith* (verse 2)
        E. *Benevolence* (verse 3)
        F. *Conviction* (verse 3)
    II. LOVE IS EFFECTIVE—ITS SUPERFLUITY (verses 4-7)
        A. *Patient not Impatient* (verse 4)
        B. *Sympathetic not Unsympathetic* (verse 4)
        C. *Generous not Greedy* (verse 4)
        D. *Unostentatious not Boastful* (verse 4)
        E. *Humble not Proud* (verse 4)
        F. *Courteous not Rude* (verse 5)
        G. *Selfless not Selfish* (verse 5)
        H. *Good-tempered not Bad-tempered* (verse 5)
        I. *Indulgent not Vindictive* (verse 5)
        J. *Benevolent not Malevolent* (verse 6)
        K. *Shelters not Exposes* (verse 7)
        L. *Credulous not Suspicious* (verse 7)
        M. *Optimistic not Pessimistic* (verse 7)
        N. *Constant not Inconstant* (verse 7)
   III. LOVE IS ETERNAL—ITS SUPREMACY (verses 8-13)
        A. *Unfailing* (verse 8)
        B. *Progressive* (9-12)

I. LOVE IS ESSENTIAL—ITS SUPERIORITY (verses 1-3)

Paul shows how essential love is for the Christian by placing it alongside the other spiritual gifts and graces and thereby showing love's superiority. It is essential because it is superior to:

A. *Eloquence* (verse 1). The ability to talk like an angel is as nothing without love. Such talking becomes mere noise. The preaching may be "sound" and "orthodox" but if it lacks love then it will be of no use.

B. *Prophecy* (verse 2). Preaching is both *foretelling* and *forth*-telling the things of God. We may be able to explain the Book of Daniel or the Book of Revelation, be well-equipped to preach about the Second Coming, explaining the signs of the times, and so on, and yet if our hearts lack love it is valueless.

C. *Knowledge* (verse 2). Some have the ability to investigate and understand the Bible mysteries. To the world a mystery is "something obscure or incomprehensible" (Oxford Dictionary); in the New Testament a mystery is "a revealed secret" (Dr. C. I. Scofield). Some have the ability to understand the deeper truths of Scripture regarding the kingdom of God, the Body of Christ, the cross for the Christian, and yet if their heart is not fiilled with love it will avail them and others nothing at all.

D. *Super-faith* (verse 2). Some believers may have a mountain-moving kind of faith, but without love it will avail little or nothing.

E. *Benevolence* (verse 3). Others may be rich in this world's goods and generous to a degree. But if they give away to good causes without their sincere motive being love for the recipients then they might as well have held on to their money.

F. *Conviction* (verse 3). It is possible to hold on to one's convictions to the point of martyrdom, but if love is not present in the heart then the witness and testimony to the truth has been belied.

The love-less life then is a negative life. It may be a life of excitement, attainment and self-satisfaction, but the life-of-love is positive for love is superior to all other gifts and when present enhances them and makes them worthwhile and God glorifying.

II. Love Is Effective—Its Superfluity (verses 4-7)

Paul now deals with the positive, with what has been called "the over-plus of love." The true believer is one whose heart knows the fullness and the fruitfulness of love. He possesses enough and to spare. He has a superfluity of love, and that love is:

A. *Patient not impatient* (verse 4). It "suffereth long," or as we say today, "It counts ten before it speaks"! There is a waiting period before we reply and give way to anger. When wronged we prefer to remain silent and are content to leave vengeance with God.

B. *Sympathetic not unsympathetic* (verse 4). "Kind" means tolerant of, considerate of others, sympathetic toward. When expressing our point of view we take into account the feelings of others and their differing point of view.

C. *Generous not greedy* (verse 4). "Envieth not" means that there is no begrudging others what they have, their possessions or their position in life.

D. *Unostentatious not boastful* (verse 4). There is no display ("vaunteth not") of what we have or are; no seeking for the admiration of others; no self-advertisement, no boastful swagger in walk or manner. "Itself" reminds us that love never talks of love. The man who is "proud of being humble" is usually a "showy" Christian without real love in his heart.

E. *Humble not proud* (verse 4). "Not puffed up" reminds us of Aesop's frog who blew himself up to gigantic proportions until he exploded! The believer with love in his heart does not go in for self-inflation. He has no airs and graces but is humble and gracious.

F. *Courteous not rude* (verse 5). The loving believer does "not behave himself unseemly." We live today in a world that is fast becoming ill-mannered. Old-fashioned etiquette is on the wane. "Be courteous" says Scripture. Love is always polite and not ill-mannered. The Christian is not rough or coarse in speech or manner, not brusque or brutal—he does not call a spade a spade for the sheer love of it!

G. *Selfless not selfish* (verse 5). Twentieth-century man is one who insists upon his "rights." But love "seeketh not her own." The Christian is more concerned with the rights of others than his own rights. He is more concerned with giving others pleasure than finding pleasure for himself. He knows that "it is more blessed to give than to receive." True joy is found in loving, selfless service.

H. *Good-tempered not bad-tempered* (verse 5). "Provoked" has no "easily" in the Revised Version, which makes it more difficult for the Christian trying to live the love-life. The Christian is one who is never provoked at all, at any time. He never finds any excuse for losing his temper, neither illness or when defending a righteous cause. He is never "touchy" or irritable but constantly sweet-tempered.

I. *Indulgent not vindictive* (verse 5). There is no harboring of wrongs for the believer "thinketh no evil." He does not believe malicious scandal. He has no desire to "get even." He knows that mud always brushes off when dry.

J. *Benevolent not malevolent* (verse 6). The loving man does not laugh when another is "caught." He does not make capital out of another's faults or weaknesses. He does not explore the possible weakness in another and then gossip about them. He overlooks such things, "rejoicing in the truth" rather than "in iniquity." He is glad when others prosper. If a minister or evangelist, he has no "professional jealousy" in his heart toward a more successful servant of God.

K. *Shelters not exposes* (verse 7). Paul's idea here is similar to the modern umbrella. Love "beareth all things"—it is like an apron or umbrella. Love is always wanting and willing to shelter the man who has strayed, the man who is "down."

L. *Credulous not suspicious* (verse 7). Love "believeth all things." The Christian is not cynical, pessimistic, one who probes and tests everything and everyone with a suspicious mind. He always looks for some good point, some favorable characteristic.

M. *Optimistic not pessimistic* (verse 7). Even when disappointed the believer looks on the bright side—"hopeth all things." Knowing that there is something bad in the best of us and something good in the worst of us, he always looks for the best, optimistic that the word of testimony spoken will bear fruit in the other's life.

N. *Constant not inconstant* (verse 7). Love "endureth." It is persevering not irresolute. The true Christian continues to lavish affection on others when others do not appreciate it. He gives love even when that love is unrequited.

III. Love Is Eternal—Its Supremacy (verses 8-13)

Love is not only superior, above all other divine gifts, but it is supreme—highest in value as well as highest in rank or degree. Why? Because these other gifts will pass away whereas love is eternal and immortal like God Himself.

True love is:

A. *Unfailing* (verse 8). Making a slight change of letters we can say that true love is *unfading*. It never loses its freshness, its bloom. Tongues, they will fail and fade out but love is perennial. Love never "dates" like a scientific textbook. As Paul will tell us in verse 13, love is one of the three great lasting things—faith, hope and *love* (last but by no means least).

B. *Progressive* (verses 9-12). The apostle takes his illustration from the growth of a man through the various stages: babyhood, childhood, youth, man, maturity, old age. So love progresses, growing in depth, intensity, strength and inspiration.

We dare not close without noting the first verse of the next chapter—"Follow after love," or as some modern translators put it: "Make love your quest." It is an intense word, a word of effort. It means more than reading about love, studying love—we must put it into practice with strenuous effort. Love must so dominate our lives that it will lead to dynamic living.

Have we got it? Are we doing it on the individual level? Does love characterize our church fellowship? Are we noted for it in our church or chapel? Do visiting worshipers perceive it, feel it, as soon as they enter the building? The church of Ephesus was hard-working, diligent, disciplined, orthodox—yet she lacked one thing, *love*. She lacked the essential ingredient that would have transformed all others. Nothing can take the place of love—it is essential!

GIVING GENEROUSLY NOT GRUDGINGLY

II Corinthians 9

The second letter to the Corinthians is more joyful in tone than the first. Church discipline has been exercised and the many disorders, difficulties and divisions dealt with. Paul writes this letter, far less severe in manner, to vindicate his own ministry (key word, "ministry"). His theme is, "The Sacredness of the Ministry." This is thus a very human letter and deals with a variety of subjects as the following outline shows:

INTRODUCTION—THE GREETING (1:1,2)
I. EXPLANATION (1:3—6:10)
   The Trials, Travels and Triumphs of an Evangelist
II. EXHORTATION (6:11—9)
   A. *A Plea for a Complete Separation*
   B. *An Appeal for a Special Collection*
III. EXONERATION (10—13:10)
   The Ability, Affection and Authority of an Apostle
CONCLUSION—THE GRACE (13:11-14)

Chapter nine, our "famous" chapter, comes in the second main division of the letter in which the apostle is appealing for a special offering to be made for the needy believers of Jerusalem. The appeal begins in the previous chapter and there Paul reveals his businesslike methods and organizing ability. Collectors have been arranged; all is open and aboveboard, for in the finances of the Christian Church there must never be anything suspicious so that the world can lay the charge of religion being a "money-making racket."

Here then are abiding principles of Christian giving. Paul's main emphasis is on giving generously not grudgingly and he proves his point by Apology, Theology and Doxology:

I. APOLOGY (verses 1-5)
   A. *Readiness*
   B. *Reputation*
II. THEOLOGY (verses 6-14)
   A. *Giving*
   B. *Gaining*
III. DOXOLOGY (verse 15)
   A. *Marvel*
   B. *Motive*

I. APOLOGY (verses 1-5)

We use the word "apology" in the original sense of "an explanation" or "a reasoned defense," not in its accepted modern meaning of "regretful acknowledgment of an offense." In these first five verses the apostle is setting down his reasons for writing about Christian giving. The first word of the chapter is "for," which would be better rendered "Of course!" It is really quite unnecessary for him to be writing about this "delicate" matter (as today we term church finance) for two reasons:

A. *Their Readiness.* Verse 2 puts it: "the forwardness of your mind," or as it may be translated—"your willingness, eagerness, or readiness." There is the idea of alacrity behind it, the Greek implying predisposition or something already decided. These Corinthians were noted for their zeal in sacrificial giving; they did not have to be "worked upon" or "worked up" by an eloquent appeal.

B. *Their Reputation.* The generous spirit of these people had become widely known. Paul had himself boasted of it to others, using their giving as an example to stir up similar generosity among the Macedonian Christians. He had boasted that their gift was ready a year ago; now the collectors are coming and he does not want their reputation and his boasting to suffer by their default.

Then he does seem to apologize in the modern sense of the term. He says that he is sorry to be sending Titus to them with the collectors. He does not want them to be offended by the arrival of the messengers. They are only coming because he knows the money is waiting; they are not coming as a matter of "coveteousness," that is, to "wring out" the money from them. They are coming "as a matter of bounty," that is, because their spirit of generosity is so well-known.

II. THEOLOGY (verses 6-14)

Theology is the "mother" of all sciences, dealing with God's nature and attributes, His relation to man and the universe. Twentieth-century Christianity is just beginning to realize that all faith and practice should have a theological basis. Thus the various denominations are studying the theology of baptism, the theology of the Communion service, the theology of the ministry and church government, and so on. The theology of church finance is also an important subject. In the past appeals for money have been divorced from doctrine. The offering has frequently been divorced from worship as if it is an intrusion. Some have favored boxes at the door and no offering plates or bags being passed from pew to pew. Beguiled by worldly criticism of religion as a money-making project we have failed to appreciate this apostolic doctrine and Christ's teaching about money.

Paul's theology of giving can be summed up in three words: Giving is Gaining. Using a farming metaphor or gardening illustration he shows how anything sown results in a harvest and the harvest depends on what and how much is sown. Little seed means little harvest. Much seed results in much harvest. The sowing (or giving) should be done "cheerfully" (verse 7). That does not mean that we must sing a hymn or chorus during the offering. The Greek here for "cheerful" means "hilarious"—sowing with hilarity, not grudgingly, not counting out the seeds sparingly, but scattering them freely to the wind. It makes us think of a children's party where an adult throws a bag of sweets into the air and all the children scramble for them. The idea here is of lack of restraint accompanied by enjoyment. Note that there is no hint of "tithing" here; we shall see why later. But even tithing is to be a joyous affair and not a grudging adherence to a legal standard. Tithing is only a bare minimum, not a grudging maximum.

Nor is there any hint here of giving for what we can get back. Giving is gaining, but our motive must never be gain. The apostle is thinking of heavenly gain for earthly generosity. Some, of course, want to see what they are getting before they think of giving, which is the reason so many churches have sales of work, bazaars and other money-raising efforts. That accounts for missionary giving as it is in some churches—far less than giving to local evangelistic enterprises. In evangelism we can usually see *at the time* what we are giving to; missionary giving is a long-term policy.

How can we be so daringly hilarious in our giving? What are our grounds for such faith? Paul tells us (verse 8). What we have and hold has been given us from God. If we give it back to Him for His work then He will see that we do not suffer hardship. The apostle uses a great theological term, "grace," and uses it in an unrestricted sense, "every form of bounty" or "everything you need" (J. B. Phillips). He quotes a Scriptural promise in support (verse 9). A good man will not be impoverished by his giving but can go on giving from a store that is being ever-replenished (Psalm 112:9). In other words, the more we give, the more we gain!

As a further illustration Paul once more turns to nature—seedtime and harvest. As God blesses the labors of the farmer when he sows, so God will bless the man who sows by charitable acts. The word in verse 10 for "ministereth" is interesting. In classical Greek it was used of the rich man who paid for the chorus in a theater. This word for patronage by a rich person is now applied to the divine generosity of a beneficent God.

In verse 11 the apostle implies that Christian giving results not only in the generous supply of temporal, material needs by our heavenly Father but enrichment "in everything," that is, spiritual blessings as well. Many "tithers" can testify to the wonderful spiritual blessings that have come as a result of tithing.

God Himself is pleased and blessed as the Christian gives. The recipients of the gift thank God as well as the human donors and so giving is gain indeed, for God gains further glory as a result of human generosity.

J. B. Phillips explains verse 13 best by translating it: "Your giving proves the reality of your faith. Men thank God that you practise the gospel you profess to believe in." A true Christian who lives in subjection to the Gospel, who lives by the Gospel as well as for the Gospel, is one whose life is really and regularly conducted by God's standards.

A further gain from giving is that the recipients of our gifts will pray for us (verse 14). How much prayer we need! Are we missing the prayers of other Christians because of our lack of generosity? What better recompense for giving could we wish for than that we should be remembered before the throne of Grace by others.

III.   DOXOLOGY (verse 15)

The contemplation of the results of Christian generosity makes the apostle rejoice and sing aloud the praises of God. He thanks God for being the Supreme Giver and for inspiring giving in the hearts of His people. Here is why we commented on the apostle's lack of emphasis on tithing at the beginning of the chapter. "Lay aside" now says the great Paul. Who can think in terms of a minimum contribution of one tenth when God has been "hilarious" in His giving, bestowing on us a gift that is indescribable in human words—"His unspeakable gift" —Jesus Christ."

Paul's mind is taken up with a thought to which neither he nor anyone else can give adequate expression or description—God's gift of a Saviour to the world. No wonder the next chapter in this letter is in an entirely different vein. There is a long pause between the two chapters while the apostle sings his doxology. Here, first of all is:

A. *A Marvel.*   Such a great deal could be said about God's great gift, and yet when all was said nothing would have been said for it defies adequate explanation. It can lead only to "speechlessness and adoring awe and wonder" (G. Campbell Morgan). Jesus was rich, yet for our sakes He became poor (literally "a pauper." Oh, the marvel of such condescension!

Next, Paul mentions:

B. *Our Motive.*   What stronger motive for generous giving could there be than God's gift of His Son? Such sacrificial giving on God's part ought to inspire our sacrificial giving. When we think of the needs of God's missionary servants, the evangelistic home needs, the building of a new church in a needy neighborhood, here is our inspiration and motive, here is our true pattern—to see our money stamped with "the image and superscription" of Jesus Christ who gave Himself that we might live.

LIBERTY NOT LICENSE FOR LIVING

Galatians 5

The letter to the Galatians is the most intense, passionate and personal of all the Pauline epistles. Paul is appealing to his readers to turn away from "the different gospel" that has attracted them. They have gone back to a strict adherence of the law of Moses and have forsaken their new-found liberty in Christ. They are again in bondage and so Paul refers to them as "foolish Galatians." His theme, therefore, is, "The Nature of Christian Freedom" (key word "liberty"). Our "famous" chapter is the climax of his argument, and a great clarion call to "stand fast." First we must understand the whole of the apostle's appeal by noting the divisions of the letter:

    I. HISTORICAL (1, 2)
        A. *The Derivation of the Gospel*
        B. *The Defense of His Apostleship*
    II. DOCTRINE (3, 4)
        A. *The Function of the Law*
        B. *The Superiority of Faith*
    III. PRACTICAL (5, 6)
        A. *The Delights of Liberty*
        B. *The Dangers of License*

The apostle's argument has gone something like this: Some people believe that for a Gentile to become a Christian he must first become a Jew and be circumcised, submitting to the ritualistic law of Moses. Such a rite does not make a person a child of Abraham. Faith, however, does make a person a son of God and an heir with Christ. The era of faith has superseded the era of law and to return to the law would be a retrograde step. Now in this "famous" fifth chapter Paul returns to the subject of circumcision, stating that to return to that rite would mean, logically, a return to keeping the whole of the law, and so salvation would once again become a matter of law-keeping. The Chapter can be divided and subdivided as follows:

    I. THE MEANING OF LIBERTY (verses 1-12)
        A. *Not rites and ceremonies*
        B. *But faith and works*
    II. THE MISUSE OF LIBERTY (verses 13-15)
        A. *Indulgence of Self*
        B. *Influence Upon Others*

III. THE MAINTENANCE OF LIBERTY (verses 16-26)
   A. *The Works of the Flesh*
   B. *The Walk in the Spirit*

I. THE MEANING OF LIBERTY (verses 1-12)

Christian liberty must be something very important if believers are to "stand fast" (be firm and unwavering) in it and not become "entangled again," that is, become like a slave in shackles or an oxen in harness. The Revised Version margin has, "With freedom did Christ set us free." That is why our freedom is so important, because it was wrought out and won for us on the cross by Christ our Saviour. On the cross the Jewish observances were abolished once and for all when the veil was rent in two. Liberty is no longer—

A. *Rites and ceremonies.* Verse 2 specifies that circumcision was binding upon the Jew of old, and as binding as baptism is for the believer in Christ. But baptism is not a rite to be observed for its own sake; it does not secure salvation. If circumcision or baptism could save then Calvary was in vain and the grace of God could be rejected.

Positively liberty is—

B. *Faith and Works.* The faith is in God and the works are toward men. Faith must come first, for we are saved by faith and not by works. Faith is the root, works are the fruit. New Testament faith, however, is always worked out in practice; faith without works is dead. Someone has said: "We recite the creed—that is what we believe; we repeat the Commandments—they tell us what to do." The motorist is free to drive where he chooses, taking any road he wishes, but the highway code makes sure that he keeps to the highway and does not drive on the sidewalks. A musician is free to play or compose what he chooses, but he must at the same time obey the rules of music.

This all seems clear to many Christians today and we wonder how the believers of Paul's day managed to add to their faith this belief in the efficacy of the law. But are there not Christians today who are entangled with "isms?" If they had not answered the advertisement in the paper or listened to the radio program of the false cult, then they would not have become entangled with this religion that has so much of the Old Testament in it—Seventh Day Adventism and the Jehovah's Witnesses to mention but two.

Verse 11 tells us that times and habits have little changed. The important and illustrious preacher is still slandered and misreported. Some were saying that Paul himself preached circumcision. How can that be, he asks, for if he had done so he would not have been persecuted for preaching the offense of the cross. His message is one of belief in the Atonement, not the saving power of ordinances. Such critics, says Paul, deserve to be excommunicated (verse 12). "Cut off" means expelled from the Church, not mutilated or incarcerated.

II. THE MISUSE OF LIBERTY (verses 13-15)

Unless the real meaning of Christian liberty is understood there is a danger of misinterpretation and misuse. "Occasion" here is a military term meaning "base of operations" or "starting point." It has behind it the idea of violence. Figuratively it means an "opportunity." Liberty, then, is not to become a believer's base or starting-point for sinful actions and excesses. They were not saying as some were saying, "Because we are saved and under grace and not under law we can live as we please."

Two misuses of liberty are mentioned:

A. *The Indulgence of Self.* Liberty is not synonomus with license, for that results in self-indulgence of the flesh. Liberty certainly does not mean adopting the attitude "I can do as I like and please myself." Liberty is far removed from carnal indulgence in worldly pleasures and pursuits to the detriment of the spiritual life. Licentiousness, sexual excess, gross immorality, allowing the baser passions to have free play—this is not Christian liberty but self-indulgence.

B. *Influence Upon Others.* Liberty is not throwing overboard with alacrity the whole law. The law is summed up in love (verse 14). Liberty is thus loving service, gladly done as a delight and not as a duty. "By love serve one another" says the apostle (verse 13). Liberty is thus the promotion of one another's welfare. The law of love, which is true liberty, affects our behavior toward one another, preventing dissension, discord and division.

III. THE MAINTENANCE OF LIBERTY (verses 16-26)

In verse 7 the Christian life has been likened to a race, a pilgrimage. "Walking" for Paul meant the Christian's habitual conduct. Liberty, then, has to be maintained daily, moment by moment each day. First there is the negative side, it is not maintained by—

A. *The Works of the Flesh.* "Flesh" does not mean the physical body of a man, but the Christian's pre-conversion way of life, his unredeemed, carnal nature, his undisciplined passions and desires. Thus if liberty were synonomous with license then the Christian would be free to commit adultery and other sins of the body.

The positive aspect of liberty is—

B. *The Walk in the Spirit.* The believer must live in and by the Spirit who indwells him. By admitting the Spirit of God freely and wholly into the life the result will be a life of "fruits" and "fruitfulness." The "fruits" (verse 22) listed are not the natural virtues of an unregenerate "decent living" man. Fruit suggests spontaneity, sweetness, appetite. By contrast how laborious and irksome are the works of the flesh. This fruit is a divine gift, the direct operation of the Holy Spirit upon the new God-given nature of the Christian. The words of the Authorized or King James Version have changed their meaning over the years. A translation like the *Amplified Bible* gives these "fruits" in modern English form. Together they constitute a picture of the Spirit-filled Christian, the believer walking in the Spirit. There is a great difference between living in and walking in the Spirit. Living in the Spirit means that the Holy Spirit has wrought the New Birth, giving spiritual life in place of the deadness caused by sin. Walking in the Spirit is submitting to the Spirit for guidance, thus living in the will of God. It is possible to live in the Spirit yet not walk in the Spirit, but it is impossible to walk in the Spirit without first having the life of the Spirit.

In the last verse is a final warning by the apostle. Summing up the characteristics of these Galatians Paul puts his finger on the very things that stop them from being steadfast in the faith, standing fast in their liberty. They are vain, quarrelsome and envious—these are their weak points, and they are all-too-common among Christian people today. Not understanding the meaning of liberty, we misuse it, forgetting to maintain it.

FOREWARNED AND FOREARMED

Ephesians 6

The letter to the Ephesians may have been a "circular" letter for the place-name is omitted from certain manuscripts. The contents of this letter were considered so important by the Apostle Paul that his plan was to send it to several different Christian fellowships. As the theme is, "The Essential Nature and Character of the Church," it is easy to see that it had, and has, universal application. The key word is "church" and the key text 5:30.

There is a natural division in the letter, the first half being doctrinal and the second practical, so the outline of the epistle is as follows:

I. DOCTRINAL (1-3)
   The Church's—
   A. *Conception* (1)
   B. *Construction* (2)
   C. *Consummation* (3)
II. PRACTICAL (4-6)
   The Christian's—
   A. *Calling* (4)
   B. *Conduct* (5)
   C. *Conflict* (6)

It should be noted that a secondary theme in this letter is that of the Holy Spirit (closely connected, naturally, with the Church), and under the same two divisions of Doctrine and Practice occur these two subdivisions: 1. The Range Defined (the Spirit seals, enlightens, unites, occupies, teaches and strengthens); 2. The Results Demonstrated (the Believer keeps the unity, does not grieve, bears the fruit, becomes filled, wields the sword of, and prays in the Spirit). It is important to keep the two themes in mind for the Church and the Spirit are inseparable. When separated then worldliness enters the Church. The revival so desperately needed by the Church is a Holy Spirit revival.

This "famous" chapter then comes at the end of the letter and forms the final subsection of the practical half of the whole epistle. It concerns the Christian's conflict and we entitle it *Forewarned and Forearmed*.

The outline of this chapter is this:

I. CHILDREN AND PARENTS (verses 1-4)
II. SERVANTS AND MASTER (verses 5-9)
III. BELIEVERS AND FOES (verses 10-12)
IV. SOLDIERS AND EQUIPMENT (verses 13-17)
    A. *Helmet*
    B. *Breastplate*
    C. *Girdle*
    D. *Sandals*
    E. *Sword*
    F. *Shield*
V. AMBASSADORS AND BOLDNESS (verses 18-20)
VI. MESSENGERS AND ENCOURAGEMENT (verses 21-24)

In the previous chapter the apostle has ended on a domestic note, he has written of the relationship between husbands and wives. Now he continues this domestic scene by writing of—

I. CHILDREN AND PARENTS (verses 1-4)

Jewish family life was characterized by solidarity. The modern trend of "communal streets" where children are "equally at home in any home" would be shunned by them. It is because of this breakdown in family relationships that the western world is where it is today. Little or no parental discipline has resulted in ever-increasing juvenile delinquency. Writing to Timothy Paul stresses that one qualification for office in the Christian Church is the ability to exact obedience from one's children. Today with many parents only concerned with work and making money the children are left to go their own way. The "free discipline" schools have helped to foster this lack of emphasis upon discipline.

The apostle says here that children are to "honor" and "obey" their parents—but they will only do this to those who exercise, in love, Christian discipline. Chastisement must be accompanied by explanation; it must be followed by prayer after the administration and reinstatement to a position of favor after repentance has been seen.

Does the phrase "in the Lord" mean that this applies only to Christian children, and that non-Christian children can please themselves? The words "in the Lord" are not so much connected with children, or parents, but "obey." If parents make a request of their children that is in accord with divine commands, then that request is "in the Lord" and it must be obeyed. In other words, if unbelieving parents make demands of their non-Christian children, and these demands are morally in keeping with the moral code of Almighty God, then such parents can expect their children to be obedient. The obedience is to God rather than to parents. Thus parents must not expect their children to please their every whim, but only to be obedient to reasonable requests based on divine ethics and morality.

To make this easier for the children the apostle stresses the other side of the relationship: parents are not to provoke their children to wrath. Fathers as head of the family are especially mentioned, but it applies to mothers as well. We must not be unreasonable in our exercise of discipline. We must not be too severe, thus making our children bitter or resentful or rebellious. Punishment must only be given when we have "cooled off," not in a fit of temper. Positively we must bring our children up in the "nurture and admonition of the Lord," that is (according to J. B. Phillips' translation), "with Christian teaching and Christian discipline," making it our primary purpose to fit them for life here below and life in heaven above.

The result of observing this will be the divine bestowal of a promised blessing: "that it may be well with thee, and that thou mayest live long on the earth." We may expect to live happily together for a long time; no stresses and strains of family relationships will take their toll of our physical well-being. Further, to take concrete examples, if by parental example we keep them free from the slaves of smoking and strong drink, we shall insure them freedom from certain killing diseases.

II. SERVANTS AND MASTERS (verses 5-9)

The scene now changes from family to industrial relationships, from parents and children to employer and employee.

Home life is responsible for many social and moral ills in twentieth-century society, but industrial relationships have also brought hardship to many. Irresponsible workmen, lack of conscientiousness in work and a loss of the dignity of labor, has meant the dying out of some of the older crafts. Money-grabbing bosses, men with little or no integrity, have "sparked off" strikes and stoppages.

For the apostle the secret of efficiency and smooth-running is again obedience (verse 5). The worker is to do his job with "fear and trembling," or as Weymouth translates it, "with respect and anxiety to please." Not with "eye service," that is, conscious of being watched over by the foreman, but knowing that we are under divine oversight —Christ is watching! Whatever we do we do for Him, to increase His glory. This may not result in a "rise" from our earthly employer but it will result in a reward in heaven, and—

"The Master praises, what are men?"

asks the hymn writer.

Verse 9 shows the reverse side of the coin. Masters, employers, are to be respectful. They are to refrain from threats and govern by respect and love. They are not to "throw their weight about." They may be earthly masters but they have a heavenly Master to whom they will ultimately be responsible, and there is "no respect of persons with him"—He takes no notice of rank or position when dealing out His rewards.

We must remember at this point that in the main the apostle was writing to *slaves*. If these are his injunctions to them then what is expected of us? What a transformation would come over the industrial scene or the commercial scene if we lived by these precepts!

III. BELIEVERS AND FOES (verses 10-12)

Everywhere the New Testament talks of the Christian life as a war. Paul seemed more conversant with military life and terms than many others. He frequently uses military illustrations to press home a spiritual truth. He sees the Christian as a soldier and in verse 10 he tells us that the Christian soldier must be strong for the battle (later he will describe our equipment for the fight). Our strength, however, is not our own but Christ's. Powerful enemies necessitate a might that we do not possess ourselves.

We must put on God's armor, that is, for the defensive and the offensive. A small boy once saw a book in a book store that contained the words on the dust cover, "Uniform with this volume . . ." He went in, bought the book, and then demanded the uniform! The believer's book, the Bible, contains the uniform, the Christian's armor, which if put on does not leave us vulnerable at any point. We are fully equipped against "the wiles of the devil."

Paul describes the believer's foes, his deadly enemies. They are not "flesh and blood"! So often Christian people "personalize" their enemies. We would bear far less resentment and utter far less harsh criticism if only we realized that our real foes are not men and women. Our foes are the powers of darkness and evil. They certainly make use of men and women, using them as Satan's tools, but our foe is the devil himself.

"Spiritual wickedness in high places" (verse 12) does not mean evil and wickedness among men in high positions, rather "wicked spirits in the lofty regions of the air."

The believer has enemies to contend with within and without. Sin proceeds "out of the heart." Daily we have to deal with that which is within us. But sin also abounds in the world and we have to make war against the evils of our time, immorality, disease, drug addiction, drinking, blasphemy, and all the rest that characterizes our day.

IV. SOLDIERS AND EQUIPMENT (verses 13-17)

In the previous section we were *forewarned;* now we are to be *forearmed*. The apostle describes our tough armor with which to face a terrible enemy. It protects us from head to foot, each piece of armor meeting some particular need. Our adversary is Satan. Each piece of armor combats a certain characteristic of Satan.

A. *The Helmet*. Satan is "a deceiver." He deceives the head, eyes, ears and mind of the believer, so God has provided the "helmet of salvation." The Roman helmet covered head, eyes and back of neck. So God's helmet defends us against the devil's deceits and delusions. We have a salvation and a hope of salvation (a present salvation and a future salvation to be consummated) as our equipment against the wiles of the deceiver.

B. *The Breastplate.* Satan is also "the accuser," so we have a breastplate with which to counteract his false charges against our character. It covers breast and back, protecting the vital organs of the body, especially the heart. But Christ (whom we have "put on") is our righteousness and so God looks at us through His own Son.

C. *The Girdle.* The girdle is the first piece put on by the Roman soldier; it ties all else together, preventing loose pieces from hampering movement. Satan is "the liar," the father of lies, and so we need the "girdle of truth," encircling and supporting, counteracting Satan's lying contradictions. We are kept true to God's Word against all the untruths and half-truths of Satan. The motto of Spurgeon's College, London, is: "Et Teneo Et Teneor—I hold and am held." We hold to the truth, and the truth embraces us.

D. *The Sandals.* Satan is "the hinderer" so God has provided us with military sandals or shoes. The devil will do all he can to obstruct the Christian's path, hindering his progress along the highway of holiness in the service of the Gospel. These shoes, with their long "greaves" or shin guards, provide ample protection from the sharp-pointed sticks in the traps of Satan, the pits that he digs along the pathway to the Celestial City. These sandals are "shoes of preparation of the gospel of peace." "Preparation" means alacrity or swiftness. The hinderer tries to make us go slow. The days are getting short; the night cometh. Satan does not want the world converted so he slows us up in evangelism.

E. *The Sword.* The Word of God is the Christian soldier's sword, his one weapon of attack. Satan is "the tempter," but when he tempted our Lord in the wilderness he fled as the Saviour attacked him with "It is written . . ." "The Bible says" is our sword. We must know the Word and use the Word. Satan discovered its cutting power and piercing strength.

F. *The Shield.* The order of equipment we have given is not the Scriptural order, but an order that shows how we are protected from head to foot. The Roman foot soldier's shield was door-shaped and he could kneel or crouch behind it and again be covered from top to toe. Satan is "the destroyer" so we need the "shield of faith" to come between us and him. Only God's shield can keep off the fiery darts, the flaming arrows of Satan. Dr. A. T. Pierson states: "It is Jesus Himself who comes between me and the devil. How blessed is that verse I John 5:18, 'The Only-Begotten of God keepeth him, that that wicked one toucheth him not'."

V. AMBASSADORS AND BOLDNESS (verses 18-20)

The scene changes from the battlefield to the prison cell, and the characters are no longer soldiers but ambassadors. Paul is an ambassador for Christ and he is confined to prison. An ambassador is a ruler's representative in a foreign land. No greater affront can be given to another nation than to imprison its ambassador. Yet even in prison Paul is able to serve his King and speak forth his message with boldness. For this he needs the assured prayers of other believers on his behalf. They were to pray for one another (verse 18), always, all the time, constantly, not intermittently; but especially were they to pray for him as Christ's ambassador (verse 19). The temptation of gospel ambassadors is to "water down" the Gospel, or deliver it in a half-apologetic tone of voice. God's message must be given with boldness, without fear or favor. An ordinary ambassador does not tamper with the message, neither must the Christian ambassador. We must not be ashamed of our King or His royal decree.

Do we pray sufficiently for ministers of the Gospel? Do we remember other Christians and their daily witness and testimony to the unsaved? The Gospel in public and in private must be proclaimed with boldness—"as I ought to speak."

VI. MESSENGERS AND ENCOURAGEMENT (verses 21-24)

The scene is the same but again there is a change of characters. Being confined to prison he is sending a written message by a personal messenger, a common practice with Paul. In his second letter to the Corinthians he especially commends his messengers: "They are the messengers of the churches, and the glory of Christ. Wherefore shew ye to them, and before the churches, the proof of your love, and of our boasting on your behalf" (II Corinthians 8:23, 24). This became a common feature of early Baptist life in Great Britain. Churches had their "messengers" who went from place to place encouraging and exhorting, bringing cheer to small companies of Christians.

Paul knew that his various churches and converts would be concerned about him, as he was concerned about them, and so Tychicus became his messenger of encouragement. What a ministry this is, the ministry of encouragement! Some expect it only from the pulpit. The Scriptures exhort: "Comfort one another," and again, "Edify one another." We do not need to be preachers for we can "admonish one another in psalms." Here is Paul, an ambassador in bonds, in need of encouragement himself and yet his one thought is the encouragement of others. He was going to continue a bold ministry and his boldness would bring him further hardship, but he thinks only of encouraging others. When did you last encourage your minister at the close of a Sunday service? When did you last encourage a missionary on the field by writing a letter? When did you last encourage a young Christian? Are you an encourager? The Church has many *dis*couragers; become an *en*courager.

THE IMITATION OF CHRIST

Philippians 2

Although written from a prison cell this letter is full of joyous optimism. "Joy" is the key word and occurs sixteen times in various forms (joy or rejoicing). The theme is, "The Duty of Christian Optimism." Joy is connected with prayer and preaching, witnessing and healing, victory over anxiety, and much more. It is a joy that is not worked up; it is not dependent upon circumstances without; it comes from within, being first sent down as a gift from God. It enables us to live above our environment. The outline of this letter is:

The Christian rejoicing in—
   I.   Suffering (1)
  II.   Service (2)
 III.   Struggle (3)
 IV.   Strength (4)

The "famous" chapter, *The Imitation of Christ*, is the second division of the letter—"The Christian Rejoicing in Service." It is a wonderful chapter of the Word of God because Christ is central to it. Our Lord's lowly service is the believer's pattern.

A much-printed devotional book is Thomas à Kempis' *The Imitation of Christ*. Here in this chapter we have the example, the pattern to be imitated. The world today needs to see Christ in us.

An outline of chapter 2 is this:

   I.   The Sharing of the Spirit (verses 1-4)
  II.   The Standard of Christ (verses 5-11)
 III.   The Salvation of God (verses 12-18)
 IV.   The Sincerity of Men (verses 19-30)

I. The Sharing of the Spirit (verses 1-4)

Two modern translations are helpful at this point. Dr. Moffatt: "So by all the stimulus of Christ, by incentive of love, by all your *participation in the Spirit* . . ." Dr. Weymouth: "any common *sharing* of the Spirit."

The apostle makes a fourfold appeal in this first subsection: by Christ's consolation (encouragement), love's comfort (persuasive power), communion of the Spirit (fellowship or sharing), and human compassion (tenderheartedness). All these will cause the Philippians

248

to live together humbly, lovingly, so bringing joy to God and their Christian leaders.

Besides these four C's of comfort, communion, consolation and compassion, there are four L's—"Let nothing . . ." "Let each esteem . . ." "Look not . . ." "Let this mind . . ." Regarding the first, "Let nothing be done through strife or vain glory," John Trapp the Puritan commentator says: "Those hell-hags who set the church on fire!"

Paul then is describing the ideal church in which there is loving unity, each member holding in high esteem the others. When it is so then the world looks on amazed. It ought to be so for the same Holy Spirit indwells us all—we share the common life of the Spirit of God.

Verse 3 implies the same sort of cliques as Paul mentions in his first letter to the Corinthians. A group in the church were maneuvering to get their own way and gather a following behind them. Self-seeking and self-exaltation are two prevalent forms of sin among believers. Rivalry and discord can enter a Christian fellowship so easily, even a church that is fundamentally orthodox in doctrine. Only the Spirit-shared life can prevent it. Paul saw no reason why this life in harmony should not characterize the Galatian church, and to press his argument a stage further he turns their eyes from the Holy Spirit to the Lord Jesus Himself.

II. THE STANDARD OF CHRIST (verses 5-11)

The great missionary Hudson Taylor used to call these verses "Five Steps Downward and Two Steps Upward." The five down are:

1. "Made himself of no reputation." Previously in the form of God Himself, the same in appearance and essence, Jesus consented to come to this earth without such distinction, laying aside the rank and dignity that were His in heaven.

2. "Took . . . the form of a servant." He looked like a servant, performed the duties of a servant, and was looked upon by others as a servant. What infinite condescension! The Son of God was willing to take to Himself the lowest rank of mankind—that of slave.

3. "Made in the likeness of men." He became subject to man's weaknesses and infirmities. He needed food and clothing, rest and relaxation like other men. Like them He became weary and exhausted. Like them He was "tempted in all points," He experienced every kind of temptation, physical, mental and spiritual.

4. "He humbled himself." Even in the humble condition of a slave He went still further. He had no aspirations or ambitions for greatness. John Trapp comments: "The Sun of Righteousness went ten degrees back in the dial of His Father."

5. "He became obedient unto death." He yielded to God's will in all things, even when He knew it would result in the termination of life.

And he did not shrink from the worst known form of death—crucifixion.

The two steps upward are:

1. "God highly exalted him." "Wherefore" is written by Paul to show
us that this was God's reward for His Son's five downward steps. It
was an appropriate reward. He who stooped so low is now lifted cor-
respondingly high, exalted to the very throne in glory.

2. "Given a name which is above every name." Having stepped down
to be called Carpenter, Man of Nazareth, Man of Sorrows, He is now
called Saviour, Redeemer, Mediator.

In those seven steps is the standard for all believers in Christ.
He alone must be our pattern. It can be summed up in the theological
term *Kenosis* or self-emptying. It is the opposite of self-enrichment,
something to be grasped at. So the believer who would live in harmony
with other believers within the framework and fellowship of the
Church must be willing to empty himself and adopt the standard set
by Christ. In all that we do we must show forth Christ. His "mind"
must be in us, we must think like Him, and speak like Him, and act
like Him, living a self-emptying, self-denying life, saying "He must
increase and I must decrease."

III. THE SALVATION OF GOD (verses 12-18)

Conscious of our failings and shortcomings, our failure to achieve
the standard set by Christ, we must nevertheless spare no efforts to
"work out our own salvation." We must do it with "fear and trembling"
(I Corinthians 2:3), that is, with sensitivity, anxious to escape the
dangerous mistakes that damage our testimony to the unsaved.

This is essentially an outworking of what has been worked in us
by the Holy Spirit. God "worketh in you," says Paul in verse 13. The
sovereign God, through sovereign grace, has saved us. That same
grace will work in us until we are "blameless and harmless, without
rebuke," until we are in such a state of sanctification that others will
have no accusation or criticism of us to make.

The world will see that we are as light in the world, stars shining
brightly in a dark night by which men can pinpoint their position and
find their way. Through our spreading of the Gospel we shall dispel
the darkness of sin. Perhaps Paul was thinking of the Colossus at
Rhodes and not stars, that great lighthouse of the ancient world. Well,
Christians are to be like a lighthouse, encircled by the sea but en-
trenched upon the rock and entrusted with the light.

IV. THE SINCERITY OF MEN (verses 19-30)

Contemplating the future Paul hopes to send two sincere, helpful,
encouraging men to the Galatian church—Timothy and Epaphroditus.

Timothy is "likeminded" (verse 20) to the apostle, "a man of equal
spirit" is the literal translation. He was a man who would "naturally"
or sincerely care for them. His special fitness for the task was that "he

had a heart to care for them." A man of intelligence and gifts, perhaps superior in mental power and spiritual gifts to the Galatians themselves, yet Timothy made them subservient to his pastoral care of these people. He has been described as "a true-hearted and large-hearted Christian."

Epaphroditus means "charming," and here was a man who obviously lived up to his name. Paul refers to him in five different ways, a brother, a fellow-worker, a comrade in arms, a messenger and a minister. Perhaps the choicest note about this man is that he had been seriously ill and at the time of writing he has learned that his illness was causing others to grieve and sorrow on his behalf. He wished therefore that he could have kept his sickness to himself. Compare that with some Christians today who seem to "enjoy bad health" and never cease from describing their symptoms to derive sympathy from others.

"Let such men be held in reputation" says Paul. It is right to honor such sincere men by giving them a large place in our hearts. We need to turn to the apostle's letter to the Colossians to find Paul's real reason. Such men are a gift of God, the ascended Lord of glory, to His Church!

LIFE ON THE HIGHEST LEVEL

Colossians 3

The apostle wrote this letter to a people he did not know personally. Four times we are told he had "heard" of them and their faith in Christ. What he had heard was disturbing (Bible commentators call it "The Colossian heresy"). Idolatry, secrecy, mythology, philosophy—all were mingled with the Christian faith. Holy days, Jewish observances, angelic powers—these were superseding Christ. No wonder "pre-eminence" is the key word and the apostle's theme, "The Absolute Supremacy of Christ." The answer to their heresy was to put Christ first in everything, in their personal lives and in the life of the Church.

The following outline can be given of the contents of this letter:

I. The Preface of the Writer (1:1-8)
II. The Prayer of the Apostle (1:9-14)
III. The Person of the Saviour (1:15–2:3)
IV. The Position of the Church (2:4—23)
V. The Principles of the Life (3:1–4:6)
VI. The Peculiarities of the Workers (4:7-18)

The "famous" chapter forms part of the fifth section, "The Principles of the Life." Paul is concerned about Christian living. For our own sakes and for the sake of the non-Christian, the Christian life must be lived upon the highest possible level. *Life on the Highest Level* is therefore our title for this chapter. So many are content to live it on a low level, their spiritual lives barely distinguishable from the ordinary life of the unregenerate person.

Our outline of this "famous" chapter is:

I. The Precepts for This Life (verses 1-11)
   A. *Sought After* (verses 1, 2)
   B. *Christ-centered* (verses 3, 4)
   C. *Self-denying* (verses 5-11)
II. The Practices of This Life (verses 12-25)
   A. *In the Church* (verses 12-17)
      1. Forbearance and Forgiveness (verses 12, 13)
      2. Love and Peace (verses 14, 15)
      3. Ministry and Testimony (verses 16, 17)
   B. *In the Home* (verses 18-21)

I. THE PRECEPTS FOR THIS LIFE (verses 1-11)

Beginning with the Resurrection of Christ the apostle proceeds to explain how the Christian life should be one that has no place for the mundane things of the worldling. The believer has now been raised to a new, high level of living. The first precept for this high level living is—

A. *Sought After* (verses 1, 2). "Seek those things" writes Paul, that is, "reach out for them" (J. B. Phillips), "give your heart to the heavenly things."

The Christian life is not one of ease and comfort; it is a pilgrimage upon the hard, dusty road of life. The slogan "Let go and let God" has been misunderstood by many. It does not mean that the Christian has nothing to do himself. Life is warfare, cross country running, a marathon run. We must strive for mastery, we must train to increase our stamina. We must possess a correct attitude of mind toward worldly things. They must be relegated to their proper place—spiritual things must come first. Being thus heavenly-minded does not, of course, make us of no earthly use! It means that we see all things as God sees them and we see all things in relation to Him.

B. *Christ-centered* (verses 3, 4). "Your life is hid with Christ" writes Paul, and adds: "Christ, who is your life." One modern translation puts it: "Christ, the secret center of our lives." It has been suggested that "hid" refers to a valuable treasure hidden away in a place of security. The believer's life then is like a precious jewel deposited in the strong room of a bank, only it is safe for time *and* eternity. It is not entrusted to *our* keeping; *He* keeps it safe. Ought not this One who both saves and keeps be the very center of our lives, pre-eminent in all things?

C. *Self-denying* (verses 5-11). Paul has already stated in verse 3 that the Christian is "dead" to the world, to sin and to self. Now he tells us how to remain "mortified." What does he mean? If already dead how can we continue to die? What does "mortify" mean? This has been called "the hardest text in all the Bible." Of mortification John Trapp says: "It must be done or we are undone." In English "mortify" means to be affected with gangrene. The Greek word is stronger, it means "to deaden" or "subdue." Paul is saying that we are dead once and for all when we are converted—dead to our old nature, our old self. Now we have to mortify, deaden, subdue the sins themselves. It is like a surgeon who removes all dead or diseased tissue after the re-establishment of healthy circulation. Note the apostle's list of things to be mortified. A modern translation will explain them best (verse 5, 8, 9).

II. THE PRACTICE OF THIS LIFE (verses 12-25).

Precepts are meant to be put into practice. Vices are to be taken over by virtues. After "putting off" there must be a "putting on." This higher life must be put into practice in three spheres:

A. *In the Church* (verses 12-17)

1. Forbearance and forgiveness (verses 12, 13). A catalog of virtues are given for the believer to "put on." The result of this "over-all" will be a willingness to forbear and forgive. Sometimes it is easier to do the first ("to suffer fools gladly") than the second! But suppose Christ had not forgiven us. We should be as ready to forgive as He was.

2. Love and peace (verses 14, 15). As in I Corinthians 13, love is supreme, the "golden chain of all the virtues" (J. B. Phillips). Older commentators looked upon love as being the Jew's outer garment that kept all others in place, or, in the words of John Trapp: "The loops that held the Tabernacle curtains joined." In the same way "peace" or harmony is to be evident, it is to "rule in the Christian's heart." The Greek word gives us our English word "umpire." When quarrels and misunderstandings occur between Christians then Christ's peace is the arbitrator.

3. Ministry and testimony (verses 16, 17). The Word of God and Christian teaching is to be so deep-rooted in us that it will govern all our thinking and acting. We are to minister to one another; we should not rely on a one-man ministry (see Ephesians 4:12). If we cannot minister to one another in speech then it should be in song— encouraging each other with a Psalm, a hymn or a spiritual song. Psalms and hymns have stood the test of time; they are set compositions. Spiritual songs are outbursts of praise such as negro spirituals or evangelical choruses. You say you have not got a good voice? It is the inward grace more than the outward sound that really matters.

B. *In the Home* (verses 18-21). So many Christians seem to be one thing in church and other in the home. The home is the most difficult place in which to witness and live a consistent Christian life, but it is a most important place.

1. Husbands and wives (verses 18, 19). Paul has been greatly misunderstood with regard to his attitude toward women and the Christian life. He always goes back to God's original intention for man and woman as set out in Genesis. Women have become emancipated politically, and that is a good thing, but in the realm of the Church of God there is often a hankering after an unnatural emancipation. Paul urges certain obligations on both sides, to husband and wife. The woman is to be willing to "submit"; the man is to "love" and "reverence," which does not mean "subdue" if the woman refuses to

"submit"!

2. Parents and children (verses 20, 21). Obedience is emphasized on the part of children. Modern psychology says that children must be left free to please themselves; the Scriptures state that it is not a question of them pleasing themselves but pleasing God. The way to please Him is to obey godly parents. Fathers are not to discipline too severely (they are not to break the will of the young; they are not to nag and so discourage their children that they become sullen). Note that mothers are not mentioned here, yet today the disciplining of children is often left to the mother to perform.

C. *In the World* (verses 22-25). Although no longer *of* the world, the Christian is still *in* the world, this work-a-day world in which we have to conduct our daily business and in which we have to witness to our faith in Christ. For Paul much of this world was in the home, for he speaks of the relationship between the master of the house and the domestic slave. For us that would be the employer-employee relationship, the world of commerce or industry. In such an area there must be—

1. Obedience and sincerity (verse 22). The Christian does what he is told to do by one in a higher position. Our obedience is sincere obedience, based on God's Word, not an attempt to curry favor and receive promotion. By our submission to authority we show that we hold God and His Word in awe.

2. Conscientiousness and recompense (verses 23-25). Work is not to be "slap-dash," workers are not to be "slackers." The Christian is not a clock-watcher, ready to drop his tools as soon as time is up. He does not do just enough work to "get by." He is conscientious and consistent in his daily work for it is a testimony to the reality of his faith. Such an attitude does not go unrewarded. We may not receive promotion in our job, but God Himself will reward us. We may, of course, be given a greater position of trust by our employer, but ultimately our reward is in heaven, for we have worked to please God and not men.

THE DANGER OF DATE-FIXING

I Thessalonians 5

Paul's theme in the two letters to the Thessalonians is the return of Christ. "Coming" is the key word of both the first and second letters. In this first letter he stresses, "The Imminence of Christ's Return," that is, its nearness and suddenness. He is writing to Christians who have become slack and lazy in their daily occupation, and in their Christian testimony and service. Some have played "hooky" from work. Others are perplexed about their saved relatives who have already died. What will be their position at the Second Advent? These problems the apostle sets out to answer in his letter. In outline form the letter appears like this:

The Lord's Return and the Believer's—
  I. SALVATION (1)
  II. SERVICE (2)
  III. SANCTIFICATION (3)
  IV. SAFETY (4)
  V. SOBRIETY (5)

It will be seen that the fifth and last section is our "famous" chapter. We entitle it, *The Danger of Date-fixing,* for obviously Paul foresaw the "cranks" that would arise down the centuries who would mislead many with their unscriptural predictions about the return of Jesus Christ. He knew something of their ingenuity and their infamous interpretation of God's Word that would turn some from the glories of the personal return of the Saviour to lesser mechanics of Bible study such as the Irvingites and the Jehovah's Witnesses indulge in. This kind of prophetic study merely panders to the flesh, to the carnal nature of man. It is not in the least God-glorifying.

Our outline of chapter 5 will be:

  I. INSTRUCTION (verses 1-11)
      A. *Times and Seasons* (verses 1-3)
      B. *Night and Day* (verses 4-8)
      C. *Life and Death* (verses 9-11)
  II. EXHORTATION (12-22)
      A. *Officers and Offices* (verses 12, 13)
      B. *Discipline and Duty* (verses 14-16)
      C. *Prayer and Preaching* (verses 17-22)

III. Benediction (23-28)
    A. *Sanctification and Security* (verses 23, 24)
    B. *Supplication and Salutation* (verses 25, 26)
    C. *Authority and Autograph* (verses 27, 28)

I. Instruction (verses 1-11)

This opening subsection can be compared with Acts 1:7—"It is not for you to know *the times or the seasons,* which the Father hath put in his own power."

A. *Times and seasons* (verses 1-3). "Times" refers to any indefinite period of time; "seasons" means a fixed, definite time. The plural is used to indicate an infinite variety of times and seasons.

Paul tells the Thessalonians that he need not write of these times and seasons, for they know already the teaching laid down by Jesus of the end of the age and the Day of the Lord. The apostle's aim is to cure them of restlessness and idle speculation, the sin of date-fixing, when only God Himself who has mapped out the timetable knows the times and seasons. The phrase, "thief in the night," should not make us think of stealth or secrecy (like a burglar), for the Second Advent will be an open and visible manifestation. The illustration is of a sudden, unannounced arrival. "They" in verse 3 refers to the wicked upon whom sudden destruction will fall. Thus we see that Jesus is coming again before all the world is converted. "As travail" refers to the birth pangs of the Messiah.

B. *Night and Day* (verses 4-8). A change of emphasis is brought out by this illustration. Christ will come suddenly, but Christians should be awake, not asleep like the five foolish virgins. Christians are "children of light," they have been enlightened by the Holy Spirit (verse 5), and so they should live in daylight, ever wakeful and active. It should be impossible to surprise them or catch them off their guard. The unconverted will be asleep and unconcerned but the converted man will be sober, not stupefied. Nighttime is the time of sleep and inactivity; day is the time for being awake and working. Christians must be perpetually awake and on the lookout for the coming of the Lord. They must be clad in their armor (cf. Ephesians 6), although Paul only refers here to the breastplate and the helmet, the one guarding the heart and other guarding the head, showing how believers must not let their emotions run away with them nor miscalculations mislead them regarding the Second Advent.

C. *Life and Death* (verses 9-11). If we are unsaved at the return of Christ then we shall have every reason to be afraid; but the saved person, saved by the death of Christ, need not fear. Whether he is awake or asleep, alive or dead, when Jesus comes he will go to be with the Lord.

All this Paul has been writing for the comfort and edification of Christians (verse 11), to alleviate sorrow and bereavement and establish in the faith. So they are to continue (they had been doing it) to comfort and strengthen one another. How rarely we mention the Second Advent to one another! We listen to sermons on the subject, but how rarely do we comfort some bereaved believer at the graveside by referring to the coming again of our Saviour when "the dead in Christ shall rise first."

II. Exhortation (verses 12-22)

The church at Thessalonica had appointed overseers. They are not named, neither are the offices they filled, so we refer to them as:

A. *Officers and Offices* (verses 12, 13). They may have been pastors, teachers, evangelists, deacons or elders. It is not important. The office is more important than the officer.

Although only a small fellowship Paul urges them to "know" these officebearers in the church. Perhaps they had been cold, distant, formal. They were to get to know them personally and take their spiritual difficulties to them. Yet these men were "over you," that is by appointment of the Lord. Part of their oversight was to "admonish," or warn of danger, exhorting to better things, rebuking if any went astray.

In spite of the fact that some may have been admonished, they were still to respect and hold in high esteem the officebearers. If they could not adopt that attitude toward them as mere men then they must do it for the sake of the good work they were doing. Yes, the character of some Christian servant might be repellent, but if he is serving the Lord and God is blessing the work that he does, then we must hold that man in high esteem for his works' sake.

Finally they were to be "at peace among themselves." John Trapp adds: "So shall your Pastor have a better life and be able to follow his work with more content and comfort." If the pastor is forever maintaining peace among quarrelsome members, that hinders him from going about his pastoral work and the preparation of his sermons.

B. *Discipline and Duty* (verses 14-16). "Exhort" is the same as "admonish." As in Colossians Paul emphasizes that the ministry is more than a one-man affair. All members are ministers of one another, comforting, correcting, supporting, being patient with each other. "Feebleminded" does not imply some lack of mental power, but rather "dispirited or downcast." "Be patient toward all men" has been translated (in the light of the previous word "weak"): "Set your shoulder and shore them up." How we need to act as a buttress to weak church members!

Vengeance (verse 15) is to be left to God; we need not seek to repay harsh criticism. Our conduct to one another and to those outside the Church must be the same.

In verse 16, after "rejoice evermore," we must insert "in the

Lord" as Paul has written in his letter to the Phillipians. This kind of joy has nothing to do with natural disposition; it is not a happiness that depends on what happens; it is rejoicing in who and what God is and does.

C. *Prayer and Preaching* (verses 17-22). Prayer is to be without ceasing in the light of the Lord's return. We must have our morning and evening prayers daily, and perhaps family devotions. We must attend the regular meetings of the church for prayer; and always we must live in close and constant communion with God the Father. Prayer must be the Christian's "vital breath" and "native air." And prayer must never be separated from praise. "In everything give thanks." In *everything*—is that possible? Job found it possible even in death: "The Lord gave and the Lord taketh away; blessed be the name of the Lord." This rejoicing and praying (some say it refers to verse 12 onward) is the will of God.

At the same time the Spirit is not to be "quenched" (reminding us of the altar fire that was never allowed to go out). Fires go out through neglect, because of lack of air or by throwing water upon it. So may the Holy Spirit be expelled from the life or from the church —not the Holy Spirit Himself but His gracious influences.

Preaching is *fore* and *forth*-telling (see I Corinthians 14:3). It is called prophesying, because in Paul's day the preacher frequently took his text from the prophets as did Peter on the day of Pentecost. Preaching is not to be despised as it is today, with films and so on substituted in its place.

It is said that verse 21 relates to the trial of precious metals by fire, or the acid test for gold. So the believer must test what he hears and reads by an appeal to Scripture. If it is in accord with Scripture then it is right and must be held fast. If it is not in accord with Scripture then we can throw it overboard.

Finally, because Jesus is coming again, the believer must "abstain from all appearance of evil." Even when going into a tavern to distribute tracts it could look to an outsider as if we were going in for the purpose of drinking alcohol. The words may also be translated: "Abstain from every form of evil."

III. BENEDICTION (verses 23-28)

Paul's letters always begin with greetings and end with benedictions. Here the blessing is rather more lengthy than usual. It incorporates:

A. *Sanctification and Security* (verses 23, 24). The apostle prays for entire sanctification. Man is tripartite, soul (the real self), spirit (the life-principle), and body (the entire physical organism). It reminds us of the temple courts leading into the holiest place of all. So the entire man must be sanctified by the Holy Spirit. This work of sanctification depends entirely on Christ, His grace, His faithfulness in sending the Spirit of Holiness.

B. *Supplication and Salutation* (verses 25, 26). Paul's often-repeated request is one for prayer for himself and for his ministry. Like us he was tempted and temperamental, tried and tested. Perhaps his words are here connected with what he has just written, for surely the best way to achieve personal holiness is through prayer.

The holy kiss (verse 26) was on the forehead and was woman to woman and man to man. It was a ceremonial kiss, believed to precede the Communion service, among early Christians. A Puritan commentator says: "Our very civilities should savour of sanctity." J. B. Phillips gives the modern counterpart: "A handshake all round please."

C. *Authority and Autograph* (verses 27, 28). "I charge you" is the formal phrase for putting a person on oath. Perhaps Paul was calling a special church meeting or a meeting of the elders or deacons. The subject matter of his letter is so important that it was not to be read at the ordinary breaking of bread service but a special meeting was to be called on his apostolic authority.

The closing verse, our common benediction today, was Paul's frequent autograph to a letter. If, as it has been said, Paul told the Thessalonians in this letter, not to be afraid, asleep or ashamed at the coming of the Lord, then here is the secret: "The grace of our Lord Jesus Christ."

SIGNS OF THE TIMES

II Thessalonians 2

The Thessalonians misunderstood Paul's first letter. His emphasis was upon "imminence" and they had taken that to mean "immediacy." They had thus become very unsettled. This second letter is to re-assure them. Paul again emphasizes the sudden return of the Lord but he also indicates some of the signs of the approach of the advent. His theme is thus, "The Inspiration of Christ's Return." The letter may be given in the following outline form:

I. PREFACE (1)
   Salutation and Inspiration
II. PROPHETIC (2)
   The Advent and the Events
III. PRACTICE (3)
   Service and Discipline

Section two, the prophetic section of the letter, is our "famous" chapter. As there is a danger in date-fixing, so there are difficulties in reading the signs of the times. In past decades over-jealous students of prophecy have hailed successfully the invention of the internal combustion engine, the vacuum cleaner, radio and television (and now flying saucers), as being fulfilled prophecy and a sign that the coming of the Lord is near. Dr. J. A. Finlayson once wrote: "The attempt to find in Scripture support for a supernatural, or at least a supra-mundane object (i.e. a flying saucer) only goes to prove that Scripture can be used and abused to support any fancy we choose to hold. (It is) needless dissipation of (a Christian's) energies to allot any of his time to speculation." The Bible is quite clear in telling us that there will be supernatural, divine phenomenon before the advent of Christ. They will be happenings in the realm of nature and not the inventions of mankind. Paul is greatly concerned about these happen-ings, but at the same time he emphasizes spiritual verities. An outline of the chapter then is:

I. EXHORTATION (verses 1, 2)
   A. *No Agitation*
   B. *No Consternation*
II. PREDICTION (verses 3-12)
   A. *The Apostasy* (verse 3)
   B. *The Antichrist* (verses 3, 4)

C. *The Agency of Restraint* (verses 5-7)
D. *The Activities of Antichrist* (verses 8-12)
III. RECOGNITION (verses 13, 14)
A. *Election* (verse 13)
B. *Sanctification* (verse 13)
C. *Glorification* (verse 14)
IV. INJUNCTION (verse 15)
A. *Stand fast*
B. *Hold fast*
V. SUPPLICATION (16, 17)
A. *Courage* (verse 16)
B. *Confidence* (verse 17)

I. EXHORTATION (verses 1, 2)

The apostle's exhortation to the Thessalonians is a dual one:

A. *No Agitation.* "Shaken" means "tossed on a wave like a ship at sea in a storm"; "troubled" means "unsettled" or "thrown off balance." This is often the result of sinful date-fixing and wrongful reading of the signs of the times. It is on record that in 1843 seventeen persons were admitted to a mental hospital in Worcester, Mass., U.S.A., because of a deranged condition caused by a certain expectation that Christ was to come back. And this is meant to be a comforting doctrine! It is not meant to produce fear or consternation.

B. *No Consternation.* A television play in England resulted in jammed telephone wires to the producer. Russians descending on London and taking over the government of the country had been a little too realistic! Consternation was caused in the minds of many viewers. So in Paul's time false teachers, with a pretended spirit of prophecy, were frightening people. They had even misunderstood Paul's first letter and that had unsettled some. But Paul infers that they had been receiving other letters with a forgery of his name ("as from us") on the bottom.

Well, the same exhortation is necessary today. On the one hand we have the liberal theologian who dismisses the doctrine of the Second Advent, or spiritualizes it, denying a personal, visible return of Christ. On the other hand we have unscholarly, imaginative booklets and pamphlets that do damage to the doctrine, taking away the glory and majesty of the event. Others dwell on the subject so much that they neglect to preach "the whole counsel of God."

II. PREDICTION (verses 3-12)

This is the main section of the chapter. Here the apostle gives his readers the true, unmistakable signs of the climax of the age.

A. *Apostasy* (verse 3). The word means "a falling away," but here it is *the* falling away. There have always been fallings away in every century. Some have departed from the faith, and statistics reveal declining churches, lack of conversions, and all the rest. But before the return of Christ we shall see *the* apostasy—a falling away such as had never been seen before. There will be no doubt about this religious revolt. All that evangelicals have held dear for centuries will be scoffed at and denied. The apostasy will be intellectual, moral and spiritual. It will be within the Church as well as without.

B. *The Antichrist* (verses 3, 4). As there will be *the* apostasy so there will appear *the* man of sin, the "son of perdition." Prophetic students have for almost two thousand years successively labeled this man the Emperor Nero, Napoleon, Stalin, some Roman Catholic pope. Some now label the World Council of Churches as the Antichrist when they consider the apostasy of their beliefs. All we know is, that that man will claim to be superior to God, will attempt to supersede Him, claiming His honors, His attributes, His powers, sitting in His Temple in Jerusalem. Of his activity we shall see something in later verses.

C. *The Agency of Restraint* (verses 5-7). There will be a "restraining power" at work, something or someone who holds back the Antichrist. Again there have been attempts to "label" this restraining power. Some government or other has been named as being God's instrument, and certainly history reveals that governments are in God's hand and often contribute to His purposes. Once again, however, Paul reminds us that we must look on a supernatural level. This restrainer is "an apocalyptic figure" as is the Antichrist. He may be one of the fallen angels.

D. *The Activities of the Antichrist* (verses 8-12). When all restraint is removed then there will be an advent of the Antichrist before the true advent of Jesus Christ. The Antichrist will be revealed, but his manifestation will be short-lived, for the brightness of the Lord's coming will destroy the Antichrist. His activities will be Satanic, a real exhibition of the powers of Satan and hell: lying wonders that will deceive and delude the unsaved, God allowing them to be so deceived because of their rejection of Christ. These unsaved, sinful, abandoned wretches will become enraptured with the person of the Antichrist and infatuated with his errors, with *the* (again the definite article) lie as opposed to *the* truth—Jesus Christ.

III. Recognition (verses 13, 14)

Paul now turns with some sense of relief from the unsaved to the saved. He recognizes three things about the true believer.

A. *His Election* (verse 13). The believer has been chosen, divinely selected. It is an individual and an eternal election and so a matter for great thanksgiving. All the apostasy and activities of the Antichrist cannot affect the man or woman who has been chosen from before the foundation of the world.

B. *His Sanctification* (verse 13). The Holy Spirit who wrought the New Birth in the believer is now working out the Christian's spiritual sanctification. In spite of the sinfulness of the world the believer has the *Holy* Spirit working in him, making him more and more Christlike.

C. *His Glorification* (verse 14). The culmination of sanctification is glorification. One day the believer will be "perfect even as he is perfect." When the Christian is "with Christ" he will not only see Him but be like Him, sharing in, possessing the same glory as the Saviour.

IV. INJUNCTION (verse 15)

In view of the believer's election, sanctification and glorification, that is, all that God is doing for him, he should himself do two things in return:

A. *Stand fast.* The apostle is referring to temptation and persecution. Our natural instinct is to succumb to the first and run away from the second. We must stand fast.

B. *Hold fast.* The latter helps the former. The Christian must hold fast to the "traditions," that is, "the things delivered," the doctrines, faithfully and perseveringly, this helps us to stand fast in the faith precepts, promises of God, oral and written. By holding fast to them, against Satanic and worldly opposition.

V. SUPPLICATION (verses 16, 17)

Paul ends by making a prayer to God through Jesus Christ His Son. He has a two-fold request on behalf of those to whom he is writing. He prays for—

A. *Courage* (J. B. Phillips translation of "consolation" and "comfort"). We sometimes speak of "the consolations of religion" and indeed there are such. If we are not careful, however, we can wish for a Christianity that is all comfort and no challenge; all encouragement and no exhortation; all cheer and no correction. The purpose of this doctrine of the Second Coming of Christ is to bring "comfort" in difficult days and to stir us to be courageous in witness. Others must know this great truth that Jesus is coming again.

B. *Confidence.* "Stablish" implies a witness in word and work, by speech and act, by life and lip, that will be given without faltering, with no sense of uneasiness or unsteadiness. Again we see what a practical doctrine the Second Advent is—it makes for strong, courageous, steadfast Christians in a world that totters on the brink of eternity.

QUALIFICATIONS FOR CHRISTIAN MINISTRY

I Timothy 3

This pastoral epistle is personal in character, and very practical, dealing with the pastoral work of the Church. Timothy was converted as a youth when Paul visited Lystra, and now the recipient is probably about thirty years of age. The apostle's aim is to encourage Timothy in discouragement and to exhort him to preach the pure Gospel, fulfilling a faithful ministry. "Order" is the key word and the theme is, "The Function of the Christian Church." An outline of the letter and contents is as follows:

I. THE TEACHING OF THE CHURCH (1)
   Edifying not Controversial
II. THE WORSHIP OF THE CHURCH (2)
   Public Prayer and Women's Place
III. THE OVERSIGHT OF THE CHURCH (3)
   Elders and Deacons
IV. THE MINISTER OF THE CHURCH (4, 5)
   His Walk and Work

"The Oversight of the Church," chapter 3, forms our "famous" chapter of the Bible, and we are immediately reminded of the apostle's letters to the Colossians and the Thessalonians in which he stresses that the Church's ministry is the job of the whole fellowship and not one man. Members are to edify, admonish and exhort one another, by singing and by speaking. In this chapter then we have the *Qualifications for Christian Ministry*, and they have been described as qualifications that "ought to characterize all good Christians." If all Christians did possess these essential qualifications for officebearing in the Church then it would be extremely difficult to elect men to office! Our outline of the chapter is:

I. THE ELDER'S DUTY AND DIGNITY (verses 1-7)
   A. *His Private Life*
   B. *His Domestic Life*
   C. *His Spiritual Life*
   D. *His Social Life*
II. THE DEACON'S QUALITY AND QUALIFICATIONS (verses 8-13)

A. *His Character*
B. *His Doctrine*
C. *His Experience*
C. *His Family*
III.   THE MEMBERS' BEHAVIOR AND BELIEF (verses 14-16)
A. *Their Propriety*
B. *Their Certainty*

Today in many of our churches two New Testament offices have been combined in one man. Instead of having deacons (looking after finance and fabric) and elders (giving oversight to the spiritual and pastoral work of the church), we expect deacons to do both. Or perhaps an unscriptural office is created for the practical side of the church's affairs—a board of trustees or a committee of stewards. In this chapter we shall see the essential qualities and qualifications of elders and deacons.

I. THE ELDER'S DUTY AND DIGNITY (verses 1-7)

In verse 1 Paul speaks of "desire." C. H. Spurgeon used to call it "holy ambition." Too many are fond of saying, "I like to take a back seat." The important thing is to distinguish between "desire" and "loveth to have the pre-eminence." The first is a Holy Spirit influence and prompting; the second is our carnal nature rearing its ugly head.

"Bishop," presbyter or elder, comes from a word meaning "to inspect, care for, see over," thus the noun is "overseer." In classical Greek it is used for the care of the sick and in early Baptist life it meant a man on the lookout for inquiring souls after a gospel service, and one who helped in sick visitation. Here we have a description of—

A. *His Private Life* (verses 2, 3). "Blameless" does not mean "perfect" but "without charge of immorality held against them."

The elder was to be a married man and "the husband of one wife"—which some say meant no polygamy, and others that he was not to marry again when his first wife died. He was to be "vigilant" or sober, temperate in the sense of free from excess in any direction. Then too he was to be "sober" in the sense of having a sound mind, able to reason well, not under the control of bad temper, giving way to excess of passion. He must be a gentleman, of "good behavior," that is well-mannered, courteous, modest and neat in dress. "Given to hospitality" is one reason why he should be married! "Apt to teach" means capable of instructing others in the fundamentals of the faith (following up the pastor's converts). "Not given to wine" inferred that he kept good company and did not frequent the company of those habitually partaking of too much alcohol. He was to be peaceable and peace-loving ("no striker"). He must not be avaricious, "not greedy of filthy lucre," living only for gain. He must be "patient," mild and gentle, forbearing and considerate, not a " brawler," one who likes a quarrel and is all the while disposed to fight. And finally he was not to be a covetous man. In other words the elder was to be as much unlike the general run of men of the world as it is possible to be!

B. *His Domestic Life* (verses 4, 5). He must be able to "rule his own house"—again the implication is that he is married. His children must be "in subjection" and "grave." That does not mean long-faced children, subject to him like slaves. The father was to be serious-minded, not fickle and frivolous, so that implicit obedience would be given him by his children. The argument is: How can a man be expected to look after a great number of church members if he cannot look after two or three of his own children?

Finally, he is not to be a novice, one newly come to faith in Christ. He must be spiritually mature, his faith having been tried and tested. If he is to instruct others then he must be well-grounded himself. A new convert elected an elder would be in danger of becoming proud of his prominent position in the church and so would fall into Satan's sin (he fell from heaven because of pride).

C. *His Social Life* (verse 7). The qualifications of an elder must stand the test of the world outside the church as well as the members inside. The world must be able to testify to his consistent life. No matter how spiritual a veneer a man may put on in the fellowship, if his business associates in the world do not approve of his life and conduct then he is unfitted for spiritual ministry and position in the Church. By taking office unworthily he will bring reproach upon the Christian faith and church. Satan will see to it that those outside the church will talk and point the finger!

II. The Deacon's Quality and Qualifications (verses 8-13)

"Deacon" is a word that was used by the ancient Greeks for "errand boy," impressing upon us that all church officers are servants of the church. These men in the Early Church dealt with the finance of the church and the fabric of the church, the offerings for the poor and the church properties. We have to note:

A. *His Character* (verse 8). "Double-tongued" is used nowhere else in the New Testament. Literally it means "uttering the same thing twice" and then came to mean "speaking one thing and meaning another." Deacons then must be utterly truthful, men of their word. It can also be used of "tale-bearers," so deacons must be men of strict confidence.

B. *His Doctrine* (verse 9). A "mystery" in Scripture is a spiritual truth hidden from men in general but revealed to someone privileged. We often read that God "made known" His mysteries to Paul. Deacons then are men rich in spiritual discernment, even though by virtue of their office they deal with temporal things. They are men who have a real grasp of Christian doctrine.

C. *His Experience* (verse 10). As the elder must not be a "novice" so the deacon must be a man who has "proved" himself. The first seven deacons ever elected, we read, were men "of honest report."

D. *His Family* (verses 11-13). Like elders they must be men of one wife, and this time the qualifications of the wives are also set out. Why? It is thought that the early deacons did a lot of house-to-house visitation (perhaps distributing the money for the poor, or conducting the breaking of bread services), and their wives could have spoiled this spiritual ministry by gossip, repeating what their husbands saw and heard. Deacons' wives are to be "grave," serious-minded, not "skittish," frivolous or false accusers ("slanderers"). They must be "faithful in all things"—faithful to the Lord, the truth, the Church, their husbands and families.

III. The Members' Behavior and Belief (verses 14-16)

Paul obviously does not regard Timothy as the permanent pastor for he himself is going to make certain alterations on his next visit. What he now writes is for all the members of the fellowship. There are no definite articles here so commentators are agreed in saying that all Christian congregations are being addressed and advised by the apostle. "Thou mayest know" (verse 15) is translated in the Revised Version—"Know how *men* ought . . ." Here then is a word to all church members.

A. *Their Propriety* (verse 15). High standards have been fixed for elders and deacons. Now a certain standard of propriety, of good behavior, is expected of all members of the church. We should behave ourselves in God's House. There should be no whispering to one another before a worship service begins, and after an intense, earnest gospel appeal at the end of an evangelistic service we should again see that we do not detract from the solemnity of the occasion by idle gossip. After the end of the weeknight prayer meeting we should remember in whose presence we have been, and what tremendous things we have been asking in faith.

It is the "house of God," that is why we have such a sense of right deportment. Paul does not mean a building first of all, but a fellowship built of "living stones." It is a fellowship meeting within the walls of a building that has been erected and dedicated to the glory of God. Dare we sing—

> We love the place, O God,
> Wherein Thine honour dwells,

and then conduct ourselves unworthily? The Church is the "pillar" and "ground" of truth, the bulwarks and buttresses of divine truth. These architectural terms explain something of the spiritual, doctrinal, and theological aspects of the Christian faith. The visible Church of God on earth preserves the truth of God. We must be careful how we behave in it so that we do not bring it into disrespect with the world.

B. *Certainty* (verse 16). "Without controversy," that is, undeniably, with certainty. The Church stands for certain truths: the Incarnation (God manifest in the flesh), the Vindication of Christ (the Holy Spirit's refutation of all false charges laid against Him), the Ministration of angels (who attended our Lord at every stage of His life), the Proclamation of the Gospel (to the Gentile world as well as to God's chosen people), Redemption (the salvation of the world through the blood shed at Calvary), and Exaltation (the reception into glory of the risen Christ). These are some of the main truths entrusted to the Church and which the Church must guard from error. These truths must govern our behavior. These are the truths which we must hold if we would become overseers of the flock of God, elders or deacons.

ON ACTIVE SERVICE

II Timothy 2

The theme of the second pastoral letter to Timothy is "The Minister's Fidelity to the Truth." Again the apostle writes to encourage his spiritual son. This was the last letter written by the great apostle and so special attention must be paid to its teaching. The key word is "loyalty" and the letter's outline is:

I. THE CHARACTER OF THE MINISTER (1, 2)
   A. *Zeal, Courage and Fidelity*
   B. *Diligence, Patience and Separateness*
II. THE CONDUCT OF HIS MINISTRY (3, 4)
   A. *In Time of Change*
   B. *In Face of Death*

The "famous" chapter comes from the first main division of the letter and the second subdivision. Our title is taken from J. B. Phillips' rendering of verse 4—"No soldier *on active service* gets himself entangled in business, or he will not please his commanding officer."

Our outline of this important chapter is:

I. THE MINISTER'S CHARACTER DESCRIBED (verses 1-7)
   A. *Soldier*
   B. *Athlete*
   C. *Farmer*
II. THE MINISTER'S CREED DECLARED (verses 8-13)
III. THE MINISTER'S CONDUCT DEFINED (verses 14-26)

The true minister of Christ must suffer hardships like a soldier on active duty. He will be persecuted, criticized, tempted, and so must be strong enough to stand up to this active life. Paul first deals with the minister's character:

I. THE MINISTER'S CHARACTER DESCRIBED (verses 1-7)

It is important to note the tense of the Greek used—"Be continually strengthened." The Christian minister needs daily physical and spiritual strength, for in that strength he is to teach others the truths of the Gospel.

"Commit" means "to deposit," so ministers of the Gospel are guardians of God's truth.

We must be strong enough to "endure hardships," that is, put up with a soldier's privations. *Three* illustrations are given here, however, a military one, another from the field of sports, and an agricultural one.

A. *Soldier*. Regular, rigorous training is the policy of the military, plus "toughening-up" courses from time to time. Mock battles have to be fought in peace time, endurance tests have to be carried out, also trials initiated. The soldier is away from home and friends. Sometimes he is sent to a hot climate or to a cold country. He must be fit for service anywhere. He must not be a part-time civilian, taking on a civilian job while in the army. Children play at soldiers, of course—it is part of their growing-up process. When tired or cold they can forget their game and go indoors to bed. Some Christians only play at being soldiers, but Paul says we are to be *real* soldiers if we are in the ministry, for we are in the front line of the attack.

B. *Athlete*. Paul may have in mind the runner or the wrestler. Both need to go into training to attain stamina for the race or conflict. Both must keep to the rules of the sport. They must watch how they discipline themselves, taking due regard of weight and diet. So the Christian must discipline himself and get himself into peak condition for service.

C. *Farmer*. The man who cultivates the earth should be "first partaker of the fruit" says Paul. Does he mean, "the first one to partake of what he has grown"? He might mean: "Any man who would reap a harvest must first work to produce a harvest." Labor must precede reward. So the Christian in full-time service must work hard to produce a harvest and rejoice in his reward for fruitful service.

These three illustrations then speak of devotion, discipline and diligence. There must be devotion to duty like the soldier; discipline of one's powers like the runner or wrestler; and diligence in work like the farmer.

II. The Minister's Creed Declared (verses 8-13)

Paul, as a minister of Christ, now declares his beliefs. Here is a doctrinal statement which he urges Timothy to pass on to others.

He begins by stating his faith in the Resurrection, which presupposes his faith in Christ crucified. By reminding Timothy that Christ was of the seed of David he emphasizes his belief in the humanity of Christ. By going on to the Resurrection he shows his belief in Christ's deity. In the first we have the virgin birth, and in the second the resurrecting power of the Holy Spirit. And this is not only the creed that he holds himself, as his personal beliefs, but it is the burden of his preaching—"his evangelizing as well as his evangel" (I.V.F. commentary).

The result of preaching such a creed brings the preacher trouble. In Paul's own case it was bonds, that is, fetters, chains, the prison cell. But that did not fetter the Gospel. The messenger may be enchained, but the message is free and goes out into the world setting sinners free. For that reason Paul was prepared to go on enduring hardship. In order that men might be saved he was willing to suffer indignity and persecution of all kinds. What befalls the individual Christian minister is as nothing when set side by side with the progress of the Gospel.

This creed is worthy of being adopted by all Christians for it is "a faithful saying." It is believed by some commentators that the short, pithy sayings in this section once formed part of an early Christian hymn sung by martyrs to inspire one another to live faithfully even in the face of death. If we suffer with Christ, says Paul, then one day we shall reign with Him. If we go to our deaths then one day we shall live forever with Him. And He may come again before we are called upon to die.

Then comes the darker side of the picture: suppose we go under? Suppose we should deny our Lord and our allegiance to Him? Then one day He will have to deny us, for it would be a denial of God's nature to be unfaithful in these things.

III. THE MINISTER'S CONDUCT DEFINED (verses 14-26)

Creeds can be recited or sung. They can be argued about. Controversy about them can wage hot and strong and people can be alienated from each other. Timothy then is to minister so that he wins divine approval by the proper handling of the Word of God.

Two men, it appears, had been failing in their ministry on this very point. Uttering false, heretical teaching about the Resurrection (the bodily resurrection of believers), they had nevertheless gained a following. This particular form of heresy was like a "canker." Our minds immediately think of a canker or worm in an apple. The illustration is wrong; it is too weak. The Greek word gives us our word "gangrene." This false doctrine was cancerous and well-nigh incurable; it had gotten such a hold.

A note of hope follows, however, "the foundation of God standeth sure." There was a steady, rock-like remnant in the Church who had not been swayed by these men. And this foundation stone had a "seal" on it. It was customary then, as now, to put the builder and architect's names upon a stone in the building. The "seal" or inscription read: "The Lord knoweth them that are his," that is, no one can deceive God; He can discern between the true and false, the nominal churchgoer and the genuine born-again Christian. The second inscription was: "Let every one that nameth the name of Christ depart from iniquity." God not only knows His own; His will is that they should live holy, pure lives.

Continuing his theme of the church as a building Paul reminds Timothy that in a great house there is no uniformity or level of importance for the utensils in it. Not all furniture and fittings are of the same material, shape, size and usefulness. Some cost a great deal; others are cheap. Some are for cooking meals, others for scraping mud off shoes. Some are for eating and sleeping while others are for garbage or refuse. So within the Christian community some are called to prominent positions (elders, deacons, pastors and teachers), while others perform humble tasks (stewards, caretakers or janitors). But we are all in the great house, we all have a place and function to perform. It behooves us to keep ourselves away from contaminating, sinful influences that will render our service useless.

"Flee youthful lusts" first of all, declares Paul. As a young man Timothy is to turn his back on the temptations common to one at his time of life. This is also a word to much older Christians, for sometimes they hanker after the desires and pleasures of youth once again. Positively, our time and thinking must be taken up with "following righteousness," practicing regularly those things that are good and virtuous, living the true life of faith. And we must love all men. C. H. Spurgeon once said that he would rather spend all eternity with some people than half-an-hour with them on earth! Yes, in heaven we shall "be changed." The only way to love and "get on" with some Christians down here is to think of them changed and ready for eternity. That helps us to live "at peace" (in perfect harmony) with others.

Once more there is a negative. Trifling and unedifying questions, the raising of controversial points that cannot finally be settled this side of heaven, must be avoided, for they only cause heated arguments. The true servant of God is not to "strive," that is seek to be victorious in argument, "get one over" a brother Christian, for the mere sake of being the victor. By contrast the true pastor of his people will be gentle and not quarrelsome, ready to instruct others patiently in the things of the Spirit, even those who have willfully embraced error. Thus will they be led to repent of the error of their ways and receive God's forgiveness and be restored to fellowship.

How little have we learned the apostle's lessons today. We shall see how Jude speaks of "contending for the faith" later in these studies. It does not mean rudeness of speech and behavior, an attitude of mind that repels instead of attracting. Courageous exposition can still be courteous. The apostle's last word, however, is to the modernist, liberal theologian, the one who is not faithful to his calling, who does not hold to the creed as defined in this chapter. Such a man is in the snare of the devil, entangled, confused, intoxicated. Our attitude toward such a man must not be a bitter spirit of condemnation. We must love him and with meekness instruct him so that he might become "sober" (Paul's word is translated "recover") again after his sinful intoxication.

PIOUS BELIEFS OR PERSONAL BEHAVIOR?

Titus 2

Written in between the two letters to Timothy, this letter to Titus is another pastoral letter by Paul. Titus, like Timothy, is another of Paul's sons in the faith.

The key word is "ideal" and the theme: "The True Church of God." Things were not in an ideal state in Titus's church, however, and so the apostle writes to Titus about the church's organization, doctrine and practical piety. Our outline then is:

    I.   ORDERLY ORGANIZATION (1)
        A. *Its Nature and Necessity*
   II.   SOUND DOCTRINE (2)
        A. *Its Comprehensiveness and Authority*
 III.   PRACTICAL PIETY (3)
        A. *In Civil and Social Life*

This "famous" chapter is about sound doctrine then, and the apostle emphasizes orthodoxy. It is possible to be orthodox and spiritually dead, as it is possible to be evangelical and yet not evangelistic. Orthodox belief must always result in true Christian living or behavior. This chapter may be divided into the following sections:

    I.   TITUS And—
        A. *The Old* (verses 1-3)
        B. *The Young* (verses 4-6)
        C. *The Preacher* (verses 7, 8)
        D. *The Employed* (verses 9, 10)
   II.   PAUL And—
        A. *The Past* (verse 11)
        B. *The Present* (verse 12)
        C. *The Future* (verses 13-15)

I. TITUS and—

    A. *The Old* (verses 1-3). In the previous chapter Paul has dealt with the need for exposing harmful, false teaching. Now he exhorts Titus to give out "sound doctrine" or healthy teaching (Revised Version). This kind of teaching is greatly concerned with Christian conduct. J. B. Phillips entitles this section in his translation of the

New Testament—"Good character should follow good teaching." The title is insufficient. Good teaching should result in good characters *and* good conduct. The best counteraction to false teaching is to let the world see lives that are morally and spiritually healthy. All ages and both sexes, and differing social sections of the community are dealt with here, beginning with the old.

The old are the most neglected section of the community in Christian and non-Christian spheres. Today's emphasis is on youth. Paul's order is: fathers, young men, little children—the order given by his brother apostle, John.

The old men are to be "sober" or watchful. Some young Christians seem to imagine that the older, more mature believers never have any temptations. The devil sees to it that there are special temptations for the old as there are for the young.

These elderly men are to be "grave," that is venerable, serious, revered for their sane and serious attitude to life, especially as they are soon to pass from it into eternity! Perhaps it also means that they are to be restrained in dress. They must also be "temperate." Self-restraint must be imposed. There must not be excess in any field of life. The older Christian must be on an even keel, keeping his balance well in all things. He may not be sound in body at that age, but he can and must be "sound in faith."

The old women must be characterized by "holiness." They must not be "false accusers" or slanderers (the word is applied to the devil himself elsewhere in Scripture; Satan is the Accuser!). They too must be temperate in the sense in which we generally understand it—"not given to much wine," and they must be "teachers of good things." Let them pass on Biblical teaching to the younger women.

B. *The Young* (verses 4-6). Young wives are to be serious-minded ("sober"). They are to "love their husbands" and "love their children." Again and again the New Testament writers emphasize the sanctity of marriage and home life. Domestic bliss is not a dream but a reality for the Christian couple. So these women are to be "discreet" (the same as "temperate" in verse 2) and "chaste"—pure in heart as well as body. Then they are to "keepers at home," that is, home-lovers, domesticated, not "gadabouts," ever away from home for one reason or another. "Obedient to husbands" underlines the Biblical concept of the headship of man in spiritual things. And all these qualities are to be cherished and guarded so that "the word of God be not blasphemed," that God's Word shall not be discredited.

The young men are also to be "sober-minded," serious in deportment and steady in behavior. The worldly attitude, "You're only young once," implying that a young man can "sow his wild oats" and "kick over the traces," is quite unscriptural. Yes, we are only young once. In a little while young men are old men and will have to take the place of the older men in the church. How can they take the place of the present "pillars" of the church if they are not trained in these important characteristics and graces.

C. *The Preacher* (verses 7, 8). The pastor of the flock must be "a pattern of good works," a practical model to his congregation or membership. His pulpit utterances and his daily life and example must tally. In doctrine there must be "uncorruptness," "gravity" and "sincerity," which some think are characteristics of the teaching rather than the teacher. How this contradicts the modern jovial-evangelist style of preaching, the "anything-for-a-laugh" attitude.

D. *The Employed* (verses 9, 10). Is the apostle now giving us a description of slavery in Crete? The people of Crete were called "liars, beasts and gluttons." Slavery was a terrible thing in those days. Yet Christian slaves, objects of abject misery to the world, were to "adorn the doctrine of God"! They could preach the Gospel by lip to their master and mistress, but by their lives they could testify to the reality of their faith. Their work must be done willingly and cheerfully, with no back-answering and no grumbling and contradicting. They were not to steal their master's goods. They were to be faithful on every possible occasion. What an example to workmen today! Is our boss an overbearing character? Then by our silent witness, the way we do our work, we adorn the doctrines we believe.

II. PAUL and—

A. *The Past* (verse 11). Having instructed, advised and exhorted Titus Paul now makes a declaration of his own belief and behavior. Here is a remarkable summary of doctrine—foundation facts —that if lived out as well as believed in will result in others becoming believers.

He uses the past tense that signifies a definite, completed act. Christ came, Christ died (the Incarnation and the Atonement). He came to offer a universal salvation (He offered it to all men, Jew and Gentile alike).

B. *The Present* (verse 12). If that salvation is received then it makes life in the present entirely different. Negatively we abandon certain things: "ungodliness" (all that is anti-God), "worldly lusts" (the insatiable desire for pleasure, power, possessions and position); positively we seek to live lives that are "sober" (restrained) and "righteous" (just and right as regards our fellowmen). We are "godly" in the sense of living to please God.

C. *The Future* (verses 13-15). We look to the future for Christ's return in glory, remembering how He died to redeem us and to make us "peculiar" or in a special sense His own. If only we thought more of the Second Advent then we would be more "zealous of good works."

There then is the doctrine, the beliefs that should result in good behavior. A good life is not enough by itself without the doctrine, and the doctrine without the good life will only cause men to "despise" us, that is, say that we are not worthy of their attention.

TWO-WAY FELLOWSHIP

Philemon

This letter is the shortest written by the Apostle Paul. A prison letter, it is nevertheless very personal in tone, and in spite of its brevity is a literary masterpiece. Here is a great example of Christian dignity, courtesy and affection. If the Christian cannot write to a fellow Christian in this strain then he might as well not set pen to paper.

The subject matter of the letter is rather delicate. Paul's friend Philemon, perhaps the pastor of the church at Colossae, has had a slave called Onesimus. Onesimus, after embezzling his master's goods, has run away to Rome, but there has come in contact with Paul and with Christ. Onesimus has been converted. So Paul uses fifteen arguments in favor of Philemon receiving back his runaway slave on a different footing, not only as a slave but as a brother in the Lord. Philemon is to *forgive* Onesimus. "Forgiveness" is the key word of the letter, and the theme is, "The Outworking of Christianity."

As there are no chapter divisions in this letter we shall have but one outline:

    I. SALUTATION (verses 1-3)
        A. *The Writer*
        B. *The Recipients*
    II. PAUL'S PRAYER FOR PHILEMON (verses 4-7)
    III. PAUL'S PETITIONS TO PHILEMON (verses 8-21)
    IV. BENEDICTION (verses 22-25)
        A. *The Blessing*
        B. *The Blessed*

It is Dr. G. Campbell Morgan who points out the "Two-way Fellowship" of this letter. He calls it "two-sided" fellowship (*Searchlights from the Word*), that is, fellowship between Paul and Philemon and Onesimus, and fellowship with the Lord Jesus Christ. Paul can only write to Philemon as he does on the basis of this two-way fellowship being effectual and acted upon. The circumstances were such that this two-way fellowship was possible; now he hopes it will become actual.

Often the fifteen arguments of the apostle are overlooked in studying other matters in this "half sheet of paper" (as someone once called this letter), so let us review them briefly before studying the letter in detail under the divisions of our outline

"Take Onesimus back," writes Paul, "because . . .

1. You are always doing good, so continue in well-doing;
2. It comes within my authority as an apostle to ask this of you;
3. I waive my authority and ask it for love's sake;
4. I am old, so respect the plea of an old person;
5. There is a spiritual relationship (father and son) between Onesimus and myself;
6. He that was once unprofitable is now profitable;
7. I love him as myself;
8. I am denying myself his company and help in sending him back to you;
9. So great is his change of heart that he will be yours forever;
10. He will come back as more than a mere servant;
11. He comes in my place, for I cannot come to you yet awhile;
12. I give my word that he will give satisfaction;
13. You are so much in my debt;
14. It will give me joy and comfort;
15. I have always had a good opinion of you, knowing you always do more than I ask."

Then, too, the three applications of this letter are sometimes missed by the one who reads "on the surface" of God's Word. There is a social application—the Christian attitude toward slavery in Paul's time is dealt with here. In the words of the Inter-Varsity *New Bible Commentary*: "To preach brotherly love between master and slave ultimately makes slavery meaningless." Thus it is possible to call this letter a "charter of emancipation," although it does not strongly denounce slavery as social workers and philanthropists have done since. It attacks the problem on the highest level.

There is also a personal application. The Christian faith, when adopted by employer and employee, does not abrogate the old relationship; there is, however, a new relation which bears upon the old.

Finally, there is the evangelical application. In this letter is "a mosaic of gospel truth." The great truth emphasized is the New Testament doctrine of "identification." Paul identifies himself with Onesimus as Christ identifies Himself with the sinner. We are accepted by the Father because we are *in* Christ.

I. SALUTATION (verses 1-3)

The writer is Paul, and he describes himself as "a prisoner," not of Rome but of "Jesus Christ." Timothy is with him, and together they salute Philemon who is a brother in the Lord and a fellow laborer in the Lord's service. Apphia was probably Philemon's wife and Archippus perhaps their son, an evangelist in that district. Finally there is a church fellowship in Philemon's house and Paul seems to expect that his letter will be read when they are gathered together for worship or prayer, maybe when Archippus is giving a report of his work.

II. PAUL'S PRAYER FOR PHILEMON (verses 4-7)

As in Philippians Paul here tells us that he prays constantly for various fellow Christians. He has great cause for praise as well as prayer on Philemon's behalf for he has heard, doubtless through Onesimus, of Philemon's "love and faith." It is good to know that even when Onesimus was "outside Christ," a sinner in Philemon's home, that he noted the piety and faith of his master. We never know what effect our personal lives have upon the unsaved, even though we do not see them converted.

The apostle's great prayer on behalf of Philemon is that "the communication of thy faith may become effectual by the acknowledging of every good thing which is in you in Christ Jesus." Literally it means that Paul is praying that Philemon's faith might be *operative* ("effectual") or effective in producing results. This might have reference to Philemon's preaching gift, and Paul is thus praying that he might see many conversions as a result of his preaching of the Gospel. On the other hand it may well mean that Philemon's faith is to produce fellowship—two-way fellowship, between himself and his Lord and between himself and other Christians. Or Paul's prayer could be that he wants Philemon's faith to blossom out in greater personal spiritual attainments, Christian virtues and graces and active Christian good works. At any rate these possible interpretations give Christians today sufficient reason for praying the same prayer for each other: that our faith might become "effectual."

III. PAUL'S PETITIONS TO PHILEMON (verses 8-21)

Paul now appeals on behalf of Onesimus to Philemon and presents the fifteen arguments in favor of the slave being received back and restored to favor. Philemon could, of course, have had Onesimus crucified as a runaway slave and thief. Historians tell us that "death by crucifixion was no unusual penalty for a heathen master to inflict for such offences." It seems logical to suggest that Philemon took heed of Paul's petitions and saved the life of Onesimus—the letter would hardly have been preserved for us otherwise.

It has been pointed out therefore that Onesimus was literally saved *from* a cross *by* the cross. Because the blood of the cross had saved Philemon, he forgave Onesimus and the slave was saved from death by crucifixion by the crucifixion of Christ. Martin Luther comments: "We are all the Lord's Onesimi." Yes, we are all sinners; we all deserve to be punished (and "the wages of sin is death"), but we are saved by the cross.

Having considered in our introduction the fifteen arguments we will not spend time reviewing them again. In this section, under the heading, "Paul's Petitions to Philemon," we will continue to stress important, and often overlooked points. For instance, in verse 16 Paul refers to Onesimus as his brother and Philemon's brother. We know that it was spiritual kinship with Paul, but was it not a flesh and blood relationship with Philemon? "In the flesh" is the phrase Paul uses. Onesimus Philemon's own brother? Why not, for in those days relatives were sold into slavery for a variety of reasons. Dr. G. Campbell Morgan states: "When Paul says that Onesimus was a brother to Philemon, not only in the spirit but in the flesh, he means it. I have no doubt that Onesimus was a slave to his brother."

The characteristic note of these petitions or pleas to Philemon is in the two words "but now" (verse 11). These two short words are favorites of the apostle. Dr. James Stewart comments: "Again and again they break out of his argument like the sudden note of a trumpet or the beat of a drum." Listen to these examples from other Pauline correspondence: "The end of those things is death. *But now,* being made free from sin." Or: "Ye were without God in the world: *but now* ye are made nigh." Every word of Paul's letters has been carefully selected under the inspiration and guidance of the Holy Spirit. These "but nows" make a fascinating and rewarding study. Onesimus can sing:

> What a wonderful change in my life has been wrought,
> Since Jesus came into my heart.

Paul can see the transformation and so he can write to Philemon of his slave's former condition and then add, "but now." It is the "but now" that supplies reasons for his return and restoration. It is the "but now" that gives Paul the opportunity and courage to write his petitions down and send them to Philemon. It is the "but nows" that will tell in our lives; it is the "but nows" that will influence others for Christ and make them desire Him and the salvation He offers.

So Paul can ask Philemon on behalf of Onesimus for forgiveness, restoration, favor, generosity, because of the "but now," the fantastic change that has come over Onesimus since receiving Christ as his personal Saviour.

IV. BENEDICTION (verses 22-25)

A. *The Blessing.* Having begun by assuring Philemon that he was praying constantly for him, he now expects Philemon to pray for him, and that prayer will be answered so that he will obtain his release from prison and pay Philemon a visit. This would give Philemon additional incentive in receiving back his former slave.

The apostolic blessing is a familiar one to readers of his letters (verse 25). In it he emphasizes the importance of the grace of God and the spirit of man. A Puritan once put it: "A grain of grace is worth a world of wealth." The spirit is the immortal part of man and grace is eternal. Paul's benediction then is not for time alone but for eternity.

B. *The Blessed.* "Your spirit" and "your prayers" are in the plural possessive and so the benediction is all-inclusive—Philemon, his family (verse 2) and his friends ("the church in thy house"). The blessing also comes from friends of Paul (verse 24), men we surmise who voluntarily took it in turn to share the apostle's imprisonment.

THE WESTMINSTER ABBEY OF THE BIBLE

Hebrews 11

The letter to the Hebrews was written to show "The Superiority of Christianity" (key word: "better"). It was written by an unknown author (although tradition has it that it is a Pauline epistle) to Hebrews or Jewish Christians. Their spiritual danger was that they inclined to go back into Judaism with all its legalism. The letter points out the superiority of the Christian faith over the types and figure, examples and shadows of the Old Testament.

An outline of the letter may be given in the following form:

    I. INTRODUCTION (1:1-4)
   II. CHRIST SUPERIOR TO PRINCIPALITIES AND POWERS (1:5—2)
  III. CHRIST SUPERIOR TO PROPHETS AND PRIESTS (3—7)
  IV. CHRIST SUPERIOR TO INSTITUTIONS AND ORDINANCES (8—10:18)
   V. THE SUPERIORITY OF FAITH (10:19—13:17)
  VI. BENEDICTION (13:18-25)

Our "famous" chapter, the well-known chapter on faith, forms part of the fifth main division of the letter—"The Superiority of Faith."

In Westminster Abbey, London, lie the mortal remains of the famous. There are to be found tombs and statues of poets, politicians, philanthropists, playwrights, preachers, and many other famous people in different walks of life. Hebrews 11 has frequently been referred to as *The Westminster Abbey of the Bible,* for in these forty verses are named nineteen well-known people from the Old Testament.

Here is more than an interesting catalog of "Heroes of the Faith." Here are words of encouragement for all Christians in the hour of discouragement, temptation, persecution or affliction. These heroes and heroines of long ago are set before us to inspire us to live by faith as they did.

The chapter may be studied under the following headings:

    I. FAITH DEFINED (verses 1-3)
   II. FAITH ILLUSTRATED (verses 4-38)
       A. *The Martyr, Confessor and Preacher* (verses 4-7)
       B. *The Patriarchs* (verses 8-22)
       C. *The Leaders* (verses 23-31)
       D. *The Judges and Prophets* (verses 32-38)
  III. FAITH CONSUMMATED (verses 39, 40)

I. FAITH DEFINED (verses 1-3)

The writer's aim in this chapter is to show that in God's sight faith is necessary for all worth-while achievement and endurance. This he does by definition and illustration.

His definition is really a description, for who can adequately define faith? Faith, according to this writer, deals with things immortal ("things hoped for") and things invisible ("things not seen"). Nevertheless faith is as real as substance; it is not shadow. Faith is "assured confidence and settled expectation" (I.V.F. *New Bible Commentary*). Because the writer's forefathers in the faith lived by this kind of faith, God has favored them by having their faith spoken about and recorded for all time in Scripture ("a good report"). This same faith enables us to understand the natural, material, created world, and the things of the spiritual world. Faith is thus a firm confidence in unseen and future realities. The writer is not dealing with that personal saving faith that results in conversion. He is writing of faith in its general and comprehensive concept, faith that enables the saved man to live by faith. This faith enables us to connect our present life, our daily walk and work as Christians, with the future world—heaven and God and Christ, the consummation of the age, time becoming eternity.

II. FAITH ILLUSTRATED (verses 4-38)

All the illustrations are Scriptural. Men of faith are brought to our view and notice—all Old Testament characters in chronological order.

A. *The Martyr, Confessor and Preacher* (verses 4-7). The martyr is Abel, and Abel's faith enabled him to make a blood offering and so overcome the death that had passed upon him through his first parents. Thus Abel's faith in his sacrifice and in the way he offered it is the writer's illustration to us today. Through faith (illustrated by his sacrifice) he was reckoned as righteous, and the present tense ("speaketh") impresses upon us the value of Abel as an example today.

Enoch walked with God when the rest of his contemporaries were unbelieving. He confessed his allegiance to God in the face of bitter opposition and hatred. As a result of his faith, in an age when we read of others "and he died," Enoch was "translated." As the Sunday school scholar put it: "One day Enoch and God walked so far away from home that God said, 'You'd better come home with me now'." Faith's reward was that Enoch passed into immortality without seeing death and the grave. This will the coming of Jesus Christ do for believers still alive at that time.

Abel's faith speaks of sacrifice; Enoch's of the Christian's walk. The preacher is Noah, and his faith gave him grace in the eyes of the Lord. Faith enabled Noah to be obedient to the word of the Lord and build to His plan. He believed that what God promised would come to pass. As a man of faith God used him to witness and work among those of his generation and become the instrument of salvation for some. Such was Noah's faith, that it stood the test of time and the opposition and mockery of the world.

B. *The Patriarchs* (verses 8-22). Abraham begins a new period of history in the lives of God's ancient people. He became the father of a divinely-chosen nation. By faith Abraham obeyed the divine command to go and possess an inheritance for God's people. He did not know where he was going but he had faith in God to guide him. His wife, Sarah, also a woman of faith, believed that in barrenness God could give her a child.

The great trial of Abraham's faith was the offering of his son Isaac upon the altar. Believing in the faithfulness of God he took his son and waited for God to save him. Faith then is the belief that in the darkest hour and in the midst of seeming unsolvable problems God can deliver.

Isaac showed his faith by going against his natural feelings and blessing Jacob before Esau. The sin of Jacob in obtaining the blessing did not alter Isaac's conviction that he was doing the will of God.

So Jacob and Joseph looked beyond their own deaths to the time when God's people would enter the Promised Land of Caanan again.

C. *The Leaders* (verses 23-31). God's people were privileged to have Moses as their leader out of Egypt, through the wilderness toward the Promised Land. Through Moses they received the divine law. All that became precious to the Jews, they owed to Moses and his leadership and his great faith. He deliberately refused to enjoy a life of ease and luxury, preferring rather to live with the people of God, believing them to be such, believing that they were a people of divine destiny. His faith enabled him to suffer reproach with the Israelites and not live a life of idolatry with the Egyptians. His faith was such that not only did he live by it, but God's people as well. They became inspired by his leadership, and although they sometimes murmured and rebelled, they rallied to him again and again. By faith he led them through the Red Sea; by faith he instituted the Passover feast; by faith he fed them and led them through the wilderness.

Under Joshua's leadership the walls of Jericho fell down and the city was captured and plundered. The city of Jericho was walled and defended. God's people did not subdue it by force of arms but by faith. Israel believed that God could conquer the city for them, so in faith they followed the divine instructions, marching around the walls, blowing their trumpets, and then marching in. So today walls fall down by faith, the walls of ignorance, unbelief, superstition and sin.

In Jericho we find Rahab, a harlot, a Gentile, and yet she is joined with these people of faith. By contrast with the other inhabitants of Jericho who were "disobedient," she had faith. Nothing saved Rahab but faith. She had no merits of her own; she was known as a gross sinner. But she put the scarlet cord, by faith, in her window and was saved. Faith in the scarlet blood of Christ alone saves today.

D. *The Judges and Prophets* (verses 32-38). The writer is now forced to summarize. He could go on giving instances of men and women of faith but time and space do not allow him to do so. He specifically mentions Gideon, and obviously he has in mind his outstanding achievement with three hundred men; Barak, who led Israel in battle against Sisera; Samson, who defeated the Philistines, calling down the strength of God to help him; Jephthah, son of a heathen prostitute, who defeated the Ammonites by faith; David, whose faith is well-illustrated in the Psalms that he wrote as well as the deeds that he wrought; Samuel, who manifested great faith early in life.

"And of the prophets" adds the writer, but they are nameless. It has been conjectured that "subdued kingdoms" could refer to many Old Testament prophetic characters; "wrought righteousness" is again a general term applicable to many; "obtained promises" means that they received promise of blessings upon their descendants for what they were themselves doing on God's behalf; "stopped the mouths of lions" must surely refer to Daniel; "quenched the violence of fire" could refer to Shadrach, Meshach, and Abednego; "escaped the edge of the sword" could refer to Elijah when he ran away from Ahab; "out of weakness were made strong" could refer to Hezekiah who was granted recovery and extension of life by God's intervention; "waxed valiant in fight" is amply illustrated in the books of Joshua, Judges, Samuel and Kings; "turned to fight the armies of the aliens," that is, the constant enemies of Israel, the Philistines, Moabites, Ammonites and Assyrians; "women received their dead raised to life again" as happened to the widow of Zarephath whose child was restored by Elijah; "tortured, not accepting deliverance," that is, they would not recant when offered freedom from instruments of torture, and would not renounce their faith; "trial of cruel mockings and scourgings," the usual accompaniment of a martyr's death; "bonds and imprisonments," chains and prison cells; "stoned," a common Jewish punishment—Zechariah, the son of Jehoiada the priest, was stoned; "sawn asunder," tradition says that the prophet Isaiah was thus sawn up lengthwise beginning at the head; "tempted" probably tempted to throw incense on the altar of a heathen god, thus renouncing their faith; "slain with the sword" as in the case of the eighty-five priests killed by Doeg; "wandered about in sheepskins and goatskins," having been driven from home; "destitute, afflicted, tormented" general terms including the specific forms of hardship mentioned in the previous verses.

What a selection of names and persons. Some are of royal blood, some have prophetic utterance, some are from the lowest class imaginable, prostitutes are placed in the same category as priests. Like the "residents" in Westminster Abbey, who all have the one characteristic of greatness, these in the Westminster Abbey of the Bible all have the common characteristic, faith! Nothing else matters. Nothing else need be noted, either their faults or failings nor their sins and shortcomings, it is their faith that is all-important as an inspiration to us.

III. FAITH CONSUMMATED (verses 39, 40)

Although all these people were outstanding persons of faith in that they believed God and His promises to them, none of them received the full and final fulfillment of promise. That all continued to look into the future for such consummation of their faith. By contrast, the man of faith today is permitted to enjoy those better things promised to the people of faith so long ago. We are permitted to see and enjoy what they only looked forward to experiencing. God reserved for us, His Christian people, the crowning blessing, the consummation of faith. How much more then ought our faith enable us to live as these men and women lived, courageously, daringly, victoriously. We dare not have ordinary faith in the light of this chapter, but extraordinary faith. The key word of Hebrews is "better," then how much better should our faith be than theirs. Our faith in Christ is far superior to theirs. They looked for a Messiah; for us He has come, living and dying and living again. The promised blessing now is His glorious return to take His people to be with Him forever.

HEARERS AND DOERS

James 1

In James we have "A Description of True Religion," the key word being "ethics." The first of the catholic letters, correspondence to Christians in general about general Christian teaching, James emphasizes the importance of practical Christianity.

An outline of the letter is:

    I. FAITH AND WARNING (1)
    II. FAITH AND WITNESS (2:1-13)
    III. FAITH WORKS (2:14-26)
    IV. FAITH AND WORKS (3:1-12)
    V. FAITH AND WISDOM (3:13-18)
    VI. FAITH AND WARFARE (4:1-17)
    VII. FAITH AND WEALTH (5:1-6)
    VIII. FAITH AND WAITING (5:7-12)
    IX. FAITH AND WEAKNESS (5:13-20)

The apostle begins right away by being "ethical, practical, forceful" (G. Campbell Morgan). In the first chapter James warns against a faith that is not expressing itself daily in deeds. We must be more than hearers of the Word, we must be doers as well, putting into practice what we hear and take in. "That Word is only of real value as it is obeyed, as what it enjoins is done. There is no profit, but rather the reverse, in hearing, if there be no doing" (G. Campbell Morgan).

Our "famous" chapter outline then is:

THE SOURCE OF—
    I. TRIALS AND TEMPTATIONS (verses 1-15)
    II. GOOD AND PERFECT GIFTS (verses 16-21)
    III. THEORETICAL AND PRACTICAL RELIGION (verses 22-27)

So many Christian people talk glibly about bad weather, bad health, wars, accidents, disasters, taking it for granted that God sends them all. Others, by contrast, place all ills squarely upon Satan. It is very necessary to know from what source these things come, and in this chapter the apostle warns against forming a wrong conclusion. First he tells us of the source of—

I. TRIALS AND TEMPTATIONS (verses 1-15)

Addressing himself to "the twelve tribes," that is, all Christian Jews ("twelve" being a collective term), James strikes a note of warning about the Christian's reaction to temptation.

Temptation for the Christian, especially for those Jewish Christians who were living in a Gentile world, is "divers" or "variegated, or multi-colored." There is an innumerable variety of temptations with which Satan can confront or subtly attract the believer. Yes, temptation is the work of the devil; trials, as we shall see in a later verse, come from God.

Most Christians become discouraged by temptation. James affirms that we should be filled with joy, (verse 2). Trial and temptation bring out the best in us. They deepen our faith and result in "patience" or better still, fortitude or endurance. In time, endurance makes us "perfect and entire," that is, really mature, complete and grown-up. Because temptation does this for us we welcome it rather than shun it.

Some temptations are so subtle, and some trials so severe, that the believer becomes perplexed. Human wisdom cannot supply the answer; nor can it help us bear what has to be borne. We must ask God for divine wisdom, knowing that He is willing to give it and does not rebuke ("upbraideth not") us for asking. The request must be made in faith, without any doubt or hesitancy in our minds as to whether God can or will give this wisdom and understanding to us. Some are like the storm-tossed waves of the sea, they sway this way and that way with indecision. They are completely unstable. Such a person cannot expect God to give wisdom. A believer in that state of mind is "double-minded" or has divided affections. He wants the best of both worlds and finishes up by having neither. A condition of answered prayer then is consistency and steadfastness.

The next verse seems to be an abrupt change of subject matter at first sight. Actually the apostle is mentioning one common form of trial, a marked change in circumstances (the "brother of low degree" suddenly "exalted"). Poor people who become Christians do not suddenly acquire material riches, but they do become joint-heirs with Christ and are thus spiritually rich. In that they can rejoice more than if they had become millionaires. So the man rich in this world's goods who is converted finds that he is now at one with Christians in humbler walks of life and his money is seen in its true light. It is not his but is on trust to him from God. He could lose it at any time. Thus rich and poor are alike within the fellowship of the Church. What light this sheds on our faith. It is suitable in wealth and in poverty. Whatever may be our position in life or our place in society our faith is sufficient.

Developing the idea of the loss of wealth or life still further the apostle says it can be as quick and as sure as the hot summer's sun withers the grass and dries it up, and causes the flowers to wilt.

The man who endures trials and temptations is "blessed" or happy. He will receive a reward for his endurance. It will not be given in this life. God may not even see fit to remove the trial while here below. But there will be a reward in heaven—"the crown of life." The apostle must have been thinking of the victor's crown at the ancient games. Being of laurel leaves it soon faded. God's crown for the tried and tested believer is unfading. This is not the crown given to all who receive eternal life through belief in the Son. This is a special crown for endurance under trial.

Then follows the warning about knowing the true source of trials and testings. These are sent by, or permitted to come upon the believer, by God Himself. Temptations, on the other hand, that is, enticements to do evil, can never be from God. They are from "below" not from "above," from hell not heaven, from Satan not God. If they did come from God and we succumbed to the temptation then we would excuse ourselves saying, "Well, God sent the temptation upon me." Knowing the true source of temptation we can offer no excuse. We are tempted when we yield to evil desires, uncontrolled thoughts and passions—these are from within a man, implanted by Satan. When we fall into the temptation and sin then "sin" has become like a child born to us, and in turn sin gives birth and results in spiritual death. Death is always the "end product" of sin, and it all starts with some subtle temptation.

II. THE SOURCE OF GOOD AND PERFECT GIFTS (verses 16-21)

Now James warns us about forgetting the true source of good and perfect gifts. God does not send temptations to the Christian, but He does send good things. He is the author and giver of all good gifts. We are not to "err" about this matter. We are to make no mistake, for if we do we shall deceive ourselves. It is none other than God who sends everything good upon us.

He is "the Father of lights," that is, the One who created all physical, moral, mental and spiritual light. He is also the unchanging God ("no variableness, neither shadow of turning"), unfailing and unalterable in nature and purpose. He does not move like the sun and moon. He has made us as Christians, "a kind of first fruits of his creatures," the "cream" or "hand-picked" ones of all created things.

Because of our position of privilege and favor we should be "swift to hear, slow to speak, slow to wrath." We must be quick in listening to God's Word, but slow in expressing ourselves about it (thinking and deliberating first), and slow to lose our temper even when provoked. An angry Christian just does not "go," is not in accord with our new righteous natures. So we must have done with "all filthiness and superfluity of naughtiness"—we must deliberately "throw overboard" the sinfulness that tends to swamp us, and overflow us. In its place we must put the Word of God in our hearts as securely as when we make a graft to a fruit tree or rose bush. Since the Word of God is able to save our souls it is a powerful, mighty thing, the only substitute for all that is sinful and impure.

The two "wherefores" must be noted (verses 19, 21). All that James has said the Christian must do must be done because of who

God is and what He has done. In view of His being Almighty, Omnipotent, Creator and Provider, and since He is the only source of good, then we must hear His Word, receive it into our heart in place of sin.

III. The Source of Theoretical and Practical Religion
(verses 22-27)

James continues, the "but" of verse 22 being better rendered "and." "Wherefore," because of all that God is and has done for us through His Word, it must be more grafted in our hearts. Having heard it, we must be "doers" of the Word. To hear only is to accept the theory of Christianity. In God's Word is both theory and practice. The Bible is the source of theoretical and practical religion.

For James the Bible is like a mirror. We take a quick look in the mirror in the morning, to shave or part our hair, and then we go about our daily business and do not look at ourselves again until we wash before going to bed at night. So it is possible to take a quick look into God's mirror, reading a few verses at the beginning of the day, and then we forget all about what we have read. The man who remembers what he has seen in God's looking glass and puts it into practice during the day, is a doer as well as a hearer of God's Word and he is "blessed in his deed." When truth is received, then responded to, then acted upon, the believer will be blessed, made happy in his heart, mind and conscience. His witness in the world will be owned of God. He will feel God's influence in his own soul first, then he will bring to bear an influence upon the world.

It is possible to give the appearance of being religious ("if any man seem to be religious"). Church going, hymn singing, money given to good causes, these make a man seem to be religious, but what do people hear when he opens his mouth to speak? Can he "bridle" his tongue or does his tongue run away with him like a horse that has escaped the bit and bridle? Coarse speech, swear words, temper—these conflict with seeming religious acts. A man may deceive himself in this way, but not God or other people.

The true test of a man's religion is its practical love—"visiting the fatherless and widows in their afflictions"; its pure living—"keeping unspotted from the world"; and the source of both these is the Word.

The Mirror of God reveals that our Christianity must be marked by piety, ours is a "pure" and "undefiled" religion; by purity, for we must keep "unspotted" from the world; and by practice, visiting "the fatherless and widows in their affliction." There is a spiritual side, an ethical side and a practical side to our faith.

WHAT THE ANGELS LOOK INTO

I Peter 1

Peter was the first disciple to confess that Jesus was the Son of God. He was also the first to deny his Lord at the crucifixion. After the Ascension, however, he lived up to his new name of "Rock" and took the leadership of the Early Church fellowship. Those days were times of severe persecution and so Peter's first letter is one of comfort. Dealing with "suffering" (key word), his theme is, "The Sufficiency of God's Grace." An outline of the letter is as follows:

    I.   Salutation (1:1, 2)
   II. Salvation (1:3-12)
  III. Sanctification (1:13–2:10)
  IV. Submission (2:11–3:7)
   V. Suffering (3:8–5:11)
  VI. Salutations (5:12-14)

Our "famous" chapter then includes the apostle's opening salutation, his view of salvation, and part of what he has to say about sanctification. No wonder Dr. G. Campbell Morgan says: "What a wonderful chapter this is!" In it is Christian experience and privilege, and Peter can only write about it as he does because he has sought the help and direction of the Holy Spirit. The things here set forth are the very things into which angels desire to look. If they, with their high intelligence, desire to study the various aspects of eternal salvation, then how much more should we.

Our division of the chapter will be:

    I.   Salutation (verses 1, 2)
   II. Salvation (3-12)
       A. *Already Reserved*
       B. *To Be Revealed*
  III. Sanctification (verses 13-25)
       A. *Exhortation*
       B. *Expectation*

It has been noted by commentators that there is no logical sequence in Peter's letters as in Paul's. Some have even said that the last word with which Peter ends a sentence gives him his thought for the first word of the next! Thus there is little or no unfolding of argument or progress of thought. There is, however, a sense of unity running through I Peter and he begins in the usual way with a—

I. Salutation (verses 1, 2)

Calling himself by the new name given to him by the Saviour, Peter declares his office and authority—"an apostle of Jesus Christ." He is one who has been commissioned or sent, a messenger. He has ability and warrant. "Of Jesus Christ" implies "appointed by Him and answerable to Him." Notice it is "an" not "the" apostle, so there is no grounds here for apostolic supremacy and turning him into "Pope" Peter!

He is writing to "the strangers" ("the elect exiles," Amplified Version), that is, Christian Jews dispersed throughout the regions mentioned, the provinces which made up Asia Minor. They were "elect" because chosen and called of God, not for any special fitness but because of His sovereign right to choose. "According to the foreknowledge of God the Father," because He had a plan and purpose for them. Divine election is always through an agent ("through sanctification of the Spirit") and for a special purpose—sanctification. Another reason or explanation of their election was: "unto obedience and sprinkling of the blood of Jesus Christ," that they might obey God and because the blood of Christ had been shed for them.

Finally comes the apostolic blessing—"Grace unto you, and peace, be multiplied." Grace and peace are two great New Testament words. Grace—God's free, unmerited favor or "love in action" as it has been called; Peace—a Hebrew word of greeting implying reconciliation and rest. "Multiplied" is an exhortation to progress. We can never experience too much of God's grace and peace as Christians. "May it abound to you," Peter is saying, or "May it be conferred on you in abundant measure."

II. Salvation (verses 3-12)

Besides writing about two aspects of salvation ("Already reserved" and "To be revealed"), Peter uses two great terms: "regeneration" and "begotten."

First, however, is a eulogy about the Fatherhood of God. He is not the Father of all men as some state, only their Creator. He is the Father of our Lord Jesus Christ and all who belong to Him as adopted sons by faith in Christ Jesus. How much we owe this Father in heaven! Our relationship to Him as son is "according to his abundant mercy"— we do not deserve such favor, it is unmerited, but He has extended His mercy. Spurgeon puts it: "No other attribute could have helped us had mercy refused." Well, this mercy has "begotten us again." This is a salvation—

A. *Already Reserved.* By the mercy and Spirit of God we have been born again. The Resurrection of Jesus from the dead gives us our hope (always a certainty in the Bible) of eternal salvation reserved for us in heaven. It is a "living" hope for it is imperishable and un-fading.

Salvation is always *from* and *to*—from sin, self and death, to an "inheritance," a property or possession, an heirship. Saved from hell to all the glories and riches of heaven. And this consummation of salvation in heaven is already reserved. The salvation is "reserved" and the saved person is "kept" for it (verses 4, 5). God is looking after our inheritance and He is looking after us, so nothing can happen to harm us or our salvation. Peter is using a military term—garrisoned or fortified. But note how Peter adds "through faith"—we must do our part. There must be staunch fidelity and truthfulness on the part of the believer. Faith in God's Word, faith in God's promises, faith in His power—these enable God to keep us.

How can He be keeping us "unto salvation" when we are already saved? There are three tenses of salvation: have been saved, are being saved, shall be saved. Saved in the past tense is our conversion; being saved in the present is our sanctification; shall be saved in the future is the believer's glorification, the completion of the whole process. This final aspect of salvation is—

B. *To Be Revealed.* "Ready to be revealed in the last time." The final phrase means "at the last hour," that is, after the Second Advent and judgment. "Revealed" is an interesting and important word. It means "the drawing aside of a veil or curtain to reveal whatever is behind." God's salvation is already accomplished; one day it will be shown us. Our inheritance and our consummated salvation, our glorification with Christ is ready to be revealed.

Before we receive (verse 9) this inheritance, this completed salvation, however, there are trials and temptations to be endured. This need not make us sorrowful or afraid. Our salvation, past, present and future, is so great that we can "greatly rejoice" (verse 6) even in the midst of affliction or persecution. We must look upon these things that come upon us as a purifying process, a testing of the genuineness of our faith. We must come out of the test like pure, refined, genuine gold.

What Peter is impressing upon his readers is: suffering is only temporary, it is not eternal; it seems common to all men but it is not inevitable ("if need be"); it is always providential and not accidental; and it distinguishes the genuine from the counterfeit. The secret is to keep our eyes on the Saviour, "whom having not seen ye love" (verse 8). He is out of sight (with our physical eyes) but not out of reach ("though now ye see him not, yet believing"); so by personal appropriation ("receiving the end of your faith") the Christian can enjoy his present salvation and past salvation experimentally, and his future salvation by anticipation.

What a salvation it is! Again Peter gets carried away. He tells his readers that both men and angels have "searched" for it. The prophets "did their utmost to discover it" (J. B. Phillips), searching intensively. The prophets were forward looking men—they saw into the future and they spoke about the future. Their great concern was to discover the time of fulfillment of the message given to them. They foretold the coming and the sufferings of Christ, and while not having a full understanding of what they prophesied, they nevertheless ministered to their own and future generations about these certainties of salvation.

The apostles, Spirit-inspired like the prophets of old, also ministered to their generation about these stupendous facts of salvation. So stupendous are the facts that even the angels "look into," that is, bend down, stoop to see, them. The angels in heaven are full of wonder at what God is doing on earth for the salvation of mankind. Being spiritual beings they know not human flesh and its frailty, and so they are restricted in their search. Moffatt says: "They long to get a glimpse of it," but they are left wondering, admiring, but not fully understanding.

III. SANCTIFICATION (verses 13-25)

"You are saved to serve" the young convert is told. It's not that simple. In the New Testament sanctification always follows salvation, then service. It is only the "clean vessel" that is fit for the Master's use. Sanctification is the continuing work of the Holy Spirit of conviction and conversion.

This third section of the chapter begins with "wherefore." All that Peter is now going to write is based on what he has just written.

Alan Stibbs in the Tyndale Commentary on First Peter heads this section: "The Challenge to Live Differently." Salvation must result in transformed conduct. Belief must affect morals and ethics, character and conduct. The saved person must become holy in word, thought and deed. First, then, from the pen of Peter we have—

A. *Exhortation.* "Gird up" or brace up your mind, exhorts Peter. It is the word used of Peter girding his fisherman's cloak around him before stepping on to the sea to walk to Jesus. It is the word used of Peter by our Lord when prophesying his old age and another would "gird" him. It implies energy, unrestrictedness. Holiness of life and character for the Christian is "shirt-sleeve" Christianity—we must mean business. We are not to let our Christian characters become moulded by our pre-conversion desires (verse 14). "In all manner of conversation," that is, in every department of our lives we are to be sanctified, taking as our standard the holiness of the One who called us. We dare not question this exhortation for "it is written"—Peter is quoting from the Word of God.

Note Peter's three-fold exhortation: "Brace up," as one about to take a journey, run a race, or fight a battle. "Be sober," that is, go into disciplined training, being temperate in all things so that the walk, race or fight will be successful. "Be holy," taking no lesser standard than the divine standard. We are not to take Wesley or Thomas à Kempis or other great "saints" as our standard, but God!

Exhortation is followed by the note of—

B. *Expectation.* "The revelation of Jesus Christ" is our spur to sanctified living. The Second Advent is a doctrine of comfort and hope in Scripture; it is also a most practical teaching for it inspires holy living and dedicated service. John calls it a "purifying hope" (I John 3:3).

In the light of this Peter urges his readers to do three things;

First, they are to pray to the Father. Holiness must be made a matter of prayer in the light of our Lord's return. There are many books on prayer for Christians today, but few contain prayers for holiness, yet no man can purify himself but must pray—

More holiness give me.

Second, they must look to the future. The return of Christ must be a continual incentive for holy living. When He comes will He find us living fragrant lives, lives of fruitfulness? Or will He find us flirting with the world?

Third, they must consider God's favor. We have been redeemed with the precious blood of God's Son. We are of the company of the elect.

Fulfilling these conditions will result in obedience to right doctrine ("purified your souls in obeying the truth"), love to all Christians ("unfeigned love of the brethren"), and acknowledgment of the enduring nature of the Word of God ("which liveth and abideth for ever"). Thus the chapter ends with a tremendous comparison between things that change and things that are unchangeable; things that are temporal and things that are eternal. Mere mortal men perish like the plants and vegetation of the natural world—none of us can resist the ravages of time. But while bombs may destroy buildings and empires may decay and fade away, God's Word will outlast time and flourish in eternity. Such is the Christian's expectation, and such is the word "which by the gospel is preached unto you." The Word of God is living and life-giving. It lives forever and it bestows life upon spiritually dead men and women that they might live forever.

PETER'S BEEHIVE

II Peter 3

Since writing his first letter false teachers with corrupt doctrines have entered into the church and so Peter writes a letter of warning. "Corruption" is the key word, Peter dealing with both moral and doctrinal corruption in this second letter. The theme is, "The Developing of Christian Character." A Christian must have a true, steadfast character to combat such corruption, such enticement on the part of false teachers. The apostle warns, too, that such false teachers and teaching will abound more and more toward the end of the age. Again, therefore, the Second Coming of Jesus is prominent in this letter.

An outline of the letter may be given in this form:

I. SALUTATION (1:1, 2)
II. FAITH'S GROWTH AND GRACES (1:3-21)
III. FALSE TEACHERS AND TEACHING (2)
IV. FUTURE GRACE AND GLORY (3)

We entitle this "famous" chapter *Peter's Beehive* because the subject of the return of Christ is dealt with in this way: in the light of the Lord's return Christian's are to "*be* mindful" (verse 2); "*be* not ignorant" (verse 8); "*be* diligent" (verse 14); "*beware*" (verse 17); and we might comment on "grow in grace" (verse 18), *be* planted first!

The following is a convenient division of the chapter:

I. ARGUMENTS AGAINST THE ADVENT TRUTH (verses 1-4)
II. AFFIRMATIONS FOR THE ADVENT TRUTH (verses 5-10)
III. APPLICATION OF THE ADVENT TRUTH (verses 11-18)

I. ARGUMENTS AGAINST THE ADVENT TRUTH (verses 1-4)

This "famous" chapter is an important chapter because the apostle begins it by reminding the readers of his purpose in writing the whole letter: "to stir up your pure minds by way of remembrance." Peter wants them to remember the warnings given by the prophets and apostles of the last days. At the same time they must remember that there will also be people who will have seeming plausible arguments against the advent truth. There will be "scoffers," that is, those who will treat the whole truth of the Lord's coming in a light-hearted fashion, deriding, ridiculing and mocking such an idea. Peter must have been meaning a special class of person for there always have been, and always will be, those who scoff at truth in a general way.

He may have been referring to a certain sect that had arisen in opposition to Christian advent truth. Their character is described in the words, "walking after their own lusts," that is, they gave full play to sensual indulgence and appetite.

When they asked, "Where is the promise of his coming"? they were really asking, "Where is the *fulfillment* of that promise?" They were spiritually blind and so could not see any signs or indications of the return of Christ. Notice how irreverently they referred to the prophets and apostles: "the fathers," that is, those old men, those "cranky" old men with their wild dreams and talk. In spite of their predictions these men died without Christ returning. And now the world is going on as usual—"all things continue as they were from the beginning of creation"—the fixed, natural laws that govern the world continue to function. Their argument was that the course of nature had not been interrupted, as it should have been prior to the return of Christ.

These arguments against advent truth the apostle now counteracts with—

II. Affirmations for the Advent Truth (verses 5-10)

"Be mindful" in the first section, is now followed by the injunction "Be not ignorant." Peter is going to teach believers certain facts about the advent.

The first apostolic affirmation is that the divine word must never be doubted. Scepticism is a sin. By God's word the heaven and earth were created; that same word has pronounced about the Second Advent. As the world came into being at the word of God, so the Lord will return again according to that same word. Besides that, God spake and water covered the earth to flood it. In the same way fire will descend upon the earth in judgment in the last days.

Peter's next affirmation is that heaven's time and earth's time are two different things. "One day is with the Lord as a thousand years," so how can they scoff at unfulfilled prophecy and say that God has not fulfilled His promise? A long period of time with us is but a brief moment with God. We have only a short span of life and so life passes quickly for us. God is eternal and lives forever and so time is of longer duration for Him. God is not "slack" as men are slack when they delay; He is rather "longsuffering" toward us, delaying the return of Christ to enable men to come to Him in repentance and faith. He does not want to see men die eternally and so He gives ample opportunity for men to obtain eternal life. "Any seeming delay is to be interpreted as dictated by merciful compassion" (I.V.F. commentary).

The third affirmation is that the Day of Christ, whenever it comes, soon or late, will come suddenly and unexpectedly, "as a thief in the night." It will also be audible—there will be "a great noise." The word used here was often used of the whizzing of an arrow in flight. Here it seems to stand for the roaring of fierce flames as they melt and dissolve the earth and all that is in it. The whole emphasis, of course, is upon what God is going to do. Some people affirm today that a nuclear war, an atomic explosion, will cause the end of the world. The world will only come to an end when God wills it. He will burn it up and lay it aside as an unused garment in His own time.

III. APPLICATION OF THE ADVENT TRUTH (verses 11-18)

"Be diligent" (verse 14) and *"Be*ware" (verse 17) are the two injunctions in this practical section of the chapter. "Be diligent" means to be conscientious in performing our daily duties, and patient in bearing our trials, and faithful in living holy lives. "Beware" means that we are to "be aware" of being led into error about these advent truths by false teachers.

In view of the burning up of the earth, the destruction of the world as we know it, we ought to be living lives conspicuous in "holy conversation" and "godliness," that is, unblamable daily conduct and Godly piety. The awesome events to come should weigh upon us to such a degree that we are induced to live holy lives. Because time and the things of earth are so transient we should be concentrating on eternity and spiritual matters. "Earth is our lodge, and heaven our home." Walking on earth we set our faces toward heaven and live as if already there. Daily we look not for death but for the Lord's coming, hastening it on, urging it on by our very desire to see it. We look for God's "new heavens and a new earth"—the ones that shall exist after the first are destroyed by fire, after the general judgment.

Those, then, are what we look for, and in the light of such expectation we live diligently so that when the Lord returns He finds us working out our salvation. Already redeemed by His precious blood and our faith in His atoning work, but knowing that "faith without works is dead," we daily serve Him, diligently and consistently. And all the time we are trying to become more holy. Because we are soon to stand in His holy presence we seek to become "without spot and blameless." Yes, this is a "purifying hope"!

To add argument to his affirmations and applications Peter refers to Paul's writings, inferring that his readers will also be acquainted with the Pauline correspondence. Because of Paul's inspiration and authority, his wisdom and teaching, as well as his own (Peter's), they must "beware" of being led away into error. What excuse will they have for going astray after such sufficient warnings? They have been faithfully and fervently warned and so should not be unlearned or unstable.

Their final guarantee of steadfastness will be if they "grow in grace." In order to *grow* one must first *be* planted (the fifth "bee" in Peter's beehive). Only the man who is "in Christ" can grow up unto Him in all things. Only the man who knows Christ can grow in knowledge of Him. As we continue in God's grace then that grace will surround us and uphold us; it will be the very atmosphere in which we live and breathe and grow and keep on growing. Only continuous growth and knowledge is the final guarantee of not falling into error of doctrine.

So Peter closes his letter with a benediction: "To him be glory, both now and for ever." The words "for ever" are unique, as we should expect after the subject matter of the epistle. The Revised Version margin puts it, "Unto the day of eternity." The Day is the theme of the letter and this "famous" chapter. The dawning of that Day will be the coming of the Lord in majesty and power and glory. Then to Him "be glory" now, and until that Day of glory comes.

A WONDERFUL RELATIONSHIP

I John 1

John's "companion" to the fourth gospel contains the word "know" thirty-two times. In an era when error was rampant and had crept into the Christian Church it was important to know the truth. The gospel, then, tells us how to be saved (20:31), and the epistle how we may know that we are saved (5:13), that is, Christian Assurance.

The key word is "fellowship" (key text, 1:7), and the theme: "Living in the Light." An outline of the letter is as follows:

I. WALKING IN THE LIGHT (1, 2)
II. WRESTLING BY THE LOVE (3, 4)
III. WITNESSING TO THE LIFE (5)

The theme of the "famous" chapter, the first, is "Walking in the Light," and so we entitle it *A Wonderful Relationship,* for true fellowship, walking in the light, is a right relationship between the believer and his Lord. The whole chapter has to do with this fellowship and is in this form:

I. ETERNAL FELLOWSHIP DEFINED (verses 1-4)
II. FALSE FELLOWSHIP DENOUNCED (verses 5, 6)
III. TRUE FELLOWSHIP DESCRIBED (verse 7)
IV. UNBROKEN FELLOWSHIP DEVELOPED (verses 8-10)

John sets our thoughts upon eternity first of all with—

I. ETERNAL FELLOWSHIP DEFINED (verses 1-4)

Jesus was pre-existent with God before the world's creation. Josiah Conder expressed this truth in hymn form:

> Thou art the everlasting Word,
> The Father's only Son.

Next, John brings his readers to time present, declaring that the eternal Christ is the same Jesus he has seen, heard and touched. The Eternal One became manifest in time on earth.

All this is being written by John so that his readers might come to believe more firmly and that there might be a closer bond of fellowship between themselves and him. He defines true fellowship as eternal for it is "with the Father and his Son." As Christians we are partakers or sharers in the divine nature; we share the divine attributes of holi-

301

ness and happiness, purity and truth; and in Christian service we are "labourers together," with one another and with the Trinity. Having the same divine, resurrection life makes us spiritually and eternally united.

Our fellowship with others, of course, depends upon the reality of our fellowship with 'God. It is only effective with others as it is vital with God. When there is a lack of loving fellowship with one another it is because we are not experiencing true fellowship with our Heavenly Father. Unbroken fellowship with the Father results in unbroken union with the fellowship of God's people.

II. FALSE FELLOWSHIP DENOUNCED (verses 5, 6)

Sad to say there are those who know what real, eternal fellowship is, but they are willing to deceive themselves with a lesser, false fellowship because they are unwilling to pay the price of true fellowship. If we continue to live this life of false fellowship we are "liars" and "do not the truth."

What is this false fellowship? It is "walking in darkness" instead of walking in light. When the Christian continues in flagrant sin and disobedience he is walking in darkness. God is light; sin is darkness. To *say* that we have fellowship, and *having* fellowship, are two different things, John points out. It is the difference between professing and possessing. In John's day there were those professing to have fellowship yet their sinful lives denied it, revealing that they did not possess what they professed. Their lives were blatant lies. Light stands for sincerity. They were insincere and so were walking in darkness. Light stands for perception but these people had no perception of spiritual things. Light stands for transparency, but their lives were not empty of deceit and guile.

III. TRUE FELLOWSHIP DESCRIBED (verse 7)

What a vast description within the compass of one small verse! There is a condition ("if") and two resultant consequences. The condition is: "If we walk in the light as he is in the light." Forsaking false fellowship we walk in fellowship with God as Christ walks in fellowship with the Father. The startling phrase is "as he is in the light." Our lives must be as clear, as transparent, as shining, as His.

One result of walking in the light like that is fellowship with one another and "the one with the other." This is two-way relationship—fellowship on the horizontal and the vertical. Horizontally we have fellowship with other believers; vertically we have fellowship with God. Nothing comes between to mar our fellowship with either.

The next result of walking in the light is that we become washed in the blood. Close fellowship with the Father makes us sensitive to evil in any form. As soon as we sin in word or thought or deed we come to the cleansing fount in order that every stain might be washed away and so the fellowship is not marred. In the blood of Christ we find complete, continual and certain cleansing which results in close and continual fellowship with a Holy God, His Holy Son and the Holy Spirit. That close communion with the Trinity results in common interests about the kingdom of God and co-operation in service that men and women might be won for that kingdom.

IV. UNBROKEN FELLOWSHIP DEVELOPED (verses 8-10)

Such fellowship with God and our fellow men is so choice and sweet (a foretaste of heaven itself) that we shall want to maintain it and develop it at all times. In the closing verses of the chapter John tells us how it can be done.

First, if any sin is coming between us and the Saviour then we must not overlook it. By doing so we deceive ourselves. Sins must be confessed, knowing that if we do so God is faithful and just to forgive us. What John is telling us to do then is to come to God, through Christ, every time we sin, as we came the first time when we were converted. The way to develop and maintain fellowship is to come to God as we did when that fellowship was first begun and experienced. Sin must always be dealt with on the basis of repentance and confession, the cross and the blood, faith and not works. God has made no other provision for sin, whether in the life of the non-Christian or the converted person. This issue cannot be evaded. If we say we have not sinned then we make God a liar. for He has said in His Word that we have. How can a saved person deny the Word of God, the very Word that saved us? If we do so then that Word is not in us, nor the living, incarnate Word, Jesus Christ.

This, of course, is a great blow to pride. On the human level, husbands and wives, close friends, know how difficult it is to confess that we have wronged another or that we are in the wrong. It has to be done before there can be a renewal of the close marriage union or the friendship. So it must be done between Christian and Christian in the fellowship of the Church. So it must be done between the believer and God. This is one of the high roads that lead to revival in the Church and in the world.

ADVANCED THINKING

II John

"The Sole Sufficiency of Scripture" is the Apostle John's theme in his second letter. The key word is "truth" and the key text verse 4. The purpose of his writing is the "many deceivers" who are deluding Christian people. The times are apostate—days of spiritual declension. But in the midst of it all he delights in finding a woman and her children who are faithfully witnessing to the truth. As the letter has only one chapter we shall have but one outline to give:

    I. SALUTATION (verses 1-3)
   II. THE BELIEVER'S PATH (verses 4-6)
       Truth and Love
  III. THE BELIEVER'S PERIL (verses 7-11)
       Apostasy and False Cults
  IV. CONCLUSION (verses 12, 13)

We call this chapter *Advanced Thinking* because the Revised Version translation of "whosoever transgresseth" (verse 9) is "everyone advancing." The false teachers of John's day considered themselves "advanced teachers." They were the modernists, the liberal theologians, people who thought they knew better than God Himself. The advanced thinker, says John, advances until he is right out of Christianity —he has gone too far! So have many theologians and Bible college teachers today. Their speculations have taken them right out and right away from the Word of the Lord.

First let us note the apostle's—

I. SALUTATION (verses 1-3)

It is to "the elect lady." Some say a specific church, others one particular woman, perhaps a widow. "Elect" or chosen could refer to an individual or to a fellowship for a church is an *ecclesia*, called-out ones gathered together into a fellowship. If a church is meant then the "believing children" must be recent converts. Perhaps it is easier to think of her as a woman, a widow (or a woman with an unbelieving husband), with several children. At any rate not only John loves them but others who are faithful to the truth as well.

Added to the ordinary benediction used is the phrase, "in truth and love," which are going to be written about in later verses as the believer's path which he must walk in the world. Obviously they were a family who were promoting truth and love wherever they went.

II. THE BELIEVER'S PATH (verses 4-6)

John speaks now from personal experience with her children. He has not listened to hearsay about their Christian witness; nor has anyone written to him. "I found" he says. Their witness and testimony was conspicuous and could be seen and heard—he had seen and heard them. They were "walking in truth," that is, they were living according to the truth, the truth of God's Word. And they were "walking" in truth, that is, continuing in it, steadfastly, day after day. By life and by lip they were showing God's truth to the world. No one could deny the truth of the Gospel when they looked at it personified in these young people. Nietzsche, the German philosopher said, when dismissing Christianity: "I can believe the redemption when you Christians begin to look redeemed"! Here were young people whose redemption was real.

The next part of the believer's path is love. "To walk only in love would make us soft," declares Dr. Graham Scroggie, "to walk only in truth would make us hard; but walking in truth and love we become strong." This John urges because it is an old commandment, not a new one. "From the beginning," from the time that the Gospel was made known, it had been emphasized that Christians were to walk in love, exhibiting love, promoting love in others. "See how these Christians love one another" the ancient historian recorded.

Love, the apostle defines as "walking after his commandments," that is, obedience at all points to the divine requirements.

III. THE BELIEVER'S PERIL (verses 7-11)

Along the pathway are to be found deceivers. false teachers, men and women who deny the Incarnation, the manifestation of God in the flesh. Such deceivers are "antichrists," people opposed to Christ or those who set themselves up in place of Christ.

In the face of these people, with their false doctrine, the true Christians are to "look to themselves," or be on their guard. Being open to attack and surrounded on all sides by teachers of error, they must guard themselves. Not only must they not imbide the new, false teaching, but they must not lose the truth they already have, thus becoming apostate. The greater their faithfulness in this respect, the greater their reward in heaven.

Those who do depart from the true doctrine about Christ, His deity or divinity, denying Him, have had no real knowledge of God ("hath not God"). But those who continue faithful to the true teaching about God and Christ have an intimate union with them.

The false teacher, the representative of the false cult, must under no circumstances be invited into the believer's home. To welcome them into the home, and to bid them "Godspeed" when they leave, would be to countenance what they are doing. Such an impression must not be given them. The professing teacher of a false cult—the Jehovah's Witness, the Mormon, the Christadelphian, and so on—must be kept on the doorstep. The believer can make his witness across the threshold. He must not buy any literature or take any free literature regarding the false sect for again that would give the impression that we are interested in what they are trying to do. Any sort of Christian farewell would be misconstrued as wishing them success in what they are doing and so would make us "partakers of his evil deeds," comrades or companions or confederates in spreading false doctrine.

IV. CONCLUSION (verses 12, 13)

Because of haste or weakness or ill health the apostle must bring his letter to a close. He has much more to say but time and duty will not permit it. In any case, some things are too difficult or too personal to put down on paper with pen and ink. He proposes to visit this lady to whom he is writing, when able. "Face to face" is a phrase that implies conversation of a confidential nature, emphasizing the correctness of our exposition, that he could not write more by very nature of what he wants to say.

In closing this correspondence the apostle includes greetings from another lady, "thy elect sister," at whose house he may have been staying when he wrote to "the elect lady." Certainly this second lady knew he was writing and knew to whom he was writing for she was willing that her own personal regards be sent.

The letter is short and simple, but it deals with important and vital doctrines. It instructs in the faith and it warns against those who deny the foundation facts of our faith. To go beyond these fundamentals is not to "advance," but to take a retrogressive step, contradicting the Word of God.

DIVINE HOSPITALITY

III John

"Hospitality" is the key word by which to remember the theme of the third letter of John. The apostle's theme is, "The Duty and Delight of Christian Entertainment," the key verse being verse 8—"We therefore ought to receive such, that we might be fellowhelpers to the truth."

The second letter of John was written to "an elect lady"; this third letter was to a man. In the second letter we saw some people to whom hospitality was not to be extended—leaders of false cults. In this third letter we are told to whom it should be extended. In both letters there is set on record the joy of pastor or parent when it is known that children are "walking in truth."

We entitle this chapter *Divine Hospitality* even though the Christian entertainment is being offered by men to men, for the spirit in which the hospitality is to be given is divine—we are to tender hospitality as if God were doing it ("worthily of God," verse 6). Here then we see what kind of a host God is—how He treats His guests.

Once again a single outline will serve our purposes for this "famous" chapter comprises the whole letter:

    I. CONGRATULATION (verses 1-4)
   II. EXHORTATION (verses 5-8)
  III. DENUNCIATION (verses 9, 10)
  IV. COMMENDATION (verses 11, 12)
   V. SALUTATION (verses 13, 14)

These five notes of congratulation, exhortation, denunciation, commendation and salutation are sounded loud and clear, and their notes ring around three characters: Gaius, Diotrephes and Demetrius.

First, the letter opens with—

I. CONGRATULATION (verses 1-4)

Gaius is greeted and congratulated upon the good report John has received from those who have been in Gaius' company and noted his steadfast faith and consistent walk. Spiritually Gaius is in "peak condition"; physically he seems to be indisposed or infirm for John wishes him prosperity of body as he has prosperity of soul. His spiritual condition is such that his witness has resulted in his own children coming to a knowledge of the truth as it is in Jesus.

Once more we must remember that the times were perilous and false teachers were on the increase. How happy John is that he has such a staunch champion of the truth as Gaius and when he has gone to be with the Lord his children are there to take up the torch. Happy the church today which has a rising generation of born-again young people to take over from the "pillars of the church" when they go to their eternal rest. And what a lesson John gives us here. He is now an old man at the time of writing. So many old people are impatient with the young—John encourages them, prays for them.

II. EXHORTATION (verses 5-8)

Gaius is well-known for his acts of hospitality, but now the apostle exhorts all believers to practice it. The example of Gaius is to be emulated. He has opened his house to "brethren" (Christians well-known to him) and "to strangers" (Christians from other districts, perhaps sent to him by John). In every local fellowship there are the widows and widowers, the lonely, the sad, to whom we can offer hospitality. Every now and again there are visiting ministers, evangelists, missionaries, and other Christian workers who need rest and refreshment in a congenial Christian home. Gaius has many who could, and had, borne testimony to his kindness in providing hospitality. Have we?

Many of these Christian workers needed to be "brought forward" on their journey, that is, facilitating their traveling arrangements, furnishing them with provisions or other gifts for the rest of the journey. And this was to be done "after a godly sort," as though God were doing it (literally, "worthy of God," Greek). Now anyone who has had any dealing with Almighty God, His provision and protection, knows that He is always lavish and that He gives only of His best. God's gifts are "good and perfect." God does not give grudgingly but willingly. He "spreads" His table before us; it "groans" (as we say) with food. "Come and dine"; "come for all things are now ready," says God. These then are the lines on which we proceed as Christians when we offer hospitality: an open house, a spread table, the very best that we can afford, even if we go without something ourselves we give the best to others.

In verse 7 John reminds us of a good reason for thus being hospitable—"for his name's sake they went forth." Ministers, missionaries, and others only travel about and need hospitality because they are upon the Lord's work. They must therefore be kept by the Lord's people and not the Gentiles, those outside of Christ. Some churches, with many hundreds of members, put up the visiting preacher at a non-Christian hotel! By giving this hospitality ourselves to the servants of the Lord we are engaging in their Christian work with them, being "fellow-helpers to the truth." Note then: the obligation of hospitality ("we therefore *ought* to receive such"); the opportunities for hospitality ("such"); the object of hospitality ("fellow-helpers to the truth").

III. DENUNCIATION (verses 9, 10)

John has written a previous letter ("I wrote unto the church") now lost, in which he probably commended certain Christian workers to the care of the church. Or the words may be taken to mean: "I would have written to the church," that is, rather than to a private member. However he knew of the bad influence of one of the members, Diotrephes. This man he now denounces, and since John is often called "the apostle of love," we may assume that he is here "speaking the truth in love."

Diotrephes was a man who "loveth to have the pre-eminence" among his fellow church members. How he loved to be first in everything! We do not know if he was an officer of the church or an ordinary member, but we do know that he was arrogant, aspiring to prominence, self-assertive, and too fond of assuming authority. He "receiveth us not," writes John, meaning that Diotrephes did not recognize John's apostolic authority. *He* was the one who was going to rule in that church; he was going to "lord it" over others. He may have had a personal dislike of John, or a secret grudge against others in the fellowship. Perhaps he did not welcome "outside" or "foreign" interference. At any rate he was going to get the church under his control and turn a democracy into an autocracy. New Testament democracy is really theocracy, but Diotrephes was the sort of man who would not even acknowledge the right of God to rule. A man who loves to have the pre-eminence himself cannot at the same time give Christ the pre-eminence in all things.

John writes that he hopes to make a personal visit to Gaius and the church, and when he does then he will exert his apostolic authority and "remember his (Diotrephes') deeds which he doeth," that is, would take measures to stop him and punish him, exercising true church discipline. Diotrephes has been guilty of "prating against" John, which means literally "to overflow with talk." Diotrephes was a foolish gossip, and he expressed himself about others without first thinking what he was going to say. His conversation was also malicious, and "against" John. Diotrephes was malicious and vindictive; he spoke harmful words with the intent of doing harm, wounding John personally and spoiling his character with others. And not content with that he persuaded others to think and speak as he did. There is nothing so contagious as malicious gossip.

Diotrephes was also inhospitable. Traveling servants of the Lord had visited the church but Diotrephes had not opened his home to them. Perhaps that was as well, for if he had given hospitality he might have laid the table with "minced preacher" or "carved apostle"! But his inhospitable spirit had gone even further: he had forbidden others in the church to open their homes. Those who went against his advice and gave hospitality he had them turned out of the church (or it may mean that he had the traveling preachers turned away).

IV. COMMENDATION (verses 11, 12)

The third character brought to our notice in this early Christian fellowship is Demetrius. He is commended to our attention after the apostle urges his reader (Gaius) or readers (for surely the letter would be read in the church) not to follow bad examples like Diotrephes but good men. The man who is doing good is more closely following God. The evil doer "hath not seen God." The man who professes to be a Christian but does no good is only a nominal believer—he is not really saved.

Demetrius may have been the bearer of the apostle's letter. We do not know for sure who he was or in what way he was connected with this church. We may assume that he was, like Gaius, hospitable, and for that reason he earns the apostle's commendation. Not only are there reports of his goodness and good deeds ("good report of all men"), but it was a certain fact ("of the truth itself"). John is glad to be able to add his own personal testimony—"and ye know that our record is true."

It has been conjectured that this Demetrius is the same man as the silversmith who stirred up a riot in Ephesus when Paul was there. It is only conjecture. If it were a certainty then what a transformation has come over him! He who was once opposed to Christianity has now embraced it and is furthering it; he who once sought to turn others against Christ's preachers is now entertaining them in his own home! We do not know if these two are one and the same, nor if Demas (a contracted form of Demetrius) mentioned in II Timothy is the same as either or both.

V. SALUTATION (verses 13, 14)

As in his second letter, John expresses the view that he would rather visit and speak "face to face" than put pen to paper any longer. He has more important and confidential things to say and a personal interview will be better than a letter. He has said a great deal already on a very personal note, and things written are likely to be misconstrued, especially where men like Diotrephes are concerned.

"Our friends salute thee," writes the apostle, informing us that he and Gaius had mutual friends in the Lord. "Greet the friends by name" is John's concluding remark. The apostle wants to be remembered to Gaius' fellow church members one by one—individually, not collectively. The lowest of them was as important as the highest. This is probably a quiet condemnation of the attitude of Diotrephes. Those pre-eminent or prominent, and those who only "stand and wait," serving in the background, all are incorporated in the apostle's salutation and benediction—"Peace be to thee"—May all felicity, blessing and happiness be yours. As Matthew Henry comments: "The apostle who had lain in Christ's bosom lays Christ's friends in his heart."

A CHANGE OF MIND

Jude

In this brief letter, Jude, the brother of James, an evangelist of the Early Church, gives us the cause and course of the prevailing apostasy of his time. "Apostasy" is the key word and the theme is, "Loyalty to the Truth." In the midst of apostasy there must be a contending for the faith once and for all delivered.

Jude has changed his mind, however, since beginning his letter. His original intention was to write about salvation, but the Holy Spirit changed his mind and he now writes about contending for the faith. Once again the one outline will suffice for the letter and the "famous" chapter are one and the same:

    I.   INTRODUCTION (verses 1-4)
          Greeting and Purpose
   II.   APOSTASY ILLUSTRATED (verses 5-7)
  III.   APOSTATES DESCRIBED (verses 8-16)
  IV.   ORTHODOXY SAFEGUARDED (verses 17-23)
   V.   CONCLUSION (verses 24, 25)
          Doxology and Benediction

I. INTRODUCTION (verses 1-4)

The first four verses are Jude's inscription and salutation, his greeting and explanation of his purpose in writing. Little is known of the one writing, Jude (a form of Judah), but "servant," meaning bondslave, tells us all we want to know. This man is completely at the disposal of Jesus Christ as was the Apostle Paul. It is a most suggestive word, describing the utter committal of a man to Christ, branded with the mark of ownership.

He writes to true Christians, not superficial believers, for they have been called and kept (election and eternal security), by contrast with those about whom the writer is going to describe in his letter.

Praying upon them God's mercy, peace and love, with a desire that it be multiplied beyond measure, he exhorts them to "contend for the faith"—"struggle as in a fight," "compete as in a race." It is a positive word of action, not a mere negative word of opposition. They are to define, defend and declare the faith once and for all delivered to the saints. What this faith is, orthodoxy in its fullest possible sense, dogma and practical holy living, we shall see as the letter proceeds.

This contending for the faith is necessary because "there are certain men crept in unawares." They are "ungodly" men who have come within the circle of the church fellowship and their presence and influence has brought about false doctrine, misrepresentation of the truth, and immorality of life. The doctrines of grace have been abused by these men so that licence has been given for corrupt, carnal, immoral indulgence of the body.

II. Apostasy Illustrated (verses 5-7)

Three examples are now given from the Old Testament of apostasy, illustrative of the belief and conduct of those who have secretly and stealthily entered the church to which Jude is writing.

The first illustration is of the Israelites who were delivered out of Egypt. Among them were unfaithful Israelites, people who identified themselves with God's people but were apostates in belief.

Next, there were the angels who fell from their position in heaven, being cast out because of their sin (some commentators affirming that they desired the daughters of men).

Thirdly, there was the destruction of Sodom and Gomorrah, whose sin was that of fornication.

In every case there was judgment: the apostate Israelites were destroyed; the angels are kept in everlasting confinement until the day of judgment; and Sodom and Gomorrah were burned.

These illustrations were to be an example to the apostates. Apostasy can never be countenanced by God—it must be dealt with by judgment. And the judgment will be perpetual, eternal.

III. Apostates Described (verses 8-16)

Jude now turns from Biblical examples to the very men who are causing the apostasy in the church. "Likewise"—these false brethren are acting in precisely the same way as the examples given. They are defiling the flesh and despising the lordship of Christ, denying the true right to oversight of church dignities. By contrast Michael, the archangel, did not use violent speech even to the devil when he was disputing about the body of Moses. The devil claimed Moses' body as a murderer, which was blasphemy. Michael restrained his speech and left it with the Lord—"The Lord rebuke thee."

By contrast the apostates are guilty of violent, abusive speech, scoffing at anything they do not understand. They have no spiritual understanding and so emphasize the physical, becoming morally perverse. They live life only on the animal level and can only be compared with such as Cain, Balaam, Korah, who sinned in the very same way.

Jude then describes these apostates in a series of vivid metaphors. They are "spots in your feasts"—literally it means they were like hidden rocks, perilous to sailors. Without real love in their hearts to Christ they were nevertheless joining in the Christian love-feasts that preceded the celebration of the breaking of bread or Communion service.

They were like "clouds without water" or clouds that give no rain, useless, driven hither and thither by the wind but doing no good. These apostates were weak in character and absolutely useless to the cause of Christ—no attention should be paid to them.

"Trees whose fruit withereth"—autumn trees without fruit; trees producing no harvest, doubly spiritually dead.

"Raging waves of the sea"—never at rest, always throwing up on the beach flotsam and jetsam.

"Wandering stars"—a star or planet out of its fixed course, lawless. So these apostates have violated God's law and are "out of orbit."

What a description of apostate modernist, liberal theologians, men who deny the value of the Atonement yet conduct the Communion service; revolting at the blood yet announcing hymns like "There is a fountain filled with blood"! How these same men are driven hither and thither after the latest, fashionable theological trend—the New Theology or "God Is Dead" thinking, for instance. What little fruit they produce—their churches never witness conversions for the Gospel is not preached. Like the raging sea and wandering stars they are restless, always searching, always changing their ideas and emphases.

Appealing to *The Book of Enoch,* an early religious writing well-known to the New Testament writers (probably written in the second or first century B.C.), Jude says that these apostates were prophesied by Enoch. *The Book of Enoch* was apocalyptic literature and contained teaching about the coming Messiah and His reign. This man saw, with prophetic vision, the apostasy of the Church centuries after his lifetime. He also saw their judgment and sentence. They would suffer the same fate as the "ungodly," that is, those without Christ.

IV. ORTHODOXY SAFEGUARDED (verses 17-23)

The faith once delivered (verse 3) is always taken to mean the orthodox faith of the Christian Church, the foundation of all our dogmas, creeds, statements of faith, and general sound doctrine. By evangelical Christians we mean the evangelical faith of the conservative evangelical (Great Britain) or the fundamentalist (America) as opposed to the modernist or liberal school of theology. The words "The faith," however, imply more than creed or dogma; they mean "faith as a whole" or "faith and works," belief and behavior. Sound doctrine can be defended up to the hilt but if the life does not tally with the doctrine then that defense is useless. The Gospel in its entirety is belief and life. True orthodoxy is what is preached and believed and what is practiced and worked out in daily life. This view of "the faith" Jude now expands and urges that it be safeguarded.

Once again there is an appeal to Scripture by Jude. He reminds his readers of certain apostolic warnings regarding "mockers" that should arise at the end of the age. Jude's "mockers" are the same as Peter's "scoffers." They separate themselves from true evangelical brethren and do not possess the Holy Spirit. True Christians are not to be confused by them. Charming as they may appear to be, cultured and educated as well, they are to be avoided like the plague. Christians are to build themselves up in their holy faith and resort to prayer. There is nothing like doctrine and prayer to counteract apostasy. Bible study and praying in the Spirit builds strong Christians able to withstand false teachers and false teaching. This kind of building-up will enable them so to live that they will be kept in the love of God. God will be so pleased with their spiritual growth that He will be able to act toward them in love and not in judgment. At the same time they must look "for the mercy of our Lord Jesus Christ unto eternal life." The future expectation of eternity will serve as a spur to the building-up process.

Toward the apostates there must be the following attitude: there must be "compassion," pity and love. Then a different attitude ("making a difference") must be adopted to others—they must be "saved with fear." Either by making them afraid, by telling them of the judgment reserved for the apostate, or by speaking to them with fear of being contaminated, the eternal salvation of these false teachers must be sought. Thus they will be snatched from hell fire. It must be done however, very carefully, so that the "garment is not spotted by the flesh," so that the true Christian is not contaminated by their sinfulness. Like God Himself, who hates sin but loves the sinner, the true evangelical Christian must love the one who has departed from the true faith while hating the false theology that he propounds.

V. Conclusion (verses 24, 25)

The writer ends his letter with words that are both a doxology and a benediction. Surrounded by false teachers, tempted to lapse into a false faith, Jude reminds the church of God's keeping power. He is able to keep them from falling and to present them faultless, unblemished, untarnished. When they thus stand in the presence of God it will be with exceeding joy (that is, a wild kind of joy, sheer exultation) because of the victory they have gained. Taking their eyes off their present surroundings and difficulties Jude lifts them to the glory of God and His utter supremacy, past, present and future. He assures them of God's power ("He is able") of His preservation ("to keep you from falling"), and purpose ("to present you faultless"). Dr. Weymouth brings out the true sense of this doxology benediction in his translation into modern English:

> Now to Him who is able to keep you from stumbling, and cause you to stand in the presence of His glory free from blemish and exultant —to the only God our Saviour through Jesus Christ our Lord—be glory, majesty, might, and authority, before all time, now, and to all time! Amen.

THE UNVEILING OF JESUS CHRIST

Revelation 1

The Book of Revelation is the "finale" (key word) of the Word of God. Its theme is "Jesus Shall Reign!" Yet this book receives less attention from Christians than many a longer book in the Bible. After all, it is the only book in God's Word that promises a blessing to the reader!

In these pages the Lord Jesus Christ is set forth in a very special way, and so Satan tries, and succeeds, in keeping Christians from it. Here in Revelation is pronounced the defeat and doom of the devil.

Among those who have and do study it there is great controversy. Some have a Preterist interpretation (looking upon the book as recording past history); others have a Futurist interpretation and say that it is yet to be fulfilled. Some say it is fulfilled and others unfulfilled prophecy. Yet others look upon it in an idealist way, seeing in its pages pictorial representation of certain great principles. An outline of the book in its own words seems to tell us to keep all these interpretations in mind:

    I.   THE THINGS WHICH THOU HAST SEEN (1:9-20)
    II.   THE THINGS WHICH ARE (2, 3)
    III.   THE THINGS WHICH SHALL COME TO PASS (4-22)

The first chapter is perhaps the most famous and well-known, and in it we see what John saw—a risen and glorious Christ. An outline of the chapter is as follows:

    I.   THE INTRODUCTION (verses 1-3)
        The Caption
    II.   THE CHRIST JOHN KNEW (verses 4-8)
    III.   THE CHRIST JOHN HEARD (verses 9-11)
    IV.   THE CHRIST JOHN SAW (verses 12-18)
    V.   THE CONCLUSION (verses 19, 20)
        The Commission

I. THE INTRODUCTION (verses 1-3)—The Caption

The caption or title of the book is given—"The Revelation" or unveiling. It means the removing of a veil of ignorance or obscurity. Note that it is not *A* Revelation but *The*. There are other revelations of Jesus Christ in the Bible but this is *The* Revelation.

It is the revelation "which God gave." It is God-inspired, God-communicated. And it is about "things which must shortly come to pass." Not about *all* future events, some, that is, the most important ones. Those who give us their detailed charts from eternity past to eternity future should remember that not all has been revealed, they have many gaps in their charts which will never be filled in until the Lord returns.

These events are "shortly" coming to pass. Does John mean soon, quickly, in the near future, with speed? His phraseology implies suddenness, a series of events coming about suddenly, without much warning. And we must keep in mind Peter's statement about heavenly mathematics—"a thousand years" in God's sight is "but as a day."

God "sent and signified" this revelation to John. He sent it by one of His angels and gave some sign by which John knew that it was authentic.

Verse 3 contains the promised blessing—a double blessing—upon those who prophesy aloud in the assemblies and upon those who hear it read and expounded.

II. THE CHRIST JOHN KNEW (verses 4-8)

First, John salutes the seven churches in Asia, giving them a true apostolic blessing. Then he begins his description of the Christ he knew personally. "Is," "was," and "to come" sum up the portrait of the Christ John knew. A pre-existent, ever-present and eternal Christ, the Son of God is here. And this is more than a message from John to the seven churches for he writes, "and from Jesus Christ" (verse 5). Jesus Christ is described as a "faithful witness," One who is entirely reliant, worthy to be relied upon, for He is the "first-begotten of the dead," the first Person to have risen from the dead. He is also a "Prince," and thus John gives all pre-eminence to Him. He is King of kings and Lord of lords.

No wonder John breaks into a doxology beginning: "Unto him that loved us." To use the old English expression He has not only loved but "laved" (washed, cf. "laver") us. Some say that it should read: "Unto him that loved us and *loosed* us from our sins." Washed is more in keeping with the rest of New Testament teaching about the blood of Jesus Christ.

"Kings and priests" it is said, should be translated, "a kingdom *of* priests." Peter speaks of "a royal priesthood" (I Peter 2:9). Kings remind us of dignity, royalty and exalted rank; priests remind us of lowly service and sacrifice. Kings reign over their subjects; Jesus conquered sin and death and they are now subject to Him. Priests served the living God in the Old Testament times. So Jesus stands in the presence of the Father "ever living to make intercession for us."

Verse 7 is a notable verse on the Second Coming of Christ. John tells us that when Christ returns there will be precision as to the manner of His coming; he is exact regarding the spectators of that coming; and he is definite as to the results of that advent.

It was common then to use the first and last letters of the Greek alphabet to denote the completeness of anything. The law had to be kept by the Jew from A to Z. Here it refers to the eternal nature of our Lord. Some manuscripts have "God" and not "Lord" in verse 8 and so we are brought back to verse 4. "The Almighty" gives weight to this interpretation.

III. THE CHRIST JOHN HEARD (verses 9-11)

John heard Christ because he was "in the Spirit on the Lord's day." Perhaps that is why so many do not benefit as they ought from Sunday services in our churches and chapels—they are not *in the Spirit*. Commentators say that John is referring to some special state of mind and spirit, having had an influence from without brought to bear upon us, putting us in an attitude of elevated devotion. Thus we receive a holy religious enjoyment in our worship of God. At any rate John himself seems to be experiencing this. Yet he was an exile, a prisoner on the Isle of Patmos. He was a martyr, banished by a cruel despot to a rock-bound island in the Aegean Sea, deprived of the "fellowship of kindred minds," yet enjoying communion with God Himself on His own day.

What did John hear? A "great voice, as of a trumpet." It was the voice of Christ, and it seemed to come through a trumpet. This loud voice directs John to put on record what is revealed to him. Like John Bunyan later, John was prevented by captivity from preaching but not from writing. He is to write a book that will be circulated to seven churches. How often the printed Word goes where the spoken word will not reach. How often when the preacher dies, he "being dead yet speaketh" because he has written books and they are left as a legacy to the world.

The fact that seven churches are mentioned does not mean that this revelation was not sent around to more than seven. These seven were typical of many others. The needs of these seven were typical of the needs of many more, with their lukewarmness, wealth, backsliding ways, poverty, and false doctrine.

IV. THE CHRIST JOHN SAW (verses 12-18)

Note that John *turned* to see. How often we are looking in the wrong direction and refuse to turn to God's direction! Lot's wife looked back when she should have looked forward. Peter looked at the sea when he should have looked at the Lord. The prodigal looked away from home to the far country.

What a glorious sight met John's gaze! He had always looked to the cross of Calvary in order to see Jesus. Now he sees Him standing among seven golden candlesticks or lampstands. Christ was "in the midst" of them. If only churches would give Him His rightful place!

John is depicting under inspiration a nighttime scene. The world is in sinful darkness and churches are God's light in the world. Jesus Himself is the true Light of the world, the churches reflecting His light.

Now comes what Dr. G. Campbell Morgan calls "the most marvellous and entrancing vision of Jesus Christ contained in Scripture." Here John reveals His seven-fold glory—

First, there is His *robing*: He is not dressed as Priest but as Judge, signifying His authority among the churches—He is sole Head and Lord. The girdle speaks of the fidelity of His love. It is around His breast, encircling His heart. If it had been around the waist it would have spoken of service; here it speaks of His eternal love for His Church.

Next, His *appearance*: John begins with the head and the hairs. They are as white as wool or snow. Purity and eternity are symbolized here, also beauty and strength. Absalom was renowned for the beauty of his hair, and Samson's strength lay in his. Our Lord's eyes were like a flame of fire, speaking of infinite and infallible knowledge; penetration is meant—nothing is secret or hidden from Him. Remember, nothing goes on in the Church that He does not see, and hear! Those petty quarrels, those under-the-surface grumblings—all are seen by Him. His feet were like burnished brass, refined in a furnace. This symbolizes victory; He is the Leader of Hosts, the Church militant, overcoming all opposition. The voice was like "many waters," or rather, a waterfall! And out of His mouth was a two-edged sword, condemning and commending, as we see in the messages to the seven churches. Finally His countenance was like the sun. The sum total of His features, eyes, lips, expression, could only be compared with the sun. The sun bathes the world in beauty. No longer is He the Man of Sorrows, acquainted with grief.

What would we have done if such a vision had been granted to us? John "fell at his feet," the proper place, the position of humility. John is overcome and falls as if dead. He is prostrate before such majesty and beauty. But graciously the hand that in His earthly ministry cleansed the leper and raised the dead, lifted John to his feet again, restoring him, reassuring him, recounting to him who He was. John then realizes that this has been illusion or delusion or hallucination— this is the resurrected and glorified Christ. He has keys in His hand, showing that there is no empire to which He does not have admission.

V. THE CONCLUSION (verses 19, 20)—The Commission

Once more the commission comes to "Write." Past, present and future events must be put on permanent record for the help of others.

Finally the mystery of the seven stars in verse 16 is explained in the last verse of the chapter. A "mystery" is something obscure or hidden until it is made known. It is something spiritual and super-natural, and it can only be made known by one who has the God-given ability to do it. Thus the Holy Spirit reveals the meaning to John. The seven stars and the seven golden candlesticks are but symbols, they stand for seven angels and seven churches. There is a spiritual, suitable explanation of the symbols. So throughout the book, for the diligent reader there will be other symbols made known by the Spirit of illumination and interpretation. Where no explanation is given we must beware of human conjecture. The end of the chapter then is an onward-looking finish. To find out more about these seven churches and God's messages to them, we must read on. Then, when we have understood the messages to the seven churches, we shall want to go deeper still and understand something of the consummation of all things.